THE SISTERHOOD

"The Sisterhood, 1977," Vertamae Grosvenor, Alice Walker, Lori Sharpe, Toni Morrison, June Jordan, Nana Maynard, Ntozake Shange, and Audreen Ballard. Box 184, Folder 12. MC 1061 Alice Walker Papers. Stuart A. Rose Manuscript, Archives, and Rare Book Library, Emory University, Atlanta, Georgia; Reprinted by permission of The Joy Harris Literary Agency, Inc.; Courtesy of Alice Walker

The Sisterhood

HOW A NETWORK OF BLACK WOMEN WRITERS
CHANGED AMERICAN CULTURE

Courtney Thorsson

Columbia University Press
New York

NATIONAL
ENDOWMENT
FOR THE
HUMANITIES

The National Endowment for the Humanities: Democracy demands wisdom.
Any views, findings, conclusions, or recommendations expressed in this book do not
necessarily represent those of the National Endowment for the Humanities.

Columbia University Press
Publishers Since 1893
New York   Chichester, West Sussex
cup.columbia.edu

Library of Congress Cataloging-in-Publication Data
Names: Thorsson, Courtney, 1978– author.
Title: The sisterhood : How a network of Black women writers changed
American culture/Courtney Thorsson.
Description: New York : Columbia University Press, 2023. | Includes bibliographical
references and index.
Identifiers: LCCN 2023020614 | ISBN 9780231204729 (hardback) | ISBN 9780231555678 (ebook)
Subjects: LCSH: American literature—20th century—History and criticism. |
American literature—Women authors—History and criticism. | American literature—
Black authors—History and criticism. |
Women authors, Black—United States. | Feminism in literature. | Community life—
United States—History—20th century. | LCGFT: Literary criticism.
Classification: LCC PS228.W65 T48 2023 | DDC 810.9/928708996073—
dc23/eng/20230727
LC record available at https://lccn.loc.gov/2023020614

Printed in the United States of America

Cover design: Julia Kushnirsky
Cover photograph: "The Sisterhood, 1977," Vertamae Grosvenor, Alice Walker, Lori Sharpe,
Toni Morrison, June Jordan, Nana Maynard, Ntozake Shange, and Audreen Ballard.
Box 184, Folder 12. MC 1061 Alice Walker Papers. Stuart A. Rose Manuscript,
Archives, and Rare Book Library, Emory University, Atlanta, Georgia;
Reprinted by permission of The Joy Harris Literary Agency, Inc.;
Courtesy of Alice Walker

CONTENTS

Introduction   1

Chapter One
"Revolution Is Not a One-Time Event"   11

Chapter Two
"An Association of Black Women
Who Are Writers/Poets/Artists"   43

Chapter Three
"To Move the Needle in Black Women's Lives"   74

Chapter Four
"A Community of Writers Even if
They Only Slap Five Once a Month"   105

Chapter Five
"A Regular Profusion of Certain/Unidentified Roses"   129

Chapter Six
"The Function of Freedom Is to Free Somebody Else"   146

vi

CONTENTS

Chapter Seven
"Making Use of Being Used" 172

Conclusion 205

ACKNOWLEDGMENTS 215

PERMISSIONS 219

APPENDIX 1. MEMBERS OF THE SISTERHOOD 221

APPENDIX 2. MEETINGS OF THE SISTERHOOD 229

NOTES 231

INDEX 269

THE SISTERHOOD

INTRODUCTION

Look at the picture in the opening pages of this book: Vertamae Grosvenor, with her regal height on the far left; Alice Walker, her coat on and bag slung across her body as if she's ready to walk out the door; Toni Morrison, unimpeachably cool in her leather duster and gold jewelry; June Jordan, standing on the far right in a striped hippie dress and no coat—it's her apartment, so she's not dressed to head out into a cold February evening in New York; Nana Maynard, seated on the far left, the only other woman not in a coat—perhaps she planned to hang around after the others left; dead center in a crouching trio, Ntozake Shange, Lori Sharpe, and Audreen Ballard, all smiling, Shange looking like she was caught in the middle of a laugh. Look at these women: squeezed together happily to fit into the picture, gathered around a framed photo of Bessie Smith, in a room with the high ceilings and architectural molding characteristic of prewar apartments in the city, in warm light but with shadows that show it is evening stretching into night. Every one of the women looks straight into the camera.

This photo, "The Sisterhood, 1977," has become the subject of legend among readers, scholars, and writers since it first appeared in print in Evelyn White's *Alice Walker: A Life* in 2004. I saw it for the first time in graduate school when Farah Jasmine Griffin told me there was a photo that I absolutely had to see in White's new book. I rushed to get a copy, opened to the section of photos in the middle of the book, and saw this stunning image of powerful, smiling Black women writers, some of whom I recognized right away and others whose faces and names were new to me. White's caption describes the photo this way: "A group of black women writers in New York who met informally during the 1970s. Back row, left to right: Verta Mae Grosvenor, Alice Walker, Lori Sharpe, Bessie Smith, Toni Morrison, June Jordan. Seated, left to right: Nana Maynard, Ntozake Shange, Audrey Edwards."[1] I put a sticky note on the page so the photo would be at hand anytime I needed to look at it and started taking notes about this group of women who called themselves "The Sisterhood." Five years later, Cheryl Wall, knowing that a project on The Sisterhood was bubbling in the back of my mind, told me excitedly that she had spotted references to the group in June Jordan's papers at Harvard. A request for records from that archive led me to an agenda and minutes for one meeting of the group. This was my first thrilling clue that The Sisterhood was not just a group of women who got together once in a while, but rather an organization that met on a regular basis to tackle specific issues.

A couple of years later, I made my first trip to Alice Walker's archives in Atlanta. Sitting in an ornate, high-ceilinged room at Emory University's Rose Library, I held a physical copy of The Sisterhood photo for the first time. I turned it over and saw a handwritten note from June Jordan: "Dearest Alice: Remember the days when you needed that doublebreasted overcoat? Much Love to you Always."[2] The names of the women were there too, in purple ink and different handwriting. This told me at least two things: first, that the "Love" visible in the photo was real and lasting—"Always"—and second, that Walker knew this group was important enough to go back later and make sure that all the names of the women were on the back of the photo.

Like anyone else who has looked at the photo and recognized even only two or three of the women in it, I knew from the start that it documented something important. This image now regularly circulates on social media as a source of inspiration, and a few books and essays include the photo or briefly describe the group.[3] More than a decade after first holding "The Sisterhood, 1977" in my hands, I learned that the purple writing on the back had misidentified Audreen Ballard as Audrey Edwards.[4] Both women were in the group and both were important journalists, editors, and activists, but Ballard is the one in the photo. A quick note on the back of an archival photograph became solidified in cultural memory, as many later reproductions of the photo and descriptions of The Sisterhood repeated this misnaming. This is an important reminder that there is so much more to the story of The Sisterhood than one iconic photo.

The Sisterhood: How a Network of Black Women Writers Changed American Culture draws on members' poetry, fiction, essays, meeting minutes, correspondence, biographies, and interviews to uncover and narrate the everyday work of The Sisterhood to secure publication, publicity, and recognition for Black women writers. This image records more than one incredible Sunday in February 1977. Rather, it's a window into the everyday, collaborative work among Black women writers that changed literary history.

∾

In 2006, as "The Sisterhood, 1977" photo began to circulate, Alice Walker described the formation of The Sisterhood in an interview with Amy Goodman:

> Well, The Sisterhood was the brainchild of myself and June Jordan, because we looked around one day—we were friends—and we felt that it was important that black women writers know each other, that we understood that we were never in competition for anything, that we did not believe in ranking. We would not let the establishment put one of us ahead of the other. And so, some of us were Vertamae Grosvenor, Ntozake Shange, Toni Morrison, June Jordan, myself, and I think Audrey Edwards, who was at *Essence*, and several other women that I don't tonight remember.[5]

Walker went on to recall details from the first meeting of The Sisterhood at June Jordan's home: the women ate gumbo and gathered for a photo around a framed portrait of Bessie Smith as if she were a member of the group "because Bessie Smith best expressed our feeling of being women who were free and women who intended to stay that way."[6]

A few years later, Walker reiterated her words about The Sisterhood in an interview with scholar Rudolph Byrd: "June and I were rebels of the first order against ranking of any kind imposed beyond ourselves. We thought we must create a space for black women writers to honor each other, to know each other, so that nothing from outside could make us fight over anything. Or even feel competitive. This was The Sisterhood's purpose. We met only a few times while I was still in New York."[7]

It matters that The Sisterhood resisted "ranking" and "competition" among Black women writers. In the way repetition makes myth, though, these accounts leave out a lot of useful information. What did it look like to practice Walker's declaration, "We would not let the establishment put one of us ahead of the other"? How did The Sisterhood work to resist "competition" and "ranking"?[8] What are the ways that Black women writers worked to "honor each other"? What does it mean that there were many members not in the now famous photo and whom few accounts name? These questions and practices matter for literary history and for Black feminist organizing right now.

The Sisterhood's collaborative labors, including conflicts and the group's eventual dissolution, are as informative, useful, and inspirational as the 1977 photo. Like any group, they disagreed and argued. This is not surprising given that, while they shared the goal of transforming literary culture, there were many differences among them. Sisterhood members came to New York City from a variety of geographic and economic backgrounds. During the two years the group met, members worked as writers, editors, teachers, students, and journalists in a wide variety of outlets, often as the only Black women in their workplace. Some were well established in their fields, others were at the start of their careers, and several were pursuing graduate degrees. Their ages spanned about thirty years, from young members in their early twenties who had just graduated from college, such as Renita Weems and Judith Wilson, to members in their late forties and early fifties, such as Paule Marshall and Rosa Guy, who had both helped create earlier collectives of Black writers and artists. Zita Allen was regularly publishing articles in her role as *Dance Magazine*'s first African American dance critic, and Audreen Ballard had worked at *Redbook* and was a contributor and editor at *Essence*. VèVè Clark was completing her PhD and teaching at the University of California, Berkeley, but traveled to New York for meetings of The Sisterhood.[9] Audrey Edwards had recently completed her MA at Columbia University and was working for *Black Enterprise, Family Circle*, and *Essence*. Phyl Garland, an established journalist and author of *The Sound of Soul* (1969), was teaching in the School of Journalism at Columbia, where she would soon become the first tenured African American professor. Vertamae Grosvenor, author of *Vibration Cooking: Or, The Travel Notes of a Geechee Girl* (1970) and *Thursdays and Every Other Sunday Off* (1974), was writing essays about food and culture for *Essence, Ebony*, and other outlets. Jessica Harris was the book review editor at *Essence* and a member of the English Department faculty at Queens College. Margo Jefferson was on staff at *Newsweek* and about to start as an assistant professor of journalism at New York University.

Patricia Spears Jones was the grant program director for the Coordinating Council of Literary Magazines.

These women brought many and varied skills as writers and intellectuals into the city apartments where The Sisterhood met. They also faced serious obstacles to putting those skills to use, both in their individual working lives and in their collaboration as The Sisterhood. Outside the group, they faced daily encounters with racism, misogyny, and homophobia. Inside the group, they navigated dissent among members about its purpose. These external and internal pressures led to the breakup of The Sisterhood after just over two years. In those two years, however, these women made Black feminist writing central to magazines and trade publishing, and they laid the foundation for Black feminism in the academy.

They worked together under enormous pressures during a period of increased visibility for and public attacks on Black women. The Sisterhood accomplished a lot in this short period, and the two years they met mattered for the rest of their lives and careers. Their Black feminist collaboration—including dissent and dissolution—offers a model for collective action to change cultural institutions. They believed in the power of literature as an agent of political and social transformation. The Sisterhood contributed to the creation of literary celebrity for a few members, especially Alice Walker and Toni Morrison. Members read, reviewed, and taught one another's books. They helped establish Black studies and African American literary studies in the academy. Most immediately, in the years after The Sisterhood stopped meeting, they wrote books that defined the 1980s as a spectacular decade for Black women writers in the United States.

Some of the many works that Sisterhood members published just from 1980 to 1990 are Alice Walker's *The Color Purple* (1982); June Jordan's *Passion: New Poems: 1977–1980* (1980) and *Civil Wars: Observations from the Front Lines of America* (1981); Paule Marshall's *Praisesong for the Widow* (1983) and a reissue of her 1959 novel *Brown Girl, Brownstones* with a new afterword by Mary Helen Washington (1981); Ntozake Shange's *Sassafrass, Cypress & Indigo* (1982) and *A Daughter's Geography* (1983); Audre Lorde's *Zami* (1982) and *Sister Outsider* (1984); Renita Weems's *Just a Sister Away* (1988); and Toni Morrison's *Tar Baby* (1981) and *Beloved* (1987). Among other accolades that Sisterhood members earned in the 1980s, Shange won an Obie Award; Jordan received a National Endowment for the Humanities Fellowship; Lorde, Morrison, and Walker each won an American Book Award; and Morrison and Walker won Pulitzer Prizes for fiction. The 1980s remains unrivaled in terms of visibility for writings by African American women.

This stunning body of work from the 1980s is not a matter of suddenly increased output but rather of a time of increased recognition in terms of prizes, readership, publication, and academic study of Black women's writings. Members of The Sisterhood were active participants in a cohort of Black women writers and intellectuals who created that recognition and struggled to navigate the dangers of their increased visibility in the literary marketplace and the academy. The story of The Sisterhood is one of hard, everyday, largely unseen labor that made that spectacular period possible.

The Sisterhood was more formal and structured than most writing about it has suggested.[10] After Jordan and Walker convened the first meeting in early 1977, the group met at least once a month for over two years, kept minutes of their meetings, and collected dues. Members took turns hosting the group in their New York apartments. The thirty or so women who attended one or more meetings of The Sisterhood understood that they could always bring one guest to any meeting as long as that guest was a Black woman writer, academic, journalist, or editor. In practice, this meant that members were "really just high achieving women who loved literature. . . . Feminists who loved literature who were trying to move the needle."[11] The members of The Sisterhood were cofounders June Jordan and Alice Walker; journalists and editors Zita Allen, Audreen Ballard, Audrey Edwards, Phyl Garland, Margo Jefferson, Susan McHenry, and Diane Weathers; culinary writers Vertamae Grosvenor and Jessica Harris; poets Patricia Spears Jones, Ntozake Shange, and Audre Lorde; novelists Rosa Guy, Paule Marshall, and Toni Morrison; scholars VèVè Clark and Judith Wilson; theologians Rosemary Bray and Renita Weems; and other women writers and activists who worked in a variety of spheres including television, radio, K-12 education, law, and nonprofit foundations.[12]

They decided to name themselves "The Sisterhood" because the term signified a kinship forged in political consciousness in the 1960s. Their name reflects the group's vision of collaboration rooted in love for self, for one another, and for Black women's writing.[13] They called it "The Sisterhood"— always capitalized in their meeting minutes and correspondence—right from the start, claiming the importance and potential of the group to shape the world far beyond their own careers and lives. "Sisterhood" has an openness; it names a group that could have turned out to be almost anything—a press, a professional association, a book club, a writing workshop, or something else altogether. Over the course of two years, they worked through, figured out, and revised "The Sisterhood" to mean a group that worked to get Black women's writings published, read, reviewed, studied, and taught. They used their personal and affective bonds to struggle together to transform public culture.

Patricia Spears Jones wrote to the members in 1978 that there was something "profound" in "a meeting place for a group of Black Women who share certain sensibilities as women, intellectuals, Blacks etc."[14] Sisterhood members knew this was true in the late 1970s and, years later, they recognized even more clearly how important The Sisterhood was, not just for their own lives and careers but also for literary history. Margo Jefferson reflected in 2018,

> We were a consciousness, Black, feminist, literary consciousness-raising group, and that was both formal, meaning literature and scholarship being done . . . and a kind of airing of problems with our work, at our jobs. And we were trying to formulate basic, practical [ways of] getting through things and preserving your integrity. And that is a form of consciousness-raising and support, practical support. But we were also trying to identify, name this space, where literary and scholarly and journalistic people, many of whom were progressives—that was an absolute given—could function. I mean, in that way June and Alice helped, being some of the founders, that makes perfect, perfect sense.[15]

Jefferson described the group in nuanced and insightful terms that refer to the specific details of their late 1970s work, their radical imagination for a changed future, and the long-term effects their work had on the broader culture.

A place exclusively for Black women was an absolute necessity for these teachers, journalists, editors, and writers. In the 1960s and early 1970s, as activists, they had experienced the racism of the white Women's Liberation movement, which depended on the domestic labor of Black and Latinx women to get white women out of the home and into the workforce, and the sexism and homophobia of some civil rights and Black Power groups, which depended on endless and invisible labor from Black women but focused attention almost entirely on a few charismatic Black men leaders. By the mid-1970s Sisterhood members were navigating intense hostility at their jobs in workplaces dominated by white men.

The Sisterhood was a place to read and talk about Black women's writings and to get a break from the overwhelming whiteness of their day jobs. Jefferson reflects, "I cannot tell you what a relief it was to have this other life," meaning a life among Black women, because she and others were "alone" or "one of the few" at "white institutions" from academic departments to publishing houses to "*Newsweek, Time,* or even *Ms.*"[16] The women of The Sisterhood strategized to "formulate basic, practical [ways of] getting through things and preserving your integrity." "This space" was a foundation for their "literary and scholarly and journalistic" and "progressive" work advocating for Black women's literature and liberation in hostile institutions such as universities, magazines, newspapers, and book publishers.

From its modest beginning, The Sisterhood went on to set and achieve ambitious goals, and then stopped meeting in early 1979 as pressures on individual members and dissent within the group grew. For some, the demands of their paid, professional work as writers, editors, and scholars became difficult to balance with the unpaid or underpaid work of political, literary, and academic organizing. Class and generational differences and varying degrees of success in the literary marketplace also meant that different members wanted and needed different kinds of support from The Sisterhood; this gave rise to arguments over the group's purpose. As Black women writers became more visible, they struggled to control the terms of that visibility. Members disagreed in private and in print about Michele Wallace's *Black Macho and the Myth of the Superwoman* (1978), which was the subject of extensive media coverage and public debate. The virulence of racism and sexism at the dawn of the Reagan era, federal disinvestment in social welfare, and a sense of despair after years without any one movement setting a clear agenda for Black liberation all contributed to the group's dissolution. Against all odds, amid these obstacles to collaboration from within and outside of the group, The Sisterhood made substantive changes to the content of popular magazines and helped get Black women's books published, reviewed, and recognized. They also developed intellectual communities and wrote books that would matter in popular and academic American culture for decades to come.

～

The Sisterhood: How a Network of Black Women Writers Changed American Culture makes three interdependent arguments. First, in its complexity, contexts, and legacies, The Sisterhood is both a model for Black feminist collaboration and a cautionary tale. Second, the group's collaborative labor in the 1970s dramatically increased the visibility of African American women writers, especially novelists, in the 1980s. Third, the story of The Sisterhood and Black feminism during this period is also a story of shifting relationships among political organizations, literature, and the academy. Members of The Sisterhood, like other Black women writers and scholars, moved their intellectual labor from political organizing in the 1960s and early 1970s to literary organizing in the late 1970s and then, in the 1980s and beyond, into colleges and universities.

In the chapters that follow, I weave in and out of The Sisterhood's two-year life, using archival materials and interviews alongside close readings of Sisterhood members' novels, poems, and plays to help tell the story of their collaboration. This is not a group biography, but I do seek to capture these Black women writers at a pivotal time in their intellectual lives.[17] *The Sisterhood* proceeds chronologically from the mid-1960s to the present and travels spatially from political to literary to academic spheres, all grounded in New York. However, the group's legacies reach beyond their late 1970s moment and defy any single linear story. The spheres these women occupied also overlap and shape one another, and The Sisterhood's influence reached far beyond New York. I echo and reflect these temporal and spatial aspects of the group's work in this book by sometimes leaping back or forward in time and by often attending to multiple spheres and locations of work at once.

This book must sometimes break chronology because the story of Black women in politics, literature, and the academy is partly a story of backlash and setbacks. I title chapter 1 for Audre Lorde's assertion that "revolution is not a one-time event" because repeated erasure and resistance make it necessary to advocate for Black women's writing and chart Black feminist intellectual history again and again, including right now.[18] One urgent example of this necessity is that LGBTQ women and their vision were central to The Sisterhood and Black feminism in the late 1970s, but this became less apparent as Black feminism and African American literature solidified in the academy in the 1980s. Today, The Sisterhood's twenty-first-century descendants, including writers Alexis P. Gumbs and Mecca Jamilah Sullivan, are putting queer visions, politics, and possibilities at the center of their writing.

Other erasures, too, require the repeated telling of Black feminist intellectual histories. Farah Jasmine Griffin writes that "a small but significant cadre of black women writers and scholars" made it so that "by the mid-1990s black feminist literary studies was one of the most intellectually exciting and fruitful developments in American literary criticism." However, by the mid-2000s, academic departments were already erasing or marginalizing this lineage of Black women doing Black feminist literary studies. In her "Retrospective of Black Feminist Literary Criticism," Griffin points out that "the black women scholars who pioneered the study of these texts [by Black women] were becoming less and less visible—not only as members of university faculties but also in the footnotes of a voluminous scholarship devoted to black women's writing."[19] The stakes of Griffin's essay are to name the Black women scholars who made the study of African American literature possible, clarify the ways those scholars shaped the study of literature in general, offer new ideas rooted in a Black feminist intellectual tradition, and identify the material consequences of these moves in terms of employment, citation, and other conditions that are necessary for the continued production of Black feminist writing. This work is ongoing and remains urgent. Understanding Black women's work as a determining force for politics, literature, and the academy is part of what is at stake in telling the story of The Sisterhood.

"The Sisterhood, 1977" photo is an inspiration and a model for the work still needed and still being done right now in political organizations, literature, and the academy. This book approaches the 1977 photo and the story of it with the kind of love and rigor that defined the group—the kind of love and rigor that Farah Griffin and Cheryl Wall instilled in me as the way to study and teach African American literature. With every passing year, I believe more deeply in the transformative power of African American literature as I see former students carry the inspiration, desire for racial justice, and capacity for critical thought that they learned from this literary tradition into their work and lives as lawyers, parents, bankers, school board members, writers, activists, and teachers. It is my responsibility as a white woman scholar of African American literature to use the privilege of my whiteness, institutional affiliations, and skills as a literary scholar to get as many people as possible to read, reread, and better understand as many books as possible by Black writers. The Sisterhood historicizes and narrates some of the important and vast amount of work Black women did to make the late twentieth century a time of a spectacular visibility for Black women writers and to make it possible for people, including me, to study, teach, and learn from Black women's writing. It is my hope that this book will help us understand their remarkable achievement, the costs of their work, and the labor that remains to be done.

Chapter One

"REVOLUTION IS NOT A ONE-TIME EVENT"

When Audre Lorde asserted that "revolution is not a one-time event," she issued a call: "As Black people, if there is one thing we can learn from the '60s, it is how infinitely complex any move for liberation must be." The " '60s were characterized by a heady belief in instantaneous solutions" that brought both "promise and excitement," but also put Lorde in an impossible bind: "Either I denied or chose between various aspects of my identity, or my work and my Blackness would be unacceptable. As a Black lesbian mother in an interracial marriage, there was usually some part of me guaranteed to offend everybody's comfortable prejudices of who I should be."[1] Some civil rights and Black Power groups defined Blackness so narrowly that it did not seem to include queer people and women, much less "a Black lesbian mother" in "an interracial marriage." In the 1970s, Black feminists refused to check any part of their "identity" or their "work" at the door and pursued "revolution" not as a spectacular "one-time event," but rather as a lifetime commitment to working every day for Black women's liberation.

The early 1970s saw a shift away from the "heady belief in instantaneous solutions" that Lorde described and toward less visible but still potent forms of political activism. Toni Cade Bambara describes the decade:

> We didn't *seem* to be in a period of intense political activity as we defined its terms in the sixties. We were trained by the sixties to perceive activity, to assess movement and progress, in particular modes—confrontation,

uncompromising rhetoric, muscle flexing, press conferences, manifestoes, visible groups . . . the working of the seventies, while less visible and less audible
and less easy to perceive, to nail down and define, were no less passionate and
no less significant.[2]

Bambara describes a move away from marches and sit-ins and toward consciousness raising, study, and the unglamorous work of making the places
one inhabited every day—homes, offices, classrooms—less racist, sexist,
and homophobic. This shift happened throughout the 1970s as three key
sites of collective action laid a foundation for The Sisterhood: the Black Arts
Movement (BAM), Black feminist political organizations, and Black feminist
literary scholarship.

Each of these influences on The Sisterhood flourished in a time full of
possibility quickly followed by justified disillusion. In the 1960s, freedom
rides, sit-ins, and marches led to national civil rights legislation, and student
demonstrations made inroads for Black students, Black faculty, and Black
studies at some colleges and universities. Along with these gains, there were
massive losses, especially the 1960s assassinations of leaders Malcolm X,
Martin Luther King Jr., and Fred Hampton. In the 1960s, the civil rights
movement pursued justice through voting access, electoral politics, and legislation. At the start of the 1970s, Black activists carried some of that 1960s
optimism and highly visible activism into a new decade, BAM was in full
swing, and Black feminist political organizations were gaining momentum.
There was still a sense of possibility for social and political change.

It was hard to sustain activism in the dispiriting political landscape of the
United States in the 1970s. By 1973, the country was in a recession and the
labor movement was in decline, fighting to hold on to hard-won workers'
rights. By the middle of the decade, the civil rights movement had become
a painful example of the ways that incorporation into existing structures of
power had done very little to increase racial justice. At the same time, the
Black Power movement was in steep decline, due largely to years of harass-
ment, surveillance, and murder by the federal government. The material
conditions of daily life for many Black Americans became increasingly dire
due to government disinvestment in public services. The highly visible forms
of activism such as sit-ins and marches that characterized the 1960s no longer
seemed viable by the mid-1970s, when the last major civil rights legislation
was a decade old, the Black Arts and Black Power movements had begun to
wane, and neither had achieved the liberation or revolutionary changes that

activists had hoped for and worked toward. Activists were rightly cynical about the possibility for change in the United States, and many were reevaluating how to create "movement" in new and "significant" ways.

In the 1970s, as now, struggles for racial justice and the reassertion of racism played out in education. The Supreme Court's 1978 decision upholding affirmative action in *Regents of University of California v. Bakke* continued the slow work of racially integrating education in the United States that had begun with *Brown v. The Board of Education of Topeka, Kansas* in 1954. However, *Bakke* was not a step on a linear path toward racial justice in higher education but rather exemplifies the way American institutions work to confine Black freedom dreams. The *Bakke* decision did far less than what students in the City University of New York (CUNY) open admissions movement had briefly achieved just ten years earlier by bringing many Black and Latinx students into college. *Bakke* also did less to increase African American access to college than California's free in-state tuition program, which Ronald Reagan fought to dismantle during his years as governor. In the 1970s and '80s, free tuition eroded by degrees at CUNY, UC schools, and California community colleges, within the broader national context of the defunding of higher education.[3]

A sense of fading political possibility was sharp in New York. In the early 1970s, "New York City stood for urban liberalism, an example of the role that government might play in addressing problems of poverty, racism, and economic distribution."[4] President Gerald Ford, along with city, state, and other federal officials working closely with corporations, used New York's fiscal crisis to prescribe what would become "an age of austerity," involving a dramatic withdrawal of government support and producing "not only budget cuts but a political mood of bleak hopelessness" among Americans, and New Yorkers in particular, who suffered from the contraction of the public sector, the waning power of unions, and severe cuts in education, health care, and social services.[5] The retrenchment of segregation in housing and education and the Reagan administration's foreclosure of Black freedom dreams were right around the corner. Ronald Reagan, first as governor of California and then as president, was the most prominent of the many politicians who marshalled white racism to ensure the rise of the right and the loss of protections for Black people, workers, women, and poor people. By the close of the 1970s, racial and gender justice were even more out of reach, and activists were rightly cynical about accomplishing sociopolitical change in the United States.

Amid and despite the increasing sense of futility and doom, The Sisterhood and other Black feminist collectives saw a horizon of possibility. In the absence of one national mass movement or one charismatic leader, members of The Sisterhood and their contemporaries practiced Black radical politics on the terrain of culture and in collectives. Woman-of-color feminisms, Black feminism, anthologies including *The Black Woman* (1970), organizations including the National Black Feminist Organization (NBFO), and collectives including The Sisterhood seized on the 1970s as a time in which the work of liberation was both urgent and open to radical reimagination rooted in local, everyday work.

In this shifting political landscape, The Sisterhood gathered in 1977 to use literature for Black women's liberation. They set their sights on culture, wrote across genres for various kinds of publications, and ultimately moved into the academy. They came together at a moment when legislation and electoral politics were working to re-entrench white supremacy. A turn to cultural institutions and networks—publishing and the university—was a logical and effective response to the sense that direct political action no longer had the power to make city, state, or federal governments instruments of racial justice. In the 1970s, progressive Black thinkers and writers were gaining increased access to the culture industry and institutions of higher education. New York City, as the center of the publishing industry and with a greater density of universities than any other place in the United States, was fertile ground for The Sisterhood's advocacy for Black women's writing. The literary publishing world and the academy were adept at incorporating a performative mandate of increasing racial diversity without doing the work of radical structural change. The women of The Sisterhood understood this; some of them would later write about the exhaustion and isolation of being lone Black women in their workplaces. This generation of Black women intellectuals faced overt sexism and racism, and they closely observed the strategies that these institutions developed to appear less racist while preserving racist outcomes.[6] Sisterhood members grappled with laboring in the institutions they worked hard to gain access to while also trying to survive. I explore this struggle for access and survival at colleges and universities in detail in chapter 7. In this chapter, I study the ways that the Black Arts Movement and Black feminist political organizations set the stage for The Sisterhood while Black feminist literary scholarship developed alongside and made possible the group's work and lasting influence.

≈

The Black Arts Movement (BAM) was the cultural arm of the Black Power movement. BAM insisted that Black art and literature were necessary to Black liberation. The movement began around 1965, waned by 1976, and was a crucial force in shaping the careers of Black women writers— Ntozake Shange, Toni Cade Bambara, June Jordan, and Audre Lorde, among others—who went on to write poems, novels, plays, and essays that were a feminist revision of the Black Arts Movement.[7] Many Sisterhood members began their careers as writers during the apex of BAM. Shange and Jordan, among others, are recognizable as BAM writers in their innovative use of diction, spelling, capitalization, and punctuation that resisted the constraints of white American English. Jordan, Lorde, and other members published their early work in Black Arts Movement anthologies, in book series such as Julius Lester's Black Poets Series at Dutton (which included Jordan's *Some Changes*), and at presses such as Dudley Randall's Broadside Press (which was also publishing works by Gwendolyn Brooks and Sonia Sanchez in this period).[8] Even members who did not think of themselves as part of BAM learned from that movement to demand and create spaces—classrooms, editorial meetings, academic journals, book reviews, and anthologies—where Black writing was understood on its own terms. Partly through experiences with BAM, the women of The Sisterhood understood text in general and anthologies in particular as powerful tools for Black liberation.

BAM writers, such as LeRoi Jones (Amiri Baraka), Larry Neal, Sonia Sanchez, and Don L. Lee (Haki Madhbuti), believed that Black literature must have its own authors, readers, teachers, editors, scholars, reviewers, and publication outlets. From Larry Neal and Amiri Baraka's anthology *Black Fire* (1968) to Haki Madhubuti's Third World Press, BAM developed texts and institutions on the premise that African American writing was by and for Black readers and should be evaluated according to its own specific criteria as part of a long Black aesthetic tradition. From the mid-1960s to the mid-1970s, the Black Arts Movement generated an outpouring of anthologies of Black writing. As it did during the Harlem Renaissance, the anthology form explicitly declared Black writing as part of a distinct, racially specific body of work that ought to be read, studied, and taught in its own context.

In 1970, Toni Cade Bambara began a decades-long feminist adoption and revision of BAM with *The Black Woman: An Anthology*. She used the form of the anthology to create a community on the page.[9] *The Black Woman* insisted on the importance of dialogue among African American women by including transcripts of consciousness-raising sessions. It also brought together a number of writers who would later participate in The Sisterhood: Vertamae Grosvenor, Audre Lorde, Paule Marshall, and Alice Walker. Bambara's *The Black Woman* is both a Black Arts movement anthology and a feminist gathering. Seven years before The Sisterhood began to meet regularly, this book established that a shared publication venue could be an important unifying space for a diverse group of Black women writers.[10]

~

Black feminist political organizations served as precursors, foundations, and cautionary tales for The Sisterhood. The National Black Feminist Organization (NBFO), the Third World Women's Alliance, the National Alliance of Black Feminists, and the Combahee River Collective operated from 1968 to 1980.[11] Although none of these groups focused primarily on publishing or publicizing Black women's writings, each was an important predecessor for The Sisterhood. These groups were "formal organizations that helped shaped black feminist consciousness" in the years before and during the 1977–78 meetings of The Sisterhood.[12]

The NBFO and the Combahee River Collective most directly shaped The Sisterhood. Florynce "Flo" Kennedy, a lawyer and activist, and Margaret Sloan, a founding editor of *Ms.*, started the NBFO in May 1973 when a group of "about thirty Black women came together to share what it meant to be Black, woman and feminist."[13] Sloan and Jane Galvin Lewis led the council of the NBFO, which went on to organize regional conferences with workshops addressing matters including "the struggle for child care, welfare, women's liberation, politics, the church, media, labor force, homosexuality, cultural arts, female sexuality, prisons, addiction and education." Eleanor Holmes Norton and Shirley Chisholm were among the speakers at the first conference, held in New York in December 1973. Founding NBFO member Beverly Davis recalls a swell of attention following the group's 1973 press conference and that the group was "born" in an "atmosphere of profound contradictions" between Black women's concerns and the white women's liberation movement.[14]

Sisterhood member Vertamae Grosvernor explains the racism of "Women's Lib" in a searing and hilarious critique in her book, *Thursdays and Every Other Sunday Off: A Domestic Rap by Verta Mae* (1972). Grosvenor uses poetry, letters, newspaper articles, scholarly histories, and conversations to write in a first-person, collective "I" voice, speaking for African American domestic workers from slavery to the 1970s. She asserts that although domestic laborers often agree not to speak or write about what they witness in white homes, she "decided to sign a contract to tell what we have seen working in service for some 300 odd years."[15] She writes about the women's liberation movement: "Is there enough money to send for a girl from the South or the Islands, or, as of late, South America, to keep house for you, mind your overindulged brat, while you go to Women's Lib meetings?" and "These days, Miss Anne is sister Anne. Having decided that the sisterhood is powerful, she and her sisters don't care who answers the door, cause they ain't home nohow. They are out to lib and the children are in a day care center. Now who do you think is staffing the day care center? While Ms. Anne is out solving the feminine mystique, who is cleaning the house?"[16] *Thursdays* concludes with a letter from "Aisha (slave name, Beulah)" to her former employer that reads, in part, "I would suggest you schedule your bra burning demonstrations in the latter part of the afternoon. That will give you time to clean, shop and finish most of your pre-dinner preparations."[17] In these critiques of the ways white women's liberation depends on Black women's work, Grosvenor uses humor as a weapon and points out the conditions that made separate Black feminist political organizations such as the NBFO, the Third World Women's Alliance, and the Combahee River Collective necessary.

Two legislative victories of the women's liberation movement illustrate the divide between Black and white feminist agendas: the June 1972 passage of Title IX, which barred discrimination in education on the basis of sex, and the January 1973 Supreme Court decision in *Roe v. Wade*, which protected the right to choose to have an abortion. These crucial changes in legislation were both important and reflective of the goals of a white women's liberation movement that repeatedly excluded the agenda of Black feminists. Reproductive rights and ideas about work were areas of major difference: access to abortion was one part of white feminists' efforts to move increasingly into the public sphere. Black women in the United States, on the other hand, had a long history of fighting to care for their own homes and families. While the NBFO and other groups supported the right to abortion, Black feminists had long conceived of reproductive justice more broadly, to include the right to terminate a pregnancy but also access to health care and child care so that women who wished to do so could safely carry pregnancies to term and safely raise children. Black feminists had always sought the access to education that Title IX protects, but they also wanted to transform higher education, to make universities sites for practicing and producing more justice and safety for more people.

The NBFO, like other Black feminist political organizations, understood that meeting basic needs—education, health care, child care, parental leave, *and* access to contraception and abortion—are all essential to racial and economic justice. The initial NBFO press conference and high-profile speakers made the specific needs and concerns of Black women visible. To this end, the NBFO issued a "Statement of Purpose," sent members a questionnaire about feminism, held consciousness-raising sessions, circulated a bibliography of recommended reading, established a speakers' bureau, and worked to change the portrayal of African Americans on television.[18] The "Statement of Purpose" is a thrilling exhortation, a one-page manifesto asserting that the NBFO exists "in order to address ourselves to the particular and specific needs of the larger, but almost cast aside half of the Black race in Amerikkka, the Black Woman." The group clarifies intersecting oppressions: "Black women have suffered cruelly in this society from living the phenomenon of being Black and female in a country that is *both* racist and sexist." The NBFO uses the statement to reject roles as "breeders," "castraters," and "strong . . . matriarchs" in favor of diverse, self-defined identities, and makes clear that their work will strengthen both "the current Women's Liberation Movement" and "the Black Liberation Movement" by charting a path that, unlike these movements, is not plagued by racism and sexism. The statement concludes with a call to Black people from Black women: "We must, together, as a people, work to eliminate racism from without the Black community which is trying to destroy us as an entire people, but we must remember that sexism is destroying and crippling us from within."[19]

Black women read this inspiring "Statement of Purpose" and took up its charge, starting chapters of the NBFO all over the United States under the leadership and guidance of Sloan, Galvin-Lewis, and others, all of whom were unpaid. These leaders and the rest of the coordinating council "tried to develop an open and egalitarian form of cooperation among themselves and the members," which resulted in both governance by "consensus" and "open conflicts" at meetings.[20] In 1974, the NBFO continued to expand its reach by holding conferences in Atlanta, Detroit, and Washington, D.C.[21] By the time they sent out the third issue of the NBFO newsletter in September 1975, the editors were able to include contact information for chapters from Atlanta to Detroit, Houston, and Kansas City. Each chapter, and often each smaller group within those chapters, had its own areas of focus and activism, such as organizing for gay and lesbian rights, forming a credit union, protesting sexist state laws, helping members find employment, and operating rape crisis centers.[22] The NBFO's most active period ended in 1975, but chapters of the organization continued to operate through 1979.[23]

Many members of The Sisterhood participated in and learned from the NBFO. Lori Sharpe was a cofounder, and Margo Jefferson read her work at an early NBFO writers' workshop. Other Sisterhood members were also key figures in the organization's development: Judith Wilson helped start a newsletter and Alice Walker collaborated with Faith Ringgold (an important visual artist, an arts activist, and Michele Wallace's mother) to run a workshop on "Black Feminists and the Cultural Arts" as part of a 1973 NBFO conference.[24] Through this work, Sisterhood members learned practical skills necessary for running conferences and editing newsletters. In the NBFO and other political organizations, they also experienced the necessity and relief of creating and inhabiting spaces for Black women to do their collaborative work.

The Combahee River Collective (1974–1980), another important immediate predecessor and interlocutor for The Sisterhood, worked on all kinds of projects in the Boston area, including creating a battered women's shelter and taking part in labor organizing. Combahee, like The Sisterhood, treated political activism and writing as interdependent, and both groups cared about the relationship between literature and politics. Sisters Barbara and Beverly Smith were among the founders of Combahee. Their activism began with their participation in the struggle for public school integration as high school students in Cleveland, Ohio, in 1964 and later as volunteers with the Congress of Racial Equality (CORE).[25] Barbara would go to earn her undergraduate degree from Mount Holyoke, then pursue a graduate degree in English at the University of Pittsburgh. Beverly joined the staff of *Ms.*, and both women worked with chapters of the NBFO.[26] Barbara recalls in an interview with Keeanga-Yamahtta Taylor that she taught her "first course on Black women writers" at Emerson College in Boston in fall 1973, around the same time that the NBFO conference in New York served as a "springboard" for "starting an NBFO chapter in Boston, which eventually became Combahee."[27] With other Boston women, including Demita Frazier, Barbara and Beverly started Combahee in 1974 as a "radical" Black feminist organization whose work differed from the "reformist" agenda of the NBFO.[28] As Combahee put it in their 1977 statement, they decided in 1974 "to become an independent collective since we had serious disagreements with NBFO's

20

"REVOLUTION IS NOT A ONE-TIME EVENT"

bourgeois-feminist stance and their lack of a clear political focus."[29] Judith Wilson recalls that the "NBFO went up in flames" during what was "basically a conflict between straight feminists and lesbians."[30] Robin Kelley describes the split: "the left wing of the NBFO abandoned the movement after a year because it failed to address the needs of the poor and spoke exclusively to heterosexual women"; Combahee members "came from different movements in the Boston area, including the Committee to End Sterilization Abuse," and "nearly all of the women had worked together to bring attention to a series of unsolved murders of Black women in Boston."[31]

The women of Combahee organized for Black women's safety in Boston, a city known for both its racism and its academic institutions. The universities in the area drew Black women intellectuals, and they relied on each other to survive the racism of their city and workplaces. Combahee, like other Black feminist organizations of the 1970s, challenged the sexism of Black power movements and the racism of feminist movements. It differed from the NBFO by directly addressing homophobia and by emphasizing the ways class oppression intersects with other forms of oppression. Their regular retreats were "for black feminists and lesbians."[32]

In 1976, Combahee "decided . . . to become a study group." Although they had been reading one another's writing and studying various texts together for years, this was an intentional turn toward literary organizing. At their spring 1976 retreat, Combahee members decided to prioritize "the possibility of starting a Black feminist publication" and planned "to gather together a collection of Black feminist writing." The Combahee River Collective Statement, produced the following year, asserts, "We feel that is it absolutely essential to demonstrate the reality of our politics to other Black women and believe that we can do this through writing and distributing our work."[33] Like Sisterhood members, Combahee members had experience in civil rights actions such as sit-ins and marches in the 1960s and in less visible but equally vital political work in the early 1970s, organizing conferences and addressing issues such as access to health care. In 1976, the group made an intentional turn to the creation, distribution, and study of African American women's writing as crucial forms of political work. Like Sisterhood members, Combahee members wrote for "other Black women."

Combahee's belief in education and literary study as radical political work happened and remains visible today because, as Kimberly Springer observes, Barbara Smith's "talents as a writer put her in a privileged position in a movement that valued connecting the personal to the political through the written word and verbal acuity in academic circles, as well as in a thriving under-ground feminist press."[34] Farah Griffin notes that Combahee's "fame is less a result of its greater activism [than other Black feminist groups] than of the fact that the collective left an eloquent document, 'A Black Feminist State-ment.'"[35] Combahee put writing and literature at the center of Black feminist politics. This was possible partly because Black women writers and the liter-ary scholars discussed later in this chapter were bringing Black feminist liter-ature into trade book publishing and university classrooms. The importance of literature to Black feminist politics is also one legacy of the Black Arts Movement, which asserted the absolute necessity of literature, theater, visual art, and music in any work for Black liberation. Combahee members took part in civil rights movement activism, BAM, and Black feminist political organizations. By 1976 some members were increasingly tied to the academy; this eventually manifested as a split between those who became academics and those who did not. They may have disagreed over whether one needed a classroom to study Black women's writing, but all agreed that literature mattered for political work.

Barbara Smith and other members' skills as writers made Combahee especially influential on literary studies in the academy. Smith's scholarly grounding—she pursued a PhD at the University of Connecticut and was among the first members of the Modern Language Association's Commis-sion on the Status of Women in the Profession from 1975 to 1978—shaped the increasingly literary focus of the collective and fostered her contact with Sisterhood members. She was in graduate school and on the MLA commis-sion at the time she helped write Combahee's "A Black Feminist Statement."

The prose of the statement is precise and direct, but also passionate and persuasive, as in this framing of their position:

> Many of us were active in those movements (Civil Rights, Black nationalism, the Black Panthers), and all of our lives were greatly affected and changed by their ideologies, their goals, and the tactics used to achieve their goals. It was our experience and disillusionment within these liberation movements, as well as experience on the periphery of the white male left, that led to the need to develop a politics that was anti-racist, unlike those of white women, and anti-sexist, unlike those of Black and white men.[36]

The writing here is specific and clarifying, contextualizing the origins of Combahee in the early 1970s among a group of women who carried both "experience and disillusionment" out of Black liberation movements. Readers today immediately see that the statement called for intersectional politics decades before Kimberlé Crenshaw defined "intersectionality." The document remains a touchstone for readers and activists in part due to the power of the prose. The lines above subordinate "the white male left" into a clause, putting it, rather than the Black women writing the statement, on the "periphery." The memorable syntax of "anti-racist, unlike those of white women, and anti-sexist, unlike those of Black and white men" also uses the order of words to prioritize the "anti-racist" and "anti-sexist" Black women writing this statement over "white women" and "Black and white men." Combahee always capitalized "Black" and "Lesbians," a choice that identifies Lesbians as a political classification in addition to a sexual identity. The statement unfolds with precision, force, and eloquence over four numbered sections. It concludes with this inspiring, sermonic, future-oriented sentence: "As Black feminists and Lesbians we know that we have a very definite revolutionary task to perform and we are ready for the lifetime of work and struggle before us."[37]

∾

BAM was a cultural precursor and partial ideological foundation for The Sisterhood. The NBFO and Combahee served as precursors and training grounds for the group. At the same time, Black women scholars made space in the academy for Sisterhood members' writings. By the time many members entered academic institutions in the 1980s as professors, visiting lecturers, and writers-in-residence, Black women had established Black studies and African American literary studies in colleges and universities. These scholars built on the claims of the Black Arts Movement and Toni Cade Bambara's *The Black Woman* that literature is important common ground for the work of liberation and they made the university a place for the study and dissemination of Black literature.

One important site of convergence for Black feminist literary scholars was the SEEK (Search for Education, Elevation, and Knowledge) Program, in which Toni Cade Bambara, Barbara Christian, Jessica Harris, June Jordan, Audre Lorde, Barbara Smith, and Toni Morrison taught in the 1960s and '70s.[38] SEEK began at City College of New York in 1965, and state legislation expanded and codified it in 1966 to "provide access to CUNY senior colleges for students who graduated from high schools that had not prepared them for the rigors of college."[39] SEEK students were more likely to be poor or working class, first-generation students, Black, or Latinx than the general college student population in New York. Although SEEK provided access to higher education for many young people, it also came to alibi or stand in for a lack of structural reform to public K–12 education.[40] Like other progressive pockets at universities from the 1960s to the present, the program also functioned as a site of Black feminist collaboration: because the courses did not have a prescribed curriculum, teachers tended to collaborate on and swap assignments, syllabi, and teaching strategies in ways that brought Black feminist writing and ideas into their classrooms.[41] Scholar Nellie Y. McKay was a student in the SEEK Program at Queens College in the late 1960s, and it "transformed McKay's life."[42] Barbara Christian asserted that she "got into African American literature" because of SEEK. In order to find, read, and teach works that her Black and Puerto Rican students in the program "could relate" to, Christian found herself in the 1960s "excavating . . . texts that were no longer available" in a teaching "experience" that "would turn me around in terms of what I felt literature was about."[43] Christian and McKay are just two of the major Black feminist literary scholars whose experience in SEEK remained an important influence on their teaching and writing throughout their careers.

In the late 1960s and early '70s, as SEEK was going full force in New York, students' direct political actions all over the United States helped establish Black studies programs and made changes to racist policies at their schools. One reason members of The Sisterhood and Black feminist academics saw potential in the academy as an instrument of political change is that they had personal experience with political action on campuses. At Bennington College, Judith Wilson was "very involved in campus politics," helped start the Black Student Union and, after reading Simone de Beauvoir's *The Second Sex* (1949), identified as a feminist and led a campus women's group.[44] In 1968, as an undergraduate, Ntozake Shange participated in protests at Barnard College and Columbia University against racist, sexist, and militaristic policies. She went on to become the second director of Northeastern University's Afro-American Institute, which was established in response to student demonstrations in Boston. Audre Lorde brought soup and blankets to students at City College as they "set up barricades, occupied buildings, and forced an end to all classes," demanding that the college move to open admissions in order to give Black and Puerto Rican students equal access to education.[45] June Jordan describes this moment: "In every sense, from faculty petitions to student manifestos, to the atmosphere in the cafeteria and the bathrooms, City College signified a revolution in process. Nobody was eating, sleeping, thinking, or moving around anything except the issues at stake."[46] The actions at City College resulted in an open admissions policy that, as Roderick Ferguson describes it, "transformed" "a predominantly white institution to one . . . made up of a majority of black and brown students."[47] As Jodi Melamed explains, student efforts "to broaden access to universities, to validate new knowledges, and to make ending racial inequality a practical (not merely rhetorical) aim of university education" had a period of real success such that "by the early 1970s more than five hundred black and ethnic studies programs had been founded on university campuses" in the United States.[48]

These changes inspired students and faculty to believe that they could fight racism in and through higher education. However, in later years and decades, the academy absorbed and tempered the most transformative possibilities held out by student actions of the late 1960s and early 1970s. Despite these crushing setbacks, June Jordan's experience of a "revolution in process" on campuses was part of the intellectual formation of Sisterhood members, nearly all of whom were either taking or teaching the very first classes focused on Black women's writing at their schools. The atmosphere of revolution and the success of student actions in changing academic policy defined Wilson, Shange, Lorde, Jordan, and other Sisterhood members' early experience of the academy. As college students and teachers, they participated in, benefited from, and built on the student protests of the late 1960s. Undergraduate students' political demonstrations in 1968 and '69— and again in 2015—were among the most effective ways to push academic institutions to establish Black studies units and hire Black faculty. Sisterhood members gained a foothold for the study of Black women's writing partly because of those protests. Sisterhood members were also among a cohort of Black women scholars who faced a backlash to these specific gains alongside the long-standing and ever-persistent racism and misogyny of their academic workplaces. Yet some continued (and continue today) to take on the ongoing, everyday work of creating, running, and defending Black studies programs, centers, and departments.

Then, as now, the institutionalization of Black studies matters for Black liberation politics outside the academy. Black studies departments operate in relation to Black community organizing and with the support and critique of organizers and writers outside of the academy. In 1975, Sisterhood member

Lori Sharpe wrote "Supplemental Guidelines for Black Women" in a pamphlet about feminist organizing and consciousness raising. She recommended a discussion question: "Black studies—is it a passing phase?"[49] Sharpe's discussion question shows that Black studies was a subject of feminist political organizing alongside issues such as domestic violence and reproductive justice. Sharpe wrote the guidelines for groups that worked on a wide variety of practical projects such as access to health care, protection from domestic violence, food security, and child care. Even though academia was not the focus of these groups, many members became academics, and they believed in Black studies. In turn, Black studies scholars, including scholars of African American literature, operated from the start with a sense of obligation to the student protesters and community organizers who helped make their scholarly work possible.

In the same years they offered material support to student demonstrators and taught the first college courses about Black women's writing, this cohort of intellectuals argued for Black women's poetry, fiction, and drama as legitimate objects of study and emphasized a tradition of Black women's scholarly writing. This work to identify and support Black women's creative and scholarly writings took place in classrooms, in books and journal articles, and at conferences. Two exemplary courses in this period were Sonia Sanchez's 1969 literature seminar "The Black Woman" at the University of Pittsburgh and Audre Lorde's 1970 "series of lectures on racial stereotyping, institutionalized racism, and the stages and mechanics of oppression, wedding them to discussions of race, class, gender, black history, and literature" at John Jay College of Criminal Justice.[50]

A crucial moment in this creative and scholarly activism happened in 1973, when poet Margaret Walker organized the Phillis Wheatley Poetry Festival at Jackson State College in Mississippi and invited June Jordan and Alice Walker to participate. The Wheatley Festival claimed its namesake— a women poet—as the foremother of African American literature, thus elevating a writer whom some in the Black Arts Movement had critiqued and dismissed as insufficiently radical. The festival brought together Black women poets and scholars, insisting on the overlap between those two roles. Dana Murphy describes it as "coauthored by Margaret and over twenty Black women writers who gathered to read their work in Phillis's honor."[51] In keeping with a conference named for Wheatley, Alice Walker read her now canonical essay "In Search of Our Mothers' Gardens" in front of an audience for the first time at this gathering. Audre Lorde was there too, along with a stunning

roster of poets and scholars including Lucille Clifton, Mari Evans, Paula Giddings, Nikki Giovanni, Carolyn Rodgers, and Sonia Sanchez.[52] Gwendolyn
Brooks gave a poetry reading, and Nina Simone performed "Young, Gifted,
and Black" with the Jackson State College Choir. Margaret Walker presided
over the program and read from her poetry.[53] Although gatherings of poets,
thinkers, and musicians were common in Black Arts Movement circles, it
was extremely rare, perhaps even singular, in 1973 to hold an academic conference on a university campus focused entirely on Black women's poetry.
Margaret Walker helped ensure the future study of these women's poetry and
scholarly writing by creating, "pre-circulating," and cataloging in the Jackson
State Library a "bibliography" of "all known published works by the writers
and scholars who agreed to read at the festival" as an act of "Black feminist
academic literary canon formation at a time when such scholarship had little
presence in US English literature departments."[54]

In the early 1970s, scholars were doing the work of simultaneously creating
Black feminist literary criticism and securing a place for that criticism in
academic departments. Mary Helen Washington was "part of the small band
of scholars who, in 1970, inaugurated the first Black Studies program at
the University of Detroit."[55] The importance of literary studies to the development of Black studies made textual recovery and a Black women's intellectual tradition central to the discipline from its beginnings.[56] Washington
recalled in 1997 that, "Many of the texts we now consider classic African
American texts were being brought back into print in the 1970s, but their
life in print was erratic and unpredictable, and there was almost nowhere to
go for critical commentary."[57] Washington's work as an editor, scholar, and
teacher provided and enabled a "life in print" and "critical commentary"
for the works of Black women writers. Her indispensable collections *Black
Eyed Susans* (1975) and *Midnight Birds* (1980) gathered, published, and thus
made possible the study of writings by Paule Marshall, Toni Morrison, Gayl
Jones, Gwendolyn Brooks, Alexis De Veaux, Ntozake Shange, Alice Walker,
and Toni Cade Bambara, among others. Washington's scholarly introduc-
tions to both volumes and her essay "Teaching *Black-Eyed Susans*" (1977)
make clear that the goal was to promote the study and teaching of Black
women authors. "Teaching *Black-Eyed Susans*" outlines thematic and historical approaches for teaching the works of contemporary Black women
writers collected in the book and situates those contemporary works in a
long line of Black women's writing, from Frances Harper's *Iola Leroy* (1892)
to Alice Walker's *Meridian* (1976).[58] Like the many anthologies of the Harlem

Renaissance and Black Arts periods, Washington's volumes asserted the need for and made possible the study of African American writing as a distinct body of literature with specific formal and thematic characteristics. Scholarly, institutional, and editorial labor such as Washington's; reading groups; and conferences such as the Wheatley Poetry Festival made it possible to recover, read, and teach works by Black women writers and "fostered the enthusiastic study of contemporary Black women writers" into the 1980s.[59]

Across the 1970s and '80s, Washington and other scholars created a contemporary Black feminist literary criticism. Then and today, Black feminist literary criticism is committed to the recovery of out-of-print and understudied works by Black women and asserts that poetry, fiction, and drama by Black women offers ways to understand identity, systems of power, and history. Robin Kelley writes, "The radical black feminist movement . . . expanded the definition of who constitutes a theorist, the voice of authority speaking for black women, to include poets, blues singers, storytellers, painters, mothers, preachers, and teachers."[60] Black feminist literary criticism, in the mode of the Black Arts Movement, Combahee, and The Sisterhood, takes it as given that "poets" "storytellers," and "teachers" are "theorist[s]" with "authority." Black feminist literary criticism rejects binary thinking and instead takes a both/and stance that accepts multiple, sometimes seemingly conflicting, ideas or sources of knowledge as true. For example, Toni Cade Bambara's 1980 novel *The Salt Eaters* treats tarot, astrology, and physics as equally true and useful sources of knowledge; her 1970 anthology *The Black Woman* brings together in one volume essays that demand access to birth control pills and other essays that describe contraception as part of a larger racist medical agenda. Scholars doing Black feminist work attend to the way intersecting forms of identity such as race, class, gender, and sexuality work together to shape individual and collective experience. They study and teach African American women's writing as a distinct and specific tradition that is part of a broader African American literary tradition.

Black feminist literary scholars established these commitments and methods in the 1970s, which made them and their many students skilled readers of the works that members of The Sisterhood created during and after the years that group met. As Barbara Christian was writing *Black Women Novelists: The Development of a Tradition* (1980), which would become a foundational work of Black feminist literary scholarship, she was also teaching contemporary Black women's literature, which required the extra labor of locating the books she wanted to assign. Offering one of the countless examples of how laborious it often was to recover of out-of-print and understudied books by Black women, Christian writes, "it was virtually impossible to locate either the works of many nineteenth-century writers or those of contemporary writers, whose books went in and out of print like ping-pong balls. For example, I xeroxed *Brown Girl, Brownstones* (please forgive me, Paule) any number of times because it simply was not available and I wanted to use it in classes I had begun to teach on Afro-American women's literature."[61] In 1977, as The Sisterhood met and as Christian was teaching their works, Sisterhood member Paule Marshall's 1959 novel *Brown Girl, Brownstones* was already out of print. Nella Larsen, whose novels *Quicksand* (1928) and *Passing* (1929) would later be widely studied in African American and American literature courses, had died in obscurity with her novels out of print in 1964. Black women writers and scholars established the recovery imperative as a tenet of African American literary studies even before the field codified in the academy. Alice Walker, appalled in the early 1960s that Jean Toomer's *Cane* (1923), W. E. B. Du Bois's *Black Reconstruction* (1935), and Zora Neale Hurston's *Mules and Men* (1935) were not readily available, located rare copies of each at university libraries and "Xeroxed them and stole somebody's rights, but it was the least I could do if I wanted to read them over and over again, which I did."[62] As Farah Jasmine Griffin describes, this generation of Black feminist literary scholars did three key forms of work: "locating, teaching, and writing about earlier 'lost' texts," creating "a critical vocabulary and framework for discussing works by African American women," and theorizing both "that body of work as well as the critical practices of black feminist critics."[63] These three tasks remain central to African American literary studies.

The recovery work of Sisterhood members and their contemporaries was not only about making it possible to read and teach writings by Black women from the nineteenth century or from the Harlem Renaissance. It was also about making sure their own writing would stay in print and reach readers. This effort proved successful for a number of their books, such as Walker's volume of essays, *In Search of Our Mothers' Gardens*, which has been in print consistently since its 1983 publication.[64] The increased availability of Black women's writings from earlier periods shows in the ways that contemporary Black women writers explicitly engage these works. Thulani Davis wrote in 1987 that, although Black women writers had long understood themselves as working in a tradition, "Morrison, Alice Walker, Gayl Jones, Toni Cade Bambara, Gloria Naylor, Sherley Anne Williams, Ntozake Shange, and others are the first generation to have a body of work on the black woman's condition readily at hand."[65] The recovery and study of Black women's writings from earlier periods shaped the form and content of the Black women's renaissance of the 1970s and '80s.

As The Sisterhood sought publication and publicity for Black women's writings, literary scholars were making a place in the academy for the study of those works. Nellie McKay and Claudia Tate were in graduate school together at Harvard among a cohort of Black women who were "in the process of becoming literary critics" and "met regularly in each other's homes to discuss books by Black women" that were not part of their formal education. Alienated by the racism and classism at Harvard, McKay officially withdrew in 1971 to accept a one-year teaching position at Simmons College. As other Black women intellectuals would later find in The Sisterhood in New York, she found respite from the "alienation" of elite white institutions in "a coterie of Black women in Boston, many of whom had descended on the city for academic jobs or graduate study."[66] These "African American women who were all working on degrees" met regularly in the early 1970s in the Boston area and included Black feminist intellectuals Thadious Davis, Hortense Spillers, Andrea Rushing, and Barbara Smith.[67] Along with Mary Helen Washington, Barbara Christian, and others, they were creating institutional structures and developing methods that would make it possible to seriously and regularly study and teach Black women's writing in universities across the country for decades to come. This was not easy; scholars of Black women's writing faced resistance from hiring committees and from publishers. Christian wrote, "When I began sending out sections of *Black Women Novelists*, practically all academic as well as trade presses commented that my subject was not important," and McKay recalled that her department chair at the University of Wisconsin-Madison told her that an interview with Toni Morrison was "not real scholarship" and would not help her get tenured.[68] Both women pursued their research agenda despite the constant resistance from white gatekeepers, and both saw the study of Black women's writing grow in their lifetimes as a result.

The relationship between writers and scholars was reciprocal and interdependent; greater interest in Black women's writing grew out of and supported these scholars' works. Christian wrote in 1989, "I believe if it were not for the incredible publicity that Toni Morrison's *Song of Solomon* received in 1978, and the fact that one of my chapters was devoted to her work, I would not have been able to publish *Black Women Novelists* when I did."[69] Christian's manuscript was rejected by twenty-seven presses before finding a home at

Greenwood Press largely because, as scholar Arlene Keizer puts it, "the idea of a tradition of Black women writers was not legible at all to academic publishers in the late 1970s."[70] The attention that *Song of Solomon* earned was due to Morrison's literary achievement, but also to the work of Sisterhood members and their contemporaries who supported the book through writing reviews and scholarly pieces, teaching the novel, and organizing readings and book parties. It is almost impossible to account for the amount of work over the previous decade that went into making 1978 the year Morrison began to secure her unique position in American literature and the year Christian became the first Black woman to get tenure at UC Berkeley.

Scholars of African American women's literature built a readership for Black women's texts, especially novels, by writing about those works in both academic and general-interest publications. These literary scholars were fighting an uphill battle to establish the legitimacy of African American literature as an area of study. At the same time, they insisted on writing about Black books for a broad audience in venues that might not count for promotion and tenure at their university jobs. This meant working as both academics and public intellectuals to pursue two different and simultaneous publishing endeavors, writing both the peer-reviewed books and articles necessary to earn tenure and the articles, book reviews, and interviews that appealed to a wider audience.

Barbara Christian wrote insightful reviews of Black women's books in scholarly journals such as *The Women's Review of Books*, *The Black Scholar*, and *Callaloo*. While she was director of Black studies at the University of Detroit, Mary Helen Washington reviewed Toni Cade Bambara's collection of short stories *The Sea Birds Are Still Alive* in *Ms.* magazine in 1977. Claudia Tate interviewed Sisterhood members and other Black women writers in the 1970s for what would become *Black Women Writers at Work* (1985), an inspiring and useful collection of candid interviews with Maya Angelou, Gwendolyn Brooks, Audre Lorde, and Alice Walker, among others. Tate's volume was reviewed in academic journals and remains a crucial resource for scholars of Black women's writing, but she wrote it for anyone interested in Black writers. *Black Women Writers at Work* reached a broad, general audience, going into multiple reprintings and editions in the first few years after publication. Well-known white novelist Anne Tyler reviewed the book for *The New York Times*, asserting that "Claudia Tate, who teaches American literature at Howard University, is looking forward. Her subjects are part of a group that is just now taking on full voice."[71] In early 2023, Haymarket Books reissued *Black Women Writers at Work* to much excitement among scholars and contemporary Black women writers.

Barbara Christian describes the early 1970s as a period when "the articulation of the possibility of a tradition of Afro-American writers occurred not in a fancy academic journal, but in two magazines: *Ms.*, a new popular magazine that came out of the women's movement, and *Black World*, a longstanding black journal unknown to most academics and possibly scorned by some."[72] The journal reached both academic and general readers, most of whom were Black. Founded in 1942 as *Negro Digest* and imagined as a Black alternative to *Reader's Digest, Black World* became a popular forum that by the mid-to-late 1960s included discussions of Black Power and Black cultural nationalism. As discussed in the next chapter, The Sisterhood enlisted *Essence*, initially a less political publication than *Ms.* or *Black World*, to articulate "a tradition of Afro-American writers" for an audience larger than the readership of any academic journal. Writing for both academic and popular audiences, taking part in activism on and off campuses, and recovering Black women's writings for use in their classrooms and the broader world, these Black feminist intellectuals spoke to, from, and for multiple audiences. This intertwining of political, literary, and academic work defined Black feminism from the moment it entered the academy.

These Black feminist intellectuals achieved what Ann duCille describes as "a seismic reshuffling of what had been a stacked deck, with aftershocks that continue to reverberate throughout American letters and the US academy." DuCille explains that Black women's novels became far more visible in the last quarter of the twentieth century in part because, in the 1970s and '80s, a "generation of university-educated artists and academics of color cultivated their own black female gardens . . . furiously producing and publishing new works of their own while also constructing for that work its first black female interpretive community." This new "interpretive community" was a group of scholars able to write about and teach formally innovative novels by Toni Cade Bambara, Gayl Jones, Toni Morrison, and others who employed nonlinear time, shifting point of view, and Black vernacular knowledge. DuCille names a cohort of "newly minted PhDs," including Frances Smith Foster, Trudier Harris, Hortense Spillers, Mae Henderson, and Cheryl Wall, "who would become the premier scholars and critics of a new body of literature and field of study." As this group was completing their doctoral degrees, Black women novelists, including Gayl Jones, Paule Marshall, Toni Morrison, and Sherley Anne Williams, took teaching jobs at universities.[73]

The scholars who set the table for the study of Black women's novels brought new objects of inquiry and methods into the academy in the same decades that Black women's literary fiction in the United States became more visible. Early courses in Black women's writing began to establish a network that was part of the foundation for The Sisterhood. Renita Weems was an economics major at Wellesley, where she took one course on Black women's literature taught by Hortense Spillers, who was completing her PhD at Brandeis.[74] As an undergraduate at Bennington College in the early 1970s, Judith Wilson read books by Ralph Ellison and Richard Wright, but found few opportunities to study and write about Black women's literature in her classes. She expanded her education by pursuing independent studies and by interning at Publisher's Weekly; The Black Scholar; the San Francisco Chronicle; and Ms., where she went on to work as an associate editor. At Publisher's Weekly, Wilson met Toni Morrison, then an editor at Random House. A Black woman "clerical worker" told Wilson that Morrison was a novelist— "You know that Toni's published a novel, right?"—and loaned her Morrison's first novel, The Bluest Eye.[75] Wilson recognized that The Bluest Eye was doing something new, with its "eye-opening" attention to the "issue of color consciousness" and the way Morrison was "turning her back, in one sense, on white audiences. And really focusing on our experience."[76]

The women who would become The Sisterhood also studied Black women's writings outside of college classrooms. Margo Jefferson, in her "first full-time job" as a book critic for Newsweek, identified as a "progressive Black feminist" and entered a period of "fervent reading" in fields including Black studies; she describes this as her "adult education" through study "with friends."[77] Self-directed study was common among Black women intellectuals in the 1970s. The Sisterhood came together partly to satisfy their desire to read and talk about Black women's writings and partly as a reprieve from the overwhelming whiteness of their workplaces as they pursued their careers in New York.

Black feminists carved out spaces where they could organize and exchange ideas. Feminist bookstores were one key place to gather and network. Renita Weems remembers Womanbooks on the Upper West Side as one of several "feminist bookstores" that "were hugely important to the success of women's literature in the 70s" that "all of the novelists in the Sisterhood frequented and owed a debt to." Weems relied on Womanbooks to help her build a "reading list" and as a "comfortable" place to hang out.[78] This was by design; co-owner Eleanor Olds Batchelder recalls, "people would come do research at Womanbooks, because we didn't mind if they used the books there. We had a big table. So they would come and spend days and just use the books gently on the premises."[79] Weems went to Womanbooks "almost every day or every other day after work to find something to read to get me through the evenings or whatever, to back to work, to this job that I absolutely hated" at Merrill Lynch. A desire for serious engagement with Black and women's writing led Weems to feminist bookstores and eventually to The Sisterhood. She spotted a posting on the bulletin board at Womanbooks that read, "Are you interested in reading Black women's books? I am too, please give me a call." Responding to this notice led Weems to Rosemary Bray, who was an editor at *Essence* and a recent Yale graduate. Bray invited Weems to come along to a meeting of The Sisterhood.[80]

The mission of feminist bookstores to simultaneously reach a general audience and shape an academic one was successful, as demonstrated by the fact that each time the Modern Language Association met in New York, Womanbooks had a "throng" of customers who came uptown to buy stacks of books to ship home that "provided women's studies founders with resources unavailable elsewhere."[81] Feminist bookstores of the 1970s were owned and run mostly by white women, but several advocated for Black women's writing. Bookstore owners collaborated as literary activists in ways that both inspired and echoed the work of Black feminist literary activism. The national trade publication *Feminist Bookstore News* offered instructions about "how to lobby for reprints of books" and had several successful campaigns, "including Morrison's *The Bluest Eye*, published in 1970, out of print by the mid-1970s, and reissued in 1978."[82] Feminist bookstores in cities around in the country stocked mimeographed copies of out-of-print works, just as Black women writers and readers were passing around worn originals and mimeographed copies of older works, such as Hurston's *Their Eyes Were Watching God* (1937), and more recent ones, such as Vertamae Grosvenor's *Vibration Cooking* (1970).

By 1977, the year that saw the first meeting of The Sisterhood and the publication of both the Combahee River Collective Statement and Barbara Smith's essay "Toward a Black Feminist Criticism," Black feminists had established the interdependence of political, literary, and academic spheres. At the end of 1977, Smith and Audre Lorde discussed the need for Black feminist retreats. They used the overwhelmingly white, male, academic setting of Modern Language Association conferences in Chicago and New York subversively to meet up to discuss and plan these retreats.[83] As the year came to a close, Smith was energized and optimistic. She wrote to Lorde, "quite a few of my visions for Black ♀♀ and myself came true in 1977" and "I am even more convinced that there is a kind of Black ♀♀'s cultural awakening going on now."[84]

The promise of 1977, Smith's "visions for Black" women and sense of a "cultural awakening," were real and would achieve results, though sometimes not until years or decades later.[85] Though Combahee "disbanded" in 1980, Lorde and Smith started Kitchen Table Women of Color Press and published *Home Girls: A Black Feminist Anthology* (1983), which grew directly out of Combahee and reprinted the collective's "A Black Feminist Statement."[86] Barbara Smith understood the volume as a continuation of Combahee's Black feminist work and writes in the introduction, "It is safe to say that in 1982 we have a movement of our own. I have been involved in building that movement since 1973."[87]

Home Girls documents the intellectual, political, and literary spirit of The Sisterhood, the Combahee River Collective, and Black feminism at the start of the 1980s. The anthology includes writings by Sisterhood members Alice Walker, Patricia Spears Jones, June Jordan, Audre Lorde, and Renita Weems. In editing the book, Barbara Smith drew a distinction between "political analysis and fiction" but "wanted the new anthology to represent Black feminism at the present time and retain its literary focus."[88] *Home Girls* offers queer and feminist critiques of the homophobia and sexism that Combahee and Sisterhood members encountered in the Black Arts Movement. Like Toni Cade Bambara's *The Black Woman*, it participates in a tradition of anthologies that assert a diverse but coherent tradition of Black writing and make the study of that writing possible by gathering representative works in one place. Writing about Gloria Hull, Patricia Bell Scott, and Barbara Smith's 1982 anthology *All the Women Are White, All the Blacks Are Men, But Some of Us Are Brave*, SaraEllen Strongman describes the "revisionary and resuscitating nature" of the multigeneric Black feminist anthologies of the early 1980s.[89] Barbara Smith argued that "anthologies which bring together many voices seem particularly suited to the multiplicity of issues of concern to women of color."[90]

Home Girls put lesbians at the center of Black feminist thought and made public the conversations about lesbians that had often taken place only in private. These were sometimes contentious moments, as when the homophobia of some chapters of the NBFO led members to break off and form Combahee. In her contribution, "The Failure to Transform: Homophobia in the Black Community," Cheryl Clarke writes, "The black lesbian is not only absent from the pages of black political analysis, her image as a character in literature and her role as a writer are blotted out from or trivialized in literary criticism written by black women."[91] She takes Mary Helen Washington, bell hooks, and Michele Wallace to task for not writing about "the black lesbian" in their literary and cultural criticism.

There is plenty of desire, love, and sex among women in Washington's two collections of Black women's fiction, in works by Sisterhood members, and in writings by Black women throughout the African American literary tradition. Black feminist literary scholars have attended to representations of lesbians, queer people, and women who love women in African American literature from the founding of the field on, but not as consistently as Clarke rightly demands. Her critique of homophobia had high stakes because the "omission of black lesbianism and black lesbian writers" occurred as the study of African American literature was beginning to be codified in the academy.[92] This omission of Black lesbians, if not of desire among Black women, continued into the 1980s. Barbara Christian's "No More Buried Lives," an essay on "lesbianism" in fiction by Black women, is an important exception. "No More Buried Lives" was published in 1984, but began a few years earlier as a talk at A Woman's Place Bookstore in Oakland. Christian writes, "The primarily black lesbian audience at Woman's Place was marvelous in their discussion of the books and of my essay . . . and indicated how important reader response is to our understanding of the literature's significance."[93]

The "omission" Clarke describes allows for liberatory individuality but erases the collectivity necessary for political action. "Black lesbian," like "Black woman," can, as Clarke suggests, be a necessary political category (as in a voting block) or literary category (as in the title of a course or anthology). The stakes of this erasure are that novels such Nella Larsen's *Passing* and Toni Morrison's *Sula* can be regularly taught in high school and college classrooms with little or no attention to the same-gender desire and queer elements of those novels. To not name "Black lesbians" in political and literary discourse makes it possible—even in an African American literature course or a Black women's political group—to think of all Black people as straight and all lesbians as white, which is exactly what Christian, Clarke, Lorde, and Smith were writing against.

Despite the fact that several members identified as lesbian, gay, queer, or bisexual, there was little to no discussion at Sisterhood meetings of "what would have [then] been called [the] lesbian and gay rights move-ment," although "it was assumed that everybody was down with it."[94] By the time the group met in 1977, Lorde had made a "public claim to a lesbian identity," including at John Jay College, where she rightly feared that colleagues in the Department of English would use her sexuality to undermine her authority as an advocate of an autonomous Black stud-ies department.[95] Lorde and Alexis De Veaux were part of a community of women writers in Brooklyn who identified publicly as lesbians. The homophobic "backlash" to their work was even "nastier" than what other Black women writers faced. The Sisterhood responded to these attacks on their Black lesbian members and other colleagues by visibly stepping up to support their books, public readings, and events.[96] In the title essay of *Civil Wars* (1980), June Jordan names "Gay rights" as "Civil Rights" and writes of "my loving a woman."[97] Other members of the group navigated similar complexities of their intersecting identities in their political, aca-demic, and literary labors.

As Black women writers gained visibility and faced virulent criticism, they rightly protected themselves by keeping some aspects of their personal lives off the record. The Sisterhood was built partly on close personal relationships, but the purpose of the group was to come together as thinkers and writers, and that determined their focus. Likely for both reasons, as I describe in the next chapter, these women didn't include discussions of motherhood in their meeting minutes, even though many of them had children. At Sisterhood meetings, there was little or no direct discussion of sexuality of any kind and definitely no Combahee-style assertions of "Black Lesbian" identity. Jordan's words, "my loving a woman," are an example of a focus on love and desire that she, Walker, and other members of the group tended to use rather than calling themselves lesbian, gay, or bisexual.[98] This is in keeping with the ways that they did not discuss their personal lives. The consequences of these boundaries radiated out from the group: because these women shaped mag-azines, publishing, and the academy for decades to come, they were part of the larger cultural "omission" of Black lesbians that Cheryl Clarke describes. Despite their differences in discussing sexuality, belief that the creation and study of literature is political work aligns Combahee and *Home Girls* with The Sisterhood and shows the interdependent and sometimes conflicting efforts to establish Black feminism in the academy, the literary marketplace, and the larger world.

~

Sisterhood members gained ideas, skills, and support from the Black Arts Movement, political organizations, and Black feminist literary studies. They were also already a nascent network before the group began meeting in 1977. When June Jordan and Alice Walker sent out invitations to the first meeting of The Sisterhood, they relied on existing personal and professional relationships among Black women writers in New York. Women who attended Sisterhood meetings had often met through work and then developed strong professional ties or, more rarely, close friendships. The Sisterhood was built on and sustained by a complicated set of relationships, and each meeting held a mix of professional ambition and obligation, respect for one another's writing and editorial work, as well as friendship and love. Although they did not explicitly name this as part of their strategy, the intimate ties between lovers and loving friends helped knit the group together.

When the group began meeting, whether individual members of The Sisterhood had met or not, they knew one another's work well. Walker taught Morrison's *The Bluest Eye* (1970) and wrote a letter to the *New York Times* objecting to a lackluster review of *Sula*.[99] Margo Jefferson began working at *Newsweek* in 1973 and reviewed many books by Black writers for the magazine, including *The Black Book* (1974), which Morrison edited; Walker's *Meridian* (1976); and Morrison's *Song of Solomon* (1977). Phyl Garland wrote an *Ebony* profile in August 1974 of Vertamae Grosvenor's daughters Kali and Chandra, whose remarkable achievements at the ages of just thirteen and eleven, respectively, already included poetry, filmmaking, lecturing, and activism. Jessica Harris interviewed Morrison for *Essence* in 1976 and avidly read and discussed Morrison's and Walker's novels with other scholars throughout the 1970s.[100]

In addition to writing about or teaching one another's books, some of the women had mentoring relationships prior to The Sisterhood and others used the group to create such relationships. Judith Wilson describes her work as an intern at *Publisher's Weekly* as "this little eighteen-year-old" having to "call up" Toni Morrison and other writers to get their overdue copy for the Christmas issue of the magazine. Wilson remembers, "It was so terrifying to me to make these phone calls that every morning I would come into work and before I went into the offices, I would make a beeline to the restroom and sit there and smoke and try to get my courage up." A few years later, when Wilson became a contributing editor at *Ms.* around 1974, Alice Walker "really took" Wilson "under her wing," becoming one of several "older, more experienced Black women" who would "play a mentoring role" in Wilson's career. This "was a very informal sort of thing" that white men had always done for one another in "the old boys' network."[101]

Rosa Guy and Paule Marshall offered models and mentorship to other group members. Guy and Marshall were a bit older than other Sisterhood members, were part of other networks of Black writers and artists, and were rooted in West Indian communities in New York. Guy was born in Trinidad and immigrated to Harlem as a child. In 1951, Guy asked "the white communist Philip Bonosky and the Black leftist John Killens" to create a group for Black writers. Bonosky and Killens "formed the Harlem Writers' Workshop (later the Harlem Writers' Guild), which encouraged and helped publish progressive Black writers."[102] The Harlem Writers' Guild (HWG) is a predecessor to The Sisterhood in that it brought together and worked to publish Black writers. Members included Sisterhood members Rosa Guy, Audre Lorde, and Paule Marshall. Guy recalls that HWG served primarily as a rigorous "workshop."[103] Decades later, when The Sisterhood met, Guy had just published *Ruby* (1976), the second in her trilogy of novels for young adults.

Just before her birth in 1929, Marshall's parents immigrated from Barbados to Brooklyn. In addition to being a successful novelist, Marshall was a celebrated creative writing teacher and a lifelong supporter of young writers from across the African Diaspora. In the 1970s, Marshall hosted regular gatherings of intellectuals; Guy, Jessica Harris, and Vertamae Grosvenor were among her guests.[104] By the time The Sisterhood met, Marshall had published two novels, *Brown Girl, Brownstones* (1959) and *The Chosen Place, the Timeless People* (1969), and a collection of stories, *Soul Clap Hands and Sing* (1961), and had won a Guggenheim Fellowship. Guy and Marshall were among those Sisterhood members who brought publishing experience and diasporic perspectives to the group. Marshall was well established enough to help other writers along, as evidenced by Toni Morrison turning to her in 1972 to read and comment positively on Toni Cade Bambara's collection of short stories *Gorilla, My Love* (1972).[105] Morrison, ever the relentless advocate for writers whose works she edited, sent out many letters asking for "a line or two that we can use in our promotion" to writers from John Updike, John Cheever, and Eudora Welty to Ralph Ellison and Joyce Carol Oates. She wrote Paule Marshall as part of this campaign on behalf of Bambara's short stories. This shows Marshall's stature on the literary scene in

1972. Most of the many letters repeat the same request verbatim, but those asking for "comment" on *Gorilla, My Love* from Marshall, Maya Angelou, James Baldwin, and Gwendolyn Brooks were more personal and urgent. In those letters, Morrison called Bambara's stories "sublime"; she tells Brooks that Bambara's stories are "heavy, elegant, funky, poignant, survivalist—all of the things good black writing is"; and she offers a personal note to Marshall, wishing her "a splendid and fruitful stay in Haiti."[106]

When Alice Walker and June Jordan brought The Sisterhood together in 1977, Jordan was already well acquainted with Morrison's editorial advocacy. Morrison engaged in a laborious letter-writing campaign to drum up support for and reviews of Jordan's book of poetry *Things That I Do in the Dark*. Even with this kind of effort, Black women's books, especially poetry, struggled to gain a wide readership. *Things That I Do in the Dark* was reviewed in only two publications: the Black political and cultural journal *Freedomways* and the *New York Times*.[107]

Walker and Jordan understood the challenges that Black women's writing faced and set out to overcome those obstacles through the collaborative work of a smart and skilled group of women. Walker and Jordan believed in the potential and the necessity of bringing respected writers such as Marshall, major forces in trade publishing such as Morrison, budding journalists such as Judith Wilson, and cultural critics such as Margo Jefferson together on a regular basis. The two cofounders brought a lot to the group themselves: Walker was an established writer and was good at persuading people to attend meetings, while Jordan had experience at organizing collective work.

Literary activism was central to June Jordan's life: "June was the catalyst for many projects, ideas, issues in opposition to the status quo."[108] She believed in doing this work in and through literary institutions, such as a campaign to protest the racism of *American Poetry Review (APR)*. In late 1976, just before The Sisterhood began meeting, Jordan wrote Morrison asking her to sign a "Statement on the Editorial Policy of *American Poetry Review*" objecting to the "all-white editorial board," noting the journal's failure to include "women and minority poets," and offering evidence that the journal's publication "record constitutes a racist policy."[109] Jordan "invited poets, some of whom were [or would be] Sisterhood members to her apartment in Grand Army Plaza to strategize."[110] Patricia Spears Jones, at the time just beginning her career as a poet, describes this as her "introduction into literary politics." She recalls that she first met June Jordan when Jordan was "starting a boycott of *American Poetry Review* because . . . she [Jordan] and Alice Walker both had columns in *APR*, but *APR* would not publish their poems" and the journal "barely published any poems by Black people."[111] Jordan's column, "The Black Poet Speaks of Poetry," appeared in *APR* from 1975 to 1977, and she had been working behind the scenes to change the journal for years before ending her column in protest of its "exclusionary policies." She issued a public, collective "Statement" that laments the absence of Black poetry, especially formally experimental writing and poetry reflecting a variety of women's experiences, "including lesbian experience."[112] Signatories included Sisterhood members Jordan, Jones, and Audre Lorde.[113]

The *APR* campaign is just one example of Jordan using her connections with other women and her skills as a literary organizer, both of which made The Sisterhood possible. When she and Walker founded The Sisterhood, Jordan had already published two poetry collections, *Who Look at Me* (1969) and *Some Changes* (1967, 1971), as well as a biography of Fannie Lou Hamer for young readers; her book of poems *Things That I Do in the Dark* (1977) came out right as the group began meeting. She was relatively successful and extremely busy as a poet and teacher but felt strongly that she must still and always find time for organizing Black women writers in collective action and support of one another.

Walker and Jordan had a strong connection that was an important foundation for The Sisterhood. They exchanged letters about personal and professional matters for years before they established the group and were united by what Cheryl Wall calls "their lifelong quest for a redemptive art and politics."[114] Walker reflected in 2021, "June and I were warriors connected at all times, even though we were very different."[115] Jordan was also close with Ntozake Shange; they had the kind of friendship between intellectuals where they knew the most minute and mundane details of each other's writing practices.[116] Jordan's advocacy for Black writers became a model for The Sisterhood. She collaborated with Morrison to get publication and publicity for poets, wrote department heads and deans at Yale and Sarah Lawrence in 1975 recommending Morrison for creative writing positions, and, in the late 1980s, brought together forty-eight Black writers and intellectuals to protest in print the fact that Morrison had not won a National Book Award or Pulitzer Prize.[117]

When The Sisterhood began meeting, Morrison had been the first and only Black woman editor at Random House for a decade. In 1977, she published *Song of Solomon*, the novel she regularly describes as a turning point from thinking of herself as an editor to thinking of herself as a writer.[118]

She was in the middle of a time that would be a tragically brief window of transformation in which Black women represented a statistically significant portion of novelists published by major trade houses.[119] Morrison's work at Random House built a strong network of Black writers, including many Sisterhood members and many authors whose work she did not publish. In late 1976 alone, she had business lunches, drinks, meetings, and book parties with soon-to-be Sisterhood members Ntozake Shange, June Jordan, Alice Walker, and Jessica Harris.[120] Morrison regularly offered advice to writers whose work she ultimately did not acquire or edit, such as Phyl Garland's proposed book about Bill "Bojangles" Robinson and Vèvè Clark's book about dancer and choreographer Katherine Dunham.[121] Morrison also used her connections with the Black popular press to help publicize Black women writers. She met regularly with journalist, editor, and Sisterhood member Audreen Ballard throughout the 1970s.[122] Given her skills, expertise, and position, it is not surprising that Morrison was constantly in demand as a kind of uncompensated consultant about Black writing across genres and venues.[123]

The women who coalesced as The Sisterhood in 1977 brought a diversity and depth of experience to their collective efforts to publish and publicize Black women writers. They were part of a broad, varied network of Black women writers and activists who had learned from and worked with BAM, the NBFO, and Combahee. However, The Sisterhood was distinct and exceptional in its reach into print culture and academia. The group did not ultimately create their own press or publication, but their collaborative work and individual publications transformed the literary world. The group set out to change two cultural institutions, the publishing industry and the university. They worked to increase the visibility of Black women writers and to control the terms of that visibility. This work was hard, came with a great deal of personal sacrifice, and required navigating the racism and sexism of the institutions they were entering and changing.

They worked in politics, literature, media, and academia, squeezing in time for writing their fiction, poetry, and plays in the early morning or late-night hours, outside of their paid jobs. When they first met in early 1977, Sisterhood members already had experience in political organizing, navigating academic institutions, and thinking deeply and acting justly on behalf of Black writing. The Sisterhood functioned in networks of Black feminist political, literary, and academic activism. These three phases unfolded mostly chronologically, each overlapping with and building on the others.

These women drew on their experiences in the Black Arts Movement and in Black feminist and Black Power political organizations. They brought ideas developed in Sisterhood meetings into their fiction, journalism, and scholarly books and articles and, eventually, into countless college classrooms. They laid the foundation for what we now know as a canon of African American women's literature and initiated the major debates in African American literary studies for the next several decades. Their impact on American literature, culture, and education far outlasted the two years they met on a regular basis.

Chapter Two

"AN ASSOCIATION OF BLACK WOMEN WHO ARE WRITERS/POETS/ARTISTS"

The success of Ntozake Shange's play *for colored girls who have considered suicide/when the rainbow is enuf* put a spotlight on Black women writers and intellectuals. In February 1977, when June Jordan and Alice Walker convened The Sisterhood, *for colored girls* was in the middle of a successful Broadway run. Although Walker was well-known and Toni Morrison was on her way to becoming a literary celebrity, at that year's meetings of The Sisterhood, "everyone was kind of dazzled [when] Ntozake Shange came to town."[1] *for colored girls* premiered at the Bay Area lesbian bar Bacchanal in 1974. In 1975, it moved with Shange to New York, where she staged performances at bars and cafes and regularly changed the cast and the text. Shange called *for colored girls* a "choreopoem," a work of dance and spoken poetry that she continued to revise in collaboration with directors, choreographers, and performers in each of its incarnations. As a collaborative and improvisational artist, Shange struggled with the idea of pinning down one version that would be staged night after night in a theater. Working with director Oz Scott, chorographer Paula Moss, and a cast led by Trazana Beverley as the "Lady in Red," Shange developed the version of *for colored girls* that reached larger audiences, first at the Henry Street Settlement New Federal Theater, then at Joseph Papp's Public Theater, and then at the Booth Theatre on Broadway in 1976, where it ran until July 1978. It won an Obie Award, was nominated for a Tony Award for best play, and earned Beverley a Tony in the Best Featured Actress category. As Patricia Spears Jones recalls, "Zake was the face of that poster [advertising *for colored girls*]; she was everywhere in

New York City."[2] In the late 1970s, *for colored girls* and Shange were the talk of the town.

for colored girls is a set of poems spoken by seven women, all of whom remain on stage throughout the performance. Named for the colors they wear ("lady in brown," "lady in yellow," "lady in purple," and so on) and hailing from cities all over the United States, they are potential sites of identification for any Black woman viewer or reader. They tell one another stories of house parties in Detroit, dancing to Black diasporic music in New York, sexual assault in homes and nightclubs and cars, being ready to fall in love with a boy named for Haitian revolutionary Toussaint Louverture, abortion, and domestic violence.[3] In addition to speaking Shange's words, they dance and sing along to lyrics from older traditional songs and recent pop music. This choreopoem is a series of rituals for learning to claim, nurture, and love being a Black woman, and it depends on a community of other Black women.

for colored girls continues to have a massive cultural impact. In his memoir *Dreams from My Father* (1995), President Barack Obama tells the story of taking a date to see a performance in Chicago. Obama does not name the show but describes it in terms that are unmistakably about *for colored girls*: "women took turns telling their stories, singing their songs" and "danced until they seemed one spirit."[4] He quotes the most widely known lines from Shange's choreopoem: "I found God in myself and I loved her/I loved her fiercely."[5] Although she went on to write novels, plays, poems, and children's books, *for colored girls* remains Shange's best-known work. It is an essential, truth-telling, inspiring, and forceful work of Black feminist art. *for colored girls* was radical in the 1970s and remains radical now for its representation of Black women's lives as varied, important, and sustained by their relationships with one another.

However, from the time of its Broadway debut to over a decade later, Shange and her choreopoem were targets of intense public criticism of Black women and their writing. The prominence of *for colored girls*, especially in New York, made these women more visible, and thus more vulnerable. Much of the criticism came from Black men who objected to how Shange and her contemporaries portrayed Black men. In *Ebony* magazine in 2016, scholar Kim F. Hall summarized the divided response to *for colored girls*:

> Shange's attention to the challenges to Black women's autonomy, dignity, and capacity for love resonated with many women, but it also produced a vitriolic

backlash: commentary on the airwaves and in the street was laced with misogynoir and fear. During the play's run on Broadway and for years after, Shange and other Black feminists like Michele Wallace and Alice Walker were accused of hating and endangering Black men. Sociologist Robert Staples proclaimed that in watching *for colored girls*, "One sees a collective appetite for Black male blood." Shange's lawyer considered getting bodyguards for her.[6]

Men wrote many angry complaints that Shange was airing dirty laundry or putting Black family business out in public for white people to consume. This was partly a response to Black women writers addressing domestic violence, drug use, and misogyny; partly a response to Black women writers enjoying a time of greater visibility; and largely a response to the fact that many writings by Black women in this period were by, for, and about Black women.

Cultural critic Hilton Als, unlike some of his contemporaries, was inspired by the openness and visibility of *for colored girls*. He recalls seeing it at the Booth Theatre: "It shattered the Negro propriety I knew and lived by. The force of Shange's writing seemed to say, 'Fuck the old rule of not airing your female business in front of colored men, white people, let alone the rest of the world.'" This was a "thrilling" moment of liberation for Als as a kid and remains an inspiration for him as an adult. As it did for President Obama, *for colored girls* laid a foundation for Als to engage with Black feminism. Als also saw that the choreopoem's focus on Black women made some men angry. He writes, "Shange's work was a particular target for black men, perhaps because she quite literally didn't share the stage with them."[7]

Responses to *for colored girls* began a period of intense public criticism of Black women writers. Mel Watkins in articles in the *New York Times*, Ishmael Reed in his novel *Reckless Eyeballing* (1986), and Stanley Crouch in numerous essays, interviews, and books harshly criticized or satirized Black women writers throughout the 1970s and '80s. Men staged protests outside performances of *for colored girls* in the late 1970s, much as they would in 1985 when Steven Spielberg's film adaption of Alice Walker's *The Color Purple* came to screens across the country. Male viewers and critics objected to how the film depicted men.[8] There are at least two profound ironies in these critiques. First, Shange's choreopoem and Walker's novel focused primarily on Black women. These works, and even white director Spielberg's film adaptation of *The Color Purple*, are not really about men. Second, although some Black men writers and critics resented the recognition Black women were getting, the attention for the women's writings created a wider readership, increased critical attention, and literary celebrity for Black men writers too.[9]

Black men criticized Black women writers relentlessly and in public, often for white audiences, in the 1970s and '80s. Ishmael Reed is an example worth engaging because he is a great writer and a serious thinker who regularly criticized Black women writers in ways that were not always fair but included useful and bracing critiques of the publishing industry. Unlike some of the men who protested at screenings of *The Color Purple* or, as I discuss chapter 4, took Alice Walker to task on *The Donahue Show* in 1989, Reed read and thought about these women's books. Even as he continued to criticize Walker in 2021, he also continued to read widely in Black women's literature and to differentiate among works by Black women.[10] Some members of The Sisterhood counted him as a friend, many of them read his novels, and some of them directly or indirectly helped his writings get published and publicized.

Less than two years after June Jordan organized a campaign to get more Black poets published in *American Poetry Review* and then resigned from the journal in protest, *APR* published John Domini's interview with Ishmael Reed, then best known for his novels *Mumbo Jumbo* (1972) and *Flight to Canada* (1976). Domini conducted the interview over several phone calls in 1977 while Reed was enjoying renewed attention as Avon published new editions of each of his five novels in paperback and Doubleday brought out a collection of his essays.[11] In this interview, Reed talked about the limits of working with "big publishers" and their "formulaic approach," the importance of small presses, his work with poet Al Young on the five volumes of the multiethnic *Yardbird Reader*, and the whiteness of the "counter-culture" in California.[12] Reed also criticized the "Manhattan literary and dramatic establishment" for relying on racial tokenism, including "the *one* black poetess who's usually a feminist lesbian."[13] Reed and Sisterhood members shared a concern about the "Manhattan literary . . . establishment" elevating one Black writer at a time. However, Reed undercuts the possibility of Black literary solidarity by using "feminist lesbian" as a derogatory term to refer to what he imagines as a performance of race, gender, and sexuality that serves white expectations and Black literary ambition.

Reed also sharply criticized Sisterhood members by name. He said, "the hot Afro-Americans right now are the women: social realists whose principal characters live in the ghetto or the field and are *always in the right* . . . you know, Alice Walker, Gayl Jones."[14] He thus inaccurately described the settings of both women's novels and referred to Jones as "hot," suggesting a much wider readership than her work had. In fact, at Random House, Toni Morrison edited Jones's first two novels, *Corregidora* (1975) and *Eva's Man* (1976), and had to advocate forcefully for them because they were so formally experimental; Jones just was and is not "a social realist." The irony of Reed's criticism deepens when we consider that Reed, with Henry Dumas and Leon Forrest, was one of the Black men writers whose works are not in any way "formulaic" and Morrison regularly championed. In 1974, as she was shepherding Jones's *Corregidora* through the last stages of publication, Morrison was also trying to persuade Random House to distribute Reed and Young's *Yardbird Reader*.[15]

Reed called Margo Jefferson's review of *Flight to Canada* in *Newsweek* "unfair," arguing that she was only assigned the review "because she was black" and "she's black and *feminist*, you see, kind of like the Bionic Woman . . . Seriously, she had no real knowledge of my writing." For Reed, "black and *feminist*" are traits of a fictional character ("the Bionic Woman"), rather than lived racial and political identities. He deployed "black and *feminist*" as an epithet—you can practically hear the anger in the italics—to dismiss Jefferson's substantial body of work as a cultural critic and to elide the fact that it was her advocacy that got Black novels reviewed in *Newsweek* at all. He also referred to a "manifesto published recently by a well-known black feminist poet" that criticized *American Poetry Review* for "not publishing poems by women and minority groups." In Reed's view, that unnamed poet is guilty of "hypocrisy" because she is "on the masthead of *First World* (formerly *Black World*), a magazine which publishes only blacks, and blacks of predictable ideological inclinations, at that."[16] As discussed later in this chapter, The Sisterhood did seek to make sure *First World* included writings by and about Black women, and the journal's editor, Hoyt Fuller, was an important interlocutor. However, there is not a Black woman poet on the masthead of *First World* in 1977, so Reed manages here to criticize both what he sees as the "hypocrisy" and narrow "ideological inclinations" of Toni Cade Bambara, who did work for *First World* but wrote in nearly every genre other than poetry, *and* June Jordan, the "well-known black feminist poet" whose literary organizing was surely part of the reason *American Poetry Review* published an interview with Reed. Reed and Ntozake Shange were friends and he was likely not taking a swipe at her, but it would have looked that way to readers since *for colored girls* had recently been featured in the first issue of *First World* when Domini conducted this interview with Reed.

Encounters with racism came as little surprise to Shange and her contemporaries, but the severity of Black men's responses to their works was shocking and hurtful. In a journal entry years later, Shange reflects,

> There was quite an uproar about the seven ladies in their simple colored dresses . . . I was totally dumbfounded that I was right there and then the biggest threat to black men since lynching & not all women were in my corner either. The uproar about how I portrayed black men was insidious and venal. Apparently my choreopoem hit home. There were fisticuffs in Chicago. Male students tried to shout me down at Howard University . . . It felt dangerous. . . . Nothing prepared me for the hateful response to fcg. I was devastated.[17]

This was the "dangerous" and sometimes "hateful" atmosphere in which The Sisterhood gathered. Members provided one another with a haven from the intraracial misogyny Shange describes and the racism and sexism they encountered in their workplaces, the academy, and the literary marketplace. In these seemingly impossible conditions, Sisterhood members were among the many Black women intellectuals who rallied around *for colored girls* and secured its place in the literary canon.

Marcia Ann Gillespie, editor in chief of *Essence* magazine, "was so bold that when *for colored girls* came out, she held up the print run and changed the whole cover art, everything, to talk about *for colored girls*."[18] The November 1976 issue of *Essence* featured *for colored girls* with photos of performances, an interview with each cast member, writings about Shange and her choreopoem by Barbara Lewis and Jessica Harris, and excerpts from the script of the show. Gillespie's choice to feature Shange's choreopoem paved the way for Sisterhood members' later efforts, in collaboration with Gillespie and Cheryll Y. Greene, to transform *Essence* from a Black women's beauty and lifestyle magazine into a venue for serious Black feminist writing.

Like Gillespie, Sisterhood members immediately recognized that *for colored girls* was important and took on the work of asserting its importance publicly. Nearly all of them were seeing, talking about, or writing about Shange's choreopoem. Margo Jefferson, Patricia Spears Jones, Zita Allen, and Toni Cade Bambara saw *for colored girls* multiple times and wrote reviews of it.[19] Judith Wilson saw it before most New Yorkers when it played at the Henry Street Settlement House. She pitched a piece about it to *Ms.*, but the magazine was not interested until the choreopoem began to get more attention during its run at the Public Theater. Wilson met up with Shange,

Patricia Spears Jones, Thulani Davis, and others in "Zake's circle" at a down-town jazz club, hoping to interview Shange. They talked it over and agreed that, rather than give yet another magazine interview about *for colored girls*, Shange would write a "self-interview." *Ms.* published the "self-interview," but "decided that they didn't want to put [Shange] on the cover because *Ms.* at that point had a real problem with sales. And every time they had had a Black woman on the cover, sales [went down]. And the financial interests finally won out."[20] These editorial decisions at *Ms.* were part of a larger pattern of diminishing Black women's writing and part of an ongoing struggle over the place of Black feminism and Black women in the magazine.

Michele Wallace wrote with a deep appreciation for the way Shange's Black feminism reached audiences who had rarely thought about the lives of Black women before seeing *for colored girls*. Wallace's review in the *Village Voice* also demonstrated that intense public attention trained on a Black woman's personal life can be dangerous. The piece relied on an interview with Shange and explained the ways that public performances of *for colored girls* had made parts of Shange's own interior life public as well: "Her four suicide attempts, her middle-class upbringing, and her 'feminist at eight' line are familiar now to an audience that just a year ago thought feminism and blackness, black middle-classness and pain were combinations as unthinkable as disco and Gregorian chant."[21] Just a couple of years later, Wallace's book *Black Macho and the Myth of the Superwoman* (1978) would be the subject of a backlash at least as cruel as what Shange was facing.

The creation of The Sisterhood was bookended by "intense" "Black masculinist backlash" to Shange's *for colored girls* when it started meeting and Wallace's *Black Macho* when they stopped meeting.[22] The attacks on Shange and her choreopoem made the need for Black women writers to support one another especially urgent; those attacks were part of the state of emergency that The Sisterhood came together to resist. Shange's broad smile as she crouches in the famous 1977 photo of The Sisterhood's first meeting suggests that the group was a source of sustenance and support for Black women intellectuals, a kind of healing space akin to the "laying on of hands" ritual among women at the end of *for colored girls*.

≈

Misogynist and racist reactions to Black women's writings, and especially to highly visible successes such as *for colored girls*, made it necessary for

The Sisterhood to be exclusively for Black women. Meeting minutes reveal their determination to be "an association of Black Women who are writers/ poets/artists in the broadest sense of these words." The Sisterhood would serve the "purpose of unifying us and strengthening our bonds with one another through the sharing of ourselves, our art, our experiences, our food, our love and our ideas."[23] By gathering in one place, making time, commit- ting, showing up, they provided one another with this kind of unification and strength. From the moment she joined the group at its second meeting, Judith Wilson recognized its importance, not initially as place for "network- ing" and "professional" advancement, but rather as a form of "psychological support" that came from the "experience of seeing that there were so many of us." Being in a room with a group of Black women writers and intellectuals "was just so reaffirming."[24]

In this space of affirmation, The Sisterhood accomplished many practical tasks. At the February 20, 1977, meeting, they agreed that each member would "gather names" for "the central rolodex," invite new members, and "come up with concrete suggestions and ideas about possible investors and per- sons who might be interested in becoming involved with the formation and operation of Kizzy Enterprises, Inc."[25] Experience in smaller consciousness- raising groups and in political organizations such as the NBFO taught these women cooperative practices and logistics such as "how to have a meeting" and "how to lead and how to follow."[26] Consciousness-raising groups of the 1960s and '70s were devoted to study and were often explicitly anticapitalist; The Sisterhood used those tools to different ends by engaging in professional networking (creating a "Rolodex") and participating in a capitalist market- place (planning to incorporate and seeking "investors").[27]

At the February 20 meeting, Judith Wilson became the official secretary for The Sisterhood and in that role produced an archive of the group. She "volunteered to take minutes at the Sisterhood meetings" partly because of her high school training in "notehand" that was "intended to prepare us career-minded girls for our secretarial futures" but instead proved useful to her as an undergraduate and graduate student, as a journalist, and in The Sisterhood.[28] There are varying versions of meeting minutes, Sisterhood members made their own notes on their personal hard copies, and they archived those notes in all kinds of ways. June Jordan's copy of Wilson's min- utes for the February 20 meeting, for example, are filed in Jordan's papers at Harvard with unrelated correspondence and attached to an undated note from Vertamae Grosvenor that reads, "Finally found this. See you at the sisterhood next."[29] These minutes begin with a four-part agenda and note that Audreen Ballard, Toni Morrison, and Ntozake Shange are working on various projects for the group but didn't make it to this particular meeting, then address practical matters, including how The Sisterhood could sustain itself over the long term. The women agreed that, going forward, Wilson would "keep minutes of all Sisterhood meetings and copies will be sent to all members" and "The Sisterhood will meet once a month on the third Sunday of the month. Refreshments will be 'pot luck' and sisters should feel free to bring other 'favorite things'—records, poems, etc." The minutes record the group's commitment to collaboration ("pot luck"), to having fun ("records, poems, etc."), and to documenting their collaborative work (minutes to be written and "sent to all members").[30]

In these meetings, Sisterhood members clarified repeatedly that the group was exclusively by, for, and about Black women. Unlike some other Black feminist collectives of the same period, The Sisterhood was not interested in intervening in mainstream, white feminist discourse. Many members shared Toni Cade Bambara's view: "I'm not adamantly opposed to black-white coalitions; there are some that speak to our interests, but I personally am not prepared to invest any energy in that kind of work. There are too many other alliances both within the black community and across colored communities, both at home and abroad, that strike me as far more crucial."[31]

Some members of The Sisterhood, such as Audre Lorde, did regularly participate in interracial feminist exchanges.[32] Many, including Lorde, Jordan, and Marshall, worked to establish solidarity with Black women and other women of color outside the United States. Some, such as Shange and Jordan, identified as Black cultural nationalists and others, such as Morrison, did not. Many had published their work and found community through strategic and occasional participation in the racial separatism of Black Power and Black Arts groups, even as they challenged the gender politics of some parts of those movements. Bambara called her politics "black nationalist feminism," meaning she, like members of The Sisterhood, saw no contradiction between Black cultural nationalism and Black feminism.[33] No members identified as gender separatists, but all asserted the need for a group in which every person was Black, a woman, and engaged in some form of writing.

The members knew that the group was important and worth documenting. Alice Walker is one example of a Sisterhood member who valued and preserved her own archive. Even a cursory glance at Walker's papers suggests that she thought about Black women's visible and invisible work as worth archiving from early on in her career. Rudolph Byrd writes of her adolescent scrapbooks, "there is a sense of the high value Walker attached to her own person and vision . . . There is also an awareness, at the age of fifteen, of the contributions she would make as a writer to the world of letters."[34] Walker's archive at Emory University preserves her careful organization of her print, digital, and audio materials. Alexis Gumbs explains that Audre Lorde was "an ivy league trained librarian" who "kept everything from her childhood poems to box after box of correspondence and a lifetime of journals."[35] Walker and Lorde brought this sensibility to The Sisterhood; they recognized the historical importance of their collaborative labor as it was happening.

Some members saved printed records of the group's collaborative work, including minutes, agendas, and correspondence. This record keeping began right away. Audre Lorde saved June Jordan's personal invitation, a note that reads, "This Sunday, February 6th, 2 p.m., Alice and I are having this chitlins and champagne dinner for a kind of Black Sisterhood of the Spirit. Happy Purpose. Please come. (my house.)."[36] At Walker's instruction, Abike (also known as Patricia Murray) sent a letter to The Sisterhood with detailed minutes of their first two formal meetings on February 6 and February 20, 1977, and notes about "a luncheon meeting with Toni Morrison, Audreen Ballard and myself held February 10, 1977." A month after the first meeting, the tone of these minutes is already retrospective and treats the group as important: those minutes refer to the group as "what has now become known as The Sisterhood." The group codified into something formal very quickly in the months after Alice Walker and June Jordan first issued the invitation to gather at Jordan's home in order "to have some writers/artists over to congregate, get to know each other better, eat and talk about topics of common interest and concern."[37] Audreen Ballard, Vertamae Grosvenor, Nana Maynard, Toni Morrison, Lori Sharpe, and Ntozake Shange accepted the invitation and attended the first meeting, where they drank champagne and ate gumbo (not chitlins). They posed for a photo, which became an essential document of the group.

Alongside the balance of work and play, there was, from the first meeting on, a collective decision to refuse "ranking" and "competition" among members.[38] This was not always easy given the varying visibility, age, economic status, and career stage of members. Renita Weems and her friend Rosemary Bray "were star struck" by the women who were already established writers.[39] Ntozake Shange was in the public eye with *for colored girls*, and

Morrison was well-known as a fierce advocate for Black writers as an editor at Random House. Weems did not yet think of herself as a writer and was working unhappily at Merrill Lynch, while Patricia Spears Jones was writing poetry and working for the Coordinating Council for Literary Magazines. Jones was keenly aware that "Alice was already famous."[40] Judith Wilson "felt like oh I'm so lucky to be a fly on the wall, you know, Paule Marshall here and Alice there and June."[41]

Proximity among members facilitated this literary community. There was the energy of 1970s New York, a city experiencing simultaneous economic scarcity and creative abundance. There was also the "physical proximity" of these women in Park Slope in Brooklyn and the Upper West Side and Morningside Heights in Manhattan.[42] Jordan, Maynard, and Abike all lived near the Grand Army Plaza subway stop, and Walker's home on Garfield Place was "about a 10–15 minute walk away."[43] Abike and Nana Maynard were part of a "Brooklyn Black creative community that was quite different" from the literary scene in Manhattan.[44] The Brooklyn group identified as lesbian and included many poets who had an "interest in African traditional practices, herbalism, religious practices."[45] Lorde likely connected with them as an out Black lesbian poet who was studying the African kingdom of Dahomey as research for her volume of poetry *The Black Unicorn* (1978). Jordan and Walker interacted with, supported, and had lots in common with the Brooklyn group; they differed, though, in thinking that The Sisterhood should focus on publication in popular magazines and with large trade presses.

Sisterhood members wanted and needed to earn a living from their writing, which often meant working within the confines of existing institutions, such as large trade publishers and universities. This was a turn away from the anticapitalist stance of Black feminist political groups such as the Combahee River Collective. Toni Morrison "wanted to get other people's work out" and "get more black people in [mainstream trade] publishing."[46] Some Sisterhood members, such as Audre Lorde, continued to publish works with smaller, independent, feminist, and Black presses. Lorde made this choice partly because she was wary of "media exploitation of a laudatory few of us" in ways that meant success for a few Black women writers, but little or no political change and not nearly enough attention "in the Black literary community" for "Black Lesbian writers."[47]

The Sisterhood understood the racism of the American class system but believed in reaching as many readers as possible with their work, and needed to make a living. Many of them entered the workforce during the recession that began around 1973. Although several members came from relatively comfortable middle-class backgrounds, working in New York in the mid-1970s made all of them familiar with precarious employment and financial insecurity. Rather than fully resist participation in the capitalist marketplace, they took advantage of the moment to secure employment and to change the content of mass-market media, from the pages of *Essence* to, in later years, Oprah Winfrey's television show, book club, and magazine. Members of The Sisterhood simultaneously depended on, critiqued, and worked to change magazines, the publishing industry, and eventually universities.

Individual members' choices about work depended to some extent on their financial circumstances. One clear marker of economic class difference was their homes. The Sisterhood needed apartments big enough to host meetings and, though they were committed to rotating hosting duties, only a few members had places big enough to accommodate the group. In May and June 1977, "Meetings took place at Alice Walker's well-appointed apartment on Garfield Place in Park Slope in Brooklyn or in a well-known lawyer's [Sheila Rush's] six-room apartment on West End Avenue in Manhattan."[48] Patricia Spears Jones saw June Jordan's apartment as "huge!" and "grandiose" and recalled that Jordan's and Walker's "Brooklyn apartments made our tiny Manhattan spaces feel even more claustrophobic."[49] Walker's and Rush's homes occasioned less envy than aspiration and inspiration. Jones wrote that, "There was for all of us this sense of what could happen if we worked well enough . . . got lucky enough."[50]

In these monthly meetings, "15 to 20 women from trade house editors to first-time writers would all show up," and Walker "had a way of making everyone feel at ease, no matter where they were on the publishing food chain—rank beginners and well-published authors alike really did meet and greet."[51] Jones remembers the group as "a mix because there were all these people who were incredibly accomplished and then there were younger people like me who were sort of joining in and hanging out and listening."[52] Their practice of culinary and intellectual potluck—members brought food, poems, slide shows of their travels, and other things to share—contributed to this collaborative, anticompetitive spirit. Although Walker and Jordan convened the group, others also had a leadership role, and each member shaped and determined the direction of the group, often by taking on projects specific to their expertise. Leadership of meetings was distributed to the extent that Judith Wilson had the "impression the group was founded by [Paule] Marshall, Alice Walker, and Toni Morrison."[53]

Some practices of The Sisterhood drew on members' experience with consciousness-raising sessions, and the group followed the 1975 pamphlet "Consciousness-Raising Guidelines" when it came to sharing food and taking turns hosting meetings, but not the suggestions that groups provide formal child care during meetings, despite the fact that many members were mothers.[54] There is no mention of child care in the meeting minutes, but retrospective accounts decades later refer directly or obliquely to exchanging child care as an important way members supported one another's writing. They met during a time when New York City had radically defunded child care, and some members did bring their children to meetings.[55] Federally mandated cuts to New York's Agency for Child Development caused the closure of "forty-nine day care centers" in 1977 "on top of twenty-eight that had already been defunded the previous year," and "the city and the state tightened eligibility rules," making the limited public day care that remained less accessible.[56] Politicians used New York's fiscal crisis as an excuse to defund other public services essential to children, including parks, libraries, and health care. This made the city an even harder place to be a parent and made a network of mothers who could help each other out especially important.

Parenting and child care were not agenda items at Sisterhood meetings, but the challenges of mothering and writing, usually while holding down another full-time job, appear often in the women's poetry and fiction. When the group began to meet, Rebecca Walker was seven years old and living with her mother in New York for a two-year stretch before going to her father's home in Washington, D.C., for two years.[57] Alice Walker's poem "Now That the Book Is Finished" reads:

> Now that the book is finished,
> now that I know my characters will live,
> I can love my child again.
> She need sit no longer
> at the back of my mind,
> the lonely sucking of her thumb
> a giant stopper in my throat.[58]

"Now That the Book Is Finished" first appeared in Walker's 1979 volume *Good Night Willie Lee, I'll See You in The Morning*; she likely wrote it as The Sisterhood was meeting. Toward the end of that year, in an address at

Sarah Lawrence College, Walker calls this a "self-pitying poem" and insists that it is "as much a celebration as anything" and "of course I'd loved my daughter all along."[59] She redefines the "stopper in my throat" as not a child's "lonely sucking of her thumb," but rather "the fear of falling silent, *mute*, that writers have from time to time." She describes herself and Rebecca as "Mother and child, yes, but *sisters* really, against whatever denies us what we are."[60] There is, on the one hand, a loving sense of being united against social forces of oppression. On the other hand, it is easy to imagine that a seven-year-old might find it burdensome to be treated as a sister in struggle, rather than primarily as a daughter. Walker closes her 1979 talk by quoting a "sign," really a poem, that she kept over her desk to remind her that while "Virginia Woolf had madness," "Jane Austen had no privacy/and no love life," and "Zora Hurston (ah!) had no money/and poor health," "You have Rebecca— who is/much more delightful/and less distracting/than any of the calamities/ above."[61] The relationship to motherhood here is, as in Walker's other writings, both loving and ambivalent. Her daughter is "delightful," but also comparable to "calamities" like illness and lack of love. These words to herself and the public talk in which Walker quotes them are explicitly autobiographical, reflections on her experience as a mother who writes and a writer who mothers. Like Morrison's reflections about her life as a "mother, editor, and writer," Walker's words in the Sarah Lawrence address were ones she chose carefully to deliver in public as narration of her personal life.[62]

"Now That the Book Is Finished" works a little differently than a public talk, interview, or essay. It's public in the sense that it is published and, like any poem, play, or work of fiction, it is literature that requires interpretation rooted in more than the author's biography. There is no simple correlation between the speaker of a poem and the author of that poem, and "Now That the Book Is Finished" is a representation, not a report. However, and perhaps because it is poetry rather than polemic, the poem spoke to other Sisterhood members and many readers of their works. The speaker expresses the conflict that other Sisterhood members experienced in trying to balance mothering their children and doing other forms of work. In her review of *Good Night Willie Lee* for *Essence*, Judith Wilson wrote, "These poems by Alice Walker are about the agonies and ecstasies of love, motherhood, and authorship and political struggle."[63] Wilson's list captures the sense among Sisterhood members that "authorship and political struggle" were as central and demanding in their lives as "love" and "motherhood." In "Now That the Book Is Finished," Walker could be drawing on her experience writing her first two novels, *The Third Life of Grange Copeland* (1970) and *Meridian* (1976), or the work she had begun by this time, *The Color Purple* (1982).

Like Walker, other members of The Sisterhood did not make the experience of a being mother and writer sound glamorous in their poems, fiction, and interviews. In a 2015 *Fresh Air* interview with Terry Gross, Morrison describes writing parts of what would become *The Bluest Eye* in longhand on a legal pad (which became her standard practice) and, when her baby son "spit up" on the page, she "kept writing around the puke."[64] In her 2019 eulogy for Morrison, Angela Davis remembers Morrison jotting down what would become *Song of Solomon* on those legal pads in between cooking breakfast for her sons and while stopped in traffic on her commute into the city. Davis celebrates the ways Morrison was simultaneously "fully engaged" with her fictional characters and "fully present" with her children.[65] These two retrospective accounts paint a somewhat rosier picture than Morrison's words in the late 1970s. Jessica Harris's 1976 *Essence* profile of Morrison, published about two months before The Sisterhood began meeting, directly addresses the complexities of being a working, single mother raising sons. Morrison asserts, "All of the three things I am, mother, editor, and writer, are primary to me. I couldn't live without any one." Harris writes, "Toni Morrison will say that her first responsibility is as a mother to Dino [Ford] and Slade," and Morrison describes a little of what that looked like in daily life: "I rarely have more than three or four hours as a block of time. Usually at the end of the fourth hour somebody wants lunch." In Harris's profile, Morrison offers one version of something she said often when interviewers asked how she managed it all: "I'm not entertained nor do I entertain often. I don't see the plays I want to or do a lot of other things I like."[66] She would, later on when the boys were grown, be able to do these things, but would regularly reiterate versions of her assertion, "I don't give or go to dinner parties."[67]

Alice Walker's short, free verse poem might have spoken for Audre Lorde, also a mother of two, who was wrestling with a "character" representing herself as she created the genre of "biomythography"—an experimental form of autobiography that includes elements of history, myth, and fiction—in *Zami: A New Spelling of My Name* (1982). Paule Marshall might have recognized "the child" of Walker's poem in the daughters in need of "love" that appear in almost all of Marshall's novels and short stories. In 1979, Marshall was at work on *Praisesong for The Widow* (1983), in which the protagonist, Avey Johnson, sorts through her experiences as a granddaughter, daughter, and mother as a way to find her place and purpose as a member of the Black Diaspora.

Members of The Sisterhood were well aware that their simultaneous work as mothers and writers existed in broader political contexts. Among other issues, mothering and reproductive justice were a crucial site of difference between the white women's liberation movement and Black feminism. Both movements sought freedom and choice for women. While there was diversity of thought and goals within both, freedom and choice meant different things to white and Black women. In broad terms, white women in the liberation movement sought freedom from narrow roles as wives and mothers, freedom to work increasingly in the public sphere, and the choice not to have children or to abort a pregnancy. Black feminists wanted access to these freedoms and choices but defined reproductive justice more broadly to include freedom from the forced sterilization so common for Black women that a hysterectomy was colloquially called a "Mississippi appendectomy."[68] The white women's liberation movement agenda regarding reproductive rights and mothering was just one of the ways that the movement defined "women" as meaning "white women" and thus failed to address the needs or acknowledge the concerns of Black women.

Black feminists were also responding to a broader, long-standing weaponization of Black motherhood that had a massive impact on federal legislation and policy. Daniel Moynihan's 1965 congressional report *The Negro Family: The Case for National Action* infamously described Black American families as a "tangle of pathology" in which a "matriarchal structure" was the cause of social ills including juvenile delinquency, crime, and psychological disorders.[69] As Vertamae Grosvenor put it during a 1968 radio broadcast in conversation with Flo Kennedy and other Black women, "You got a hustler like Moynihan that comes in and pretends to have a whole lot of insight when in fact all he's doing is blaming Black people for what white people did from the moment [we] came over as slaves."[70]

Moynihan's only specific recommendation in his report was for Black young men to join the armed forces to get the corrective patriarchal structure and discipline that he imagined were lacking in Black homes. The report concludes, "the programs of the Federal government . . . shall be designed to have the effect, directly or indirectly, of enhancing the stability and resources of the Negro American family." Men, including white liberals and Black nationalists, were drawn to Moynihan's patriarchal prescription and his dangerous rhetorical move of shifting focus from institutional oppression to personal responsibility. Although Ronald Reagan and Moynihan differed in party affiliation and on many policy matters, both regularly placed blame on Black women's individual choices as a way of obscuring the federal government's systemic racism. Reagan's creation in the 1980s of the myth of the "welfare queen" built on Moynihan's 1960s deployment of the castrating matriarch stereotype. With these fictions, the federal government pathologized Black mothers, especially single mothers. Black women quite reasonably sometimes chose not to publicly present or identify themselves as mothers because they did not wish to be instrumentalized as part of this racist political discourse. As members of The Sisterhood became increasingly visible in a racially integrated literary marketplace, motherhood was just one aspect of that visibility that they had to define and manage. They keenly understood the ways U.S. culture stigmatizes and caricatures Black motherhood. They were careful about what they revealed and concealed as they pursued their careers.

≈

The Sisterhood—mothers, writers, teachers, editors, activists—came together knowing that advocating for Black women's writing was an uphill battle. The group was a place where the women could identify primarily as writers, as opposed to their other roles. As Margo Jefferson says, "The Sisterhood was a . . . literary collective," and Black women "writers, academics, journalists, knew that we needed this" place to get together and talk about their work.[71] At the first meeting, they had a "lengthy, broad" discussion of "problems Black Women Artists/Writers/Poets married and single face in seeking publication of their work and surviving from day to day."[72] They identified the need for "an alternative publication and press or publishing company" that would produce a "periodical" or "literary magazine" and publish works that were out of print ("such as Zora Hurston's *Their Eyes Were Watching God*"), anthologies of Black writing, and "new Black works."[73]

Abike, Audreen Ballard, and Toni Morrison met on February 10, 1977, over lunch to determine whether Random House might distribute a new periodical that could "fill the void for a serious Black literary magazine" in terms of audience, purpose, and scope, including practical information about "survival," such as "information about and pertaining to the provision of food, clothing and shelter."[74] The Sisterhood decided that they should "form a Corporation," and Morrison suggested the names "Sapphire Enterprises,

Inc." and "Kizzy Enterprises, Inc."[75] The three determined that "Kizzy" was "extremely appropriate in view of the fact that we do consider ourselves here to stay—a group of Black Women to be reckoned with and with an important history and legacy to pass on."[76] Kizzy is the first enslaved character born in the United States in Alex Haley's novel *Roots* and in the miniseries based on that novel, which aired to a massive television audience less than a month before the first meeting of The Sisterhood.

Ballard and Morrison had substantial experience in publishing that they could use to create Kizzy Enterprises. Ballard was a leader and organizer who had served as cochair of Black Perspective, a group that organized and lobbied on behalf of Black journalists.[77] Morrison began working for the textbook publisher L. W. Singer in Syracuse in the mid-'60s and was promoted to senior editor in 1967. Random House acquired Singer in 1960 and moved some of its operations and employees to Manhattan in 1968. Morrison was among those who made the move, which became her transition from editing textbooks to editing trade books.[78] Alice Walker's experience with various presses and publications was also useful, including her role as an editor at *Ms.* magazine, which she began in 1974 after moving to New York City.[79] Just after The Sisterhood held the first meeting on February 6 and the smaller meeting on February 10, 1977, Walker wrote to Morrison, "It was wonderful seeing you among 'de sisterhood.' . . . You seem to me so wise, and like you probably know most of the turnings in the road."[80] Walker knew "the turnings in the road" pretty well herself by 1977, having already published novels, collections of short stories, and volumes of poetry and being part of a New York literary scene. This same letter includes a postscript noting that Walker plans to ask Gwendolyn Brooks to review June Jordan's *Things I Do in the Dark* for *Ms.*[81]

The Sisterhood declared itself "a non-profit association" and decided on a five-dollar membership fee, which most members paid on the spot at the March 1977 meeting.[82] At the same time, the group was working on big goals, such as Kizzy Enterprises, plans for a "periodical," and a starting a "publishing house" that could "re-issue out-of-print black books," "anthologize important black articles," and possibly establish a "distribution relationship with Random House" with Morrison's help.[83] They discussed possible sources of financial support, and Wilson urged members to bring ideas for funding sources to future meetings.[84] Variation in type and scale of projects characterized The Sisterhood's work throughout the years they met. Some projects fell to the wayside as membership changed over time.

The Sisterhood did not ultimately create their own press or publication, but their collaborative work transformed existing periodicals, and members wrote lasting, canonical works of fiction, nonfiction, and poetry during and after the years they met.

The Sisterhood's meeting minutes and agendas show that much of the group's labor consisted of the mundane, and often tedious, administrative tasks that are necessary and largely invisible in any collective action for liberation. This work included writing agendas and keeping minutes, making copies of those agendas and minutes, mailing the copies, sending letters reminding members of meetings, maintaining the address list, and countless other tasks that kept the group going. Patricia Murray kept a "central roladex [*sic*] of names/addresses for the Black Poets & Writers Clearinghouse" and briefly managed other administrative tasks that later fell to Judith Wilson, then to Renita Weems.[85] They, like all the other women in The Sisterhood, had their plates full with their paying jobs, but took on this unpaid organizing labor to help sustain the group.

The Sisterhood's third full meeting, on March 20, 1977, was the first one Audre Lorde attended.[86] June Jordan's introduction of Lorde at a poetry reading in Manhattan's Donnell Library earlier that month may have helped convince Lorde to join the group. Reading a copy of the introduction after the event, she was moved by the "approval and recognition" she found in Jordan's words.[87] By then, Lorde had published several volumes of poetry and was well-known among readers and writers of poetry, especially since her 1974 nomination for a National Book Award for her collection *From a Land Where Other People Live*. Like Jordan, Lorde made time for collaboration and literary organizing even while busy with her own writing, teaching, and parenting. These shared commitments were essential to the friendships among these women. Jordan and Lorde corresponded regularly starting in the late 1960s, when Jordan requested permission to include three of Lorde's poems in *Soulscript: A Collection of Classic African American Poetry* (1970).[88] They were able to see the many aspects of each other's labor that were invisible to a broader reading public. Jordan wrote Lorde, for example, in fall 1977: "I heard the Pat Jones-Adrienne reading was *wonderful*. All thanks to you, lady, for making these readings real,"[89] acknowledging Lorde's work as a literary organizer who made Patricia Spears Jones and Adrienne Rich's public reading in New York happen.

These were mutually supportive dynamics happening as The Sisterhood was meeting. About a month after Jordan's note to Lorde, Jones sent Lorde a card with a watercolor painting of roses on the front and note inside that said, in part, "I don't usually say prayers you know formal ones but I have for you and all Sisters facing adversity at this time . . . My Mama used to say over and over sometimes sarcastically 'Wonders never cease' and she's right. They don't stop. Like love don't stop. And courage. And friendship. Get side-tracked sometimes. But not stopped. So keep your wonder moving."[90]

Lorde had plenty of experience with racism, misogyny, and homophobia. Jones chose not to name the specific slight or "adversity" that prompted her to write this card, instead adopting her mother's sarcastic use of "wonders never cease" to refer to obstacles so countless they are hardly worth naming. This card is a relatively rare extant archival example of the voluminous personal correspondence among these women in support of one another. Jones offers that support—"love," "courage," and "friendship"—as maternal wisdom and words of encouragement between Black women poet friends.

These personal relationships outside of official meetings bolstered The Sisterhood, and they continued their discussions of "proposed publishing ventures to be organized by The Sisterhood, New York."[91] They talked about "criteria for membership" and reminded June Jordan (maybe because Jordan was inviting new people) that this had been "resolved at last month's meeting to be 'black women who are artists or artist-related.'" Jordan proposed that the group establish "a center for battered black women." Support for battered women was the kind of community work that some local branches of the NBFO had taken on, and Sisterhood members, including Lorde, were involved in such forms of activism. Other members, though, wanted the group to stick to the literary work that was in their specific skill set. The Sisterhood was especially important as a way for Black women in the media and publishing world to network, given that they were shut out of the white boys' club in those industries. Perhaps foreseeing the conflicts that would soon emerge over the group's mission, Walker reminded them that The Sisterhood's "purpose was simply to unify black women artists, not to actually carry out, as a group, all of the projects it might generate." Although they discussed it for months, The Sisterhood did not ultimately incorporate as Kizzy Enterprises; this proved one of several ideas that they explored in detail but did not ultimately realize. Walker imagined The Sisterhood as a kind of incubator from which "individual members will carry out those projects that particularly interest them."[92]

The Sisterhood did agree that images of Black women in print media needed to change. A few years earlier, the National Black Feminist Organization had called for Black women to represent themselves: "We, not white men or Black men, must define our self-image as black women and not fall into the mistake of being placed upon the pedestal . . . It has been hard for black women to emerge from the myriad of distorted images that have portrayed us as grinning Beulahs, castrating Sapphires, and pancake box Jemimahs."[93] Black feminist organizations worried that even in the Black popular press and in "reporting on the women's movement," "*Jet* and *Ebony*, the leading publications," "consistently recentered men's reactions to feminism and ignored the discrimination black women faced within the black community."[94] To address this, The Sisterhood developed plans to publish more political and literary Black women's writing as a corrective in existing periodicals that already had substantial readerships. They focused on transforming the Black women's magazines *Ebony* and *Essence*; the journal *First World*, a scholarly periodical run by Hoyt Fuller; and the mostly white feminist magazine *Ms.* At the March 1977 meeting, several members took up the need to change the content of these existing magazines. The dance critic Zita Allen encouraged the group to "try to influence major publications such as *Essence, Ms., Ebony,* and *First World* to publish more young black poets and writers"; June Jordan suggested contacting Sharyn Skeeter, poetry editor at *Essence*; and Jordan and Alice Walker planned to "discuss this problem with Patricia [Marcia Ann] Gillespie and Audreen Ballard," both of whom worked at *Essence*.[95]

In the spring of 1977, Vèvè Clark wrote an "In-House Proposal" "toward meeting 4/10/77" regarding "Publishing in Popular Magazines." This proposal reflects The Sisterhood's strategic, coordinated, and careful work "to provide encouragement and exposure to both published and unpublished writers, photographers, researchers and, particularly, poets."[96] The focus on poets grew out of the recognition that there was a far greater market for novels than poetry or short fiction. In late 1976, describing her editorial work, Morrison said, "I wish that Toni Cade Bambara would write a novel, and that Lucille Clifton would write a sustained one. Not that what they do isn't marvelous, it's just that I would be able to make more money for them in other forms. Poetry and short pieces have always been extremely difficult to sell."[97]

Clark's proposal takes up Sisterhood discussions of the need to promote Black women's poetry in *Ebony*, as a widely read black periodical with "international appeal."[98] Clark suggests that the group ask the editors to "establish a monthly, bi-monthly or weekly feature on the poetry of one black woman (per time)." Their plan was to appeal to "the largely visual nature of *Ebony*" by supplying photographs and brief biographies of Black women poets to "draw readers (and before them editors) into the poetry itself." These photos and biographies would be in portfolios that The Sisterhood put together for Black women writers and artists that "could then be sent directly to popular magazines where the format is decidedly different from literary or scholarly periodicals." The proposal reflects the group's consistent attention to members' labor, commenting, "photographers and graphic artists in the Sisterhood might consider receiving a flat-rate commission for their work," which would include taking pictures for members' portfolios and creating a logo for The Sisterhood. Clark asserts that if the group sends out portfolios of poets' work that "is consistently good for six months" they will "begin to get quick attention from editors."[99]

Ebony was a difficult target for change because the magazine had focused on entertainment since its founding in 1945. Sisterhood members saw an opening as *Ebony* increased its coverage of political issues beginning in the mid-1960s. Vertamae Grosvenor had written about food for the magazine, and Phyl Garland had been an editor and music critic there since the late 1960s. The group agreed that Garland would know how to best approach *Ebony*.[100] When The Sisterhood met on April 10, 1977, at Garland's East Village apartment, Vèvè Clark talked the group through her proposal, including pitching poets for features in *Ebony*. However, the magazine does not appear in subsequent meeting minutes and correspondence. This might be because *Ebony* was not receptive to their proposals or because, as it appears from the available records, Garland stopped attending Sisterhood meetings after April 1977. It might be because editor Hoyt Fuller had had a major falling out with *Ebony*'s publisher, Johnson Publications, resulting in "the demise of *Black World*," and Sisterhood members had close ties with Fuller and were keen to support his new journal, *First World*.[101]

Founded in the 1940s as *Negro Digest* and renamed under Fuller's leadership in Chicago, *Black World* played an important role in the intellectual trajectory and writing careers of women in The Sisterhood. The journal regularly published works of Black literary criticism and offered logistical advice on publishing to Black writers. The monthly magazine also included fiction and poetry as well as lists of new publications, performances, activism, and honors of Black thinkers, writers, and artists in the United States and the African Diaspora. Carole Parks wrote many pieces for *Black World* and served as managing editor. Contributors included Sisterhood members June Jordan, Audre Lorde, Toni Morrison, and Diane Weathers.[102]

Roderick Ferguson argues that *Black World*'s place as one Johnson Publications property alongside popular magazines like *Jet* illustrates that "the publishing world's interest in the student movements and in the Black Arts Movement testified to the fact that black culture was not simply of interest to anti-establishment radicals but to the 'establishment' as well."[103] Ferguson rightly points to the cultural and financial capital of Black Arts and other politically radical ideas in a popular Black marketplace. From the late 1960s through the early 1970s, *Black World* had subscribers who wanted to read about "student movements," such as sit-ins to demand Black studies departments, and to read poetry and essays by BAM writers such as Amiri Baraka, Dudley Randall, and Addison Gayle.[104] James Smethurst argues that this readership had shrunk so much that Johnson Publications likely shut down *Black World* because it was not lucrative and could not "sell much advertising" by the mid-1970s, when "Black Power and Black Arts movements increasingly splintered."[105]

Throughout these changes and across his career, Hoyt Fuller was concerned about the conditions of publication for African American literature and the study of those works in the academy. Fuller mentored Black women scholars and connected them to a growing body of African American literary scholarship. Mary Helen Washington says, "That extraordinary little magazine *Black World*, edited by the visionary Hoyt Fuller, turned up in my mailbox each month with announcements about the world of Black literature and culture . . . Hoyt encouraged me to be a writer and thinker when my professors at the university were interested only in their white male protégés."[106] Fuller, like Sisterhood members, shuttled among different kinds of venues and readers. After, "Johnson Publications (best known as the publishers of *Jet* and *Ebony*) shut down [*Black World*] in 1976," Fuller moved back to Atlanta and established *First World*.[107] Carole Parks joined him as managing editor and became co-editor-in-chief. Parks later worked with Toni Cade Bambara, among others, to try to keep the magazine going after Fuller's passing in 1981.

The Sisterhood built a reciprocal relationship with *First World*, and Fuller's advocacy for Black women's writing shows in every issue of the journal's short run. The first issue included book reviews by June Jordan and a photo of Ntozake Shange with the cast of *for colored girls*.[108] Subsequent issues included poetry by Jordan and Lorde as well as notices of publications, recognitions, awards, and participation in conferences by Phyl Garland, Audre Lorde, Toni Morrison, Ntozake Shange, and Alice Walker.[109] When

The Sisterhood began meeting in 1977, member Patricia Murray started keeping a copy of each issue of *First World* "for the Sisterhood's library."[110]

The relationship with *First World* demonstrates The Sisterhood's reach and investment in various publications, including relatively niche journals. At the April 1977 meeting, Margo Jefferson suggested that the group urge the West Coast feminist magazine *Chrysalis* "to include black women as much as possible," and Donna Simms suggested that members attend a meeting in Brooklyn the following week of the feminist journal *Heresies* staff to encourage them "to publish a black women's arts issue."[111] Getting Black women's writing published was a matter of coordination and strategy in these various venues, from independent and academic journals to the major feminist magazine *Ms.*

The Sisterhood had significant success with *Ms.* magazine in the sense that they pushed the most widely read feminist publication in the United States to grapple seriously with Black women and Black feminism. *Ms.* made sense as a target for their literary activism, even though it was a largely white publication. Like The Sisterhood, *Ms.* began as a group of women meeting in New York City apartments.[112] By the time The Sisterhood coalesced, several members had ties to *Ms.*, the magazine had been in print for about six years, Susan McHenry was a senior editor, and Alice Walker was on the masthead as an editor. Writer, intellectual, and activist Margaret Sloan was both a founding editor of *Ms.* and, very soon after, a cofounder of the National Black Feminist Organization. Sloan's role in the start of *Ms.* in late 1971 suggested that the magazine welcomed Black feminist thought. However, *Ms.* was uneven in this commitment over the years, in terms of both the contents of its pages and the practices in its workplace.

Judith Wilson worked at *Ms.*, first as an intern and then as an associate editor, for about three years. When she started, the magazine was "very diverse ideologically" with a "broad spectrum of feminisms," but that "changed" to an unspoken narrow, dogmatic, white feminist vision. For example, in keeping with 1970s white feminism, *Ms.* focused on access to abortion rather than Black feminism's broader agenda of reproductive justice and focused on getting out of the home and into the workplace rather than acknowledging that Black women had been in the workplace, whether they wished to be or not, since at least 1619. In a mid-1970s journal entry, Alice Walker identified "the problem at *Ms.*" this way: "what I want for the world is not what they—American white feminists—want. Or rather, it is not what the majority of editors at *Ms.* want."[113]

Margaret Sloan was the only Black woman among the magazine's founding editors and initially the only Black woman involved in the magazine's day-to-day operations. Black women at *Ms.* sometimes found themselves literally and figuratively on the periphery of editorial meetings. In response to these conditions, Wilson and five other editors resigned in late 1977. Writer and feminist activist Gloria Steinem had cofounded *Ms.* with the idea that it should "be as egalitarian as possible." To this end, although she was clearly in charge, Steinem was listed as just one among a group of editors. Another group of several women all had the title of associate editor. However, in practice, "there was an internal hierarchy that played out. In salaries, in work assignments, etcetera. In who was taken more seriously, just all of that stuff."[114] Wilson gained valuable experience at the magazine and wrote several important pieces of investigative journalism there, but she also experienced the kind of political, racial, and social pressures that most members of The Sisterhood were facing in their respective workplaces. Like Sloan, Wilson bore the unsustainable burden of demonstrating through her presence that the magazine was committed to Black women's concerns and writings, whether or not this was always true.

Maintaining distributed leadership was as difficult at *Ms.* as it was in The Sisterhood and other feminist groups. *Ms.*, however, persisted as a cultural institution, which is part of what made the magazine a smart target for The Sisterhood's efforts. It makes sense that *Ms.* was the only white periodical that the group pushed to include more Black women's writings because, even when it missed the mark, *Ms.* did engage with Black women intellectuals. This meant an ongoing process in which gains were hard-won, incremental, and uneven. For example, the magazine published Ntozake Shange's "self-interview" in 1976, but decided it was too financially risky to put Shange on the cover.[115] This might have been due to backlash to the success of *for colored girls*, but the decision was also part of a larger pattern in which *Ms.* "editors openly talked about their belief that putting black people on the cover would depress newsstand sales."[116]

As I discuss in chapter 4, writer Michele Wallace had—a few years before and separately from The Sisterhood's efforts—written Steinem taking *Ms.* to task for its lack of attention to Black women writers and proposed a regular feature on Black women visual artists. Margo Jefferson, then at *Newsweek*, had written a few pieces for *Ms.* and wrote a letter to Steinem supporting Wallace's plan.[117] The success of this pressure is apparent in the fact that Judith Wilson, just a few years after leaving the magazine partly over the unspoken racial hierarchy in the office, wrote articles as a freelancer for *Ms.* about Alma Thomas and Howardena Pindell. Published in 1979 and 1981, these articles brought important Black women artists who were not as well-known as they ought to have been to the readers of *Ms.*, which reached 450,000 people by 1981.[118]

For Wilson and some other Sisterhood members, *Ms.* was better as an occasional publication outlet than as a daily workplace. *Ms.* hired Alice Walker as a contributing editor in 1974 and put her on the cover when *The Color Purple* came out in 1982.[119] Walker and Steinem became good friends in the 1970s and remained close. At *Ms.*, however, Walker preferred roles that did not require her to be in the office regularly. Ruth Sullivan, an early white woman coeditor at the magazine, later recalled, "I think Alice felt the burden of being, as she described it, the token black woman at *Ms.* . . . when she worked in the office, it fell on her to generate the articles dealing with women of color."[120]

A version of Walker's essay "Looking for Zora," about her literal search for writer Zora Neale Hurston's grave site and figurative search for a literary foremother, first appeared in *Ms.* magazine in 1974 and has become a canonical text for Black feminism. Due in part to Walker, Wilson, and others, *Ms.* did print more and more reviews of Black women's books over the course of the 1970s and '80s, including Mary Helen Washington's review of Toni Cade Bambara's *The Sea Birds Are Still Alive* in 1977 and Bambara's review of June Jordan's *Civil Wars* in 1980. The magazine addressed the absence of Black women from its pages more systemically by hiring Sisterhood member Susan McHenry as well as Marcia Ann Gillespie, who had worked closely with Sisterhood members in her years at *Essence*, as editors in 1979 and 1980.[121] As I discuss in the next chapter, *Ms.* made an important move by supporting Michele Wallace's book *Black Macho and the Myth of the Superwoman* (1979). At a time when Wallace was hit with harsh critiques from many other publications, *Ms.* published an excerpt of *Black Macho* and put Wallace on the cover of the January 1979 issue.[122] Racist and sexist responses were very public; less visible is the work Wallace had already done in the years before then, and in collaboration with Jefferson, Walker, and Wilson, to increase the presence of Black women in the magazine.

In collaboration with other Sisterhood members and on her own for years, Alice Walker pushed Gloria Steinem and *Ms.* to include Black women. Frustrated by the lack of progress on this front, Walker resigned from the magazine in 1986. In addition to being exhausted by the burden of racial representation, she was not always taken seriously at *Ms.* In her journal in the 1980s, she drafted what would become her letter of resignation addressed to Joanne Edgar, a white founding editor of *Ms.*, and Rosemary Bray, a Black editor there who had been a member of The Sisterhood.[123] In the draft letter Walker described her experience at *Ms.* staff meetings: "whenever I spoke there was a curiously respectful silence punctuated by even more respectful chuckles. Then the business of the magazine continued . . . I stopped attending conference meetings because it became clear that what racial color there was in the magazine *I* would basically provide or represent."[124] In the letter of resignation she ultimately submitted, Walker wrote, "I am writing to let you know of the swift alienation from the magazine my daughter and I feel each time it arrives with its determinedly (and to us grim) white cover . . . It was nice to be on a *Ms.* cover myself once. But a people of color cover once or twice a year is not enough. In real life, people of color occur with much more frequency. I do not feel welcome in the world you are projecting."[125]

Walker and Marcia Gillespie both reflected on this moment in 2011 for an "Oral History of *Ms.* Magazine" by Abigail Pogrebin, daughter of Letty Cottin Pogrebin, a co-founding editor of the magazine. Walker recalled, "The proverbial straw that broke the camel's back was a *Ms.* cover showing two pregnant women, both white. This would have been such an easy cover on which to show a bit of diversity." Gillespie remembered Walker's resignation as a moment when she had to decide whether she still "wanted to be associated with the magazine" and "decided to move forward with *Ms.* because I felt there was a need to keep pressing from within."[126] Gillespie eventually became the first Black editor-in-chief in 1992.[127] The Sisterhood's progress getting Black women's writing and Black feminist thought into *Ms.* came in fits and starts, and there were setbacks. Their work had lasting results: the magazine still exists today and continues to engage Black feminist thought and Black women's writing in efforts such as the Harriet Tubman Bicentennial Project, a large-scale online project that *Ms.* launched in 2022.

Strategies for getting more Black women artists and writers into popular magazines were a frequent topic of conversation at Sisterhood meetings. As a Black women's magazine that was relatively receptive to Black feminist literature and politics, *Essence* remained prominent in these discussions. In the late 1970s as The Sisterhood coalesced, *Essence* had a significant but uneven relationship with Black feminist writers. The Sisterhood's work made meaningful change. By 1975, members and interlocutors for the group were working at *Essence*: Toni Cade Bambara was on the editorial board, Jessica Harris was the book review editor, and Vertamae Grosvenor was writing "witty and trenchant" "social commentary."[128] *Essence* published Alice Walker's writings, including an excerpt of her novel *Meridian* and an interview by Harris in the July 1976 issue. These women brought their existing relationships with *Essence* to the table at Sisterhood meetings. The magazine was also a smart target because ownership disputes and concerns about the publication's longevity made *Essence* open to change. It also had reach: in 1977 the circulation was 550,000. *Essence* did not reach 2.5 million readers, as the women's magazine *Cosmopolitan* did by 1978, but *Essence* had about 100,000 more readers each month than *Ms.* In the late 1970s, major media companies and advertisers saw potential for growth at *Essence*, as the magazine had circulation numbers "somewhere between *Cosmo* and *Ms.*"[129]

By the second full meeting of The Sisterhood in 1977, cofounders Alice Walker and June Jordan had scheduled a meeting with Marcia Ann Gillespie, then editor-in-chief at *Essence*, about the "poetry submission problem" at the magazine.[130] Gillespie was a managing editor at *Essence* when it was founded in 1970 and became editor-in-chief in 1971. She had begun changing the content in ways that aligned with The Sisterhood's goals and had gone to bat for Ntozake Shange's *for colored girls*, insisting that the magazine feature the choreopoem on the cover and throughout the November 1976 issue.[131] Even so, *Essence* was still largely a women's lifestyle and beauty magazine in early 1977. The "poetry submission problem" The Sisterhood meeting minutes refer to is that *Essence* was not regularly publishing or reviewing poetry despite the fact that Black women's poetry was flourishing. About a week before The Sisterhood's first meeting, Toni Morrison wrote journalist, editor, and Sisterhood member Audreen Ballard: "I think we've sent you a copy of June Jordan's bound galleys—THINGS THAT I DO IN THE DARK. Don't you think that a story/interview in *Essence* would be dynamite for her? She would make fantastic copy. Let me know if you agree."[132] Morrison's persuasive appeal did not get Jordan's book reviewed, but she continued to meet regularly with Ballard in 1977, and their discussions were part of The Sisterhood's efforts to influence the content of *Essence*.[133]

The Sisterhood pushed *Essence* to publish serious, sometimes politically radical Black feminist writing. One success was the publication of June Jordan's essay "Where Is the Love?" This essay came out of a 1978 academic conference but, as Cheryl Wall explained, "appealed to a readership beyond activists and intellectuals," and thus it worked in a magazine "geared to middle-class black women" who would recognize right away that the title of the essay came from Roberta Flack and Donny Hathaway's hit song.[134] Just two years later, *Essence* published Judith Wilson's positive review of Michele Wallace's *Black Macho and the Myth of the Superwoman* and, as discussed in chapter 4, used Wallace's book as an occasion to seriously explore intraracial gender dynamics across multiple issues of the magazine. In the 1980s, *Essence* published essays by June Jordan about subjects such as the devastating effects of U.S. foreign policy in Nicaragua.[135] These editorial choices declared that foreign affairs were within the purview of a Black women's magazine.

Although *Essence* proved receptive to political writing by Wallace and Jordan, other Sisterhood members had a more strained relationship with the magazine. Alice Walker's relationship with *Essence* was sometimes tense. Unlike *Ms.*, *Essence* did not consult or hire Walker as part of its 1970 launch or in its first decade of publication. Despite The Sisterhood's success in making Black women's literature increasingly central to the magazine, *Essence* declined to publish an excerpt of Walker's 1982 novel *The Color Purple*.[136] Even so, Sisterhood members Audrey Edwards and Audreen Ballard wrote for the magazine, and Edwards served as editor from 1981 to 1986. As she had done at *Ms.*, Judith Wilson made *Essence* a platform for rigorous writings on Black women artists, such as her 1986 essay "Coming of Age: A Look at Three Contemporary Artists—Howardena Pindell, Jeanne Moutoussamy-Ashe, Beverly Buchanan." The Sisterhood made *Essence* a venue for Black feminist literature and ideas. Cheryll Y. Greene sustained this shift with her editorial labor and thus kept the Black feminist element prominent for at least two decades.

~

In addition to their outward-facing work on publication and publicity, The Sisterhood developed internal procedures that reflected their politics and attended to their personal and professional wellness. They talked about "members' desire to not feel pressured to follow-up on voluntary projects, but to do so at their own pace" and how to "enhance the cohesiveness of the group."[137] As they closed the April meeting by setting the agenda for their May meeting, Walker offered to invite Marcia Ann Gillespie, author of a "recent editorial in *Essence* on depression," and Nana Maynard planned to "report to the group on Transcendental Meditation." The meeting concluded with Walker sharing slides and telling the group about a "black artists tour of Cuba." Finally, they set the next meeting for May 15 at Alice Walker's house. The minutes end with plans: "Wear walking shoes, because if weather is good, Alice will conduct a tour of Prospect Park. In addition to depression, we will also discuss such matters as forming an unincorporated association and opening a bank account for The Sisterhood at this meeting."[138] As a principle of Black feminist practice, the group stressed that their collaborative mode of organizing included care for self and others as inseparable from literary, political, and academic work.

The penultimate paragraph of the minutes for the following meeting on May 15, 1977, reads, "The meeting then turned to discussion of the topic proposed last month, depression, and there followed a general discussion of individual members problems in this area and methods of overcoming depression."[139] This sentence reveals the extent to which the group served as a source of emotional support. The brevity of this part of the minutes also suggests that they kept some of the contents of those conversations out of their written records. In all their meetings, The Sisterhood maintained a delicate balance among points of order, concrete plans, visible action, and discussion about matters professional and personal. Patricia Spears Jones wrote, "We talked about oh everything from the usual Black men versus Black women fusses to what was really good to read . . . we tried to find language to talk about who we are and what we do. How feminist were we, did that have to do with Blackness or not—and why were we asked to separate our gender from race—did anyone ask the men?"[140]

These conversations were necessarily ephemeral, and members understood that The Sisterhood was worthy of documentation. This meant that they needed to keep their own archives, which they did in Judith Wilson's meeting minutes, VèVè Clark's "In-House Proposal," the 1977 photograph of the women at the first meeting, the official correspondence that Abike and later Renita Weems wrote to the members, and, eventually, the papers that some members placed in libraries around the country. As The Sisterhood met, they wanted and needed to control the terms of their increasing visibility. They treated support among friends and colleagues as an important part of this documentation but omitted personal details, perhaps already imagining that scholars would study their meeting minutes decades later.

The Sisterhood created a sustaining all-Black, all-woman space that was both escape from and response to the backlash to *for colored girls*, the overwhelmingly white offices of places like *Newsweek* and Random House, academic departments that treated African American literature as a minor or fringe subject, and racist political discourse about Black mothers. This work to support one another was contingent and sometimes fleeting. It was also concrete and detailed, and had lasting effects. Members knew then and know now that The Sisterhood's collaboration was important for their own lives and work and for the place of Black women's writing in American culture.

Chapter Three

"TO MOVE THE NEEDLE IN BLACK WOMEN'S LIVES"

The Sisterhood's first phase was one of gathering together, supporting one other personally and professionally, and getting Black women's writing and Black feminist ideas into existing magazines. The group's second phase, starting about six months after their first meeting, was defined by new forces and pressures. Members' work and personal lives were reaching far beyond the group's home base in New York. The women were navigating dissent and burnout within the group while also facing criticism from outside. The Sisterhood's advocacy helped some members become more visible, busy, and successful in the literary marketplace, which ironically made it increasingly difficult to get all the members together for their monthly meetings.

Less than six months after the first meeting, The Sisterhood's collaboration radiated outward beyond New York and beyond the United States. On May 15, 1977, the women gathered in Alice Walker's home in Brooklyn. They continued to secure publication and publicity for Black women writers locally, but they also reached out to people in the South, especially Atlanta, and in the West, especially the Bay Area. The Sisterhood made plans for individual members to meet with editors in Atlanta and California. Patricia Spears Jones reported on the "women's art issue of *Southern Exposure*," a journal based in Durham, North Carolina; Renita Weems "stated that in such Northwestern cities as Portland [Oregon] she had seen a real commitment to art unlike what we see here"; and Phyl Garland reported on her "recent visit to Atlanta and passed around copies of *First World*" that she had picked up there.[1] The Sisterhood made significant progress with *First World* and, as detailed in the next chapter, Toni Cade Bambara was a kind of one-woman branch of the group in Atlanta.

Relationships with Black feminists in Oakland and San Francisco were important to Sisterhood members, and they regularly discussed their political and aesthetic differences from West Coast writers.[2] The Sisterhood identified strongly with its New York location. The question of its relationship to African American writers, thinkers, and artists on the West Coast came up at several meetings in passing and then occupied a significant portion of the conversation at the May 15 meeting. June Jordan reported on "her recent trip to California with NaNa Maynard."[3] VèVè Clark talked about "Valerie Bradley of the Bay Area's Black Women Organized for Action," a group that was planning to move to New York. She noted that Joyce Carol Thomas, a member of "The Rainbow Sign—Marianne Pollard's black cultural center," would be in New York soon, and Jordan promised to plan a dinner with Thomas and members of The Sisterhood. Jordan also described a "new dance, poetry and martial arts center in Oakland, California, Everybody's Creative Art Center, which is run by a sister named Halifu," and Clark described a "Latin cultural center" and a recently closed "neighborhood school in Berkeley, The Neo-Arts Cooperative."[4] Clark was especially tuned in to Black feminist work happening in the Bay Area because she was a faculty member at Berkeley, though she regularly spent time in New York. Like Ntozake Shange and others who had done collaborative projects in California, Clark was working in both visual and print media. "She was part of a group of women at Berkeley who were trying to put together material about Katherine Dunham" to create a book and a film about the choreographer.[5] With this group, Clark coedited *Kaiso! Writings by and about Katherine Dunham* in a small print run to accompany a 1978 exhibit about Dunham at UC Berkeley.

While members respected Clark and her work, they were somewhat skeptical about the multimedia projects of other West Coast women. The group talked about "the progress of black artists in the Bay Area," noting, "although there seems to be less political consciousness among West Coast artists and a lack of tough aesthetic standards, there does seem to be more experimentation, especially with electronic media."[6] The Sisterhood had a sense that Black women in New York were more progressive in terms of "political consciousness" and more successful making inroads into the literary establishment than their West Coast counterparts. They also thought of Black women in the Bay Area as more experimental in terms of performance and visual arts and more knowledgeable about new "electronic media." In a letter to June Jordan a couple of weeks after The Sisterhood discussed "West Coast artists," Patricia Spears Jones asserted that "the time for a new national poetry magazine is at hand" and that the journal *Poetry Now* could not fill this need because it "is a fine magazine that is getting better [but] is still too 'west coast.'"[7] Margo Jefferson recalls discussion at Sisterhood meetings about their "sense," possibly "cliché,'" that "a freeform experiment was going on on the west coast" with "a kind of pioneer swagger."[8] The Sisterhood saw the West as a place of possibility but doubted that the political and literary work happening there was as serious as the Black feminist work happening in New York.

Ntozake Shange had deep connections to the Bay Area. She did not share other Sisterhood members' skepticism about West Coast artistic activism. *for colored girls* premiered in Oakland in 1974, and Shange continued to collaborate with writers, musicians, and performers there throughout her career. Among writers in California, she found "a certain freeness" to collaborate with "all Third World people." In 1979, she described a liberating relationship to place and space: "The poetry of the Black Writer on the West Coast clarifies—migrations, our relationship to the soil, to ourselves in space. There is an enormous amount of space in the West, and you do not feel personally impinged upon every time you come out of your door like you do in New York and in Chicago."[9]

Audre Lorde, too, had ties to the West Coast, beginning with her poetry readings in Los Angeles and San Francisco in November 1976 and through her friendship with poet Pat Parker. However, Lorde worried that the "women's scene" in California lacked class consciousness and exhibited "patterns of unexamined racism."[10] June Jordan echoed Lorde's experience, asserting that "the feminist community in Berkeley is very strong and interconnected with the local black artists' community, although the same divisions exist there between other factions of the black community and feminists." Jordan encouraged The Sisterhood to "exchange information and support with Bay Area artists." The group wanted to "sponsor a New York" exhibit of "California women's art" and was excited about films coming out of California.[11] They were likely referring to what film scholar Clyde Taylor would later name the "L.A. rebellion," a group of filmmakers in the late 1960s and '70s creating important and experimental Black films at and beyond UCLA's filmmaking program. As Sisterhood members were experimenting with form in their writings, these filmmakers were experimenting with cinema, exploring the intersections of race, gender, and class identity in works including Haile Gerima's *Bush Mama* (1975), Charles Burnett's *Killer of Sheep* (1977), and Julie Dash's *The Diary of an African Nun* (1977), which is based on Alice Walker's short story of the same title.[12] At the May 1977 meeting, The Sisterhood discussed various ideas for film screenings of West Coast work in New York City, and Judith Wilson, in keeping with her labor to build The Sisterhood's archive and document their meetings, suggested that The Sisterhood start building their library of "videotapes or films" of "West Coast black arts exhibits and performances."[13] The group took up her idea that they might show not just films but also video recordings of live performances and art exhibits coming out of California.

As they built collaborative relationships with writers and artists in the U.S. South and West, The Sisterhood also built and maintained transnational connections. A relationship to the African Diaspora, especially the Caribbean, was central to their personal lives, politics, and writing. Sisterhood members including VèVè Clark, Rosa Guy, June Jordan, Audre Lorde, Paule Marshall, and Lori Sharpe were themselves or were children of recent immigrants from the Caribbean. Marshall's parents emigrated from Barbados, and she grew up in a Brooklyn neighborhood populated largely by West Indian immigrants. Brooklyn and Barbados both figure heavily in her fiction and nonfiction writing. Guy moved with her parents from Trinidad to Harlem when she was eight years old, and her fiction depicts friendships between young Caribbean and Black American women in New York.[14] Jordan's parents were both Jamaican. Lorde's mother immigrated from Carriacou (one setting of Marshall's 1983 novel *Praisesong for the Widow*) and her father from Barbados before they settled in New York. Patricia Spears Jones describes Sharpe as "an older woman of fierce determination and drive. Mother to two daughters and long-time divorced, she was one of the first Caribbean women to talk openly about her roots and the problems within her family outside of her own community."[15] Clark and Sharpe were, as Jones recalls, "very much from the Caribbean" and thus brought a "different kind of sensibility" to The Sisterhood, such as attending to the role of Caribbean cultures in African American identity and using Caribbean settings in their writings.[16]

Audre Lorde's essay "Grenada Revisited" (1984) illustrates the ways that ties to specific locations in the Caribbean shaped Sisterhood members' personal lives, writing, and politics. As The Sisterhood met, Lorde made the first of the two trips that would inform "Grenada Revisited." She went to Grenada in 1978 in search of a sense of "home" and to see her "mother's birthplace" and returned to the island nation in 1983.[17] Like other Black feminist writers, Lorde uses first-person narration of her individual experience to advance collective interests. She explains that the United States "sanctioned" nearly three decades of "wasteful, corrupt" rule prior to a "bloodless coup" in 1979 that "ushered in the People's Revolutionary Government (PRG)." Grenadians enjoyed a few years of a federal administration that addressed the needs of regular people: "all roads were widened and reworked, and a functioning bus service was established that did more than ferry tourists back and forth to the cruise ship"; "free medical care"; "no more school fees"; "teacher education and a planned each-one-teach-one program through the countryside."[18] Then the United States invaded in 1983, leaving the island "savaged" with "its people maneuvered into saying thank you to their invaders."[19] Lorde offers a detailed, numbered list of the Reagan administration's declared reasons for invading and dismantles each rationalization, offering copious footnotes in support of her position. Echoing Lorde's travels, her essay starts with Grenada in the late 1970s and revisits it after the invasion, describing the destruction of the country's infrastructure and its people.

Like other Sisterhood members, Lorde had a familial connection to one place that informed her politics and necessitated solidarity with oppressed Black and Latinx people globally. She wrote,

> Had the amount that the invasion cost each one of us in taxes been lent to the PRG when it requested economic aid from the U.S. five years ago . . . Grenada would have been self-defined and independent . . . What a bad example, a dangerous precedent an independent Grenada would be for the peoples of Color in the Caribbean, in Central America, for those of us here in the United States.
>
> The ready acceptance by the majority of americans of the Grenadian invasion and of the shady involvement of the events leading up to the assassination of [PRG leader] Prime Minister Maurice Bishop both happen in an america whose moral and ethical fiber is weakened by racism as thoroughly as wood is weakened by rot. White america has been well-schooled in the dehumanization of Black people.[20]

Lorde articulates here what Sisterhood members meant by Third World Feminism: an anti-imperialist, anticapitalist, antiwar liberation agenda for people of color around the world. This mode of feminism takes care with and has respect for differences of race and nation within a broader solidarity because part of its authority is rooted in individual experience, such as Lorde's search for matrilineal connection in Grenada and her life in New York. This feminism acknowledges Black women's expertise in foreign policy and puts that knowledge to use in understanding the United States as internally colonizing Black Americans. Lorde names one damning purpose of the invasion of Grenada: for "the Pentagon" to find out "whether or not Black american soldiers could be gotten to fire upon other Black people."[21] Lorde resists this violent imperialist division among Black people and redefines her own simultaneous connection to and difference from Grenadians: "Grenada is their country. I am only a relative."[22] She wrote this essay in 1984, but its roots are in the ideas she developed in The Sisterhood and other Black feminist groups in the 1970s.

This particular relationship to Caribbean identity of a Black American woman who is "only a relative" appears in Sisterhood members' writings across genres, including fiction.[23] While The Sisterhood was meeting in 1977 and 1978, Toni Morrison was at work on Tar Baby (1981). The novel is set mostly in the Caribbean but also captures the financial obstacles, physical toll, and social excitement young Black people were experiencing living in New York City in the 1970s. Sisterhood members could surely have seen their experiences in both Tar Baby's primary setting, the fictional Isle des Chevaliers, and its secondary setting, the island of Manhattan. Late in the novel, lovers Son and Jadine travel separately from Isle de Chevaliers to meet up in New York. In a scene that echoes the migrant's initial encounter with the city in novels such as Paul Laurence Dunbar's The Sport of The Gods (1903), James Weldon Johnson's Autobiography of an Ex-Colored Man (1912), and Ralph Ellison's Invisible Man (1952), Son finds New York overwhelming, hectic, and sad:

> The black girls in New York City were crying and their men were looking neither to the right nor to the left. Not because they were heedless, or intent on what was before them, but they did not wish to see the crying, crying girls split into two parts by their tight jeans, screaming at the top of their high, high heels, straining against the pull of their braids and the fluorescent combs holding their hair. . . . Like blazing jewels, the subway cars burst from the tunnels to the platforms shining with the recognizable artifacts of childhood: fantasy, manic, ego, energy, humor and paint.[24]

For Son, the city is a place of "crying, crying girls" wearing constraining and garish clothing and accessories. Jadine, a model who has lived and worked in Paris and New York, loves the "manic" "energy" of the crowded city and the access to fashion, including "tight jeans" and "high, high heels," even when both hurt. The "subway cars" are "blazing jewels" that assault Son's senses, but they give Jadine a sense of life as part of the romantic pull of the city. She loves the city partly *because* it is dirty and challenging: "New York made her feel like giggling, she was so happy to be back in the arms of that barfly with the busted teeth and armpit breath. New York oiled her joints and she moved as though they were oiled. Her legs were longer here . . . if ever there was a black women's town, New York was it."[25] She is giddy, "giggling," in motion, stretching her "longer" "legs" in this "black woman's town." The city may be a smelly, bedraggled "barfly," but its "arms" wrap around her seductively.

Son and Jadine both think of their departure from the Caribbean as "escape from the plantation," but Son would rather be in his hometown of Eloe, Florida, where Jadine is bored out of her mind.[26] For her, the city is a hard place to make it financially, but also a space of possibility and far more desirable than Isle de Chevaliers or Eloe. In her mind, the pull of the city stands in stark contrast to both the Caribbean and the rural South. Jadine travels the patterns of migration that Sisterhood members and many of their families had followed. They were each navigating the romance, drama, and challenges of a place that, for all its hardships, might be "a black women's town."

~

Even as The Sisterhood built connections across the United States and Caribbean, made inroads for Black feminist writing in popular magazines, and started writing some of the most important works of their careers, they also navigated serious obstacles. Within six months of their first meeting, there was significant dissent about the purpose of the group. The Sisterhood gathered on June 12, 1977, at Sheila Rush's home on Manhattan's Upper West Side. Patricia Spears Jones reflected on the meeting in a handwritten post-script to a letter to June Jordan:

> The Sisterhood Meeting was interesting. But I feel very strongly that we should start to act in concert. That is politically since enough established & soon to be

established writers & other media women are interested in doing something real. I would really like to sit down w/ you & talk about this. I'm good at ideas but I'm not into leading & I'm also a lot younger than most of the women in the Sisterhood but we need to do more than hold each other's hand.[27]

Jones understood that The Sisterhood had significant power as a group of "established & soon to be established writers & other media women" who could shape the literary landscape. She, like some other members, felt it was urgent to make use of this collaboration to do "something real." This sense of urgency increased over the months the group met, in part because their individual successes as writers meant that their lives were "very busy" and "intense" and that finding time to attend the monthly meetings, "trying to add one more thing to do on the to-do list," was challenging.[28]

The anxiety in Jones's letter reflects the enormous pressure on any collective of Black women to do political work for liberation. Seeing her note to Jordan for the first time since she wrote it forty years earlier, Jones said that "a problem for all Black organizations, frankly, is that we are always placed in a situation . . . politically and culturally and socially" where "the assumption is that you're supposed to somehow do something, be active in some way. And I think it's only in the last maybe two or three decades that Black people have enough kind of sensibility to come together just to hang."[29] The deeply felt urgency to help Black women's writing reach readers was "active" work for liberation, but these women also needed "just to hang" to help them recover from and commiserate over their daily experiences of racism and sexism in their workplaces. Most Sisterhood members saw the group as a way to serve both needs—to get publication and publicity for their writing and to support one another by gathering and talking in a space for Black women writers. As is the case for many feminist groups, simultaneously meeting both kinds of needs was a challenge.

Sisterhood members continued to meet and collaborate both in and outside of the formal monthly group meetings. There are no archived copies of minutes for the July–December 1977 meetings, but the group did meet during those months at the homes of Margo Jefferson, Paule Marshall, Sheila Rush, and journalist Diane Weathers.[30] Jefferson held one meeting at her home that included "lots of conversation" about "what constitutes Black feminism."[31] In this and similar discussions, members continued to strategize about practical matters of publication and publicity and write and theorize about Black feminism. They also made time to have fun. As 1977 drew to a close, The Sisterhood had a festive holiday meeting on December 18 at the Wellesley Club in the Biltmore Hotel. It was a potluck, and in addition to bringing a dish, members were instructed to bring "something to read, or sing, or dance, or even mime" and permitted to bring one woman as a guest.[32]

It was tricky to sustain support for one another, the battle to get Black women's writing into print, celebration of their successes, and each individual member's work, which usually included both being a writer and having a day job. As 1977 drew to a close, Renita Weems pushed to keep the group going. In a letter announcing the December meeting, she reminded members that The Sisterhood is a "group of women in the arts/art-related fields," lamented that "many of us have fallen by the wayside" recently, and chided that "it is both tacky and disruptive for us to be as late as we have too often times been in the past."[33] In this and other letters to the group, Weems worried about the kind of work The Sisterhood could do and whether the group could be sustained. She wrote in first-person plural, treating herself as part of the "we" to reassert the group's identity as a collective and because Weems was, in her role as "correspondence secretary," conveying the words and concerns of other members.[34]

A year after the group began, it was hard to keep meeting every month. In a note to members in late 1977, Renita Weems wrote, "Dear Sister: It is unfortunate that the Feb. [1978] meeting of the Sisterhood must be cancelled because of the unavailability of a meeting place." She noted that it was "unfair" to ask members who had recently hosted a meeting to do so again, and that this difficulty "speaks of a greater dilemma: Continued Interest in the Sisterhood," which appeared to be waning based on "attendance." She was frustrated that some members "do not even call up to ask what happened at meetings that we miss." Weems suggested that the women must recommit or the group would not continue: "There are no figure heads in the Sisterhood. Therefore after talking with a few sisters about this concern, we have decided to try to take a poll of the continued interest."[35] She included her work and home phone numbers, asked members to call her, and promised to mail the results of the poll to all members. Weems was speaking for the group, or at least for "a few sisters," but she was working alone on the detailed and mundane labor of maintaining the group's records and correspondence. She made herself available to speak to members, tracked the results of the poll, and mailed copies of those results to Sisterhood members. The burden of this work had been such that Weems's predecessor, Judith Wilson, needed to step back from her secretarial duties for the group to figure out her career path. As Wilson took a less active role in The Sisterhood, Weems was "appointed, anointed, drafted into becoming a correspondence secretary," but chose not to keep the kind of detailed minutes that Wilson had, opting instead to limit her labor to the significant task of maintaining the group's correspondence.[36]

Weems's note to the group about attendance and lateness brought conflicting ideas about the purpose of The Sisterhood to the surface. She remembers, "that postcard that I sent out just kind of blew things up" and "came across as chastising," and "people were upset, whether they spoke it or not, about who wasn't there and that how fluid things were becoming."[37] Jones was among those frustrated by Weems's postcard. In March 1978, Jones replied to Weems, copying Jordan, Walker, Sheila Rush, Lori Sharpe, Margo Jefferson, Madeline Moore, and Joan Harris on the letter. Expressing her "irritation and annoyance," Jones wrote, "As far as I am concerned and other sisters I have talked to, the SISTERHOOD is a valuable part of my life" and "is quite healthy." Jones shifted away from her earlier worries about whether they were "doing something real" and asserted instead that the "The cancellation of one meeting is not a threat" to the group and that, contra Weems's claims, "attendance has been quite consistent." Jones, by copying others on the letter, chides Weems in front of some of the group: "And the tone of your note makes it difficult for anyone to wish to open up their homes if there is going to be some kind of chastisement about it as in regards to our telephone conversation when you asked to have the meeting at my house." Jones could not host because she had a small place with "very little furniture (three chairs does not a living room suite make)."[38]

Weems and Jones's correspondence also points to the cumulative burden over time of taking care of the mundane tasks that keep a group going. Jones was frustrated that she "and other members have requested repeatedly that we be given a list of names and addresses of other members and as far as I know you have not made up that list or shown any inclination to do so. Also, some of the problems [of attendance and members staying in the loop] would be greatly reduced . . . if there are minutes read from the previous meetings. That too has not been done."[39] Jones's tone is harsh, but she is rightly naming basic practices of sustaining a group. However, these tasks were not part of her role as Weems understood it; she had only agreed to send official correspondence to members about upcoming meetings.[40]

This correspondence reflects The Sisterhood's ongoing negotiation of their purpose a year into the life of the group and shows the ways Jones's sense of the function of the group shifted over time. In an earlier letter to June Jordan, Jones described debates that cropped up in nearly every feminist organization about leadership and hierarchy and about "doing something real" versus "hold[ing] each other's hand[s]."[41] In later interviews, Walker said that The Sisterhood resisted "ranking" and "competition," but in fact, many members did sense a "pecking order" determined by age and career stage.[42] As a result of this unspoken hierarchy, younger members like Wilson and Weems, both recently graduated from college, served in secretarial roles.[43] It is also the case, though, that younger or less-established members clearly had a strong voice in the group. Weems and Jones were the ones who engaged most visibly in this debate about the direction and purposes of The Sisterhood. Although Jones was writing poetry and Weems had a sense of her path ahead as a womanist theologian, they were not yet the accomplished writers they would become.

It is difficult to run an organization that resists hierarchy and charismatic leadership in favor of shared authority among diverse members. This structural obstacle confronted Combahee, the NBFO, and The Sisterhood. Jones's frustration was partly about the ways that Weems seemed to disregard how remarkable The Sisterhood was. Jones wrote, "We all have very busy lives and to see that a number of women who would probably rest a bit on Sunday, take time and money to come together and share conversation and comradeship once a month is quite an achievement especially in New York City."[44] Jones thus both honors the "conversation and comradeship" that took work to maintain and suggests that, despite her assertions that The Sisterhood "is quite healthy," she was attuned to how fragile the group was amid the women's "busy lives" and need for "rest."[45] This connects with Weems's recollection that "people were upset."[46] Her words point to an undercurrent of anxiety in this correspondence, both about waning attendance of prominent members such as Ntozake Shange and Toni Morrison and about how formal the group's work ought to be.

The Sisterhood "started with having no dudes and no rules," and some members "bristled" at attempts to bring more structure to the group as it grew. As more women joined, it was "no longer the small intimate group of peers," and some of the original members began to attend less frequently by 1978.[47] In many cases, this was due to the demands of successful careers;

several members were now working full-time as editors, teachers, or journalists while also writing and promoting their increasingly visible books. New York offered proximity and energy that helped The Sisterhood coalesce and keep going. The city was the center of literary publishing, journalism, and academia, making it fertile ground for many members' success. However, as Jones remembers, "New York also in some ways led to the seeds of the dissolution of the organization because people . . . really did blow up. All of a sudden folks who were available to do all kinds of stuff couldn't do it anymore. Or you couldn't call somebody on the phone and say . . . let's have lunch. Not gonna happen. And, so that kind of stratifying that happens here around the success . . . became a problem."[48]

Renita Weems, too, recalls, "the name-brand people who were at the core of it, you know, sort of no longer prioritized coming."[49] This stratification is an obstacle to most literary and political groups, but perhaps especially Black women's organizations in the 1970s. Some Sisterhood members and many of their contemporaries had provided the constant, endless, unseen labor of the civil rights movement from the mid-1950s to mid-1960s while a few charismatic male leaders took center stage. This gendered distribution of labor continued in some Black Power groups. Black women had been writing, organizing, and working for liberation since before the United States was a nation, but they were getting more sustained, national attention for their writing in the late 1970s than ever before. That attention was not equally distributed. Those who "really did blow up" were navigating intense public scrutiny and those who didn't had to pick up the slack of daily labor in organizations like The Sisterhood.

As new members continued to join, founding members were attending less frequently or not at all. Some, such as Toni Morrison, were in New York but navigating the demands of careers that made it difficult to keep participating in the group. Other members began to leave the city, particularly for the Bay Area, where they found more living space, a slower pace, and sometimes secure employment at West Coast universities. Cofounder Alice Walker moved to San Francisco in late 1978, but regularly visited New York and continued to work for *Ms.*[50] The women who had served as the organizational glue for The Sisterhood by keeping minutes and conducting all official correspondence were no longer attending by the end of 1978: Weems had "dropped out" that spring after written exchanges arguing over the purpose of the group, and Wilson stopped attending meetings around the time she began her studies at the School of Visual Arts in fall 1978.[51]

During these shifts in membership, the question of "doing something real" persisted. Reflecting decades later, Weems said, that, like "every group" she has "been a part of," The Sisterhood repeatedly discussed structure and purpose:

> Why are we together? Do you think we should go to the next level? What is the next level? . . . You've got the activists and you got those who just want to read. You've got those who want to leverage their capital and the capital of having all of us in the room together to make some statements, to be more active, to do something more political, to move the needle in Black people and Black women's lives. So you've got well known writers and you've got literary agents and you've got the lawyers, . . . and you've got professors. When you've got that size of group, obviously, it is not just about reading the next chapter of somebody's book or reading someone's forthcoming book. You've got quite a bit of capital in the room. And so, yes, there were discussions about that.[52]

Like other members, Weems recognized the cultural and social capital of the group that met as The Sisterhood. She thinks back on the ways that capital came from assembling women who were increasingly successful in a variety of fields as activists, writers, literary agents, lawyers, and professors. The internal and external pressure to use it, "to move the needle in Black people and Black women's lives," was enormous, particularly in the late 1970s when no one political movement (such as civil rights or Black Power) defined Black liberation politics. For the women of The Sisterhood, this meant that the culture industry (including publishing and the university) was a primary and demanding site of their work to change Black women's lives.

The forces operating on The Sisterhood such as burnout, conflict over the group's purpose, shifting membership, increased visibility, and geographical moves shaped not just the group but also the women's individual personal lives and writings. June Jordan's poem "Letter to My Friend the Poet Ntozake Shange" gives a sense of just how much work it took to get together, stay in touch, and keep The Sisterhood going. Jordan wrote "Letter to My Friend" during The Sisterhood's active period, and it appeared in her volume *Passion: New Poems: 1977–1980* (1980). With a tone of both frustration and love, the poem depicts the difficulty of maintaining relationships amid the demands of housework, travel, and career:

> Just back from Minnesota/North Dakota
> All my clothes into the laundry or
> dry cleaners before I leave
> again
> for Oregon then California
> and my agent calls to say your business manager
> is sending me
> a Christmas present
> from you
> by messenger
> within the next two hours: will
> I be home?
>
> Jesus Christ (I think) getting nervous
> about two hours housebound
> under the circumstances
> maybe
> one of us
> better slow down![53]

The speaker is in between trips, likely to give public poetry readings, in "Minnesota/North Dakota" and then in "Oregon then California." She is in demand enough to have these reading gigs and an "agent," but not so economically flush that there's anyone else but herself to deal with housework, with the "laundry or/dry cleaners." With clothes to wash before she hits the road again, the speaker is perhaps running back and forth between her New York apartment and a washer and dryer in the basement or a laundromat down the block in addition to dropping clothes off at a "dry cleaners." Between this and other errands, she is "getting nervous" about the idea of "two hours housebound" waiting for a package to be delivered. "Letter to My Friend the Poet Ntozake Shange" stays in present tense, building urgency and this "nervous" feeling.

The Jordan figure in this poem gets a call from her "agent" with news that the Shange figure's "business manager" says "a Christmas present" is on the way "by messenger." It is absurd that these two friends, who had, for years, often spoken on the phone, hung out, and written letters to each other find their relationship mediated by people who work for them, as they each became busy in ways that required this kind of help. The speaker exclaims "Jesus Christ" silently to herself at the ridiculous notion that a Christmas gift between poets requires a staff.

This poem describes the lives of several members of The Sisterhood, but its title invites us to read it as correspondence from Jordan to Shange meant for a public readership. "Letter to My Friend the Poet Ntozake Shange" is an act of mediation and representation for public consumption—not a private letter between friends but a published work that names the two women as poets ("the Poet Ntozake Shange"), though both were writing across genres. It represents not only intimate griping among friends about the demands of housework and travel but also how domestic and poetic labor are intertwined, interdependent, and demanding in ways that put pressure on personal relationships. The speaker cautions "maybe/one of us/better slow down!" but makes clear that neither of them will. Sisterhood members managing the demands of family, home, teaching, writing, activism, and, for some, increasing visibility in the literary marketplace could surely see themselves in Jordan's depiction. It was hard work and a real accomplishment to gather once a month for substantive conversation and collaborative work. The speaker has the success that The Sisterhood wanted, especially for its poets, and that success is hard to navigate. While describing these challenges, "Letter to My Friend the Poet Ntozake Shange" also declares in public that Black women writers are in demand: they have agents and business managers and are traveling around the country to give readings.

Even as they collaborated to advocate for Black women writers, the women of The Sisterhood took varied individual approaches to their own careers. As I discuss in chapter 7, these differences eventually played out in relationship to universities. Some members, such as Judith Wilson, committed their significant talents to academia; others, such as June Jordan, leveraged academic positions to do work outside the university; while others, such as Alice Walker, kept their relationship with universities intermittent. These differences were not sites of conflict within the group, but they did sometimes draw members' time and labor away from The Sisterhood or make collaboration among members less likely. Three examples illustrate the variety of approaches and commitments: Ntozake Shange's independence from institutions, Paule Marshall's insistence on maintaining some privacy, and the place of religion and spirituality in various members' lives.

Around the time that Jordan wrote "Letter to My Friend," Shange describes her approach to getting her work out to readers and audiences independently from the publishing and academic institutions that her fellow Sisterhood members focused on:

> You don't have to wait on nobody . . . If you want to do a show, you go to your little local bar, and tell them that on—whatever their night off is—you want to use their space. And you go and use it to the best of your ability, and get paid $1.37, but get known in your community. Send out your own little press releases. Meet a printer. Have a printer do up just one page of your poems. Give them away, mail them to your friends. Give him fifty dollars and have him do a ten-page booklet. You don't have to wait. Learn how to print your goddamn self. This sense that we have to follow all the patterns established by the country and by our own habit is really quite unnecessary.[54]

In 1979, right after The Sisterhood had stopped meeting, after *for colored girls* had run on Broadway and won awards, Shange calls on Black women writers to operate outside of the cultural institutions that were beginning to pay more attention to them. This is a significant departure from the ways that members collaborated to change existing institutions. Shange's suggestion to playwrights and poets to "Send out your own little press releases. Meet a printer. Have a printer do up just one page of your poems" does follow practices of The Sisterhood of writers doing their own marketing, developing publicity portfolios, and publicizing their public readings. Shange, though, prescribed putting these practices to work outside of the existing magazines, presses, and universities that The Sisterhood was working to gain access to and to change. This necessitated the enormous amount of labor that made Jordan write, "one of us/better slow down!"[55] During the years The Sisterhood met, Shange was among its most widely known members, but she continued to approach her work in ways that were improvisational and outside of institutions, and that resisted "all the patterns established by the country and by our own habit." Advocating for Black women's writing and self-determination was Sisterhood work, but not all members did or could go about it the same way.

All Sisterhood members encountered the racism and misogyny of very narrow ideas about Black women's career options. Paule Marshall began college in the 1940s and, like "most young Black women at that time," understood "social worker or a teacher" as the two careers open to educated Black women.[56] In Marshall's 1962 short story "Reena," two daughters of Barbadian immigrants meet at a funeral for the first time in years and recount their paths since college. Reena tells the narrator that she "ended up," "Where else?," "as a social investigator for the Welfare Department." The two women are "helpless with laughter" in recognition of their shared experience as the narrator responds, "You too?" Work as an instrument of the state, including being "Someone whose dirty job it is to snoop into the corners of the lives of the poor and make their poverty more vivid by taking from them the last shred of privacy" is so common as one of the few professions available to Black women that it prompts sincere and bitter laughter.[57] These few lines in Marshall's story represent educated Black women in New York doing the only professional work they can get. They also reflect the complexity of being a public employee participating in a system that pathologizes and surveils Black people. This dialogue in "Reena" hints at the cumulative pain of intimately witnessing the results of public disinvestment in social services accompanied by extreme monitoring of private lives. Jobs as a social worker or welfare investigator appear often in Black women's writings of the 1960s and '70s. Sisterhood members were well aware of and wrote about the few expected occupations for educated Black women in cities even as they forged paths for themselves as academics, journalists, and writers.

By the time The Sisterhood met in 1977, Marshall was an accomplished fiction writer, but it bothered her that her writing had not gained a larger readership. Even so, she preferred not to give interviews or to promote her book through "television and radio appearances, book parties, public debates, cocktail parties, and the like."[58] This was a matter of both personality and generation. Sisterhood members younger than Marshall may have had a few more career options, but many of them felt more intense pressure and obligation than she did to appear in public not only to promote their own work but also to ensure the publication and study of Black women's writing. Not every member wanted to be in the public eye. Some, like Marshall, wanted attention for their books, but not for themselves. As I discuss in chapter 6, Toni Morrison, partly because fellow Black writers chose her to do so, took on the difficult task of maintaining a public self that was the face of African American literature to readers around the world.

Marshall was a prolific novelist, teacher, and literary organizer, but she was not always as visible as other members of The Sisterhood. She was a dedicated creative writing teacher and mentor to Black writers from across the Diaspora and taught fiction seminars at Virginia Commonwealth University and New York University for decades, shaping many young writers. Throughout the 1970s, Marshall hosted gatherings of intellectuals in her home. In the twenty-first century, she organized annual public readings at New York University by up-and-coming writers from around the African Diaspora, always with a catered party in her apartment on Washington Square Park afterward. In other words, Marshall was deft at and dedicated to building Black literary community from her work with the Harlem Writers' Guild in the 1950s to her passing in 2019, *and* she insisted on maintaining a degree of privacy.

Shange's independence from institutions and Marshall's preservation of her privacy are examples of how some Sisterhood members approached their careers in ways informed by but different from the group's collective efforts. Relationships to religion also differed significantly among members of the group. This was not a source of conflict, but rather one reason members turned to other collectives to help meet their needs. In their early meetings, Alice Walker advocated for Transcendental Meditation, which she studied with teachers and groups outside of The Sisterhood, and Audre Lorde was immersed in her study of spiritual practices in Dahomey, which connected her more with a community of Brooklyn lesbian poets who were focused on "African traditional practices, herbalism, [and] religious practices."[59] Several members identified as Christians, and both Renita Weems and Rosemary Bray would go on to be prominent pastors. Several of the women attended church services in the morning and a Sisterhood meeting in the afternoon on those Sundays that the group met. In a note to Morrison just before the first meeting of The Sisterhood, June Jordan suggests that members would be coming from church, or perhaps that the meeting was a kind of church for the women: "I'm looking forward to Sunday and the first After Church Supper of the Sisterhood."[60]

However, like most groups advocating for Black literature and liberation in the 1970s and '80s, The Sisterhood was secular. Weems recalls that "talk about religion (and being religious) was taboo in the Sisterhood and lots of other Black consciousness raising groups back then."[61] Religion and spirituality were in every member's writings, from the protagonist's mystic trances in Walker's 1976 novel *Meridian* to Baby Suggs preaching to other formerly enslaved people in Morrison's 1987 novel *Beloved*. Even so, religion and spirituality were not on the official agenda at meetings. During and after the years The Sisterhood met, Black women scholars who brought Black feminism into literary studies and other fields were themselves often religious but rarely centered religion in their academic work. The Sisterhood and their contemporaries set the terms for the study of African American literature and culture as a largely secular endeavor. This was and remains the case, even though uses of Christianity are a defining characteristic of African American literature from its beginnings to the present, including in works by Sisterhood members.[62]

Even as they navigated differences of economic class, career goals, and spiritual practice and engaged in substantive debate about the function of the group, a year after Jordan and Walker first convened it, The Sisterhood was still meeting once a month. Patricia Spears Jones recalled,

> Every one of the women in the Sisterhood was storming barricades . . . And at some point I think maybe, I realized that that was, because I was one of the younger people. And so a lot of other folks showed up and they were, they were a little older, they were better educated in some ways. Frankly they came from, you know, more middle and upper class families. And I come from a poor family. So their expectations of what's to be done were different. I can sort of see that now. It was annoying. But it's not unusual.[63]

Differing backgrounds, goals, and expectations among members made it hard to sustain The Sisterhood. This is "not unusual" for any kind of collective. In addition to internal differences among the women, the group faced obstacles from outside.

~

Black women writers and their ideas were becoming visible and legible to more people by 1978, partly due to The Sisterhood's efforts. Increased visibility was hard to navigate and impossible to fully control, even in places that ought to have been the most supportive, such as the annual Black Writers Conference at Howard University. Novelist John Oliver Killens created the conference as a gathering place for Black writers. Like the long-running annual Black Writers Conference that he would later establish at Medgar Evers College in New York, the Howard conference was open to the public, and journalists covered the event. Each year, the Howard conference focused on African American literature as a distinct tradition worthy of study.

This was important for scholars like those discussed in chapter 1, who were teaching the first African American literature courses at universities around the country. The conference was a chance to gather at a historically Black college with others in their field and to interact with poets, playwrights, and novelists. From the start, it included men and women writers, and the May 1978 conference program explicitly acknowledged that Black feminism was central to Black literature. June Jordan presented with Howard professor and activist Acklyn Lynch (a man), poet Sonia Sanchez, and scholar and activist Barbara Smith as part of a "public seminar" titled "Feminism and the Black Woman Writer." Jordan's opening statement—titled "Where Is the Love?" after Roberta Flack and Donny Hathaway's duet—reached a larger audience when it was later published in *Essence*.[64] The conference seemed like an opportunity to bring together scholars, writers, and a larger public audience to consider Black women writers, their work, and their feminism from a position of "love," but this panel discussion became yet another battleground.

Reflecting in 1995, Jordan remembered her excitement about the "historic, unprecedented" fact that "Feminism and the Black Woman Writer" was the closing panel at the 1978 conference. There was a "standing room only audience," and the atmosphere was tense: "the very scheduling of this seminar had managed to divide people into camps prepared for war."[65] The crowd was "jumpy," and Jordan feared the seminar would become "a fight," but "Black panelists and audience together" succeeded in really "talking" and stayed in the room until time "ran out."[66] Like the backlash Ntozake Shange faced a couple of years earlier from men who perceived *for colored girls* as an attack on Black men, the response to the inclusion of a panel about Black women writers was defensive and angry. Some attendees saw the use of the word "feminism" in the program as an attack on Black men.

Jordan's anxiety was justified by the fact that the conference at Howard was one of many occasions in which news media amplified, even exaggerated, conflict between Black men and women. Poet Tom Dent attended the full conference and wrote a brief report for the journal *Callaloo* in which he described the "seriousness and range" of Jordan's panel, noted the importance of a "panel on the history of the Black Arts Movement" "moderated by Larry Neal," and expressed appreciation for such discussions that focused on "the writers and community theatres working in the South." Dent experienced the conference as "a certain kind of *healing*" among "people who had been alienated from each other" since the recent dissolution of the Black Arts Movement.[67] The central problem he notes is not conflict between men and women, but rather waning financial support for Howard's Institute for Arts & Humanities.

Some people read Dent's short and thoughtful report, but many more read the *Washington Post* article about the conference, which focused almost entirely on Jordan's panel. *Post* writer Hollie West identified a "provocative note of black male-female relations and feminism" as the defining feature of the conference and reported that it "reached its most heated moments at the closing session when feminist-lesbian advocate Barbara Smith spoke." Smith's talk drew from her now-canonical essay "Toward a Black Feminist Criticism." One audience member, psychiatrist Frances Cress Wesling, responded with the comment, "An endorsement of homosexuality means the death of the race."[68] A panel about Black feminism that simply acknowledged the existence and rights of Black lesbians was radical and faced resistance at an academic conference about Black writing at a historically Black college. On the one hand, these conflicts were real and made it much harder for Black feminists to do their work. On the other hand, media coverage focused on and sensationalized conflicts along lines of gender and sexuality. This kind of public amplification of Black intraracial disagreement distracted from the serious work of building Black studies and African American literary studies at the very moment those fields were entering the academy.

For members of The Sisterhood, this was a time of real success but also an impossible situation of challenges from without and conflict within. They were getting Black feminist thought and Black women's writing into academic conferences, popular magazines, trade books, and newspapers. In Black spaces like the Howard conference, there was active resistance to and anger toward Black women writers, feminists, and women who (lesbian or not) enjoyed the company of other women. This resistance and anger was even more intense in white spaces like their workplaces and the mainstream press.

The pressures that were making The Sisterhood hard to sustain reached a fever pitch with the publication of Michele Wallace's first book, *Black Macho and the Myth of the Superwoman* (1978). Wallace draws from history, literature, interviews, legislative documents, and personal experience to theorize and illustrate the ways that the two "myths" in her book's title have oppressed Black people and sometimes made them complicit in that oppression. "Black macho" is militaristic, masculinist, patriarchal Black manhood like that prescribed in the Moynihan Report in 1965. Performances of Black macho harm and oppress Black women and confine and limit Black men.

The "Superwoman" stereotype is a Black woman who has no individual desires, has infinite emotional strength, and does all the labor to support men in political movements and at home, endlessly and without complaint. Toni Cade Bambara summarizes Wallace's two primary arguments:

> One—that black folks made a serious error in the '60s equating the pursuit of manhood or the public exercise of narcissistic macho with the liberation of a people, with power. Two—that the perpetuation of the strong black woman image in the black community and in the American mentality (an invention that persists in the teeth of poverty and powerlessness) sets us up for the bogus power-is-manhood equation and predisposes us all to a faulty vision and, consequently, to false steps.[69]

Bambara's summary points to just a few of the ways *Black Macho* was controversial when the book came out in December 1978. To claim "serious error in the '60s" was to criticize the civil rights movement, which some moderates (both Black and white) still viewed as a high-water mark of racial progress. To name "the public exercise of narcissistic macho" as a misguided pursuit of some Black men was to criticize the Black Power movement, whose dissolution was recent and painful for many Black people in 1978. To locate "the perpetuation of the strong black woman image" not in white people's creations alone, but rather "in the black community" was to name Black people's complicity with racist and sexist thinking and policy that keeps Black women caught "in the teeth of poverty and powerlessness."

Wallace's piercing analysis of race and gender generated discomfort and controversy. One illustrative example is her description of what she saw in the Student Nonviolent Coordinating Committee (SNCC) in the 1960s:

> Besides the more visible black male leadership, black women played an important role, as they did generally in the Civil Rights Movement. Yet women, both black and white, handled an inordinate amount of typing, coffee making, housework, in addition to their other duties . . . Black and white women might have fought this inequality [in 1960s civil rights organizations] together [but] during the summer of 1964 hundreds of middle-class white women went South to work with the Movement and, in a fair number of cases, to have affairs with black men . . . black women in SNCC complained to male leadership that they could not develop relationships with black men as long as black men could so easily turn to involvement with white women.[70]

Versions of Wallace's initial catalogue of women's invisible work in Black liberation movements were common in Black feminist writing of the late 1970s and early 1980s. Toni Cade Bambara's novel *The Salt Eaters* (1980), for example, opens with protagonist Velma Henry working to heal from the exhaustion and hurt of her decades of civil rights work that have brought her to the point of a suicide attempt. Bambara's novel includes scenes of women making flyers, brewing coffee, running meetings, writing agendas, and making up the bulk of political marches, all while charismatic male leaders periodically swoop in for brief appearances in which they take the spotlight and the credit.

After briefly explaining the "duties" of women in the movement, Wallace departs from what most of her cohort was willing to say in print. She calls out Black men's romantic and sexual "involvement with white women" for the pain it caused Black women, explains how it became an obstacle to political work, and names it as a reason for the lack of durable interracial solidarity among women in the civil rights movement. Alice Walker's 1976 novel *Meridian* depicts some of these dynamics, but Wallace saying it plainly in a nonfiction book for an interracial audience made the reception to *Black Macho* particularly volatile.

Black women's response to Black men's "involvement with white women" is just one of the subjects Wallace addresses to understand the ways that racism and patriarchy work together to keep oppressed people subjugated. These interracial relationships are of interest to Wallace primarily in terms of how they affect dynamics among Black people, especially between Black men and Black women. Her book is a work of Black feminist theory that explains that Black men and women are not immune to white American patriarchy. Although both face racism, Black men also participate in the gender oppression of Black women.

Like Shange's *for colored girls*, Wallace's book was met with harsh criticism from prominent Black men and some Black women. Joyce Johnson, Wallace's editor at Dial Press, discouraged the use of "feminist" in the marketing materials and descriptions of the book for fear it would be too incendiary. Johnson effectively lost this battle when Gloria Steinem put Wallace on the cover of the January 1979 issue of *Ms.*, excerpted *Black Macho* in the magazine, and declared it "the book that will shape the 1980s."[71] When "Gloria [Steinem] offered her the cover," Wallace was rightly cautious, and worried about "the politics" of appearing on the cover of this largely white feminist magazine.[72] The prominent feature in *Ms.*, other media coverage, and the book's status as a bestseller all increased Wallace's visibility. The subsequent backlash against her and other Black feminist writers escalated, especially from prominent Black male intellectuals such as Ishmael Reed and Stanley Crouch. Wallace later wrote, "I was torn limb from limb for being too young, for being bourgeois, for not being scholarly, for having ill intentions, and for not having solidarity with black men in these very pages [of the *Village Voice*] by both Stanley Crouch and Darryl Pinckney."[73]

The Sisterhood meetings and its members were a source of support for Wallace as she faced "a lot of attacks."[74] Judith Wilson reviewed *Black Macho* positively for *Essence*, noting that the book "gets the core of our problems with one another as men and women." She described Wallace's writing style as "Black, fast-paced, largely anecdotal and frequently quite personal" and sometimes "brilliantly sarcastic." *Essence* published writing that was "Black" and "personal," so Wilson's review framed the book in a way that appealed to the magazine's readers. Wilson reads *Black Macho* as "about hope—the hope that if we begin to know who we are and what our position in America as Black women really is, we will rise up to change it."[75] She appeals to *Essence* readers' desires for "change" and insists that Wallace's Black feminist scrutiny of oppressive conditions is necessary.[76]

Wilson's review is one example of how members of The Sisterhood read, wrote about, and discussed *Black Macho*, just as they had with performances of *for colored girls* a few years earlier. They had unanimously celebrated *for colored girls*, but they disagreed about Wallace's book. June Jordan's and Alice Walker's essays offer critiques not exactly of Wallace's arguments, but rather of the cultural landscape. In a negative review in the *New York Times*, Jordan offers an important reminder that in the 1970s, even though Black women's writing was more visible than it had ever been before, books "by and about black people" remained "negligible" as a percentage of all books published. Jordan expressed frustration that *Black Macho* was one of the few by Black women to receive substantial public attention. She also criticized Wallace's book for, among other things, seeming to erase important collaborations among Black women of the time, such as The Sisterhood and Jordan's work in 1979 with Ntozake Shange and Bernice Johnson Reagon to mount a show at the Public Theater about Sojourner Truth. For Jordan, Wallace's focus on intraracial, gendered conflict ran counter to her own efforts to "skip the idiocy of competition for the sake of a political and artistic goal."[77] The harsh review is partly a reaction to the content of Wallace's book, but even more so to the space *Black Macho* took up in public discourse. In Jordan's view, the media's focus on *Black Macho* came at the expense of getting the word out about the rich and varied Black feminist collaborative work that was happening as the 1970s drew to a close.

In a letter submitted to *The Black Scholar* in 1979 but not published until it appeared in her collection of essays *In Search of Our Mothers' Gardens* in 1983, Alice Walker offered her measured response to Wallace's controversial book. Walker found "many good things" in the book, but criticized its lack of engagement with Black women writers. She writes that Wallace "chose mainly white and black male writers" as sources for her research and "tossed in Ntozake Shange, Toni Morrison, Angela Davis, and Nikki Giovanni at the end" without accounting for the ways these women's books theorized and practiced Black women's liberation.[78] Walker laments that *Black Macho* does not take up the varied, detailed, and exciting characters from Black women's novels, such as her own titular protagonist in *Meridian* (1976), Zora Neale Hurston's Janie Crawford of *Their Eyes Were Watching God* (1937), Toni Morrison's Pecola Breedlove of *The Bluest Eye* (1970), Morrison's Sula and Nell in *Sula* (1973), or "even" Frances Harper's protagonist of *Iola Leroy* (1892).[79] She argues that Black women's novels since the nineteenth century theorize, complicate, and resist the dynamics and stereotypes of "Black macho" and the "myth of the superwoman" that Wallace examines. Walker is asking here for a different book than the one Wallace wrote, for something more like the literary scholarship about Black women's poetry, fiction, and plays that Claudia Tate, Mary Helen Washington, and others were writing in this period. Despite her misgivings, Walker provided a positive comment for the book jacket of *Black Macho*. She soon regretted it because "along with us women feminists," novelist Ishmael Reed, a critic of Walker, also supplied an endorsement. Walker was weary of expectations that she keep controversy going, and she declined requests from *Ebony* and *The Washington Post* to comment further.[80]

Perhaps after Walker declined, Toni Cade Bambara agreed to review *Black Macho* for *The Washington Post*. While Jordan and Walker worried that Wallace's best-selling book was getting too much attention, Bambara wrote, "this book deserves all the play it is getting." She described it as a study of "sexual politics" that is a "serious, well written . . . model of hardheaded but caring analysis, principled in its criticism, [and] important." Many reviews of *Black Macho* when it came out and years of subsequent critiques of the book seemed, in a heartbreaking irony, to assign the strong Black woman stereotype to Wallace. Bambara's review differed by noting that the book "is Wallace's attempt—as a young woman coming of age in turbulent times— to make sense out of the orchestrated madness that frequently characterizes race/class/sex arrangements in this country." Bambara was attuned to the fact that Wallace, at twenty-seven, was a young writer at the beginning of her career illuminating unequal power dynamics as one initial and necessary step toward political change. Bambara rightly read the book as a "challenge" for Black men and women to work together in a Black feminist movement for liberation.[81] She was keen to clarify that the problem is not Blackness or Black people, but rather systemic oppression; she emphasizes this with the useful phrase "orchestrated madness."

Sisterhood members and others also responded to *Black Macho* in academic publications. In the spring of 1979, *The Black Scholar* published an essay by sociologist Robert Staples, "The Myth of Black Macho: A Response to Angry Black Feminists." Staples criticized Ntozake Shange and Michele Wallace as two among a group of "angry Black feminists" who had failed to address class oppression and unfairly depicted Black men. The response of readers was so voluminous that the journal published a May/June 1979 special issue titled "The Black Sexism Debate," which included contributions by Audre Lorde, June Jordan, Shange, and Wallace, among other Black feminists.

Editors at *The Black Scholar* deemed Alice Walker's essay "both too 'personal' and too 'hysterical' to publish," and she withdrew it rather than make the changes suggested.[82] The journal did print Robert Staples's and Ron Karenga's critiques of the Black feminist writings that were in "The Black Sexism Debate" special issue. Judith Wilson said in retrospect, "I remember there was a whole issue of *The Black Scholar*, in fact, that essentially was repudiating these upstart women writers and all this other stuff. It was absolutely despicable. But that was what was happening at the time."[83] Even with the inclusion of writing by Black feminists, the overall effect of the two issues of *The Black Scholar* was to treat men's writing, "repudiating these upstart women writers," as serious and Black women's worth as a subject up for debate. The heated exchange in the pages of the journal was more rigorous than the version of it taking place in popular culture, but it revealed that the scholarly world was hardly a refuge for the Black women writers who were fighting for a place for Black feminism and Black women's literature in the academy. *Black Macho* continued to spark debate throughout the 1980s. Conducting the interviews for her volume *Black Women Writers at Work* (1985), Claudia Tate asked each of the fourteen authors included about reactions to *for colored girls* and *Black Macho*, not because either was necessarily a "literary touchstone" for every Black woman writer she interviewed, but because of "the undeniable fact that [*for colored girls* especially] attracted a great deal of attention, and as a result had serious effects on the literary media as it affected blacks and women."[84]

Black Macho remained a subject of media attention throughout the 1980s, partly because it tapped into what Sisterhood member and *Essence* editor Audrey Edwards described as, "the big thing going on culturally in the 80s . . . this schism . . . between Black men and Black women."[85] For a women's magazine, *Essence* had an unusually high number of men among its writers and readers. Under Susan Taylor's leadership, the magazine both capitalized on interest in gender divisions and tried to ease tensions by providing a "forum for men and women to talk to each other."[86] This was one venue for Black men's objections to what they perceived as Black women writers airing dirty laundry in public. Taylor's work at *Essence* had previously focused on style. By the time she began working as a freelance fashion and beauty writer there in 1970, she had already earned a cosmetology degree, owned a salon, and founded a cosmetics company. Overall, Taylor's vision for the magazine was relatively conservative in that she focused on "empowerment," "upliftment," and "productivity" of Black women within a heteronormative "Black family."[87]

The fact that Taylor felt compelled to address tensions between Black men and women in *Essence* suggests how central such tensions were in the lives of readers by the late 1980s, when Taylor established a new column in the magazine, "Say, Brother," to "reach out to the Black male."[88] This was a shift from Marcia Gillespie's editorial focus in the 1970s almost exclusively on Black women's voices. When Taylor said in a 1989 radio interview, "we have to agree not to disagree on certain subjects" and "we must present a united front," she was referring to her view that Black men and women ought to be "united" in front of white people and in resisting racism.

Taylor's desire for Black men and women to appear united, Black men's objections to Shange's and Wallace's works, and June Jordan's critique of *Black Macho* were all, in part, a reaction to the sensational marketing of these works in white publications, discussions, and television shows that otherwise paid scant attention to Black writing and art. White audiences and readers had a voracious appetite for public conflict between Black men and women. White media focused more on the criticism of and conflict about Black women's books than on the books themselves. This is why, in part, *Black Macho* found so many readers and was reviewed in many mainstream and niche white publications—from *Ms.* to *The Washington Post*—that were not otherwise publishing many reviews of books by Black women.

Mary Helen Washington uses the phrase "renaissance of Black women writers" to describe the 1970s and '80s as a time of dramatically increased visibility.[89] Black women's books, ironically, sometimes gained popularity from prurient white interest in Black intraracial conflict. Coverage of controversy, both real and exaggerated, was a viable financial strategy for popular magazines and daytime television shows.[90]

In this media environment, before fervor over *for colored girls* and *Black Macho* had died down, and a few years after The Sisterhood stopped meeting, Alice Walker's *The Color Purple* was published in 1982; in 1985, Steven Spielberg released his film adaptation. Both were the subject of "intense opposition" that treated the novel and the film as "interchangeable."[91] As Jacqueline Bobo explains, both versions were initially acclaimed but soon "were constructed as controversial" in the media based on the idea that these works "negatively depict black people," often with little reference to the actual content of the novel or the film.[92] "Media coverage of protests from black men" obscured the fact that many Black women readers and viewers found value in Walker's work. Bobo describes this as an inverse relationship: "in reaction to black women's favorable responses to the film, black male criticism of the film began to attain much more media space."[93] Increasingly public and aggressive objections to the film spilled over into criticism of Walker's novel and tended to group *The Color Purple* with Shange's *for colored girls* and Wallace's *Black Macho*. Filmmaker Spike Lee was among the prominent Black men who attributed the publication of both works and their success to what he viewed as their harsh portrayals of Black men.[94] Thulani Davis observed in 1987, "No one seemed to make even one cogent observation about the books black women write. Yet *much* was said about black women writers and our work."[95] Attacks were nothing new, but by the 1980s, they reached a larger audience than ever before. Shange, Wallace, and Walker in particular, but Black women writers in general, had a large readership for their Black feminist ideas and writings, but this broader reach also brought on relentless scrutiny, criticism, sexism, and racism.

One striking example is a July 1989 episode of *The Phil Donahue Show*, "Black Women Writers." A decade after the publication of *Black Macho* and more than a decade after the end of the Broadway run of *for colored girls*, and several years after protests at film screenings of *The Color Purple*, Shange, Wallace, and Walker remained targets of public misogynist attacks. These three women appeared with Maya Angelou (via satellite) and Angela Davis on the popular talk show. Phil Donahue begins by introducing the five panelists to his studio and broadcast audience. He names Angelou's and Walker's most recent books, but identifies Shange as the author of *for colored girls*, which he says "rattled this town," and Wallace as the author of *Black Macho*, establishing a focus on those works rather than anything else they had done in the past decade. He introduces Davis in a joking tone as "our most threatening guest" in reference to her past inclusion on the FBI's most wanted list. In response to Donahue's opening question about how each woman became a writer, Davis says: "It's really only been in the last two decades that there has been any kind of public presence of Black women in literature, in theory, and I think it's probably because Black women's voices have been suppressed for so many decades, for so many centuries . . . we're seeing increasing numbers of Black women, and somehow it appears threatening." Davis uses this moment to shift focus away from men's responses and toward "Black women's voices." When Donahue interrupts to turn the discussion to the more sensational topic of Davis's persecution by the FBI and her imprisonment, she keeps returning to her subject by framing her incarceration as part of a broader cultural moment in which "the government of this country felt very threatened by Black women. The fact that they would put me on the Ten Most Wanted list said something about their fear of what would happen in this country if that long-suppressed voice of Black women finally became heard."[96] Davis, in this very public forum, continues what The Sisterhood did in the late 1970s by focusing on "Black women's voices" even as others constantly push to focus on men's reaction to those voices.

Phil Donahue, a white man creating television for a largely white mass market audience, conveys some of how relentless and exhausting the backlash to these women's writings was when he says, "Alice Walker has more to do than come back to another television show and be asked about *The Color Purple* and be accused of bashing Black men." He immediately undercuts this statement before Walker has said a word about *The Color Purple*. First he shows a clip of journalist Tony Brown on a 1986 *Donahue* episode saying that Walker has written "at the expense of Black people and Black men"; then, before allowing Walker to respond, he takes the microphone to a Black man in the audience clapping vigorously in response the clip. The audience member addresses the panelists by their first names, notes that he understands the need for "honesty" in writing and asks, "Does that honesty have to be so harsh? We all have fragile egos."[97] In a rare, maybe even singular, instance of these particular five powerful Black women intellectuals gathered in one place for a conversation that will reach many viewers, two Black men who have seen Spielberg's film adaption but have not read Walker's novel voice their objections to *The Color Purple* before its author has said one word about the book. Walker briefly responds that she was not thinking about harming anyone's "ego" and is "sad" that some people's ego is "so fragile." This is typical of her compassionate response to aggressive comments and questions from the audience. She asserts later in the episode, "I have so much faith in Black men; I think I have more faith in them than they have in themselves." Before Walker has even finished responding to the question "Does that honesty have to be so harsh?," Donahue runs the microphone to another Black male audience member, who observes that "media" have overemphasized the idea that Black women's writing is criticizing Black men. Not incidentally, this is the only person in the episode to say that he has read the panelists' books. Others in the audience restate the well-worn critiques of portrayals of Black men and request that the panelists say something "positive." This aspect of the episode was a setup; as Alexis De Veaux wrote a few months later, "old anger from an invited audience of Black and Latino men was fanned off-camera by the show's producers."[98]

Despite the fact that this television show gives excessive time to male voices in an episode titled, "Black Women Writers," and despite the host and audience's fixation on conflict between Black women and Black men, the panelists break through with nuanced insights. Wallace notes, "It's also important to recognize difference, not only racial and ethnic difference but also sexual difference. The possibility of unity is not mutually exclusive from considering, as well, our differences."[99] She manages in just two sentences to articulate how calls for unity can perpetuate racism, sexism, and homophobia. Angelou consistently uses the platform of the show, regardless of the questions she is asked, to recommend important Black books, from the Oxford series of writings by nineteenth-century Black women writers edited by Henry Louis Gates, Jr., to Calvin Hernton's *The Sexual Mountain and Black Women Writers* (1987). Angela Davis historicizes the ways that "men always got the credit" in the 1960s civil rights movement even as Black women did the daily work to make that movement happen, the damaging influence of Daniel Moynihan's 1965 congressional report *The Negro Family: The Case for National Action*, and "the rise of a feminist consciousness among Black women." Davis also recalls Black men's "solidarity with women's rights" dating back at least to Frederick Douglass and W. E. B. Du Bois, whom she calls "male feminists." Shange addresses the persistent, troubling approach of reading African American writing primarily through the author's biography, as if Black writers do not have the "imagination" to create stories that do not mirror their own experiences. Walker turns the conversation to the actual plot of *The Color Purple* to describe the "transformation" of the male characters in the novel that so many of its detractors have ignored. Moving beyond the manufactured sensationalism, these women do important, precise, and radical Black feminist work on this popular, mainstream daytime television talk show.

The 1989 *Donahue* episode vividly illustrates the challenges Black women faced in their work as writers, editors, teachers, public intellectuals, and activists from the mid-1970s through the 1980s. The kind of hostility visible in the episode also happened in countless private spaces. Having a seat at the table, achieving representation—in publishing, at universities, or on television—did not protect these women from sexism, racism, and homophobia, but rather exposed them to virulent strains of each of these intersecting oppressions. The emphasis on men's reactions to Black women's writing shaped dynamics in print and on television, but also in semiprivate, everyday interpersonal interactions. At a "garden party" to celebrate one of Walker's books in the 1980s, for example, two Black male writers spent their time audibly "grumbling about how Black women were just taking over and the white publishing industry doesn't want to deal with Black men anymore." Judith Wilson interrupted them to say that it was hardly the time or place for that conversation.[100] Members of The Sisterhood and their contemporaries were constantly doing in private and in public what they did on *Donahue*: facing sexism, racism, silencing, and resistance but still writing and speaking brilliantly.

The burdens of this labor accumulated over the years The Sisterhood met and long after. Sisterhood members were "storming barricades" as the lone Black woman at most of their workplaces every single day.[101] They were striving to meet the expectation that high-achieving Black women advance racial and gender justice for others. These pressures "made everybody fiercer" in the 1970s, but they were taking their toll by the close of the decade.[102] Some members left New York, some got more recognition, and some got overwhelmingly busy as the demands of their careers increased. Many would continue "storming barricades" of the academy, the canon, and the culture industry in decades to come, but not as members of The Sisterhood.

In a 2013 interview, Sisterhood member Audrey Edwards reflected on the reaction to *for colored girls* as the first in a long period of attacks on Black women writers that defined the American cultural landscape in the late 1970s and '80s: "there was a lot of fallout from Alice Walker's book *The Color Purple*, Gloria Naylor's book *The Women of Brewster Place*, Ntozake's play *for colored girls*, you know, that had men up in arms and sometimes women up in arms."[103] In retrospect, the backlash to *for colored girls* and to *Black Macho*, respectively, marked the beginning and the end of The Sisterhood. It is also clear that those moments are just two examples of the criticism, racism, and misogyny that Black women writers dealt with in a period of American literature now regularly celebrated as a renaissance for African American women writers.

June Jordan, Alice Walker, Lucille Clifton, and Audre Lorde singing at Phillis Wheatley Poetry Festival, 1973. Photo by Roy Lewis. Manuscript Collection No. 1054. Series 8 Photographs, circa 1930–2005. Lucille Clifton papers, Stuart A. Rose Manuscript, Archives, and Rare Book Library, Emory University/© Roy Lewis Archives, 1973

Toni Morrison and Alice Walker photographed by Jill Krementz on March 15, 1974, in the kitchen of the townhouse owned by Ms. Krementz and her husband, Kurt Vonnegut. Courtesy of Jill Krementz

Ntozake Shange, 1976. Courtesy of Frank Stewart

"The Sisterhood, 1977," Vertamae Grosvenor, Alice Walker, Lori Sharpe, Toni Morrison, June Jordan, Nana Maynard, Ntozake Shange, and Audreen Ballard. Box 184, Folder 12. MC 1061 Alice Walker Papers. Stuart A. Rose Manuscript, Archives, and Rare Book Library, Emory University, Atlanta, Georgia; Reprinted by permission of The Joy Harris Literary Agency, Inc.; Courtesy of Alice Walker

Ms.

Special Report on Black Feminism

$1.00
JANUARY
1979

Breakthrough Treatment for Breast Cancer

Is Divorce Ever Final? Ten Women
Talk About Their Ex-husbands

**BLACK
MACHO
AND THE
MYTH
OF THE
SUPER
WOMAN**
by Michele
Wallace—
the book
that will shape
the 1980s

A New
Look at Job
Benefits

Exposé:
The Wrongful
Death of
Rosie Jimenez

What Does
Sarah Weddington
Have That
Midge Costanza Didn't?

Celebrating Muriel Rukeyser

Michele Wallace

Michele Wallace on cover of *Ms.* magazine, January 1979. Image used by permission of *Ms.* magazine © 1979

Audre Lorde in her Staten Island study, 1981. Image of Audre Lorde © 1981 JEB (Joan E. Biren)

Toni Cade Bambara at lectern at Southern Collective of African American Writers (SCAAW) 1988. Courtesy of Susan J. Ross

"Black Women Writers" episode of *The Phil Donahue Show* with Maya Angelou (remotely), Alice Walker, Ntozake Shange, Michele Wallace, and Angela Davis, July 1989. NBCUniversal

Toni Morrison celebrating her Nobel Prize with Mari Evans, Susan Taylor, Oprah Winfrey, George Faison, Maya Angelou, Howard Dodson, Angela Davis, Eleanor Traylor and Amina Baraka, September 1994. Eugene Redmond Collection, Louisa H. Bowen University Archives & Unique Collections unit, Lovejoy Library, Southern Illinois University Edwardsville

Chapter Four

"A COMMUNITY OF WRITERS EVEN IF THEY ONLY SLAP FIVE ONCE A MONTH"

An extended community nurtured the achievements of The Sisterhood. Many other Black feminist groups and individual intellectuals in the 1970s and early 1980s shared The Sisterhood's goals of publication and publicity for Black women writers, as well as the belief that political and social change could and should be made through culture. In this larger network of Black women literary activists, the group mattered to and benefited from the work of women who were not official members of The Sisterhood. Michele Wallace, Toni Cade Bambara, and Cheryll Y. Greene are especially important for understanding The Sisterhood's impact. Wallace engaged, sharpened, and extended the group's Black feminist ideas into literary and cultural criticism. Bambara extended their advocacy for Black women's writing into the South and was an important friend and interlocutor, especially for Toni Morrison. Cheryll Y. Greene collaborated with Sisterhood members to get Black feminist thought into Black mainstream culture on the pages of *Essence* magazine.

~

Michele Wallace is best known as the author of *Black Macho and the Myth of the Superwoman*, but that is just one work in her long career as a scholar, writer, activist, and cultural critic. Wallace is a scholar of African American cultural production and a keen observer of Black collectives. Her thinking about various organizations is visible in her archive at the Schomburg Center for Research in Black Culture, which includes copies of minutes from The Sisterhood's meetings; a newsletter, writers' workshop program, reading list, and regional conference program from the National Black Feminist Organization (NBFO); and a draft platform for the Black Feminist Organization of the National Organization of Women (NOW), all with Wallace's handwritten notes and edits. She kept track of, supported, and criticized these organizations. Her published writings and personal correspondence attend to the stakes, limitations, and legacies of Black feminist groups of the 1970s. Like that of many Sisterhood members, Wallace's Black feminist work moved from political organizations into literary and cultural organizing in the 1970s and then into the academy in the 1980s.

By the time The Sisterhood began meeting, Wallace had connections with many of its members and to its mission. She had already tested the waters of several other collectives in her search for community. When applying to college, Wallace fantasized that Howard University would be "a super-black utopia where for the first time in life I would be completely surrounded by people who totally understood me."[1] Once there, she "sought out a new clique each day and found a home in none," but did find some community hanging out with the women who "stayed in on Friday and Saturday nights on a campus that was well known for its parties and nightlife."[2] Wallace's disappointment in the colorism and sexism she encountered in college and her appreciation for being in a group made up exclusively of Black women shaped her ongoing search for and sharp critiques of other groups.

Wallace began a "black women's consciousness-raising group" in New York City in the early 1970s, and then she and her mother, artist Faith Ringgold, helped found the National Black Feminist Organization (NBFO).[3] At the same time, Wallace continued her studies at City College, where she met future Sisterhood members Audre Lorde, Toni Morrison, Alice Walker, and June Jordan.[4] She began reading Walker's work around the time that Walker led an NBFO workshop with Ringgold on Black women in the arts.[5] After earning her bachelor's degree in English in 1974, Wallace continued to seek, but not find, solidarity and support in Black spaces including the National Black Theatre (NBT). She discovered that the NBT's "brand of a consciousness-raising session" meant hearing about "the awful ways in which black women, me included, had tried to destroy the black man's masculinity."[6] The "Black Power antics" and "misogyny run amok" Wallace had encountered at Howard also plagued the NBT.[7] By the mid-1970s, she was working as a secretary at Random House while Morrison was there and later wrote that "even then, to fledgling black women writers, Morrison was a queen."[8] Wallace became a researcher at *Newsweek* with Margo Jefferson and then started teaching journalism at New York University, a position she got partly on Jefferson's recommendation.[9] The job at *Newsweek* granted Wallace "entry to all sorts of magic New York worlds from the Newport Jazz Festival to the Public Theatre [*sic*] to a variety of literary shenanigans and shindigs," but it also meant being in an overwhelmingly white office.[10]

Facing racism in white workplaces and sexism in Black educational and cultural institutions, Wallace turned to collaborations with Black women, such as with Ringgold, Jefferson, and Patricia Spears Jones to organize the 1976 Sojourner Truth Festival of the Arts, where Ntozake Shange was among the performers. The Sojourner Truth Festival was a rare, even singular, event in that it focused on Black women filmmakers. It was also "the scene of a major public confrontation between" Wallace and her mother, Faith Ringgold, "that resulted in a lot of tears" and Wallace moving out of her mother's house. By that time, Wallace had already been advocating for Black women visual artists since 1970, when, at only eighteen years old, she founded Women Students and Artists for Black Art Liberation (WSABAL) "as an activist and polemical unit" that "participated in raucous art actions at the Museum of Modern Art and the Whitney" and "occupied offices" at other New York City museums to protest the lack of Black women artists in their exhibits. By the time The Sisterhood began to meet, Wallace was connected with many of the group's members, working to change the landscape of visual art, and regularly writing for the *Village Voice*. Based on her experiences with other groups, she was also justifiably skeptical of the ability of collectives to create significant political change or provide a refuge for Black women. She was "hungry for the kind of fame" that Ntozake Shange had, partly because Wallace thought that celebrity might be the only kind of power available to Black women in the late 1970s and feared "that the possibility of radical politics was over."[11]

Wallace's commitment to Black women's literature and liberation made her an invested ally of The Sisterhood; her distance and skepticism also made her an acute observer of the group and the broader terrain of Black feminist collectives. Wallace was aware of The Sisterhood from the time of its first meeting and was at the time in a different Black feminist study group with Barbara Omolade and Sisterhood member Susan McHenry.[12] In a 1995 essay, Wallace wrote that "a more informal discussion group of black women writers called The Sisterhood began meeting at Alice Walker's house in Brooklyn. Attendees included me, Toni Morrison, June Jordan, as well as virtually every significant black female writer of the next decade."[13] Wallace is not listed among the attendees in any archived meeting minutes and Sisterhood members do not recall her being there, but she may have been at later meetings that are not documented in archived minutes. Her correspondence with Alice Walker suggests that, despite her absence from the minutes, Wallace may have attended one meeting and decided not to return.

Wallace's commitment to and experience with the Black feminist activism of NBFO and other groups with national reach may have been part of the reason she declined to attend Sisterhood meetings, despite Walker's repeated invitation. Wallace's and Walker's references to The Sisterhood appear their 1977–78 letters, which discuss *Black Macho*, literary scholarship about Black women's writing, and essays that might be published in *Ms*. In a letter to Walker of March 25, 1977, Wallace writes,

> As for The Sisterhood, I find I must devote most of my time to my book if it is ever to be finished. Also I am a little disturbed by the way the thing is progressing. I promised myself a while back that I would never seriously commit my time to any organization that wasn't feminist and working toward the alleviation of the problems of black women. If it is to be a discussion group for black women artists who understand that they are *black women*, then I may attend. But if the goal is to organize a publishing company which will reissue out-of-print works of black men, and to found a magazine which will give space to black men, I can't possibly imagine what I would be needed for. I can't understand why a group of black women would do something like that. I have a great deal of respect for you Alice, but I just can't come to the meetings as long as these things aren't seriously discussed because I'll get nasty and I try to avoid doing that. If things take a turn for the better I would be happy to hear about it.[14]

Wallace's reasons for not participating in The Sisterhood shed light on the ideologies of the group. Wallace rightly notes that, unlike the NBFO or other explicitly politically organizations, members of The Sisterhood did not always or consistently use the term "feminist" to describe their collaborative work. Most members who are still living describe themselves as feminists today, but in the 1970s, they sometimes avoided the term because it evoked the white women's liberation movement. Wallace was committed to feminism and committed to making interracial feminist groups work for the liberation of Black women. She chose her membership in various collectives accordingly.

In addition to the distinction in terminology, Wallace's concerns in this letter reinforce that the work of The Sisterhood was literary and textual. In fact, the group did make plans to "reissue out-of-print works," "found a magazine," and "organize a publishing company." Wallace did not see these goals as wholly feminist and political, perhaps because they include economic advancement within existing capitalist structures or perhaps she viewed them as too narrowly literary. For The Sisterhood the work of recovery and publication *was* political. It was also part of their broader focus on textual labor as necessary for Black women's liberation. In Toni Cade Bambara's words, they all agreed or eventually came around to the idea that writing is "a perfectly legitimate way to participate in struggle."[15] Sisterhood members were keenly aware that they were "*black women*" and were explicitly concerned with advancing the work of Black women writers, which they understood as an important political project.

Walker responded: "There is no stigma attached to not attending, just as there is no coercion *for* attending. We come if we wish. If not, that's cool. As for what we discuss: we *are* black *women*, and the least that should mean is that among ourselves we discuss what we like."[16] Walker's description of The Sisterhood as more casual than the minutes or other member's descriptions suggest was likely a poor recruiting tool when it came to Wallace. Her commitment to Black women's art and literature is clear in her correspondence with Gloria Steinem and others at *Ms.* on behalf of WSABAL. In a letter to Steinem of May 27, 1975, Wallace offers data demonstrating that "the magazine has generally not covered black women or employed black women writers to any extent that might be considered adequate or even acceptable." She notes that Margo Jefferson and Alice Walker are responsible for the "one article on a black woman singer" and "one on a black woman dancer," respectively, and goes on to point out that the few articles in *Ms.* about Black women perpetuated stereotypes in articles by "white feminists dwelling on our poverty and deprivation." The relative absence of Black women from the pages of *Ms.* amounted to a "racist policy" that Wallace urged Steinem to rectify, in part, with "a series of feature articles on black women artists."[17] Although The Sisterhood focused their efforts mostly on Black periodicals such as *Essence* and *Black World*, Wallace was arguing for exactly the increased, varied, and Black-authored representation of

Black women in magazines that The Sisterhood would also soon advocate. Wallace's proposal for a *Ms.* series on Black women visual artists is similar to Vèvè Clark's proposal on behalf of The Sisterhood for *Ebony* to "establish a monthly, bi-monthly or weekly feature on the poetry of one black woman."[18]

Wallace's correspondence with Steinem shows her investment in intervening in white feminism. Wallace, Susan McHenry, Barbara Omolade, and Audre Lorde participated in predominantly white feminist events such as the Barnard Scholar and Feminist Conference and NYU *Second Sex* Commemorative Conference, both held in 1979. They also "pursued writing and public speaking in feminist circles" and publication in feminist media.[19] Wallace writes that Steinem ought to be "interested in altering your racist image among black feminists" and makes clear that the stakes are nothing less than that "The Women's Movement is being transformed into a cultural dictatorship by racism."[20] Even the most cutting parts of Wallace's letter demonstrate her sincere investment in the movement and belief that it could and should participate in the project of Black liberation. Correspondence between Wallace and *Ms.* in the spring of 1975 indicates that editors of the magazine agreed and shows that Wallace, at the magazine's request, offered a detailed plan for a series of articles on specific Black women visual artists and specific exhibitions of their work. Her work and The Sisterhood's subsequent efforts succeeded in making Black women's visual art, political activism, and literature more central to the content of *Ms.*

From the start of her career to the present, Wallace's essays have drawn attention to works by Sisterhood members and other Black feminists. Her writings about literature in newspapers, magazines, and academic journals became part of Black feminist literary criticism that secured and educated a readership for Black women's books. In 1995, Wallace wrote an essay reviewing a new book by Stanley Crouch, a vocal critic of Shange, Wallace, Walker, and other Black women writers. Rather than respond in kind, in a move typical of her investment in Black women's writing, Wallace uses the occasion of reviewing a book by Crouch to historicize Black women's literature and celebrate Morrison's *Beloved*:

> *Beloved* is Toni Morrison's brilliant [fifth] novel, not only the linchpin of her oeuvre, but the ultimate accomplishment of black women's fiction and black feminist thought of these past twenty years since the publication in 1970 of the novels *The Bluest Eye* and Alice Walker's *The Third Life of Grange Copeland*, Maya Angelou's autobiography *I Know Why the Caged Bird Sings*, and Toni Cade

Bambara's collection of essays, *The Black Woman . . . Beloved* may be as close as we'll ever get to the dream of a black feminist theory grounded in the historical experience of the black.[21]

This review of Crouch's *Notes of a Hanging Judge: Essays and Reviews, 1979–1989* also declares Morrison's writings as both exceptional and representative of an African American literary tradition.

Sisterhood members recognized that the focus on just a few Black women writers in the late 1970s and the 1980s meant that important literature by other Black women was not receiving the popular and scholarly attention it merited. Wallace was attuned to how market forces in the 1980s led publishers to focus on a select group of writers. From her own experience with *Black Macho*, she understood the dangers of increased visibility for Black women. Though she coveted Ntozake Shange's "fame" in 1976, she regretted her own celebrity by the close of the 1970s: "I had indiscreetly blurted out that sexism and misogyny were near epidemic in the black community and that black feminism had the cure. I went from obscurity to celebrity to notoriety overnight," and "the whirlwind began over the way I looked and dressed for TV appearances, the way I spoke, what I did and didn't say . . . I don't think anybody ever realized how paralyzed with fear I usually was in any kind of public appearance . . . *Ms.* wondered whether I was up to snuff as a black feminist spokesperson (I was not)."[22] Wallace had learned that being the rare Black women writer to receive significant media attention was an unbearable weight. This was not just a painful personal experience; she understood that assigning "iconic status" to one Black woman writer forces that person to "stand in for the whole."[23] The purpose of treating one writer as singular, as *the* "black feminist spokesperson," is insidious: "its primary function is to distract us from the actual debate and dilemma with which black feminist intellectuals, artists, and activists really engaged."[24]

In 1989, ten years after the first wave of backlash to *Black Macho*, a year after Toni Morrison won the Pulitzer Prize for fiction, and as African American literary studies was gaining traction in the academy, Wallace wrote "Variations on Negation and the Heresy of Black Feminist Creativity." The essay begins with the seeming contradiction that, in the nineteen years since the publication of Morrison's *The Bluest Eye* (1970), Black women writers have written books that "address the world" and a few have achieved "ostentatious commercial success," but "the creativity of most black women writers—especially if it doesn't fit the Book-of-the-Month Club/*New York Times* bestseller mold—remains virtually unknown."[25] Wallace presented a clear-eyed analysis of the ways that the "ostentatious commercial success" of the few served as an alibi for the dismissal or marginalization of the many. She lamented, "The highly visible success of a few black women writers serves to completely obscure the profound nature of the challenge black feminist thought may pose to white male cultural hegemony." Wallace explains that "highly visible success" in the literary marketplace for a few authors does not reflect broad political and cultural shifts toward justice or equality for Black women in general. She articulates a worry that continues to plague African American literary studies: "black women writers and critics are routinely kept from having an impact on how the fields of literature and literary criticism are defined."[26] Wallace points to ways that academic discourse had begun to incorporate Black women writers without necessarily working through the real challenges that Black feminist thought presents to established ideas of history, canon formation, and knowledge that shape literary studies. She values novels by Morrison and Walker for their political, aesthetic, and theoretical richness, but also implies that their "highly visible success" is on the very same capitalist terms that radical Black feminist thought resists. In this vein, Wallace asks in 1989, "first, how the successful commodification of black feminism will be reconciled with black feminist idealism; and second, what challenges are posed by adapting critical frameworks to black feminist use."[27]

These two questions continue to matter for the theory and practice of Black feminism in political, academic, and literary spheres. The first question requires scholars and critics to consider, for example, how courses on Black women writers in an English department or successful academic and trade books by and about African American women do or do not contribute to Black feminist goals of racial, gender, and class justice. The second question requires us to proceed with caution in using ideas or terms that arise from disciplines and fields outside of African American literary studies. Wallace's caution about "adapting critical frameworks to black feminist use" might, for example, warn us not to replicate the racism of some Marxist thought or, as I discuss in chapter 7, let canon wars over the inclusion of Black texts stand in for the presence of Black students and faculty in the academy. In increasingly visible roles in academic institutions from the late 1970s to the present, Sisterhood members and other Black feminists continue to earnestly wrestle with these questions in their roles as writers, teachers, and scholars.

❧

Toni Cade Bambara was also aware of the dangers of incorporating Black feminism into existing institutions and the costs of celebrating just a few Black women writers, but she proceeded with less skepticism than Wallace. In the last quarter of the twentieth century, Bambara worked to realize the potential of The Sisterhood's Black feminism to transform the academy and the literary marketplace. She put her hands on and her mind to countless manuscripts by Black writers and projects for Black liberation. Her short stories, novels, and essays are among the most aesthetically and intellectually exciting works from the Black women writers' renaissance of the late twentieth century. Alongside her collaborations with many Sisterhood members and their contemporaries, Bambara also had a working relationship and close friendship with Toni Morrison that shaped their writings and careers. When The Sisterhood formed in New York in 1977, Bambara had been living in Atlanta for three years.[28] She was not a member of the group, but she supported their work and advanced their goals of publication and publicity for Black writers in her work with the Southern Collective of African American Writers (SCAAW), and was an essential interlocutor in matters personal, professional, and intellectual for many women in the group.

Bambara exchanged letters with Toni Morrison and Alice Walker, and other writers, sometimes offering feedback on their writing. She maintained strong ties to Audre Lorde, whom she first met when they were both teaching in City College of New York's SEEK (Search for Education, Elevation, and Knowledge) Program in the 1960s.[29] She and June Jordan wrote each other often, especially in the late 1970s and early 1980s. In one letter, Bambara describes Sisterhood member Phyl Garland's visit to Atlanta, thanks Jordan for sending a copy of the minutes from The Sisterhood's recent meeting, and writes, "Let me know what Sisterhood would like to do re: 1st World."[30] Garland, in turn, reported to The Sisterhood on her "visit to Atlanta" and "passed around copies of *First World*" at one of their meetings.[31] Bambara's letter notes the group's importance in shaping Hoyt Fuller's journal, which he started when he moved to Atlanta in 1976. Bambara, as an editorial advisor for *First World*, reminded Jordan that Fuller and his wife, Carol, lived in "hollerin distance" from Bambara's house and asked for The Sisterhood's ideas about "new writers, particular topics, format, etc."[32]

The support went both ways. Bambara wrote about and taught Sisterhood members' books, notably assigning Vertamae Grosvenor's *Vibration Cooking* to students at Spelman decades before this hybrid cookbook-memoir was recognized as a classic text of Black foodways. Sisterhood members admired and championed Bambara's books. Grosvenor and Audreen Ballard performed a dramatization of Bambara's short story "The Johnson Girls" in New York in 1972, and Margo Jefferson and Jessica Harris reviewed Bambara's short story collection *The Sea Birds Are Still Alive* for *Newsweek* and *Essence*, respectively.[33] Bambara asked Jordan to remind The Sisterhood about an upcoming party in New York for *The Sea Birds Are Still Alive* and noted that she would request that Random House contact Jordan and Ballard "with the info so she can send flyers/invitations to The Sisterhood."[34] In spring 1977, Random House sent copies to Sisterhood members Vertamae Grosvenor, June Jordan, Paule Marshall, Ntozake Shange, and Alice Walker to help publicize the book through word of mouth.[35] Patricia Spears Jones describes Bambara's efforts as an example of The Sisterhood's "networking": "The ways in which people make connections whether formal or informal, that, so that if you are Toni Cade and you have to get that book out, somebody somewhere knows of a gig in Atlanta, somebody somewhere knows there is a house there for you, somebody somewhere knows how to get you some jobs so that you can take care of your child and yourself. Those kinds of things were happening all the time."[36] Bambara was adept at building and maintaining these networks of support. She became a kind of southern branch agent for The Sisterhood in Atlanta.

As these connections suggest, Bambara believed deeply that Black writers needed to support one another. Around 1980, she observed that for any writer, but especially one trying to complete a novel, "a community of writers even if they only slap five once a month or once a season, can be so supportive. A collective, a workshop, a guild, an on-going group is even more sustaining for support and *permission*."[37] Bambara was referring broadly to forms of mutual "support" among writers, but her words also applied to the "on-going" and "sustaining" functions of The Sisterhood. She describes the way such a community can give "*permission*" to take time away from more lucrative work, family, and other responsibilities to write, to think of oneself as a writer, and to do so repeatedly over the long period of time it takes to complete a manuscript. Living in Atlanta during the terror of the Atlanta child murders, Bambara knew well how necessary that permission is. She had begun collecting the news clippings and community stories about the murders that would, over the next fifteen years, become her posthumously published novel *Those Bones Are Not My Child* (1999).[38] To write as a form of political action in response to racist violence and to stay with that work was especially important to Bambara in the 1980s.

Bambara did the same kind of collective and collaborative work in the "Blacksouth" that her Sisterhood colleagues were doing in New York.[39] James Smethurst writes that Atlanta was "a crucial site of Black Arts and Black Power," especially as "a locale in which black women had an enormous impact on the Black Arts movement, helping to generate an explicitly black nationalist feminism."[40] Like her contemporaries in New York, Bambara wrote during, after, and in relationship to the Black Arts Movement, among Black writers and intellectuals who saw no conflict in the idea of "black nationalist feminism." Black cultural nationalism and Black feminism were part of the same liberation project for Bambara and her collaborators in Atlanta; they built strong connections between academic institutions, such as Spelman College, and community institutions, such as the Neighborhood Arts Center (NAC). Bambara sustained community in many ways, from teaching writing classes at "Spelman, NAC, and her own apartment" to hosting "legendary" "potluck dinners for local writers."[41]

Bambara helped Black women writers get published through her connections with Fuller and *First World* and by establishing, with Alice Lovelace and Ebon Dooley, The Southern Collective of African American Writers (SCAAW). Like The Sisterhood, SCAAW met monthly, collected dues, and created a directory of members' contact information. SCAAW provided members with templates for materials such as a brief author biography, to encourage Black writers to assemble their own promotional packets, similar to those that The Sisterhood created for Black women writers in New York.[42] SCAAW was also a source of emotional support, letting people know about members' illnesses and losses of family so they could offer help.[43]

The collective's first annual conference took place in Atlanta in October 1978. In his address, Hoyt Fuller issued a "direct challenge to SCAAW to develop the mechanism by which you, the writer, can produce, publish and gain exposure."[44] Housed in the NAC in southwest Atlanta, SCAAW offered workshops on self-publishing, navigating relationships with publishers, and breaking into the music industry as a songwriter, as well as number of genre-specific writing workshops. The collective helped Black southern writers succeed at various stages of their careers, offering writing classes for budding young authors and workshops about getting published in mainstream magazines and at trade presses. The group also supported writers who wished to publish only with Black publishers as well as writers who wanted to do local journalism. SCAAW supplied members with a "partial listing of Black independent publishers," printed calls for submissions and freelance journalists, publicized local Black theater performances, and hosted visiting authors at events including a gathering honoring Ntozake Shange and her new book of poems, *Nappy Edges* (1978).[45]

Bambara and SCAAW were consistently committed to creating an equal playing field among established writers and beginners. Poet Nikky Finney describes her first encounter with Bambara as a moment when Bambara was in the thick of making a writers' community. Finney joined in, as one of the women who sat at a table "pressing bright flyers and their stiff edges down into envelopes," doing the "quotidian tasks" of "worker bees . . . engaged in the mundane but necessary work of organizing a conference."[46] The program for that event, SCAAW's second annual conference in 1979, lists the goals of the group:

1. to provide a forum for the exchange of usable information about publishing strategies, genre techniques, arts administration resources, grants and other funding, and survival techniques as a wordsmith
2. to provide an occasion for meetings and collaborative efforts on the part of illustrators and writers, performers and directors, editors and readership, writers and publishers, student practitioners and professionals—that can result in useable products for our total community
3. to encourage members and potential members to recognize the importance of building an organization in our own interests[47]

These goals reflect the value SCAAW placed on collaboration, various kinds of creative work, participation from "editors and readership," and practical resources. SCAAW offered panels and workshops on subjects from grant applications to poetry writing to keeping a dream journal, hosted formal discussions of subjects such as the future of Black theater, and provided a venue for more casual gatherings for African American writers and artists.[48] The group made participation accessible by keeping membership dues and conference registration fees low. This meant that SCAAW was consistently engaged in fundraising to keep the organization going, expand its reach, and offer more resources to members. The work was collaborative and the group, like Black nationalist literary thinkers across the twentieth century, believed in the importance of literary scholars and cultural critics attuned to the specific formal and thematic characteristics of African American writing.

Toni Cade Bambara chaired the SCAAW advisory committee, and every SCAAW newsletter includes a report on one or more events, usually poetry or fiction readings, that she hosted in her home. While active in SCAAW in the late 1970s and early '80s, Bambara also ran the Pomoja Writers' Guild, which was a potluck open to anyone and focused on "finding suitable channels of publication for each finished piece."[49] Pomoja was a writing workshop and an example of the way that Black feminist culture workers did not wait for the academy to accommodate them. When Spelman College rejected "the syllabus that Bambara had turned in to department heads," she "refused to miss a beat" and "simply decided to host the same workshop at her home."[50]

As with Pomoja and the NAC, SCAAW worked with organizations in and far beyond Atlanta and in and outside of academia. Newsletters reported on what was happening at The Schomburg Center for Research in Black Culture in New York; offered a training workshop in "research skills" run by scholar Howard Dodson, who was then the executive director of Atlanta's Institute of the Black World; and posted openings for academic jobs.[51] The second annual conference included activists, writers, and other culture workers. Bambara and poets Sonia Sanchez, Gwendolyn Brooks, and Haki Madhubuti gave readings, and there was an "open reading" in which "any attendee could participate." SCAAW valued and drew on many kinds of knowledge: the 1979 conference included panels on how to write for television and how to use astrology "as a tool for self-understanding."[52]

Bambara's work sustained connections among Sisterhood members, SCAAW members, and a broader network of African American writers and thinkers. She brought writer and foodways scholar Vertamae Grosvenor, editor and literary agent Cheryll Y. Greene, and Black feminist scholar Beverly Guy-Sheftall together for a panel on editing and publishing at the 1979 SCAAW conference. Consistent with Bambara's vision, she planned this panel to include discussions of both Guy-Sheftall's emotional labor in editing *Sturdy Black Bridges* (1979) and Greene's "demystification" of "contracts" with publishers and magazines.[53] From New York, Toni Morrison contributed by sending a handout of "15 ways writers can make a living, so to speak, through writing."[54]

The differences between SCAAW and The Sisterhood are useful in understanding the range and diversity of Black writers' collectives in the years after the Black Arts Movement. The Sisterhood was among those groups that worked in private to achieve public ends. They sometimes followed practices of a consciousness-raising group. SCAAW's work and goals were more public; even workshops with the words "self-understanding" in the title were open to any Black writer who registered.[55] Unlike The Sisterhood, SCAAW included men and women, published a newsletter, and organized conferences. SCAAW was like The Sisterhood in terms of its efforts to get Black writers published and publicized, but it was more like the National Black Feminist Organization (NBFO) in terms of its practices and public presence. Like both The Sisterhood and the NBFO, SCAAW refused hierarchal organization and competition, but may have been more successful in creating an antihierarchical structure. It was explicit in all planning that "little-known writers received the same billing at SCAAW events as their more famous counterparts."[56] The consistent commitment to serving a wide range of Black writers across outlets, career stages, and genres of writing may be part of the reason that SCAAW remained active much longer than The Sisterhood, holding conferences and events for at least a decade, through 1988.[57] Along with Bambara's commitment, Atlanta's historically Black colleges were a factor in SCAAW's relative longevity. Spelman College, Morehouse College, and Clark Atlanta University made the city a strong base of operations because they employed Black writers as teachers, produced a steady stream of aspiring writers, and, along with the historically white Emory University, had excellent libraries with archives of important Black writers.

Bambara's advocacy for Black writers and artists continued after her move to Philadelphia in the mid-1980s, which took her away from the Atlanta literary and activist scene and toward work in filmmaking with Louis Massiah and the Scribe Video Center. However, she continued to have close relationships with many members of The Sisterhood until her passing in 1995. One of Bambara's most important friendships was with Toni Morrison, her friend, editor, and advocate from the publication of her book of short stories *Gorilla, My Love* (1972) to the posthumous publication of her novel *Those Bones Are Not My Child* (1999).[58] Their participation in each other's careers and lives was separate from the more public-facing mission of The Sisterhood. Bambara and Morrison's relationship depended on mutual respect for their writing and a trust that they could be among the most cherished friends in each other's lives while also getting work done in their professional relationship. Bambara describes their dynamic in a 1982 radio interview with Kay Bonetti:

> The relationship that we have, which I think is ideal for me, would probably not work with other editors or with other writers[; it] is that she generally

leaves me alone. You know, once in a while she'll call and say "How you doin'?" Well we talk to each other because we're friends and because we're very much interested in each other's work as women and as members of the same community. Once in a while she may probe to find out what I'm doing and I might send her something and then we talk contract for a minute and contract is done. And when I hand in a copy, she usually reads it herself, makes some comments. She might make a few suggestions, which I take or not take. And then she turns it over to her copyeditors . . . For the most part, it's a very non-interference kind of activity on her part, for which I am very grateful.[59]

What Bambara calls "non-interference" is Morrison's trust in Bambara and her work. This mutual trust depended on the two women being "members of the same community" of Black women writers, even when separated by geography with Morrison in New York and Bambara in Atlanta and then Philadelphia. This trust also depended on being "friends" who not only were "interested in each other's work" but also thought of each other as great writers.

The editorial process Bambara describes above refers especially to the years Morrison edited Bambara's novel *The Salt Eaters* (1980), which is among the most beautiful, politically radical, and important novels of the Black women writers' renaissance of the 1970s and 1980s, or of any period of American literature. Sisterhood member Vertamae Grosvenor agreed; she wrote on a postcard to Bambara: "Salt Eaters is better than Song of Solomon Seabird!!" referring to Morrison's 1977 novel and Bambara's collection of short stories *The Sea Birds Are Still Alive* (1977).[60] Decades later, many of the essays in Linda Janet Holmes and Cheryl A. Wall's collection *Savoring the Salt: The Legacy of Toni Cade Bambara* (2008) speak to the importance of *The Salt Eaters*. The question that opens the novel—healer Minnie Ransom asks ailing activist Velma Henry, "Are you sure, sweetheart, that you want to be well?"—has become a mantra for Black women's self-care in places from yoga studios to scholarly articles.[61] Holmes and Wall describe *The Salt Eaters* in their introduction to *Savoring the Salt* as "a visionary novel that enacts the fusion of literary and political, social and spiritual perspectives. Experimental in its nonlinear narrative, it is specific in its representation of the cultural practices of African Americans. But the novel maps a larger world."[62] This message and Velma's healing in the novel resonated deeply with Black women readers who had, like Bambara's protagonist, worn themselves out in endless and often invisible labor in the civil rights and Black Power movements.

Trusting in the value of each other's writing and in their friendship made space for Bambara and Morrison to share their personal lives in ways that weren't possible for some other Sisterhood members within the context of the group. Meeting minutes document only in passing, if at all, aspects of members' personal lives, such as mothering and mental health. The group discussed these subjects but rarely put details about them on official agendas or in circulated meeting minutes. Members had all kinds of friendships outside of the group. Professional relationships may have constrained certain conversations: for some of the women, Sisterhood meetings were taking place with their current or potential editor, lawyer, or mentor in the room. Bambara and Morrison's friendship was distinct because it was understandably rare for either of them to let their guard down as much as they did with each other. The pressure that came with her visibility was acute for Morrison because of the singular place she occupied as a writer, editor, and cultural figure. As I discuss in greater detail in chapter 6, Morrison needed to construct a public persona that protected her private self. In each other, Morrison and Bambara found a friend with whom they could flourish as writers and intellectuals. They could also have a good time together, gossip about men, comment on each other's writings, and speak frankly about their lives.

Linda Janet Holmes explains how important and rare that friendship was for both women, particularly given their lives as public people:

> In conversations with cultural workers, Bambara tended to focus on the work to be done rather than her personal experiences. Conversations with Morrison included her private life. Morrison confirmed the mutuality in their friendship when she said, "There were moments when she [Bambara] revealed in conversations things that I would never repeat because she really was a very public person in her teaching, in her political activity, and organizing. But there was the other very, very private person."[63]

Over the years, particularly in the last decade of her life, Morrison referred to a network of Black women writers who offered mutual support in the 1970s and '80s; Bambara is almost always the only member of this network whom Morrison identified by name.[64] In a 2013 public conversation with writer Junot Díaz, Morrison described a figurative "neighborhood" of women, asserting "Toni Cade was excellent at" making community: "I remember her coming into my house with two bags of groceries. No one asked her; she didn't say she was coming; she just appeared. And she set the groceries down and she said 'I'll take care of the children today. You go do what you have to do.'"[65] That Morrison edited Bambara's writing is widely known; that Morrison occasionally sent Bambara money to help her get by is mentioned in a number of scholarly works; that Bambara helped Morrison with groceries, food preparation, and child care has emerged only more recently in interviews Morrison gave after Bambara's passing.

Morrison thought of Bambara's fiction as aesthetically superior to the work of their contemporaries and as coming closest to her own in terms of quality and importance. In 1977, she candidly wrote to Bambara: "Have you ever stopped to count the *living black women writing good fiction*? Tell me if you need more than the fingers of one hand."[66] In 2013, Morrison gets more specific when she describes Bambara's work as distinct in assuming a Black, feminist, woman reader: "She was already there, you know, in that attitude about to whom she was talking."[67]

Bambara wrote about and for Black women from the start of her career. The first-person narrator of her short story "Gorilla, My Love" (1972) is Hazel, a smart, bold Black girl who protects her younger brother and holds adults to account for their everyday dishonesty. When a group of kids expect to see the adventure movie *Gorilla, My Love* but find themselves instead watching a religious film, Hazel leads their resistance: "when I yell We want our money back, that gets everybody in chorus . . . and I march myself up to deal with the manager who is a crook in the first place for lyin out there sayin *Gorilla, My Love* playin."[68] Bambara uses Black Arts Movement style (capital "We" and a run-on sentence without punctuation that reads a like a poem by Amiri Baraka or Sonia Sanchez) that makes Hazel (aka Scout, Peaches, Badbird) a beautiful, brave, and specific character with one of the most distinct first-person voices in contemporary African American literature. "Gorilla, My Love" is about betrayal, not primarily the movie theater's false advertising, but rather Hazel hearing that her "Hunca Bubba," who once swore he'd marry her one day, is engaged. When her uncle says, "I was just teasin," Hazel, who is usually quick witted and clever with words, is in too much pain to respond the way she wants to: "'You a lyin dawg,' I say, when I meant to say treacherous dog, but just couldn't get hold of the word. It slipped away from me. And I'm crying and crumplin down in the seat and just don't care."[69] What makes these sentences thick with pain is that Bambara forces the reader to be right there with Hazel. Bambara takes Black girls seriously and treats them as important subjects with complex interior lives worthy of description and respect, just as Morrison did in *The Bluest Eye* (1970) and *Sula* (1973).

To assume a Black woman reader and to take Black girls seriously are political moves in a culture that constantly devalues Black women and girls. Bambara's "Gorilla, My Love" and Morrison's *The Bluest Eye* use fiction to depict the disheartening and sometimes devastating effects of racially separate and unequal businesses and schools and of racist beauty standards, respectively. Morrison's novel *Sula* tells a story of love, freedom, and pleasure in friendship between girls. Nel Wright and Sula Peace's friendship turns out to be one of the many losses wrought by the push to racial integration. *Sula* is Morrison's elegy for a vibrant, all-Black community and a novel that mourns a lost friendship. The Seven Sisters Collective in Bambara's novel *The Salt Eaters* (1980) and the tender and then broken friendship between Christine and Heed in Morrison's novel *Love* (2003) show these two close friends continued to explore the power of Black women's collaborations and friendships throughout their careers.

~

Like Toni Cade Bambara and Michele Wallace, Cheryll Y. Greene was an important interlocutor for The Sisterhood though not an official member. Like Bambara and Hoyt Fuller, she was a frequent and generous reader and correspondent for many African American writers, artists, and thinkers. She facilitated the publication of Black women's writings in her roles as executive editor and special projects editor at *Essence* from 1979 to 1985.[70] Greene created "transnational black feminist critique in what otherwise would have been a black beauty and lifestyle magazine." She began to transform *Essence* in the 1970s by writing serious, insightful reviews of books by Henry Dumas, Gayl Jones, Carolyn Rodgers, and Angela Davis, among other Black writers. In a remembrance, Alexis Pauline Gumbs describes her work: "Cheryll was active in every cultural and political aspect of the black freedom movement in the late 20th century. She instigated and supported uprisings in the representational politics of film. She was involved in the beginning of the work of the Institute of the Black World in Atlanta. She vetted films for Harry Belafonte. She corresponded with James Baldwin. She fought for the good name of Assata Shakur."[71] Gumbs's description begins to illuminate the vast and largely invisible labor Greene did to advance African American literature and liberation. Like Toni Morrison's work as an editor and Toni Cade

Bambara's work to create networks of Black writers, Greene's little-known work was an important force in literary history.

Sisterhood members were central to Greene's ambition to make a popular women's magazine a mass market venue for Black feminist thought. Her ties to The Sisterhood included Rosa Guy, who had been one of Greene's clients at the Ronald Hobbs Literary Agency in the late 1960s, as well as Morrison, who first contacted Greene in 1975 to send her a review copy of Gayl Jones's *Corregidora*.[72] Greene wrote about poetry readings by Ntozake Shange and Audre Lorde for *Freedomways* and worked with Vertamae Grosvenor, Jessica Harris, June Jordan, and Shange on their writings for *Essence*; she shepherded Lorde's 1983 essay "Black Women's Anger" through each stage to publication in the magazine.[73] Sisterhood members' essays asserted the importance of Black women's interior lives in relation to a range of social, political, and historical contexts.

The magazine also continued to put literary figures front and center, organizing a wide-ranging, five-hour conversation between Lorde and James Baldwin at Hampshire College in 1983, parts of which were later published in *Essence* as "Revolutionary Hope: A Conversation Between James Baldwin and Audre Lorde."[74] They talked about "Black masculinity" and "Black womanness," rape, and police violence, going back and forth, visibly trying to be as honest with each other about dynamics between Black men and women as possible.[75] However, "The fact that Lorde was a lesbian and Baldwin a homosexual, and that they had discussed black sexualities, was not revealed in the *Essence* version of their conversation."[76] The published piece included Baldwin's assertion that "Black men and women are much less easily thrown [than white people are] by the question of gender or sexual preference—all that jazz" and Lorde's repeated attention to "differences" among Black people, but no discussion of sexuality as one kind of difference.[77] This omission is fairly typical of *Essence*, which published writing by queer Black people but almost never directly addressed LGBTQIA identities in the 1970s and '80s. On a 2015 panel about the Baldwin-Lorde conversation, Alexis De Veaux reminded the audience that the excerpt was a small selection from a long conversation and that the published version "served *Essence*" both in drawing readers to the magazine and by "situat[ing] them [the speakers] in this heteronormative culture that was and continues to be *Essence* magazine," thus erasing their "erotic lives" from a "political conversation."[78] Even though some members of The Sisterhood identified as lesbians and all supported gay and lesbian rights, they rarely emphasized sexual identities in their efforts to get publication and publicity for Black women writers. Black feminists understood that the personal had been public and political long before white feminists made that their slogan, but some Black feminist groups and publications treated sexual identity as separate from their public and political work. *Essence*, even though it was regularly including Black feminist writing by the early '80s, did not just push sexuality to the background, but rather erased queer identities almost entirely. The stakes of this were high: omitting Baldwin and Lorde's "erotic lives" from a "political conversation" fundamentally changed the meaning of their exchange.

In the same year the conversation with Baldwin appeared in *Essence*, Lorde's essay "Uses of the Erotic: The Erotic as Power" appeared in her book *Sister Outsider* (1984). Baldwin had used sex and desire to depict complex, contradictory, and varied Black men in his fiction since his first novel, *Go Tell It on the Mountain* (1953). Their conversation as it appeared in the profoundly "heteronormative" pages of *Essence* made it possible for readers to admire and engage these writers without facing that same-gender desire was central to the way both thought and wrote about Black liberation. Greene was working at a mass market magazine that was not radical in its sexual politics, but it was likely her influence that got part of the conversation between Baldwin and Lorde—two queer, Black, radical intellectuals—published there at all.

Greene's influence on African American literature was wide ranging both in editorial jobs at *Essence* and as a literary and speaking agent, helping Black novelists, poets, journalists, and scholars reach readers. She also sustained Sisterhood members' connections to one another by bringing them together in print and in person across the 1980s.[79] The 1985 fifteenth-anniversary special issue of *Essence* was a kind of reunion in print for The Sisterhood. Greene collaborated with Sisterhood member Audrey Edwards, then executive editor of *Essence*, and worked closely with contributors, offering substantive feedback on drafts and shepherding to publication essays by Audreen Ballard, Toni Cade Bambara, Lucille Clifton, Alexis De Veaux, Phyl Garland, Vertamae Grosvenor, June Jordan, Paule Marshall, Toni Morrison, Gloria Naylor, and Alice Walker. Greene also collaborated with scholar Paula Giddings on a timeline of Black women's history.[80] Greene and Edwards used the special issue to turn away from the beauty, lifestyle, and entertainment aspects of the magazine and focus instead on novelists, poets, and essayists who were politically radical, queer, and engaged in freedom struggles in and outside the United States. In emphasizing their work, the issue asserted the coherence and importance of Black women's history and put Black feminist writers at the center of that history.

A few years later, Greene organized the 1988 *Essence* writers' retreat in Nassau, Bahamas. The retreat was both a reunion for The Sisterhood and a major gathering of Black feminist thinkers. Toni Cade Bambara, Elaine Brown, Octavia Butler, Lucille Clifton, Thulani Davis, Paula Giddings, Sonia Sanchez, and Barbara Smith were there alongside Sisterhood members Phyl Garland, Rosa Guy, Vertamae Grosvenor, Audrey Edwards, Paule Marshall, Ntozake Shange, and Renita Weems.[81] The retreat aimed to get writers excited about the current direction of *Essence*, encourage them to submit work to the magazine, and assist them with writing in a style that would work well in its pages. As editors-at-large, Greene and Edwards led sessions on writing for *Essence* and met one-on-one with authors. Alexis De Veaux, June Jordan, and Toni Morrison did not attend but each sent a letter to be read aloud at the retreat, expressing deep affection for the women gathered and support for the group and the magazine.[82] De Veaux's "message of support and greetings" wished "good luck" to women new to writing for *Essence* and concluded by addressing the established writers: "To those of you who are old hands at it, keep working to make the magazine as progressive and open as it can possibly be."[83] Morrison wrote, "If I could be with you now . . . I would make you understand better than this message will how real my affection for you is, how much delight I take in the work you are doing and how important it and you all are to me."[84] Jordan sent a poem:

> Dear Sisters,
> How much I really wish that I could come and be
> With all of you beside a warm blue sea
> Our ragged spirits hunger for new healing light
> To help us rally close and then resume the fight
> We need to wage for justice and for grace!
> Let nothing come between or otherwise erase
> The dreaming and the pride our hearts may share
> If only we attempt together what no one of us may dare!
> How much I really wish that I could come and be
> With all of you beside a warm blue sea[85]

Jordan offers ten lines of iambic rhymed verse with a couplet that opens and closes the poem with the "wish" to be there in Nassau "beside a warm blue sea." Jordan's poem seeks to "rally" her "sisters" to persist in the work of "the fight" for liberation and "justice" by writing in *Essence*. De Veaux and Morrison's letters and Jordan's poem suggest that The Sisterhood was so successful in pushing *Essence* to include work by Black feminist writers that serious, literary, political writing had become an essential element that the magazine was trying hard to sustain by the late 1980s. By 1988, readers expected to encounter Black feminist writing in what had once been primarily a lifestyle, beauty, and entertainment magazine.

In a letter to Lucille Clifton about a month before the retreat, Greene describes the goals of the gathering:

> Our purpose is to commune in a pleasant setting on the prospects and problems of the commercial magazine writing process. We editors want to engage in dialogue with writers whose primary outlets are not magazines, and we've also invited a couple of our "Veteran" writers to participate in the exchange. We are looking forward to an ESSENCE in the coming years that will contain the finest writing there is for our almost 4 million readers— sisters (and brothers) who, like ourselves, need insight, information, analysis and inspiration to deal with the wretched conditions we are now facing as we move into a new century. We hope to leave our retreat having discussed specific ideas with each of you and having made assignments with reasonable, comfortable due dates.[86]

Greene carefully planned the *Essence* retreat to serve goals much like those of The Sisterhood a decade earlier. *Essence* had managed to become a "commercial magazine" that advanced politically engaged writing by literary authors. Greene got Black women published in an outlet that reached many readers and balanced "specific ideas" and "assignments" with "reasonable, comfortable due dates." The urgency, work plan, respect for writers' labor, and attention to making care for self and others possible all echo the ways The Sisterhood collaborated in the late 1970s. Greene's letter to Clifton shows that the *Essence* retreat, and her vision for the magazine more generally, shared some core assumptions with The Sisterhood: Black women write for an audience of Black readers ("sisters [and brothers]"); Black women's literary writings (by poets and novelists "whose primary outlets are not magazines") are a valuable source of "insight, information, analysis and inspiration" for all Black readers; and literature has utility because it helps Black women "deal with the wretched conditions we are now facing."

Greene remained committed to this Black feminist work throughout her life. In the 1990s, she worked as a manuscript consultant and editor, organized the 1997 conference "Yari Yari: Black Women Writers and the Future" at New York University, and served as guest editor for a 1998 special international issue of *Essence*.[87] Dedicating her career to helping Black writers in general and Black women writers in particular get published, promoted, and paid, Greene drew on an extensive network and shaped African American literature through editing, organizing, and talking with writers about their work.

Greene and Bambara had similar goals and a shared enthusiasm for Black women writers. In one 1980 letter, Bambara invited Greene to a conference in Atlanta ("conference yes or no"), pitched a nonfiction work by an unpublished Black woman writer ("Whattaya think, lady lit agent"), and included a list of her own upcoming readings in New York ("I wanna reeeeead . . . jam as much as I can that week").[88] Bambara hired Greene to organize events in New York to promote *The Salt Eaters*. In a mode typical for both women, they used their friendship to expand each other's networks and to promote other Black writers.[89] Their correspondence across the 1970s, '80s, and '90s includes reports on their emotional, intellectual, and romantic lives; plans for visits in Atlanta and New York; reflections on each of their trips to Cuba; expressions of deep affection; and a lot of humor. In a characteristic letter, Bambara wrote to Greene in 1979: "Heading up your way. Any chance of me and the kid bunking with you (we're not adverse to sleeping on the floor) the night of Friday the 14th of Dec?" and "Have you seen the [Wole] Soyinka play? Sterling Brown just called me . . . to tell me I should see it; then he put Skip Gates on the phone who said the same thing. I suspect they've got shares in the production. Think you can get tickets for me and the kid?"[90] Alongside jokes, gossip, and affection, their correspondence was filled with practical matters. In one 1979 letter to Bambara, Greene offers ideas about Bambara's plans for SCAAW workshops; asks for mailing addresses for Mari Evans, Sonia Sanchez, and Hoyt Fuller, whom she wanted to join her speaker's bureau; and thanks Bambara for recent phone conversations. These professional plans intertwine with personal reflections. Greene wrote, "I came away from our talks with a new sense of how our lives and our struggle must be integrated on the deepest levels—self and community, spirit, mind, and body, personal and political, past present and future."[91] Letters between Bambara and Greene show that their collaborative work to advocate for Black women writers was difficult, fun, and rooted in friendship.[92]

Like The Sisterhood, Bambara and Greene worked to realize a radical abundance of possibility for Black women writers. These collaborations were not easy, but they were joyful, playful, and rooted in the respect and trust of long-standing friendships and professional relationships. The Sisterhood was a middle ground between these public and private lives, a place where friendships brought affective bonds into the room every time the group met in ways that kept these women tied together, making the time and mustering the energy to meet once a month. The trust and friendship between June Jordan and Alice Walker brought the group together in the first place. There was love and a sense of mutual obligation in the room at every meeting, but they were there to advance Black women's writing in the public sphere, to work, to take care of business.

Michele Wallace, Toni Cade Bambara, and Cheryll Y. Greene each worked with and outside of The Sisterhood in ways that show how the group's ideas and projects reached out to and depended on a larger network of Black women intellectuals. Each made sure that the Black feminist work of The Sisterhood continued to radiate outward in concentric circles far beyond New York and long after the 1970s.

Chapter Five

"A REGULAR PROFUSION OF CERTAIN/UNIDENTIFIED ROSES"

After the group stopped meeting, Sisterhood members continued to advocate for Black women's writing in magazines, at presses, and in the academy. In concert with the writing and teaching of Black feminist scholars, Sisterhood members built popular and academic audiences ready to receive their writings. Their collaboration as The Sisterhood also shaped the form and content of their own writing in the years immediately following The Sisterhood's last meeting and for decades to come, including for those who had their greatest success much later.

In a 1978 interview with Karla Hammond for *Kalliope*, a journal aimed at general readers interested in women artists and writers, June Jordan says, "This is the first time that I've ever been interviewed about my poetry in my entire life. Now I have been a published poet for over twenty years. Compare me to Adrienne Rich. How many times a week is Adrienne interviewed (*laughs*)?" and says that she is "amazed" that her "Poem About My Rights" will soon appear in *Essence*.[1] Today, "Poem About My Rights" is one of Jordan's best-known works and has been widely anthologized, including in *The Norton Anthology of African American Literature*, which is often a college student's first substantial encounter with Black literature. This is remarkable given the complexity of the poem's content. In a 1981 interview with Alexis De Veaux, Jordan explains that "Poem About My Rights" represents the ways that rape, South African racial apartheid, American plunder of Africa's resources, and other forms of racist and sexist violence around the world are part of one interdependent system of oppression: "I tried to show as clearly as I could that the difference between South Africa and rape and my mother trying to change my face and my father wanting me to be a boy was not an important difference to me. *It all violates self-determination.*"[2] In one long stanza with little punctuation, the first-person speaker moves among various kinds of violence, from the danger of being a "woman alone in the evening" to CIA assassinations of African leaders and American oil operations in Angola. With a forceful tone, the poem becomes increasingly urgent; the speaker asserts, "I do not consent" to literal and metaphorical "rape." The poem concludes with the speaker resolving to practice "resistance" and "self-determination," which "may very well cost you your life."[3] This final line is a warning from a rightfully furious speaker determined to expose and resist interlocking systems of oppression. "Poem About My Rights" exemplifies Jordan's radical Black feminist politics and poetics. Like Toni Cade Bambara's novel *The Salt Eaters*, it names the late twentieth century as a time of emergency for Black women in the United States. That this forceful, urgent, radical poem appeared in *Essence* and still appears on countless syllabi is just one indication that The Sisterhood and their contemporaries had significant success in bringing radical Black feminist thought into the two institutions they targeted: publishing and the university.

~

Former Sisterhood members kept Black feminist politics at the center of their work throughout in the 1980s, around the world and in many different forms. Although some members had gone or would head west, New York remained an important center of collaboration for literature, visual art, and political action. In the years just after the group stopped meeting, former members regularly circulated in the same social and professional circles and worked together on creative projects. Several members returned to or began focusing on visual art. This was not a coordinated turn to the visual like The Sisterhood's earlier intentional focus on magazines and book publishing but rather a matter of specialized knowledge and timing. Judith Wilson's expertise in visual arts was growing as she earned her doctorate in art history. Patricia Spears Jones and Margo Jefferson have seen nearly every exhibit of any Black artist's work in New York from the time they each moved to the city in the late 1960s and early '70s to the present. These former Sisterhood members had a lot of knowledge about and interest in visual art that they could apply to writing about those forms. They also continued to be in New York City in the 1980s, a decade of stunning, politically radical, energizing visual and performance art, much of which responded to the profound oppression of the Reagan era. This was the decade when Keith Haring painted murals on subway cars alongside graffiti artists such as Futura 2000, Barbara Kruger began showing her large-scale feminist pop art paintings, painter Jean-Michel Basquiat showed up in the video for Blondie's song "Rapture," and ACT UP staged die-ins and other performance-art-inspired actions to demand acknowledgment of and medical treatment for people living with HIV and AIDS.

Former Sisterhood members were tuned in to what was happening in New York's art galleries and museums. When journalist Diane Weathers, also a Sisterhood member, told Wilson about Linda Goode Bryant's Just Above Midtown (JAM) gallery, Wilson responded with excitement, "What? There's a Black woman with a gallery on 57th Street? You're kidding?"[4] From the construction of the American Fine Arts Society in the Gilded Age of the 1890s through at least the late twentieth century, a stretch of Fifty-Seventh Street just below Central Park and a couple of blocks from the Museum of Modern Art (MoMA) was home to some of New York's most prestigious art galleries. In the 1970s and '80s those galleries were well established places named for their art dealer owners (Krugier, Zabriskie, Emmerich, and others) that sold works by well-known, long-dead artists such as Pablo Picasso and Gustav Klimt and a few contemporary white American men artists such as Jackson Pollock, Ellsworth Kelly, and Alexander Calder. Visits to these galleries were often by appointment only. The 1974 arrival of Bryant's JAM, which focused on Black artists, was a radical addition to this cultural corridor.[5]

JAM remained important to the Black cultural scene as it moved from the Fifty-Seventh Street location to Franklin Street in Tribeca and then to 503 Broadway in Soho in 1984.[6] The 1981 JAM exhibition "Crossovers" included at least one work by Ntozake Shange, and Judith Wilson wrote an essay for the exhibit catalogue.[7] Judith Wilson and Patricia Spears Jones both saw and wrote about early performances of artist Lorraine O'Grady's groundbreaking *Mlle Bourgeoisie Noir* and *Nefertiti/Devonia Evangeline* at JAM in 1980.[8] In writing about O'Grady's work, they drew attention to Black feminist performance art, which much of the art world seemed totally unaware of in 1980. The first retrospective exhibit of O'Grady's important and large body of conceptual art would not happen until forty years later with the Brooklyn Museum's 2021 show *Lorraine O'Grady: Both/And.*

O'Grady was eighty-six years old at the time of this exhibit, which brought her wider attention than she had ever experienced, despite Wilson's efforts decades earlier to draw attention to O'Grady's work.

Wilson highlighted the existence and importance of Black visual and conceptual art in the decade after The Sisterhood met. She wrote the lead article in the December 1980 special issue of *Black Enterprise* about the business of art collecting. Diane Weathers pushed for and shepherded this special issue under the direction of publisher Earl Graves. By the late 1980s, Wilson was the biweekly art reviewer for *The Village Voice* and she, Weathers, Jefferson, and others continued to write for magazines in the city. Former Sisterhood members were regularly at offices that were close together in midtown. *Black Enterprise*, for example, was on Forty-First Street "just down the street from *Ms.* magazine."[9] The energy and sense of possibility in New York remained important for those members working in theater, visual arts, newspapers, and magazines.

As they were making some headway for Black women writers and artists and for Black feminist politics in *Black Enterprise, Ms., Newsweek,* and other publications, Sisterhood members saw one of the most successful outcomes of their efforts in the changing pages of *Essence.* As in other spheres, the work they did for and at *Essence* was both liberatory and constrained. Alexis Gumbs writes, "The magazine's history reveals an imperfect resolution for melding its perceived accountability to Black women and its mandate to sell the attention of Black women to multinational corporations."[10] Gumbs explains Black feminist writers' relationship to *Essence* in terms that also apply broadly to their attempts to get published and paid in a capitalist marketplace that they simultaneously objected to and worked within: "On the one hand, *Essence* created space—however contested—for Black feminist writers, such as Nikki Giovanni and June Jordan, to challenge the prevailing notions of home, family, and labor; on the other hand, the magazine itself reinforced" the racism, homophobia, and patriarchy of those "prevailing notions."[11] The magazine published radical writings by Black feminists alongside columns and advertisements prescribing ways Black women could conform to narrow ideas of beauty and femininity, particularly to attract and support Black men. In its eventual uses of a marketable version of Black cultural nationalism, as Gumbs explains, "*Essence* became a project that both exploited and empowered Black women."[12] This ambivalent and multipronged role makes it particularly remarkable that Black women editors used the magazine as a tool for liberation even under the conditions of simultaneous empowerment and exploitation.[13]

A letter of February 1979 from Alice Walker to Judith Wilson shows the persistence of the connections to *Essence* forged in The Sisterhood. Walker tells Wilson, "I'm glad you're at *Essence*. There are some lovely women there."[14] Wilson regularly introduced *Essence*'s readers to Black and feminist academic books, scholarly journals, and novels. Her brief, insightful reviews considered a special issue of the scholarly journal *Callaloo* about Black women poets, the Black women's special issue of the journal *Conditions*, and an issue of the feminist journal *Heresies* focused on Third World women.[15] Alongside advertisements for beauty products and reviews of prime time television shows, *Essence* published Wilson's article about fellow Sisterhood member and novelist Rosa Guy; her review of Mary Helen Washington's second anthology of Black women's fiction, *Midnight Birds* (1980); and her review of Barbara Christian's study *Black Women Novelists: The Development of a Tradition, 1891–1976* (1980).[16] Other Sisterhood members appeared in the magazine's pages as well: the September 1980 issue placed Wilson's review of Bambara's *The Salt Eaters* on the same page as Patricia Spears Jones's poem "Feeling Evil," and the September 1981 issue included Wilson's review of Jordan's *Civil Wars*.[17] As Margo Jefferson built an audience for books by Black authors through her reviews in *Newsweek* throughout the 1970s, Wilson built a Black audience for serious literature and scholarly writing through her reviews in *Essence*.

Members continued to collaborate to get Black feminist writing into university classrooms, academic conferences, and scholarly journals. In trying to change the academy, made up mostly of predominantly white colleges and universities, they found themselves fighting the same battles that had made The Sisterhood a necessary refuge. Audre Lorde gave a talk, later published in *Sister Outsider* (1984) as "The Master's Tools Will Never Dismantle the Master's House," at a New York University conference commemorating the thirtieth anniversary of Simone de Beauvoir's *The Second Sex* in September 1979.[18] Speaking at this mostly white feminist conference, Lorde critiqued, in precise and vivid terms, the ways that white feminist academics and activists had failed to address the liberation of Black women and were perpetuating racial oppression even as they worked to undo gender oppression. "The Master's Tools" reached listeners who needed to hear it: white, feminist women scholars who exercised a lot of power in marginalizing Black women and Black feminist scholarship. This was one of many instances throughout the 1970s and '80s in which Lorde did the exhausting and often disheartening work of asking white feminists to acknowledge their complicity in anti-Black racism.

Throughout her career, Lorde addressed the absence of Black women from white feminist projects. She wrote several letters expressing her anger at the journal *Chrysalis* for failing to include the Black women's poetry that Lorde had, in her capacity as poetry editor, selected for publication. In the fall of 1979, Patricia Spears Jones wrote to the journal in support of Lorde's protest and June Jordan, furious over the journal's neglect of Black women, followed Lorde's lead in resigning from *Chrysalis*.[19] Just as they had supported Jordan's actions against the racism of *American Poetry Review* a few years earlier, women who had been Sisterhood members continued to pressure literary, feminist, and academic journals to publish Black feminist writing.

Former Sisterhood members also established small presses as part of their ongoing effort to exert editorial control over Black feminist writing. Although The Sisterhood never launched its own press or publication, soon after the group stopped meeting, members did use what they had discussed at meetings to launch new presses and publications. Audre Lorde cofounded Kitchen Table Press in 1980 with Barbara Smith and Smith's partner, feminist intellectual Cherríe Moraga. Smith and Moraga moved from Boston to New York, bringing Kitchen Table Press with them, partly to be closer to Lorde, who was living in Staten Island. Smith and Moraga felt that "the major energy for building and sustaining" the press was in New York, where there was a "dynamic women's cultural scene."[20] On the West Coast, Alice Walker continued writing fiction, essays, and poetry, and she cofounded Wild Tree Press (named after Walker's property in Navarro, California), which published six books from 1984 to 1988.[21]

Former Sisterhood members who remained in New York and moved in academic circles also collaborated to pressure organizations to be more inclusive in the funding of writers and artists. In 1980, "a group of writers met in New York in response to a growing perception of their underrepresentation, as members of communities of color, in the allocation of public monies dispensed by literature programs under the National Endowment for the Arts (NEA)."[22] Lorde later recalled that "white writers weren't interested in hearing about," much less organizing to protest, "the racist distribution of NEA grants."[23] In early 1980, Filipino American writer Jessica Hagedorn and Audre Lorde formed the National Association of Third World Writers (NATTW), and Judith Wilson came on board as the group's secretary.[24] Native American poet Joy Harjo was on the board, and Sisterhood members Patricia Spears Jones, Ntozake Shange, and Lori Sharpe participated in NATTW. In March 1980, the group wrote to David Wilk, director of the

NEA's Literature Program. Wilk met with representatives of the group, including Lorde, in May 1980. Alexis De Veaux took part in the campaign to change the NEA and described Lorde's feeling that the meeting "fell far short of rectifying" the Literature Program's "discrimination against Third World Writers."[25]

The NEA was established in 1965, fulfilling the vision President John F. Kennedy had laid out of sustained federal financial support for artists, arts organizations, and arts education. Novelist Ralph Ellison sat on the first National Council of the Arts (a kind of steering committee for the NEA), and choreographer Alvin Ailey received one of the organization's first grants. Toni Morrison served on NEA panels for literature grants, and poet A. B. Spellman worked at the NEA in the 1970s. Even with these Black writers and artists present, the council's membership and grant awardees were predominantly white in the 1960s and '70s. In 1980, David Wilks may have been influenced by pressure from the NATTW and also may have known that he had a short window to make the most of NEA funding before Ronald Reagan came into office and implemented budget cuts. Whether in response to these or other forces, by the end of 1980, the NEA awarded grants to numerous Black authors including John O. Killens, Charles Johnson, Sterling Brown, Bebe Moore Campbell, and Angela Jackson as well to important Asian American authors including Maxine Hong Kingston and Frank Chin.[26] That same year, President Jimmy Carter appointed Morrison to the National Council of the Arts, and she served through 1987.[27]

Sisterhood members also pursued anti-imperial, transnational political activism around the world. The NATTW was one manifestation of the idea of Third World feminism. As discussed in chapter 3, activists developed a sophisticated Third World feminism in the 1960s and '70s. Black women who identified as Third World feminists understood Black women as a distinct political and cultural identity *and* forged solidarity with other women of color nationally and globally to combat shared conditions of oppression. Throughout the 1980s, former members of The Sisterhood connected their Black feminist writing and activism to the struggles of other Black women in the African Diaspora and of other women of color around the world, just as they had when The Sisterhood was active.

Audre Lorde remained based in New York but regularly went to the Virgin Islands, where in 1980 she helped establish the "St. Croix Women's Coalition, a counseling and advocacy community group focused upon domestic violence." With her partner Gloria Joseph, Lorde cofounded Sisterhood in Support of

Sisterhood in South Africa (SISA, which means "mercy" in Xosa), a group that distributed funds directly to women in Soweto living under apartheid.[28] In June 1983, Alice Walker and Paule Marshall traveled together in China as part of a group of women writers on a "three-week cultural exchange" that Marshall organized.[29] Walker has consistently spoken and written over the decades against nuclear proliferation, apartheid, and the Israeli occupation of Palestine. She wrote and spoke about, raised funds for, and collaborated on the film *Warrior Marks* (1993) to bring international attention to female genital mutilation in African countries. Walker defied the U.S. blockade to travel to Cuba with a delegation of artists in 1993 and met with Black liberation activist Assata Shakur, who was living in exile from the United States, and again as part of a sanctioned women's delegation bringing medical supplies in 1995.[30]

Toni Cade Bambara also traveled to Cuba several times, including in January 1985 with a group of Black women writers that included Jayne Cortez and Mari Evans as well as Sisterhood members Vertamae Grosvenor, Rosa Guy, and Audre Lorde.[31] In the pages of *Essence*, June Jordan, with Cheryll Y. Greene as her editor, published essays about the U.S. funding war against the Sandinistas in Nicaragua and about "Black People and Foreign Policy."[32] Although plenty of white feminists had protested the Vietnam War, no wave of white feminism had the kind of sustained engagement with movements for women's liberation outside the United States that defined Black feminism in the 1960s, '70s, and '80s.

As they were changing a variety of cultural institutions, former Sisterhood members continued to influence one another's writing and careers. The Sisterhood was never a writing workshop; they did not exchange and comment on members' writings at formal meetings. Outside the group, though, they provided feedback about one another's writing during and after the years The Sisterhood met. As readers and as writers, they shaped what Mary Helen Washington named the "renaissance of Black women writers."[33] Members spent the decade after their last meeting participating in a period of radically increased visibility for Black women writers. Their books published from just 1980 to 1990 include Alice Walker's *The Color Purple* (1982), *You Can't Keep a Good Woman Down* (1982), and *The Temple of My Familiar* (1989); June Jordan's *Passion: New Poems: 1977–1980* (1980), *Civil Wars: Observations from the Front Lines of America* (1981), *Living Room* (1985), and *On Call* (1985);

Paule Marshall's *Praisesong for the Widow* (1983) and a reissue of her 1959 novel *Brown Girl, Brownstones* with a new afterword by Mary Helen Washington (1981); Ntozake Shange's *Sassafrass, Cypress & Indigo* (1982) and *A Daughter's Geography* (1983); Audre Lorde's *Zami* (1982) and *Sister Outsider* (1984); Renita Weems's *Just a Sister Away* (1988); and Morrison's *Tar Baby* (1981) and *Beloved* (1987).

Like the photo "The Sisterhood, 1977," this list of books ought to arrest our attention, stun us, make us curious. These publications are among the most lasting results of The Sisterhood. All of these women would have been writers without the group, but together they shaped the style and subjects of one another's work. Their collaboration as The Sisterhood in the 1970s also built a cultural landscape of magazines, publishers, general readers, students, and teachers who were ready for their books. Many of those books, especially the novels, were widely read and reviewed. The women earned other accolades across the decade. In 1980, Shange won an Obie Award for her adaptation of Bertolt Brecht's *Mother Courage*. Jordan held a National Endowment for the Humanities Fellowship in 1982. Walker's *The Color Purple* won the American Book Award in 1983, became the first work by a Black woman to win a Pulitzer Prize for Fiction, and was on the *New York Times* bestseller list for more than eighteen months.[34] Morrison won both a Pulitzer Prize and an American Book Award for *Beloved* in 1988 and had an honorary doctorate from Harvard by the close of the decade. Lorde won an American Book Award for her volume of essays *A Burst of Light* in 1989. The 1980s arguably produced Sisterhood members' most important works. This decade remains unrivaled in terms of productivity and visibility for African American women writers.

However, the "renaissance of Black women writers" was tragically short, elevated too few writers, and was co-opted into dangerous rhetoric of first multiculturalism and then diversity, especially in higher education. That Black women writers have not since matched the visibility they had in the 1980s is a crushing loss wrought by racism and misogyny. It is important to look closely at some of the writing that grew out of and was published right after The Sisterhood's years of active collaboration before that return to the status quo. Two poems by June Jordan show how the group shaped the form and content of Black women's writing both in the years just after the group met, when these poems were published, and well into the twenty-first century, when the ideas in the poems still shape Black feminist thought. Jordan's "Letter to the Local Police" and "Poem About Police Violence," like all of her poetry and like the labor of The Sisterhood, assert that literature is political and that Black feminist politics are both public and intimate.

The white feminist tenet that the personal is political is not fully applicable to Black feminist thought for a number of reasons. When white feminists sought to enter the workplace in greater numbers, Black women had already worked outside their homes in what would become the United States since the start of racial chattel slavery in the seventeenth century. The women of The Sisterhood understood that they lived during just one chapter of a long history of Black women's private bodies and choices being put to public, political uses by white people. The personal was political when enslavers forced Black women to bear enslaved children in the antebellum era and was still political when Ronald Reagan created the bogeywoman of the welfare queen in her pink Cadillac in the 1980s. Black people's personal lives were and are subject to dangerous government surveillance.[35] Black writers and artists have consistently borne a burden of expectations that they create representational works that explicitly serve collective Black political goals. One distinct, shared feature of Sisterhood members' writings is that they treat Black women's intimate lives as inherently important and insist on Black women's right to be oblique, private, quiet, or opaque.[36] These writers understand that personal lives have political meaning in the public sphere, but they also draw on a tradition of African American writing that values intimate, individual, everyday Black life. This is a specific and radical choice in the United States, which daily devalues Black life.

In the tradition of African American authors including Frances Harper, Gwendolyn Brooks, and James Baldwin, June Jordan grounds her liberation politics in desire, intimacy, and everyday experience. "Letter to the Local Police" and "Poem About Police Violence," read together, as they appeared in Jordan's 1980 volume *Passion*, echo The Sisterhood's emphasis on balancing intellectual and emotional support for one another with activism both inside and beyond existing institutions. Jordan uses person, voice, tone, and unexpected diction to show the interdependence of concrete and abstract labors for liberation.

"Letter to the Local Police" is formatted as an unsigned letter from a new resident of Saratoga Springs, New York, to the city police. The poem takes a surprising turn when, several stanzas in, it emerges that this concerned citizen is writing to complain about "a regular profusion of certain/unidentified roses" that bloom "in perpetual near riot/of wild behavior" and threaten "promiscuous cross-fertilization" with local plants. The speaker urges the police to address this "civic disturbance in our midst" with "appropriate legal response to the roses in question."[37] The low-stakes subject, roses, paired with the intensely concerned tone initially makes the poem funny. Jordan's diction, though, turns this into a satire of gentrification and white resistance to integration. The words "riot" and "wild behavior" smack of racist complaints by white residents about Black residents, and "cross-fertilization" evokes white fear of interracial social contact, especially sex. Jordan joins a long line of African American writers using flowers as metaphors for Black women, from Gwendolyn Brooks's protagonist in her novel *Maud Martha* (1953) and Toni Morrison's Pecola Breedlove in *The Bluest Eye* (1970) identifying with dandelions because they are both beautiful and ordinary to Alice Walker's poem "Revolutionary Petunias" (1973), which connects one woman's gardening to a murder she commits to avenge her husband's killing.[38] Jordan works in this vein of floral metaphors that bind the domestic and intimate to the political and public, but her roses as metaphor for Black women function in a unique way. The reader understands that this little patch of roses in this one spot are powerful, spectacular, and beautiful because they are "wild" and "in perpetual near riot."

"Letter to the Local Police" pairs a serious tone about a relatively trivial subject with a white, first-person speaker to achieve humor and biting satire. "Poem About Police Violence," which appears in the same volume, works differently. Jordan uses repetition, a first-person plural voice, and a tone of sincerity, anger, and threat to tackle the deadly serious subject of racist state violence. The poem opens and closes with a two-stanza question:

> Tell me something
> what you think would happen if
> everytime they kill a black boy
> then we kill a cop
> everytime they kill a black man
> then we kill a cop
>
> you think the accident rate would lower
> subsequently?[39]

Jordan writes a protest against racist police brutality, speaking in the voice of a Black "we." This exploration of retaliatory violence is perhaps jarring alongside roses growing wildly. The pair makes sense, though, in part because

Jordan wrote these poems as The Sisterhood was meeting. She is writing from the same place of love for "a black boy" that was shaping Ntozake Shange's profoundly loving depiction of the youngest sister, Indigo, in her 1982 novel *Sassafrass, Cypress & Indigo*. Toni Morrison's *The Bluest Eye* (1970) and *Sula* (1973), along with Toni Cade Bambara's "Gorilla, My Love" (1972) had set a template for valuing the interior lives of Black girls. Jordan and Shange, bolstered by their exchange with these women in The Sisterhood, later wrote in this vein. Jordan's two poems quoted above differ in voice and style, but both are about the iterative action in everyday life ("regular," "perpetual," "everytime") of Black women, who are "roses" that the poem, if not the speaker, loves or a "black boy" that the poem and the speaker desperately want to protect. Like The Sisterhood, Jordan's poems recognize the importance of collective action for political change and take the interpersonal and intimate seriously as a necessary part of political work. They shuttle back and forth between big, seemingly insurmountable systemic racism and the local lives of individual people acting in, for, or on that system.

The Sisterhood's influence appears in other members' published works across genres, sometimes in surprising ways. In her work as a womanist theologian, Renita Weems brought lessons of The Sisterhood and of Black feminism into her religious writings. Borrowing a phrase from Toni Morrison's *Beloved* (1987), Weems says that the women of The Sisterhood were "friends of my mind" and that the "rich conversations" at the meetings did "eventually spill over into our, into anyone's writing or one, one being a lawyer or one being an editor or whatever . . . one's work was."[40] Weems understood her nonfiction theological book *Just a Sister Away* (1988) to be in dialogue with her fellow Sisterhood members' fiction and poetry. She took part in "a recent groundswell of literature by and about black women in the non-religious sector" by "combin[ing] the best of the fruits of feminist biblical criticism with its passion for reclaiming and reconstructing the stories of biblical women, along with the best of the Afro-American oral tradition." Weems names the book's "critical perspective" as "womanist" and credits Alice Walker with creating that term to name "a black feminist; a courageous woman."[41] *Just a Sister Away* uses the term "womanist" in the preface to lay claim to the book's place in Black feminist discourse and reinforces that claim with citations in this religious text of secular writings by Audre Lorde, Angela Davis, Paula Giddings, Alice Walker, and Margaret Walker.

Each chapter of *Just a Sister Away* examines one relationship between women in the Bible and then explores the uses and meaning of that relationship for contemporary Black women navigating their own lives. This use of scripture follows the model of feminist and Black consciousness-raising groups of the 1970s: Weems offers the book as "a resource tool and a study guide," and each chapter concludes with a section titled "Questions for Thought" meant to be used in "Bible study groups, women's gatherings, workshops, and over coffee."[42] This form of discussion echoes both consciousness-raising groups and The Sisterhood's commitment to textual study. Weems supplies guidelines for serious and piercing conversations related to issues that were on the minds of Sisterhood members and other Black feminists, such as whether cross-racial and cross-ethnic alliances among women are possible, the importance of Black women's friendships, and the power dynamics in romantic relationships between Black men and women. At the end of the chapter studying Hagar and Sarah, Weems asks, "In what ways can women from differing ethnic/racial/economic backgrounds bind together and significantly impact global politics and religious controversies?" A discussion question at the end of the chapter about Mary and Martha asks, "Do you think women should be financially compensated for doing housework, especially those women who do not work outside the home? What kind of remuneration would you propose, if any?" Weems uses collaborative textual study as a way for women to consider cross-racial solidarity to effect political change in local and "global" settings and to discuss the place and value of women's domestic labor. She encourages readers to resist competition among women and to organize their churches' women's groups to write to networks and protest violence against women in television shows.[43] Weems's prescriptions for women's religious study groups incorporates the intellectual work and political organizing of The Sisterhood, the National Black Feminist Organization, and other Black feminist groups into Black Christian thought and practice. Jordan's poems at the start of the 1980s and Weems's theological book at the end of the decade show how The Sisterhood's concerns and strategies continued to shape members' writings.

Some members published their most important and widely read works decades after the group stopped meeting. In these later works, the influence of The Sisterhood persists. In late 1978 and early 1979, as the group stopped meeting regularly during the period of intense backlash against Wallace's *Black Macho*, some members retreated from the public eye into their creative work, jobs, and families. Patricia Spears Jones remembers, "I just felt like I went into the wilderness for about ten years. I don't think I was alone in that."[44] She sought to escape the ugly attacks that she had seen happen to

Shange and Wallace. The "wilderness" Jones refers was also partly the involuntary experience of being on the outside of the commercial success that a few Black women writers achieved in the 1980s. Poets often have less commercial success than novelists, and this difference felt particularly acute for some poets in the 1980s as Morrison and Walker became literary celebrities.

Jones is among those former Sisterhood members whose body of work reaches more readers now, in the twenty-first century, than ever before. She has published numerous volumes of poetry, including *A Lucent Fire: New & Selected Poems* (2015); has won awards such as the Jackson Poetry Prize in 2017; was the honoree at The Poetry Project's 2022 gala in New York; has poems included in many anthologies; and is in demand to teach prestigious poetry workshops. This is a result of her literary achievement and hard work, but also reflects shifting conditions in the literary marketplace: forty years after The Sisterhood met, African American poetry is getting more recognition in terms of awards and reviews than it was in the 1970s.[45]

The persistence of The Sisterhood's influence in clear in Jones's poem "Glad All Over" (1995). The poem is set in Arkansas, where Jones grew up and where she, her family, and other Black people in their town faced mortal danger from the Ku Klux Klan. The speaker's mother, standing up for Black children, is the hero of the poem. In titling it after a pop song by the Dave Clark Five, "Glad All Over," Jones sets the tone for a liberated 1960s youthful exuberance. She then utterly undoes that tone with the contents of the poem. The last lines of "Glad All Over" point to the stakes of contemporary Black women's writing and literary organizing. Jones writes about the 1960s as "a decade now known as much for the pursuit of pleasure as for/political assassination, a war broadcast nightly, lawless police,/ritual murder and hard, harsh truths. Getting harder."[46] This poem recovers the '60s from a romanticized story about "the pursuit of pleasure" by asserting that it was a decade of women's liberation and sexual revolution for white people, but for Black people, a decade of "political assassination" with the killings of Malcolm X, Martin Luther King, Jr., Fred Hampton, and other Black leaders and of "ritual murder" and "lawless police." This state of emergency has deep roots and reaches into the present. Jones wrote the poem in the early 1990s, when CNN televised the racist, misogynist interrogation of Anita Hill during U.S. Senate hearings that confirmed Justice Clarence Thomas to the Supreme Court and recently established twenty-four-hour news networks subjected viewers to relentlessly repeated airings of Los Angeles cops brutally beating Rodney King and going unpunished. Jones evokes the strangeness of a state of emergency that is also perpetual with "hard, harsh truths. Getting harder," lines that echo the diction, sound, and repetition of Sterling Brown's 1931 poem "Strong Men." Brown's refrain insists that Black men were, in the 1930s, "strong men gittin' stronger. / Strong men. . . . Stronger."[47] Jones asserts that Black life was and is "Getting harder" in the 1930s, the 1960s, and the 1990s. The allusion to one of Brown's best-known poems shows Jones's investment in an African American literary tradition and is an intertextual act that claims her place in that tradition. Like other members of The Sisterhood, she is drawing on the power of African American literature to correct the historical record, offer solace amid racist danger, and articulate the complex and racially specific relationship between an individual and her community.

Like Jones, Margo Jefferson has enjoyed greater and much-deserved prominence in recent years. In the 1970s and 1980s, Jefferson was writing reviews and cultural criticism for magazines and newspapers that reached many readers. In 1995, she won a Pulitzer Prize for her cultural criticism, which appeared in *Newsweek*, the *New York Times*, *New York Magazine*, and *Harper's*, among many other publications. She went on to write *On Michael Jackson* (2006) and the memoirs *Negroland* (2015) and *Constructing a Nervous System* (2022), both of which garnered significant acclaim, including a National Book Critics Circle Award for *Negroland*. Jefferson has long been doing Black feminist work in a variety of contexts, from the NBFO to *Newsweek*, The Sisterhood, public lectures, and classrooms. Both of her memoirs extend this work and take it in a new direction by treating her interior life as a Black woman intellectual as worth serious, extended consideration through innovative first-person narrative.

Jefferson said in 2018 that she thinks back on The Sisterhood as a "Black, feminist, literary consciousness-raising group" that had lasting effects on her writing.[48] *Negroland* bears the imprint of her collaborative work with the NBFO and The Sisterhood in both formal and thematic ways. Like Toni Morrison's novels, *Negroland* is formally experimental in its use of voice, point of view, and space on the page. Jefferson regularly breaks away from linear narrative using quotations, italics, sections set off and indented as if they are stanzas of poetry, and lists. Early in the book, she lists "all manner of things" that "we in Negroland have called ourselves," from "the colored aristocracy" to "the blue vein society" and "the African-American upper-class."[49] In this memoir, Jefferson uses her experiences to consider the racial and gender dynamics of upper-class Black Americans. Over four decades after The Sisterhood met, Jefferson speaks plainly about economic class, which was a mostly unstated form of difference and sometimes a source of tension among the women in the group. She examines the ways that upper-class Black girls were raised in the 1950s and '60s to embody and perform impossibly high and narrow standards of femininity and achievement as exemplars of the race.

Like Jefferson, some other members of The Sisterhood were able to attend elite colleges, live in New York, and pursue creative or academic careers because they came from comfortable economic backgrounds. Some shared Jefferson's experience of the Black Power movement as important, welcome, but also unsettling. As a student at Brandeis in 1966, "when Black Power came along," Jefferson "used it as an excuse to stop talking to various people I felt hadn't respected or acknowledged me enough" *and* pushed herself to "be honorable in my political reading, my political opinions, my modest actions against the Vietnam War and for Black Power."[50] Writing long after these events and candidly discussing the ways intersecting race, class, and gender identities have shaped her life in "Negroland," she vividly depicts herself as simultaneously petty (using a political movement as "an excuse" to drop people who annoy her) and committed to political activism. This is utterly recognizable as the way a person around the age of nineteen relates to a political awakening. She puts this moment into a collective context as a shared experience of well-off, young Black women struggling to navigate ideas of Black Power and Black nationalism that told them "the entitlements of Negroland were no longer relevant . . . we'd settled for a desiccated white facsimile and abandoned a vital black culture." Jefferson and others would eventually find their way, but they faced a difficult moment in the mid-1960s. These young women of the Black elite felt the need to overcorrect by adopting a version of Blackness that was the opposite of how they were raised but was perhaps just as narrow: "we unmade our straightened hair, remade our pristine diction, renounced our social niceties and snobberies."[51]

Negroland tells a story that happened before and during the time The Sisterhood met, but that Jefferson could only fully write decades later, with the benefit of distance. The pressure and desire to be a pillar of Black excellence as a girl followed by the pressure and desire to be a force for Black liberation as a young woman was difficult for Jefferson and for many other Black women of her generation and economic class background. By the late 1970s when The Sisterhood was meeting, Jefferson was "a passionate feminist," despite the fact that "the women's movement was controversial in the black community" because of its racism, and she was "ready to accept" "new social and cultural opportunities" that movements for women's, Black, and gay rights were opening up. At the same time, she "began to actively cultivate a desire to kill" herself.[52]

Jefferson, Ntozake Shange, and Michele Wallace discussed their depression, anxiety, and suicidal thoughts with one another directly in private and referenced these subjects more obliquely in print in the 1970s. Admitting struggles with mental health, especially contemplating suicide, was taboo. Open conversations about these dire mental health concerns were "a privilege Good Negro Girls had been denied by our history of duty, obligation, and discipline."[53] *Negroland* takes a huge risk: Jefferson defies the strictures of how she was raised by depicting her interior life in the 1970s as painful and suicidal. She was influenced by Shange having taken on the subject of Black women's mental health publicly with *for colored girls* in the 1970s. Jefferson writes, "So, when Ntozake Shange stood on the stage of the Public Theatre [*sic*] in 1975 and spoke the words 'And this is for colored girls who have considered suicide,' my heart took flight. We were the same age. We were both doctors' daughters who'd attacked our girlhood gentility with the weapons of Black Power and radical feminism. Now we could consider—toy with, ponder, contemplate—suicide."[54]

Jefferson counted Shange among her "literary idols" because she "dared to locate a sanctioned, forbidden space between white vulnerability and black invincibility" to write about Black women's complex interior lives, including depression.[55] As a cultural critic, Jefferson was able to celebrate Shange's choreopoem in writing in the 1970s, but it was not until her 2015 memoir that she put down in print the riskier notion of desiring the privilege to "consider—toy with, ponder, contemplate—suicide." Only in this much later writing does Jefferson reveal that she felt not just the admiration for *for colored girls* that she wrote about in the 1970s but also "jealousy" that Shange was more "brave" than she was and "spite" that Shange's choreopoem had not healed Jefferson's depression.[56] Her encounter with *for colored girls* is one of many scenes in *Negroland* that show how literature shaped her life. The place of Shange's work in Jefferson's memoir is especially important because it shows that the late 1970s, New York, and The Sisterhood were formative for members' thinking and writing decades after the group met.

Chapter Six

"THE FUNCTION OF FREEDOM IS TO
FREE SOMEBODY ELSE"

Toni Morrison is the most widely read, studied, and celebrated former Sisterhood member. A *New York Times* survey in 2006 named Morrison's *Beloved* (1987) as the best work of American fiction of the previous twenty-five years.[1] Upon her passing in 2019, within hours and for months, tributes appeared in print and online; on podcasts, radio, and television; and on social media at an extraordinary rate.[2] By the late 1970s when The Sisterhood began to meet, Morrison had written three novels and edited many important books at Random House. By the end of the 1980s, she occupied a uniquely prominent position in the academic, critical, and popular literary imagination. Morrison's fiction is singular, accomplished, useful, beautiful, and formally and thematically innovative. It is also the case that The Sisterhood and other African American writers made the public Morrison possible.

When The Sisterhood met regularly in 1977 and 1978, it seemed that Morrison's greatest impact would be in getting books by Black writers published, read, and recognized. Her work as an editor and advocate did change the landscape of contemporary literature, but her own writings have had an even greater and more lasting impact on literary and academic spheres. The dramatic increase of publication, publicity, and prizes for Black women's writing in the 1980s is something to celebrate. It is also a story about the largely invisible women's work that made that decade possible and how few writers reaped the rewards. In the two cultural institutions that The Sisterhood sought to transform—literature and the academy—Morrison's place is unrivaled, earned, meaningful, and its own kind of cautionary tale about the dangers of exceptionalism and individualism.

The Sisterhood's efforts to publish and publicize Black women's literary and critical writing shaped how people read and understand Morrison's novels. This chapter brings Morrison back into collectivity, back into a network of Black women writers and intellectuals. Her novels and her advocacy for African American literature remained intertwined and interdependent throughout her career.[3] She consistently used her platform as a public intellectual and celebrated novelist to advocate for the publication, study, and appreciation of African American writing on its own terms as a distinct literary tradition. A network of Black writers and intellectuals bet on Morrison, hoping that she would be a transformative public presence in literature and the academy, and they were right.

For her part, Morrison's recollection of Black women writers' support for one another in the 1970s was selective and changed over the course of her long career. Sometimes she seemed to distance herself from the collective intellectual labor that helped secure her place in the academy and the literary marketplace. Other times, especially later in her life, she referred to her network of support, including friends and family. In a 2003 *New Yorker* profile, Morrison tells cultural critic Hilton Als about help she got from other women in New York City around the time The Sisterhood met. Als uses Morrison's words in a way that urges us to read her books alongside books by Toni Cade Bambara, poet Sonia Sanchez, and other Black women writers. He weaves together Morrison's description of the 1970s and relevant observations from Sanchez with his own analysis and framing of recent literary history:

> The women [Morrison] worked with, in particular, became some of her closest friends. "Single women with children," she said, when I asked her about that era. "If you had to finish writing something, they'd take your kids, or you'd sit with theirs. This was a network of women. They lived in Queens, in Harlem and Brooklyn, and you could rely on one another. If I made a little extra money on something—writing freelance—I'd send a check to Toni Cade with a note that said, 'You have won the so-and-so grant,' and so on. I remember Toni Cade coming to my house with groceries and cooking dinner. I hadn't asked her." The support was intellectual as well as practical. Sonia Sanchez told me, "I think we all looked up and saw that we were writing in different genres, but were experiencing the same kinds of things, and

saying similar kinds of things." Their books formed a critical core that people began to see as the rebirth of black women's fiction.[4]

The Sisterhood was part of that "critical core," and also part of the "network of women" Morrison describes. The forms of "support" among working Black women in New York in the 1970s include the child care, money, and food preparation that Morrison recounts as well as the shared experience and subject matter that Sanchez describes.[5] A decade later, in a 2013 conversation with Junot Díaz, Morrison talked about moving to New York City as a single mother and relying on a group of women "who lived not in the neighborhood together, but behave[d] that way," as if they were a neighborhood.[6]

Like other members of The Sisterhood in these years, from Margo Jefferson at *Newsweek* to Judith Wilson at *Ms.*, Morrison was, at Random House, one of very few Black women in a workplace that was producing media for many readers. Each of these women felt a responsibility to shape what their workplaces produced, especially by getting more Black women's writing in print. They were also each navigating the unrelenting pressure of representing all Black women, whether or not they wanted to. This is what made it, as Jefferson said, such "a relief" for those who were "alone" or "one of the few" at "white institutions" "to have this other life" of meeting regularly with other Black women intellectuals.[7] The stakes were extremely high for someone as visible as Morrison: she understood that her public persona, bearing this unfair burden of representation, might determine whether and how Black women had access to cultural institutions in the future. She carefully constructed her public persona during the years The Sisterhood met in the late 1970s and throughout the 1980s. Later, especially in the last twenty years of her life, once her literary status was unchallenged and unrivaled, Morrison became a bit more open in interviews and lectures about the communities of Black writers and intellectuals that had supported her work. In the early twenty-first century, Als's profile of Morrison and her public conversation with Díaz show that she was both maintaining her role as a uniquely prominent public intellectual and acknowledging the people who helped her create and inhabit that role.

Recent journalism, both before and since her passing, has paid a lot of attention to Morrison's legacy. The wide reach of her novels has resulted in a way of thinking about Morrison and her work that separates both from their historical and literary contexts. A number of writers and interviewers have made the deeply troubling move of characterizing her legacy as standing apart from an African American literary tradition. In *New York Magazine* in 2012, Boris Kachka wrote, "Having once spearheaded the elevation of black women in culture—Maya Angelou, Alice Walker, Oprah—she now finds herself struggling to cut them loose, to admit at long last what she's always believed: that she's not only the first, but the best" and thus "she belongs as much with Faulkner and Joyce and Roth as she does with that illustrious sisterhood." This way of understanding Morrison is racist exceptionalism. It posits being the "best" and writing great works of literature as dependent on separating from other Black women, on "struggling to cut them loose." It also defines being the "best" as being part of a white literary tradition "with Faulkner and Joyce and Roth" rather than an "illustrious sisterhood" of Black women writers.[8]

Framing Morrison as an exception among Black women writers and measuring her work using novels by white men as a benchmark uses Morrison to deracinate her books and erase other Black writers' work. Alice Walker founded The Sisterhood, which was an important intellectual community for Morrison and solidified relationships that mattered for the rest of both of their careers. Walker's and Morrison's writing careers are concurrent; they both published their first novels in 1970, a year after Angelou published her autobiography. Together these works—*I Know Why the Caged Bird Sings* (1969), *The Third Life of Grange Copeland* (1970), and *The Bluest Eye* (1970), along with Toni Cade Bambara's *The Black Woman: An Anthology* (1970), began a period of at least thirty years in which African American literature was visibly defined by Black feminism.

Angelou, Morrison, and Walker remain among the most widely read Black writers. Although Kachka's profile in 2012 and most of Morrison's obituaries in 2019 acknowledge her work as an editor and her friendships with Black women writers, these writings are among the popular criticism that tends to treat her as distinct from the tradition in which she wrote and to celebrate her particular literary achievements by implicitly or explicitly erasing Black history and contexts. Examples of this problem of erasure through exceptionalism abound in journalism, scholarly writing by academics who are not specialists in African American literature, and high school and college curricula. Literary scholar Harold Bloom famously defended the white Western canon during the culture wars of the 1990s, but considered Morrison among the very few contemporary writers and very few Black writers who ought to be added to college curricula. A few decades after those canon wars in English departments, scholars Joe Karaganis and David McClure created the Open Syllabus Project, which includes over 400,000 syllabi from literature courses. In this database Toni Morrison's *Beloved* is the only work by a Black woman writer to appear in the top thirty most frequently taught texts.[9] The novel is often the only work by a Black woman to appear on syllabi for survey courses in American literature. Kachka and Bloom are extreme examples, but many other critics and scholars describe Morrison as exceptional and, like those who teach *Beloved* but no other works of African American literature, thus separate her from the African American literary tradition. Morrison's *New York Times* obituary describes her "luminous, incantatory prose" as "resembling that of no other writer in English."[10] The *Washington Post* obituary notes that President Barack "Obama described her as 'one of our nation's most distinguished storytellers,'" "a judgment that was nearly unanimous among literary critics," and describes the president and the novelist arguing over whether Morrison ought to be called a Black writer, a woman writer, or neither.[11] These obituaries and the conversation with Obama celebrate Morrison's writing as both singular and universal, thus deracinating her books in two ways: claiming that they are not part of a Black tradition and that they are by, for, and about people of any race. Morrison regularly reasserted the race and gender specificity of her writing and her audience, citing it as a creative wellspring: "being a black woman writer is not a shallow place but a rich place to write from."[12]

At its worst, separating Morrison from her peers and her literary tradition creates a false dichotomy in the study of contemporary Black women writers. Kachka's profile is an egregious example because he suggests that a serious reader, teacher, or scholar of Morrison's works should reject Maya Angelou's and Alice Walker's writings in favor of reading Morrison's novels in the context of works by white men such as William Faulkner, James Joyce, and Philip Roth. Morrison consistently refused such comparisons of her work, especially to Faulkner's. In an interview with scholar Nellie McKay in 1983, Morrison made clear that there was a dire need for Black feminist criticism, saying it was the "black women's" "complex" "job" to create a "systematic mode of criticism" "from us." That "us" referred to Black women scholars including McKay, who pursued, conducted, and edited this interview in her early years at the University of Wisconsin despite the fact that her senior colleagues told her the project was not serious scholarly work and would not count for tenure review.[13] Morrison reiterated the need for Black feminist criticism, explaining that readers cannot understand her books by comparing them to books by white men: "I am not *like* James Joyce; I am not *like* Thomas Hardy; I am not *like* Faulkner. I am not *like* in that sense."[14] In televised interviews in the 1990s with Bill Moyers, Charlie Rose, and Ed Bradley, Morrison answered questions about whether she would ever write about white characters or stop writing about race. In every case, she rejected the unspoken premises that a novel has to be about white characters to be universal and that whiteness is not a race. She told Ed Bradley on *60 Minutes*, "What is interesting to me is what is going on within the community and within the community there are no major white players."[15] She does not need to name "the community" as Black because Blackness is the default in her novels.

In carefully constructing her public persona, Morrison sometimes courted exceptionalism, but she never wanted to be considered separate from the "rich place" of "being a black woman writer."[16] Kachka only got part of the story when he quoted Morrison saying, "the first book of Maya's I really enjoyed, and Alice has written at least one, maybe two books that I admire a lot ... they're very different writers, very, very different from me. . . . one self-edits and one doesn't."[17] This could mean, as Kachka suggests, that Morrison thought of her work as better or better edited than Walker's or Angelou's. "Very different," though, is also simply an acknowledgment of the diversity of style and content among contemporary Black women writers, and "one self-edits and one doesn't" could be a distinction Morrison is drawing *between* Angelou and Walker, a comment on the conditions of literary production rather than a critique of those authors, or a reference to Morrison's own experience as a professional editor. Even narrowed down by gender, form, and period to women's literary fiction of the late twentieth century, African American literature is varied and diverse. The writers themselves could acknowledge those differences while still valuing one another's work and still understanding themselves as sharing a literary tradition. Critique and admiration are not mutually exclusive. When Morrison sold *Song of Solomon* (1977) to Random House for $300,000, Alice Walker felt "a little jealous," thought of Morrison's fiction as lacking "struggle," *and* celebrated Morrison for writing "beautifully" and creating "art."[18] Walker documents in her journals that she and Morrison were more admiring of each other's work and less competitive than people expected them to be.[19] As discussed in the previous chapter, Morrison's relationship with Toni Cade Bambara shows that she valued and elevated a lot of Black writing and thought of a few writers as her aesthetic equals. She also consistently identified as a Black woman

writer working in and drawing on a tradition of African American literature and culture. Critics who write about Morrison as suspicious of Black
women's collectivity erase the role of networks in fostering her deserved
prominence. They also negate the work Morrison did to foster the success
of other Black writers and to help secure African American literature as a
distinct field of study.

$\sim$

Toni Morrison's advocacy for Black writing began decades before her most
visible success. In 1977, when The Sisterhood began meeting, Morrison had
just published her third novel, *Song of Solomon*, and was a champion for
Black women's literature. As an editor at Random House, she had acquired
important works including *Angela Davis: An Autobiography* (1974), Gayl
Jones's novel *Corregidora* (1975), June Jordan's volume of poetry *Things That
I Do in the Dark* (1977), and Toni Cade Bambara's collection of short stories
The Sea Birds Are Still Alive (1977). Morrison did far more than just acquire
and edit. She was a one-woman letter-writing campaign, sending out countless missives to magazine editors, reviewers, and scholars urging them to
read and review these Black women's books.

It was not easy to balance the demands of being a novelist, editor, and
mother. On the television program *The Writer in America: Toni Morrison*,
which aired in May 1978 on Channel 13 in New York, Morrison talked about
her first three novels and the difficulties of writing while also being a full-
time single mother and a full-time editor. She described her hope that *Song of
Solomon* might "prove to be more than a literary success" and thus allow her
to "stop writing around the edges of the day." She hoped to earn enough as a
writer to maintain her role as "head of household," a phrase she used often in
this period to name her financial and parental responsibilities.[20] By the time
that interview aired, *Song of Solomon* was a literary and financial success.
It was reviewed on the front page of *The New York Times Book Review*, was
a Book-of-the-Month club selection, won a National Book Critics' Circle
Award, and was a bestseller in paperback.[21] Morrison was well on her way
to realizing her goals of making a living as writer and being a major force in
American literature.

Morrison's star continued to rise as The Sisterhood held their monthly
meetings. She had stopped attending regularly by the time the group disbanded, but she was using her platform to advance a way of thinking she

had honed in the group and in other Black feminist collaborations. A few months after The Sisterhood stopped meeting, Morrison gave a commencement address at Barnard College in 1979, where she urged the graduating women "not to participate in the oppression of your sisters," and said that educated women needed to "pay as much attention to our nurturing sensibilities as to our ambition" and to understand that "the function of freedom is to free somebody else."[22] Her words to the predominantly white Barnard graduates about their responsibilities as women who wield the "power" of education reflect The Sisterhood and Morrison's elevation of Black writers as a whole. In keeping with the nature of The Sisterhood and especially her relationship with Bambara, Morrison puts her command in the most intimate terms: "Women's rights is not only an abstraction, a cause; it is also a personal affair. It is not only about 'us'; it is also about me and you. Just the two of us."[23] Morrison was being generous with her success, putting herself on equal footing with women graduating from college. She was also savvy as ever, using the occasion of her address at a women's college to talk about "women's rights" in a way that invited cross-racial solidarity among women but didn't erase racial difference or depend on the idea of universality that she critiqued in later essays and speeches. She called on the graduates to use their prestigious education to "free somebody else," implicitly asking them to follow her lead in using any power they might have to liberate others.

Morrison also did heroic work as an editor at Random House to advance publication, publicity, and literary status for many African American writers. She later explained to Junot Díaz that she understood her editorial efforts as a "mission" and a form of political work that she chose over participating in demonstrations in the 1960s, '70s, and '80s.[24] She championed Henry Dumas, a teacher, playwright, poet, and fiction writer whom New York City police killed on a Harlem subway platform in 1968. Morrison pushed hard to get Random House to make the risky choice to posthumously publish Dumas's experimental abstract writings. Richard So documents how much of a "statistical outlier" Dumas's novel *Jonoah and the Green Stone* (1976) was among books at Random House in terms of race, form, and content.[25] Dumas's work is not easily understood in the context of the Black Arts Movement—though he absolutely was part of BAM—and his writing was nonrealist in a time when many white publishers, reviewers, and award committees placed more value on books they understood as realist, representational, and part of a tradition of protest literature. This was a misguided set of expectations that made it an uphill battle for Morrison to get Dumas's writings published. This is also an example of how Morrison leveraged her success with popular books like boxer and activist Muhammad Ali's 1975 autobiography to acquire and edit books that would reach smaller audiences, by authors such as Dumas, June Jordan, and Gayl Jones. Morrison's impact and influence as an editor was immense. Cheryl Wall rightly asserts, "As an editor, she helped to define two decades of African American literary history."[26]

Morrison's departure from editorial work was gradual. She recalled leaving "the daily grind of editing" around 1981.[27] By that point, she had written four well-received novels, most recently *Tar Baby* (1981). As the "grind" took up fewer of her working hours, Morrison became increasingly prominent as an author. An important milestone came when she appeared on the cover of *Newsweek* in January 1981 with the title "Black Magic: Novelist Toni Morrison." This occurred, in part, thanks to a member of The Sisterhood. Margo Jefferson paved the way: since the mid-1970s, her book reviews had made inroads for Morrison's work and other African American writing in the pages of *Newsweek*. At a time when general interest magazines like *Newsweek* and *Time* still had enormous influence on American culture, appearing on the cover was a big deal. Months later in a piece for *Essence*, Judith Wilson called the *Newsweek* cover a "media triumph" that "marks the end of an era in which Black literature was most often thought of as Black male literature."[28] Writing for the *Washington Post*, Jacqueline Trescott called Morrison "the queen of the blitz," referring to media coverage from the *Newsweek* cover to Morrison's appearance on *The Dick Cavett Show*, book tour and signings, and "the front pages of key literary reviews." Trescott's article and Morrison's comments in it tied the recognition of *Tar Baby* to Morrison's network. Trescott wrote, "Her success, she feels, is collective; that her story is linked to the fate of black writers, particularly black women," and Morrison said, "My dream is that one season they will have five black books, by five black women, all at once."[29]

At the dawn of the 1980s, Morrison was thinking like an editor in wishing for "five black books, by five black women" every publishing season. At the same time, she was rapidly becoming the primary public face of African American writing. The 1981 media coverage was connected to the recent publication of *Tar Baby* but also pointed to the literary fame that Morrison would attain by the end of the decade. In 1983, she wrote to several of the authors she was editing to let them know that she was planning on leaving Random House to focus full time on her own writing.[30] She did take time off from Random House to teach at Yale in the 1980s. As I explain in the next chapter, Morrison's fifth novel, *Beloved*, came to define American literature and played a central role in defining African American literary studies, Black studies, and Black feminism in the academy. When *Beloved* came out to much acclaim in 1987, Morrison was still going in to the Random House offices about one day a week. By the time she fully left her editorial position in 1988, her position in American literature was unimpeachable.[31]

∽

As she attained an unrivaled status in contemporary American literature, Morrison understood all too well that the space in the literary marketplace for Black writing was small. It troubled her that U.S. culture focused on or celebrated only one or two Black writers at a time. The desire for a singular, exceptional figure has shaped African American literary studies in all kinds of ways, from positing W. E. B. Du Bois and Booker T. Washington as intellectual opponents to understanding James Baldwin as having an Oedipal relationship to Richard Wright, to choosing Ralph Ellison's *Invisible Man* (1952) as the only work by a Black author to include on an American literature syllabus in high school and college classrooms. It is dangerous and limiting to choose one writer at a time to represent all African American literature or to treat Black writers as always in competition with one another. Focusing on just one or two writers erases the diversity of style, genre, and subject matter in every period of African American literature. By the late 1980s, with the critical and popular success of Morrison, Walker, and others, the increased visibility of African American women novelists was undeniable. As Patricia Spears Jones notes, this visibility also depended on the marketplace, "because fiction is what trade houses published. They don't publish poetry, and if you are in New York and you are really seriously, seriously dealing with a literary life, I mean a professional life, you write fiction."[32] This period of relative commercial success brought attention to a few writers, and most of them were novelists.

Like Morrison, other Sisterhood members understood the problems of exceptionalism even while they were part of a renaissance of Black women's writing. June Jordan wrote about this deficit of imagination in a 1974 essay in *Black World*, "Notes Toward a Black Balancing of Love and Hatred," an elegant work of literary criticism about two novels: Richard Wright's *Native Son* (1940) and Zora Neale Hurston's *Their Eyes Were Watching God* (1937).

This pairing is provocative because dynamics of representation, competition, and exceptionalism meant that scholars tended to teach and write about the social urban realism of Richard Wright *or* the lush, Southern feminist works of Zora Neale Hurston, but rarely both. This was true from the time of Wright's 1930s review sharply criticizing Hurston's novel for what he saw as a lack of direct political protest through at least the 1970s. *Native Son* remained in print and widely read from the time of publication through the late twentieth century.[33] Hurston's novel fell out of print, had a rocky road to its current firm place in the American literary canon, and needed the help of The Sisterhood and Black women literary scholars to get there.

The stakes of choosing between Hurston and Wright, of elevating one Black writer, thinker, or leader at a time, were high in the 1970s. Jordan writes, "We must begin, now, to reject the white, either/or system of dividing the world into unnecessary conflict . . . it is tragic and ridiculous to choose between Malcolm X and Dr. King." She asserts that "we need" both Wright and Hurston and "should absolutely resist the superstar, one-at-a-time mentality that threatens the varied and resilient, flexible wealth of our Black future." Jordan insists on the complexity and richness of Black literature as both "protest," represented by Wright, and "affirmation," represented by Hurston.[34] We must read both Hurston and Wright and thus see "protest" and "affirmation" as modes that are both necessary for protecting and celebrating Black life. Following Jordan's lead by reading *Native Son* and *Their Eyes* together illuminates the multiple roles of literature in Black liberation. Reading them in opposition nearly erased Hurston from the canon, making it necessary for Black women writers and scholars to recover *Their Eyes* and put it back into the context of an African American literary tradition.

Hurston's *Their Eyes* is now as prominent as Wright's *Native Son* and Ellison's *Invisible Man* in high school and college classrooms. Hurston began publishing her short stories in the early 1920s and was writing fiction and nonfiction prolifically in the 1930s. After the 1937 publication of *Their Eyes* and despite Wright's negative review, as Henry Louis Gates, Jr., argues, Hurston was "the dominant Black woman writer in the United States" until around the early 1950s. However, she soon fell into "dark obscurity" and was "virtually ignored after the early fifties, even by the Black Arts movement in the sixties," which might have logically celebrated the all-Black world of most of Hurston's writing. Her novels remained obscure and out of print until the 1970s, when Black women began to circulate, teach, and write about her work.[35] We could attribute this neglect to aspects of Hurston's content or style. In truth, though, in the double bind of racism and sexism, *Their Eyes* is one of countless important works by Black women writers that have been ignored, fallen out of print, or gone understudied for long periods of time. Scholar Cheryl Wall's *Women of the Harlem Renaissance* (1995) studies Hurston in the context of two other Black women writers of the period: novelist, columnist, and editor Jessie Fauset and novelist Nella Larsen. Hurston, Fauset, and Larsen were each major figures during the Harlem Renaissance of the 1920s and '30s, and all three of them died in the early 1960s in obscurity, with their works out of print. Recovering *Their Eyes* was a collective endeavor that included scholars at the Modern Language Association meeting demanding that the novel be reprinted, Black women scholars teaching the novel in English and Black studies classes, and Robert Hemenway's 1977 biography of Hurston.[36]

Alice Walker understood the forces of exclusion at work: in the early 1970s, she made a point of recommending Hurston's writings to several Black men writers and scholars and telling each of them, "Of course you know Zora—and all women, especially if they were black—had great problems being a writer." She then recorded each of their dismissive comments in her journal. The responses include novelists Ernest Gaines and James Alan McPherson saying they've never read Hurston's work despite Walker's recommendation and despite being asked at public events about connections between Hurston's fiction and their own.[37] These dimissals further spurred Walker on to act as Hurston's fierce posthumous advocate. She found and marked Hurston's grave in 1973 and, that same year, gave June Jordan a copy of *Their Eyes Were Watching God*.[38] In a 1974 issue of *Ms.* magazine, Walker wrote about her journey to claim Hurston as a literary foremother and to find and mark her grave site. Jordan's essay about *Their Eyes* and *Native Son*, "Notes Toward a Black Balancing of Love and Hatred," appeared alongside an essay by Mary Helen Washington about *Their Eyes* in *Black World* in 1974. The two essays show that the recovery of *Their Eyes*, though spearheaded by Walker, was a collaborative effort of Black women writers and intellectuals. Jordan celebrates Hurston's novel for representing "the happiness of an all-Black town/universe" in 1974 when "increasing numbers of us deem an all-Black circumstance/nation as our necessary, overriding goal."[39] Jordan articulates a Black feminist cultural nationalism rooted in her study of Hurston's novel, and her analysis exemplifies a trait that came to characterize Black feminist literary scholarship: reading fiction and poetry as theories of identity.

Black feminists' writings about Hurston show how they engaged in the 1970s and '80s in a tricky balancing act of celebrating individual writers who were gaining ground while also advocating for a broader array of Black women writers. Although her own work was central to the increased visibility of Black women's novels by the early 1980s, Morrison remained concerned about the narrow focus in the literary marketplace on one Black woman writer at a time. She told Judith Wilson in an *Essence* interview in 1981,

> When I publish Toni Cade Bambara, when I publish Gayl Jones, if they would do what my own books have done [in sales], then I would feel really fantastic about it. But the market can only receive one or two [Black women writers]. Dealing with five Toni Morrisons would be problematic. I'm not talking about the quality of work—who writes better than I do and stuff. I'm just talking about the fact that, in terms of new kinds of writing, the marketplace receives only one or two Blacks in days when it's not fashionable.[40]

These conditions of "the market" and its inability to grapple with "five Toni Morrisons" at once were factors in all Black women writers' careers. Bambara and Jones absolutely achieved the level of "quality," if not the number of books or sales, of Morrison's body of work. Black women writers were arguably "fashionable" in the 1980s, but even then, only one or two at a time. Morrison is pointing out that this idea of a small market for books by Black authors was pervasive in publishing and treated as common sense even though, as her own success as both an editor and novelist shows, it was not true. The persistence of racism and white dominance in both publishing and the academy explains, in part, the differences in prominence among Sisterhood members. During the renaissance of Black women writers and continuing in the present, publishers treat visible success in terms of sales or prizes as evidence of a dramatic increase of books by Black writers being published. However, these exceptions actually reveal the status quo of white writers dominating publishing.[41]

The stakes of celebrating one Black writer at a time remain high.[42] As Michele Wallace pointed out in 1991, *Beloved*'s "very warm critical reception by the mass media and book industry" in 1987 and 1988 did not produce "commensurate changes in the status or condition of black women in general," and while Morrison's exceptional success might suggest that "black women writers are now enjoying a certain vogue as publishable authors," that claim conceals how few Black women writers actually benefited.[43] The path to success was narrow and required massive collaborative labor to create an audience, from Margo Jefferson's reviews of Morrison's early novels in the 1970s, to Alice Walker and other Sisterhood members teaching Morrison's books in some of the first college courses on Black women writers, to Judith Wilson's 1981 profile of Morrison in *Essence* and Toni Cade Bambara's regular private correspondence offering Morrison sympathy, support, and humor. Morrison's position depends on her stunning literary achievements *and* on the network of support that included The Sisterhood and a broader group of Black writers and intellectuals who, understanding the limits of the marketplace, choose collectively to elevate her.

About a decade after the last meeting of The Sisterhood and two months after *Beloved* did not receive the National Book Award (NBA), forty-eight African American writers signed an open letter protesting the fact that Morrison had not won an NBA or a Pulitzer. The letter was "the brainchild of poet June Jordan" and it made the news even before being published in the *New York Times*.[44] In an article of January 19, 1988, Edwin McDowell reported that signatories would include Maya Angelou, Amiri Baraka, John Edgar Wideman, John A. Williams, and Henry Louis Gates, Jr., and that the letter would be printed in the newspaper on January 24. June Jordan and Houston Baker wrote a "companion piece" to the letter that was both a tribute to Morrison and a lament that James Baldwin had not won an NBA or a Pulitzer.[45] The sting of Baldwin being among Black writers slighted by prize committees was sharp in January 1988, just two months after his death.[46] Wideman described the letter as "No. 1, a tribute" and "No. 2, an announcement that a group of black writers, thinkers and intellectuals can speak collectively. There are times and occasions when that group needs to speak out on issues."[47] These writers, led by Jordan (a poet) and Baker (a scholar), used their collective platform to express sorrow and fury that Baldwin had not won a major national writing prize and insist that Morrison must receive overdue recognition.

Jordan and Baker's statement and the open letter appeared together in the Sunday Book Review section of the *Times*. The statement includes the devastating lines, "And so we have buried this native son, Jimmy Baldwin, with a grief that goes beyond our sorrow at his death. We also grieve for every black artist who survives him in this freedom land. We grieve because we cannot yet assure that such shame, such national neglect will not occur again, and then again."[48] Jordan and Baker describe a lineage of African American writers and a long history of their neglect by a racist American literary establishment: "From that actual and emblematic death we turn, determined, to the living."[49] In sermonic lines, the statement "shame[s]" prize-granting committees whose failure to honor Baldwin amounted to "national neglect." Baker and Jordan used this shame and the gravity of death to establish the unimpeachable collective authority of the writers who chose Morrison to represent "the living."

The open letter, printed just below Jordan and Baker's statement, begins forcefully: "Despite the international stature of Toni Morrison, she has yet to receive the national recognition that her five major works of fiction entirely deserve: she has yet to receive the keystone honors of the National Book Award or the Pulitzer Prize. We, the undersigned black critics and black writers, here assert ourselves against such oversight and harmful whimsy." The letter made in 1988 a claim could have come straight out of a 1960s Black Arts manifesto: "The legitimate need for our own critical voice in relation to our own literature can no longer be denied."[50] In a very Baldwinian move, these lines, with Jordan and Baker's statement, ask white readers of the *Times* and predominantly white national prize committees to understand that their racial homogeneity and lack of expertise about Black writing make them inadequate to the task of judging American literature.

In its second half, the letter changes its tone and audience, speaking directly to Morrison with love: "You have advanced the moral and artistic standards by which we must measure the daring and love of our national imagination and our collective intelligence as a people. Your gifts to us have changed and made more gentle our real time together. And so we write, here, hoping not to delay, not to arrive, in any way, late with this, our simple tribute to the seismic character and beauty of your writing."[51]

The letter did two important things: shamed the white literary establishment for failing to recognize Morrison and bestowed upon her laurels from Black writers and intellectuals. This group was a broad coalition; the fact that these particular people came together was likely as moving for Morrison as the contents of the letter.

The forty-eight people who signed the *Times* letter were important Black intellectuals and writers, including Sisterhood members Vertamae Grosvenor, Rosa Guy, June Jordan, Paule Marshall, and Alice Walker.

Houston A. Baker Jr., Henry Louis Gates, Jr., and Arnold Rampersad were each writing field-defining scholarship about African American literature. Scholars Barbara Christian, Paula Giddings, Calvin Hernton, Nellie McKay, Hortense Spillers, Eleanor Traylor, and Mary Helen Washington were transforming the possibilities of literary scholarship with specifically Black feminist methods, terms, and objects of study. Other signatories were Black women novelists, poets, editors, and activists Maya Angelou, Toni Cade Bambara, Lucille Clifton, Jayne Cortez, Angela Davis, Thulani Davis, Alexis De Veaux, Mari Evans, Nikky Finney, Cheryll Y. Greene, Gloria T. Hull, Louise Meriwether, Louise Patterson, Sonia Sanchez, and Joyce Carol Thomas.

The signatories had a shared investment in Black literature and culture, but they came together from different spheres and across generations. Margaret Wilkerson, then director of African American studies at the University of California, Berkeley, was an expert in Black dance and theater and would soon go on to serve as director of media arts and culture for the Ford Foundation. Nathan Irvin Huggins was in his sixties and well established as a distinguished historian in African American studies at Harvard. Poet Gale Jackson was thirty years old and about to see her first book, the coauthored volume of poetry *We Stand Our Ground*, in print. Richard Perry wrote novels, Jerome Brooks wrote books for children and young adults, Wesley Brown was a playwright, and professor and writer John A. Williams used formal experimentation to represent the past in his novels. Eugene Redmond was an established poet and had made an important scholarly contribution with *Drumvoices: The Mission of Afro-American Poetry: A Critical History* (1976). Luisah Teish was a spiritual teacher, dancer, and activist whose book *Jambalaya: The Natural Woman's Book of Personal Charms and Practical Rituals* (1985) was much loved and well used among Black women readers and writers. Poet Quincy Troupe had, among many other works, conducted what turned out to be the last interview with James Baldwin before Baldwin's death. J. California Cooper, John Edgar Wideman, and Sherley Anne Williams likely found Morrison's fiction compelling for its formally innovative engagement with the past. Each of them had recently written novels that, like *Beloved*, experiment with form to grapple with a history of enslavement.

A number of the signatories were Black men who had not necessarily supported earlier moments in the renaissance of Black women writers. Poet Amiri Baraka was an architect of the Black Arts Movement. Some of his early poetry was sexist, but by the 1980s he actively renounced that aspect of his work. He and his wife, the poet Amina Baraka, collaborated to edit the 1983 anthology *Confirmation: An Anthology of African American Women*, which included works by a number of Sisterhood members and was the first place of publication for Morrison's only short story, "Recitatif." Both Amina and Amiri Baraka signed the 1988 letter demanding recognition for Morrison. In the early 1970s, novelist Ernest J. Gaines had dismissed Alice Walker's insistence that Zora Neale Hurston was an important writer who must brought back into print and widely read.[52] In the late 1970s, Robert Allen (Walker's longtime romantic partner) was an editor at *The Black Scholar*, where he "had not defended [Walker's] essay/forum response to Robert Staples' sexist attack on Ntozake [Shange] and Michele Wallace."[53] Robert Chrisman, founder and publisher of *The Black Scholar*, had shepherded those attacks into print. Gaines, Allen, and Chrisman each decided to take part in the collective action by signing the letter in the *Times* in support and celebration of Morrison.

Five years before this letter, Alice Walker had won a National Book Award (then called the American Book Award) and a Pulitzer Prize for *The Color Purple*. When James Baldwin died without having received either honor and when Larry Heinemann's novel about a Vietnam veteran, *Paco's Story*, won the NBA over both *Beloved* and Philip Roth's *The Counterlife*, it was clear that the widespread acclaim for Walker's novel was an aberration, rather than a shift in the ways of the literary establishment. Black writers were especially bothered that Black woman novelist Gloria Naylor was on the NBA fiction committee that selected Heinemann's novel over Morrison's.[54] The Black writers and scholars who signed the *Times* letter came together from varied spheres to collectively assert that white prize-granting committees— even when they occasionally include one Black person—are not qualified to evaluate African American literature. In their collective statement, the signatories apply their expertise as people who do have the necessary knowledge. Recognizing the narrow confines of the marketplace, they put aside past differences and decided together that if there could be only one highly successful Black writer at a time, it would be this editor, literary organizer, scholar, and novelist, Toni Morrison.

The *Times* letter is not only a key moment in Morrison's career but also a turning point in African American literature and literary studies. The signatories used their collective cultural capital to push Black writing to the forefront of existing systems of power. Wideman's premise that "a group of black writers, thinkers and intellectuals can speak collectively" and "there are times and occasions when that group needs to speak out on issues" repeats and reinforces the Black Arts Movement claim that African American cultural production must be evaluated on its own terms by scholars, readers, and editors who understand it in the context of its specific traditions.[55] The letter offers Morrison "our simple tribute to the seismic character and beauty of your writing" from Black thinkers who write, teach, and study Black writing. The tribute is meaningful because it comes from people with expertise.

As a public statement made in 1988 in a mainstream white newspaper, the letter uses what looks like a Black Arts stance not to advocate for the cultural nationalism of BAM, but rather to hasten the incorporation of African American literature into existing U.S. institutions. This was a specific, forceful contemporary moment of understanding Black writing as excellent on its own terms while also seeking recognition for it from white institutions. That meant, to some extent, capitulating to the white literary establishment's tendency to accept only one Black writer at a time.

Morrison did not publicly express anger or disappointment about not receiving the National Book Award, nor did she ask her fellow Black writers and intellectuals to take action on her behalf. However, her disappointment and the outrage of her writer friends appeared in their personal correspondence. In a letter to Bambara in late 1987, Morrison writes that she did not realize how "bereft" she was at not receiving the NBA until she "spoke to June [Jordan]," who was "livid" about it. Morrison reports that she is feeling better after receiving a note from Bambara, and "all sorts of calls from my friends and even people who never give me the time of day saying something sweet." Morrison jokes about Black women not wanting to ask for help and expresses anger not for herself, but on behalf of *Beloved*'s characters: "it began to seem to me that Sethe and Paul D and Baby S and Stamp and Ella . . . were whooping because they had got the shaft."[56]

Morrison's friends and colleagues understood her not winning the NBA or Pulitzer by 1988 as part of a longer history of white American literary organizations, readership, and award committees failing to recognize Black writing. In the years and months prior to the *Times* letter, the importance of publication, publicity, and celebration of Black writing runs through letters to and from Morrison. Three years earlier, Henry Louis Gates, Jr., wrote to Morrison that Harriet Wilson's 1859 autobiographical novel *Our Nig*, which Gates had recently brought back into print and identified as the first known novel by an African American woman, was "nominated for a Pulitzer, but I/we won't get one."[57] Gates's "I/we" refers to himself and Wilson, but also more broadly to a pattern of African American writers being overlooked by prize committees. Lack of recognition for African American literature, including Morrison's novels, continued to anger Gates and others. A few weeks before the letter appeared in the newspaper, Gates wrote to Morrison, "I just wanted you to know how brilliant I think *Beloved* is and how pissed I am at that you did not get the National Book Award."[58]

In addition to addressing a broad public on behalf of Morrison's writing, the *Times* letter was part of an effort to publicly express appreciation for Morrison's work as a writer and an advocate for African American literature. In a televised interview shortly after the letter was printed, June Jordan and Houston Baker described it as both to and for Morrison, who appeared in the broadcast with them. Jordan said, "We wanted to really make clear to Toni our gratitude and we wanted to do that specifically in relationship to *Beloved*, but also in acknowledgement of the meaning of the life work of Toni Morrison." Baker echoed, "Our goal was to say 'we love you Toni and you are doing extraordinary work for us.'" This was meaningful to Morrison as coming from Black people, who were always the subject of and intended audience for her work. In the television interview, she says that the letter in the *Times* "is easily the most significant thing that has ever happened to me in my writing life. I write out of the culture, as everyone does, for it, through it, and in it, so a portion of that culture has said to me, 'Amen.'"[59]

In April 1988, four months after the open letter appeared in the *Times*, Morrison won the Pulitzer Prize for fiction. Though her most recent work, *Beloved*, contributed mightily, the Pulitzer is awarded for a body of work and thus recognized her earlier novels as well. Morrison went on to win many other awards, including the Nobel Prize for Literature in 1993.[60] This recognition is deserved, and The Sisterhood and a broader network helped create an informed readership for Morrison's novels. With the letter, former Sisterhood members and other Black writers and intellectuals chose Morrison to occupy a position as a singularly prominent African American writer. They chose Morrison because she had been serving and elevating Black writing in her work as editor for two decades, because she had written five beautiful and important novels, and because the racism of her not winning prestigious national awards was undeniable after *Beloved*. The *Times* letter called for "our own critical voice in relation to our own literature" and then used that "critical voice" to elevate Morrison.[61] The endeavor was wildly successful. Baker and Jordan's 1988 preface to the letter asserted, "Today, all the literate world knows Toni Morrison." This remains true in the twenty-first century.

For the forty-eight signatories, the act of collaborating publicly to demand recognition for *Beloved* established their investment in the novel as shared intellectual ground for their own thinking and for African American literary studies for decades to come. They viewed *Beloved* as especially important because its treatment of slavery participated in a literary lineage from the slave narratives of the antebellum era to the present. In 1988, connecting the novel to those earlier works became an important way to argue for a specific and distinct African American literary tradition that requires its own experts. Elevating *Beloved* was useful in establishing survey courses in African American literature as a standard offering because everyone seemed to agree that it was a massively important novel and because it was deeply connected to Black literature and history, which were rarely taught or understood in white education.

Like Morrison, *Beloved* occupies an exceptional position, which means that the attention it received depended on the exclusion of many other books. Focusing on one writer and one book obscured the diversity of African American literature. In the cases of Morrison the author and *Beloved* the novel, an exceptionalist view depended on both white scholars and critics' bad-faith misreadings *and* on Black writers' good-faith collaborative support. The *Times* letter and Pulitzer Prize in 1988, white scholars and critics' treatment of Morrison as exceptional, the Nobel Prize for Literature in 1993, and the *Times*'s own 2006 poll estimating the importance of the novel all reinforced *Beloved* as a canonical text of American literature.

In tandem with the literary achievement of Morrison's novels, the *Times* letter and Morrison's subsequent major awards helped put her and *Beloved* at the center of African American literature and literary studies. The emphasis on *Beloved* ended up making slavery even more central to Black studies than it had been before 1988. Stephen Best describes the lasting effects of *Beloved* in the academy as "directing attention within black studies straight toward the slave past and diaspora."[62] For African American literary studies, this meant focusing on the idea of a continuum proceeding chronologically from antebellum slave narratives to contemporary narratives of slavery like *Beloved*.[63]

Contemporary narratives of slavery are works of fiction that, in the decades since the civil rights movement, take up enslavement as a primary theme and have enslaved Black Americans as their primary characters. These narratives theorize the meanings of the past in the present, particularly the meanings of slavery and its aftermath for Black Americans.[64] Some, such as Margaret Walker's *Jubilee* (1966) and Sherley Anne Williams's *Dessa Rose* (1986), are set in the antebellum period and use literary conventions of nineteenth-century slave narratives such as first-person narration, detailed descriptions of brutal separation of enslaved mothers from their children, arguments for abolition, a literacy narrative, and a story of escape and fugitivity. Others, such as Octavia Butler's *Kindred* (1979) and Mat Johnson's *Pym* (2011), use conventions of science and speculative fiction to illuminate the brutal absurdity of slavery. Still others, such as Paule Marshall's *The Chosen Place, the Timeless People* (1969) and David Bradley's *The Chaneysville Incident* (1981), describe contemporary people learning histories of slavery to make sense of the present. The only contemporary narrative of slavery that reached even close to the number of people who have read *Beloved* is Alex Haley's *Roots*, both the novel in 1976 and the television miniseries, which drew a record-breaking number of viewers a few months later in 1977.[65]

Best describes the exceptional effects of *Beloved*, "It would not be going too far to add that [Morrison's] winning of the Nobel Prize in Literature in 1993 positioned *Beloved* to go on to shape the way an entire generation of scholars conceived of its ethical relationship to the past . . . a novel managed to set the terms of the political and historiographical agenda. The rise of *Beloved* moved the entire field of literary studies to a central place within African American studies."[66] He argues that the idea that "the slave past" can be apprehended has shaped Black studies in ways that limit its lines of inquiry and objects of study. Because there is no such thing as a single, clear "slave past" that can be fully understood or perceived, this is a poor foundation for collectivity. A collective Black "we" has been the goal of much African American literature and literary study, and Best explores the impossibility of that "we." Although his suspicion of recovery and collectivity pushes against the Black feminist imperatives that motivate the work of The Sisterhood and this book, his observations about *Beloved* acutely describe the novel's remarkable influence on the academy. Best is attuned to dangers of exceptionalism that shaped the novel's reception. *Beloved* "moved the entire field of literary studies to a central place within African American studies," but that was possible only because Black feminist literary critics had already spent decades defining African American studies and making a place for the field at colleges and universities.

As with the recuperation of Zora Neale Hurston, Black feminist literary criticism is committed to recovering of out-of-print and understudied works. Black feminist literary criticism also asserts that Black women theorize identity, systems of power, and understandings of history in literature (rather than only in nonfiction or academic writings). It rejects binary thinking and instead takes a both/and stance that accepts multiple, sometimes seemingly conflicting ideas or sources of knowledge as true. This work of recovering Black women's writing, treating that writing as a source of valuable knowledge, and maintaining both/and thinking allows critics to attend to intersecting vectors of identity such as race, class, gender, and sexuality and to consider African American women's writings as a specific tradition.

Best is right that *Beloved* went "on to shape the way an entire generation of scholars conceived of its ethical relationship to the past," especially in the sense that the recovery imperative aimed at bringing out-of-print and understudied texts to students and readers came increasingly to include the notion of recovery of a past defined by racial chattel slavery. This is a redefinition of "recovery" as The Sisterhood's generation of intellectuals understood it. *Beloved* "set the terms of the political and historiographical agenda" in a way that few, if any other novels have. Aida Levy-Hussen writes,

> For many critics, *Beloved* is the exemplar of black fiction's historical turn: it is the book that taught us how to read as we read now. Its lesson is construed variously, as the necessary or dangerous command, or the inscription of the impossible wish, that literary encounters with the slave past will compel a reparative catharsis for the contemporary reader. More fundamentally, *Beloved* is regarded as *the* unparalleled cultural text that confirms the register of trauma and the topic of slavery as the foremost concerns of black literary study.[67]

The uses of *Beloved* that Best and Levy-Hussen illuminate had a major impact not only on literary studies by also on Black studies as an interdisciplinary field.

Although *Beloved* occupies an exceptional place, the novel is very much part of long-standing practices in African American literature of theorizing identity, exploring meanings of the past in the present, remembering and memorializing, and offering solace. Morrison's contemporary narrative of slavery resonates so strongly because it simultaneously represents and declares unrepresentable the horrors of enslavement and other racist violence.

Beloved was able to set agendas and direct scholarly inquiry partly because Black feminist literary critics wrote articles and books, gave talks, and taught classes that asserted the novel's relationship to an existing tradition of African American literature. This work includes Nellie Y. McKay's edited volume *Critical Essay on Toni Morrison* (1988), Trudier Harris's *Fiction and Folklore: The Novels of Toni Morrison* (1991), Karla Holloway's *Moorings and Metaphors: Figures of Culture and Gender in Black Women's Literature* (1991), P. Gabrielle Foreman's "Past-on Stories: History and the Magically Real, Morrison and Allende on Call" (1992) in *Feminist Studies*, and Nell Irvin Painter's essay "Long Divisions" (2017) in *The New Republic*. These scholars ensured the life of the novel by celebrating and illuminating *Beloved* in its literary, political, and historical contexts.

A significant number of the "entire generation of scholars" that Stephen Best refers to were signatories of the *Times* letter. The letter is a document of their intellectual investment in *Beloved*, which didn't stop in 1988. Many continued to write about and teach the novel, and they trained younger generations of scholars to do the same. They, and many teachers of African American literature today, are choosing again and again to and invest in *Beloved* as an indispensable text, following in the footsteps of June Jordan, Houston Baker, and the signatories to the 1988 *Times* letter.

∼

Morrison's public persona also played an important role in the reception of her books and her place in American letters. Later in life, she regularly described "Toni Morrison" as a creation distinct from her self, whom she called by her given name, Chloe Wofford. A 2012 article in *The Guardian* quotes Morrison as saying, "That's right. And I have separated those people. My self is kind of split. My name is Chloe. And the rest is . . . that other person. Who is able to feel, or pretends to feel, or maybe really feels, or at least *reacts* to celebrityhood."[68] In a *New York Magazine* profile the same year, she says, "For the public, I have to be very severe—just keep it at bay. Otherwise they just devour you."[69] This notion of a valuable, private self that must be protected appears in other late interviews. In 2015, Morrison told Farah Jasmine Griffin, "I can't imagine that public self as the be-all for me."[70] In the documentary *Toni Morrison: The Pieces I Am* (2019), she says that using the names "Toni" and "Chloe" "is a way of dividing your life. One of those names is the person who is out there and the other one is the one who isn't, who doesn't do documentaries."[71] Morrison laughs as she says this, poking fun at the documentary even as she participates in it. She delights in keeping "Chloe" to herself as she puts "Toni" "out there," showing that this "split" is not only about being "severe" and self-protecting but also about the pleasure of having a private life as a person for whom a "public self" would never be the primary goal.

The public got a peek into Morrison's private self after her passing in Edwidge Danticat's 2019 eulogy. Danticat used the occasion of celebrating Toni Morrison to describe Chloe Wofford. Speaking to a huge number of people, those gathered at Morrison's memorial and the many others who would later watch, listen to, or read her remarks, Danticat created intimacy, just as Morrison had thirty years earlier at James Baldwin's memorial, by speaking directly to the person she was honoring: "You have giggled when you laughed and you had a twinkle in your eye when you were in the presence of someone whose company you enjoyed. You drank vodka on a cold day, just the really good stuff, and smoked cigarettes at the Louvre."[72] This Toni Morrison, this Chloe Wofford, is instantly recognizable to her closest friends. It is the Morrison who took Angela Davis on a writing retreat to Cuba so that she could complete the autobiography Morrison persuaded her to write.[73] It is the Morrison of loving, witty, playful letters to and from Toni Cade Bambara. Danticat says to Morrison: "You were the literary giant that is Toni Morrison, but you were also Chloe Wofford and you allowed me to see them both, for which I will always be grateful."[74]

Morrison spoke openly about the necessity of maintaining a "public self" more readily in her last years, but a careful negotiation of public and private was on her mind from the start of her career as a novelist and was as necessary for her writing as it was for her private life. In 1976, Jessica Harris describes Morrison as "extremely willing" to promote books she has edited but "reluctant" to promote her own work through "television guests spots, autographic tours" or other public appearances.[75] Morrison tells Harris, "I have seen 'media madness' become a disease. If I expect to write true books, I must have true feelings and perceptions of things. If I lose a part of myself to the press or the public, then I've lost a lot of myself. You can feel it. You become your name in caps."[76] Morrison protected herself and her writing partly by ensuring that the "name in caps" wasn't Chloe Wofford.

The Bluest Eye (1970) opens with a phrase that is cited regularly in scholarship about Morrison's novels: "quiet as its kept." In 1988, Morrison described this "familiar phrase" as introducing a "conspiratorial" "secret," "illicit gossip," and "intimacy." She says of *The Bluest Eye*, "In some sense it was precisely what the act of writing the book was: the public exposure of a private confidence . . . The publication (as opposed to the writing) involved the exposure; the writing was the disclosure of secrets, secrets 'we' shared and those withheld from us by ourselves and by the world outside the community."[77] As she wrote her first novel, Morrison was keenly aware of the fact that she was telling "secrets," both in the "public exposure" of Black life to a white audience and in sharing things "withheld from us by ourselves" in her examination of matters such as incest and internalized racism that *The Bluest Eye* addresses. Despite this "exposure," Morrison did not face quite the same kind of vitriolic and public backlash that plagued Ntozake Shange, Alice Walker, and Michele Wallace in the 1970s and '80s.

There are several possible reasons that Morrison endured fewer public misogynist attacks that some of her peers. The public Toni Morrison was protective; she deployed her public persona in a way that shielded Chloe Wofford. From her 1971 *New York Times* editorial "What the Black Woman Thinks About Women's Lib" to her exploration of Black beauty and intraracial colorism in her last novel, *God Help the Child* (2015), Morrison did Black feminist work. However, unlike Shange, Walker, Wallace, and Angela Davis, she did not usually call herself a feminist and was outspoken and precise about the ways that white feminism offered little that was useful to Black women. Her turn away from publicly identifying herself as a feminist was an example of her consistent precision and racial specificity: she wrote for and about Black women and she understood feminism as being about white women. Not calling herself a feminist insulated Morrison from some of the misogynist anger that her fellow writers who did claim that term faced. Morrison was almost certainly less inclined than some of her peers to talk publicly about the attacks on her work and herself that she endured in private. She was also somewhat protected by her stature. The admiration of many writers and scholars exemplified by the 1988 *Times* letter, the number of readers Morrison reached, and the respect she earned as an accomplished editor all meant that any backlash against her would be going against a consensus view.

Morrison's trajectory shows the shifting ways she understood herself and identified publicly over time. With the 1977 publication of *Song of Solomon*, she began to think of herself as primarily a novelist, rather than primarily an editor. In the 2010s, she began to speak candidly about "Toni Morrison" as a carefully constructed public persona. In addition to being an editor, novelist, and public intellectual, Morrison also claimed her place as a literary critic. In each of these roles, she celebrated and called attention to the works of many Black writers. Morrison wrote, "From the beginning, I claimed a territory by insisting on being identified as a black woman writer exclusively interested in the facets of African American culture. I made these unambiguous assertions to impose on all readers the visibility in and the necessity of African American culture to my work precisely in order to encourage wider critical vocabulary than the one in which I was educated."[78]

Like many other women in her Black feminist cohort, beginning in the 1980s, Morrison shifted a significant portion of her labor into the academy, where she helped create a "critical vocabulary" for the study of the African American literary tradition. The Sisterhood's collaborative work and Morrison's ascendance have set terms, possibilities, and limits for the study of African American literature and Black feminism in ways that scholars, critics, and readers are still grappling with today.

Chapter Seven

"MAKING USE OF BEING USED"

During the 1970s, Black women writers, reviewers, editors, and literary agents got Black women writers published, publicized, read, and better understood. The 1980s saw much of this substantial and demanding labor move into the academy, where Black women scholars had been breaking new ground. Former members of The Sisterhood and other collectives brought lessons learned in those groups to their research and writing, service, and teaching. As administrators, they helped create and sustain Black studies departments. Their scholarly writing, novels, short stories, plays, and poetry all helped establish Black feminism in the academy. The influence of their teaching is more difficult to measure, but it is a central component of The Sisterhood's lasting impact.[1]

June Jordan was immersed in the student activism that would shape The Sisterhood's political, literary, and academic work when she wrote her 1969 essay "Black Studies: Bringing Back the Person." She explains that the open admissions movement at The City University of New York succeeded in getting more Black and Latinx students than ever before enrolled in college in New York City. The energy, excitement, and effectiveness of that movement defined Jordan, Ntozake Shange, Audre Lorde, and Toni Cade Bambara's earliest experiences as college teachers. Lorde brought soup to students on strike at City College, and Shange held Black studies classes at Northeastern off campus until the university fully supported the department. These actions were practices of community simultaneously within and against a university context.

A sense of possibility shaped Sisterhood members' investment in academia for decades. Like the Black women writers of The Sisterhood, many Black feminist intellectuals were shaped by that late 1960s moment, which made it clear that student protests could make institutional change. Mary Helen Washington could have been speaking for many scholars of her cohort when she said, "My entrance into this academic world was by way of Black militancy," in her case, in response to "the 1967 Detroit rebellion" that happened while she was working on her doctorate at the University of Detroit. Washington is among a generation of Black women who chose literary study as the way to continue working for racial justice. Reflecting on her career in 2021, she said of the early years of Black studies, "All of this excitement was, in some ways, about how to transform Black communities. It wasn't about how we will make Black PhDs. That came later. And thank God it did come later because that was one way of continuing the work."[2] An obligation to "Black communities" and an element of "Black militancy" remained at the heart of the discipline, even as training graduate students became part of the work.

June Jordan and other Sisterhood members, like Washington, channeled their labor into colleges and universities to fulfill obligations to their communities, exercise their political commitments, and gain institutional authority for Black studies. In preacherly cadence, Jordan writes, "Black American history prepared Black students to seize the possibilities of power even while they tremble about purpose." She proposes that the study of African American history and literature is necessary for "the engineer, the chemist, the teacher, the lawyer, the architect," and especially "if he is Black."[3] The premise that Black studies makes people better equipped for life and able to act more justly, no matter their profession, remains a fundamental belief among many people who study and teach African American literature and history.

Many who teach African American literature year after year to hundreds of undergraduates do so because we believe what Jordan and other Sisterhood members believed: that getting students to read Black writing thoroughly is the way we can best foment racial justice. A college student who goes on to become a real estate agent or mortgage broker will be able to serve racial justice in those jobs if she has studied how racism and sexism determine the location and quality of housing available to Lutie Johnson and her son Bub in Ann Petry's novel The Street (1946). One who becomes a lawyer will be prepared to face the racism in the U.S. legal system if she has studied the many scenes in *Narrative of the Life of Frederick Douglass, An American Slave, Written by Himself* (1845) that show how the exclusion of Black people from the legal system resulted in white people being unpunished and unashamed as they assault and murder African Americans. A grade-school teacher who has studied traumatic moments of racial recognition in W. E. B. Du Bois's *The Souls of Black Folk* (1903), James Weldon Johnson's *The Autobiography of an Ex-Colored Man* (1912), or Zora Neale Hurston's *Their Eyes Were Watching God* (1937) will be prepared to mitigate or even prevent such moments among her young students. The citizen who has studied Ida B. Wells's *A Red Record* (1895) will understand current police brutality as part of systemic racist state violence and will have a set of strategies for documenting, working to understand, and resisting that violence.

African American literature can also provide solace, inspiration, and laughter, all necessary to sustain the long fight for justice and freedom. A Black feminist classroom can be a sustaining site of fun and pleasure for both students and teachers. The teaching I describe above is the heavy work of using literature to expose and explode unequal power relations in the world and, as Toni Cade Bambara often put it, to "make revolution irresistible."[4] Mecca Jamilah Sullivan captures the fact that this kind of teaching is also undeniably fun: writers including Bambara and Audre Lorde "exemplify the queer poetics of Black feminist literary pedagogy," and their teaching and writing "topples hierarchies and power structures with creative flare [*sic*], inserts new visions of joy and connection into the spaces disruption has unearthed and insists that we learn from them." In their classroom practices and their fiction and poetry, "pleasure is palpable" and crucial to teaching and learning. Sullivan, following Bambara, calls these "pedagogies of the irresistible" that happen in and beyond the classroom.[5] Every teacher who believes that literature is a tool for Black liberation and that every student needs such tools is participating in The Sisterhood's legacy. Many of them, despite the countless obstacles to Black feminist thought in academic settings, are able to keep on doing this work because of the fun and pleasure in "pedagogies of the irresistible."

∾

The slow institutionalization of Black feminism in the academy began over a decade after late 1960s campus demonstrations and around the time that The Sisterhood and other Black women's groups stopped officially meeting.

Combahee River Collective cofounder Barbara Smith, like other Black feminist thinkers of this period, turned her daily labor from organizing to scholarly writing. In a 1979 letter to Audre Lorde, Smith wrote that although she
was concerned about the depiction of Black feminism in the issue of *Ms.* that
featured Michele Wallace and *Black Macho and the Myth of the Superwoman*,
she was not going to formally respond because she was "Working quite consciously now on my dissertation and that's a priority."[6] Other Black feminist
intellectuals made this same move "quite consciously" in the 1980s to teach,
write, and lecture in academic contexts.

The women's relationships to academia varied, but all of them believed
that Black feminist thought and writing could survive at colleges and universities over the long term. They recognized that political organizations,
even important ones like the National Black Feminist Organization, could
come and go over just a handful of years. They also knew that even though
they had made Black feminist writing central to some magazines, especially
Ms. and *Essence*, magazines are necessarily ephemeral and at the mercy
of market considerations. In the 1980s, Black women writers and scholars
made their books and classrooms sites where Black feminist thought and
organizing could take root and thrive. Moving away from the reactive, often
short-term, and highly visible political organizing of the 1960s and the less
visible but briefly very effective literary organizing of the '70s, Black women
hoped to make permanent change in academic institutions by solidifying
Black studies and African American literary studies with Black feminism at
the center of both.

Members of The Sisterhood were students and teachers when the first
classes in African American literature were being taught in the 1970s through
the canon wars of the 1980s and '90s, and into the twenty-first century.
Sisterhood members who taught at colleges and universities advocated for
Black literature and Black feminist thought. They also needed the relative
economic security of academic work. Those who took on full-time academic
positions were often integrating white universities and departments; they
continued to be in the exhausting position of being the only or one of just
a few Black people at their jobs. In rare instances, like VèVè Clark and June
Jordan at Berkeley, they had each other right there for support. Individual
Sisterhood members navigated academia in very different ways from one
another. They understood they were entering racist, sexist, homophobic
institutions, and they sought to make the institutions where they worked
more just, or to use them as a source of funds, infrastructure, and authority

to do Black feminist work outside those institutions. They inspired one another to imagine various kinds of professional paths: Patricia Spears Jones remembers Clark as "one of the first scholar-creatives I ever met," meaning that Clark used the relative economic security of a university job to make art and pursue collaborative projects, including flying east once a month to participate in Sisterhood meetings.[7] Erica Edwards writes, "Black feminist literary activism mounted counterinstitutionalization projects, in effect *making use of being used*, and radically opening the institutions they passed through not only to critique them but also to create anticapitalist, anticolonial, antiimperial possibilities within and alongside them."[8] The phrase "making use of being used" comes from Paule Marshall's recollection of going on a U.S. State Department tour in her memoir *Triangular Road* (2009) but is also a guiding principle for Sisterhood members, including Marshall, who put much of their labor into the academy. Here, I offer a few examples of the varying ways these Black women writers entered the academy and leveraged institutional power for Black feminist goals.

Ntozake Shange had intermittent short-term appointments at universities and managed to make Black women's writing prominent in academic settings without getting bogged down in administrative labor. Shange earned a master's in American studies and served briefly as director of the Afro-American Institute at Northeastern University. She kept her relationships with most schools temporary, from teaching at the University of Houston in the mid-1980s to many positions as a visiting writer or artist at other universities over the years. Ultimately, she exercised her Black feminist influence most forcefully not as a faculty member but rather as an alumnae at Barnard College, where her ties were deep and lasting. She graduated from Barnard in 1970 and regularly participated in events there throughout her career. Her papers are held in the Barnard library, and Shange is among the college's most celebrated graduates. This relationship enabled the gathering of Shange's extensive Black feminist literary archive at a women's college that has the resources to preserve the materials and make them accessible. The Barnard Center for Research on Women conducted a five-year project, "Digital Shange," that used her papers "to offer students a broader understanding of African diaspora, women's history and feminist politics; an integrated study of the performing arts; and the potential for personal transformation."[9] "Digital Shange" includes student projects from performances to websites to editing Wikipedia pages as well as several incarnations of Professor Kim Hall's undergraduate class "The Worlds of Ntozake Shange" and a special issue of the journal *Scholar and Feminist Online* also titled *The Worlds of Ntozake Shange*, edited by Hall, Monica Miller, and Yvette Christiansë.[10] Shange visited campus often over the years. In 2008, accompanied by Thulani Davis, she spoke to a packed house about her participation in demonstrations at Barnard and Columbia in 1968. From the college's 2013 symposium celebrating Shange's work until her death in 2018, five years of campus events are collectively named the Shange Magic Project.[11] Her influence continues to shape campus life, scholarly events, and course offerings at Barnard.[12]

Other Sisterhood members took a more traditional academic route. Judith Wilson started graduate school while The Sisterhood was meeting and went on to earn a PhD in art history from Yale. She successfully fought to teach the work of contemporary Black women visual artists in her many classes at Wesleyan, Pratt Institute, the University of Hartford, the University of Virginia, Yale, and the University of California at Irvine. She was tenured, earned the rank of full professor, published academic articles and exhibition catalogues, and remained on the faculty at UC Irvine until her retirement. Wilson offers an example of using an academic setting to conduct Black feminist research that will endure over time. As described in chapter 5, Wilson was writing insightfully about artist Lorraine O'Grady decades before O'Grady's first retrospective exhibit in 2021. Wilson wrote about O'Grady for the *Village Voice* in 1980 and later as an academic art historian in *Lorraine O'Grady: Critical Interventions* (1991), an important resource for the many people who first learned about O'Grady's work in recent years. Wilson has done the scholarly tasks of Black feminism by centering Black women artists in curricula and writing lasting, rigorous work that helps people more deeply understand some of those artists' works.

Audre Lorde brought Black feminist thought into the academy in several ways, from teaching courses on Black women writers at Lehman College and City College to helping establish a Black studies department at John Jay College of Criminal Justice.[13] She faced resistance at all three schools, including threatening anonymous letters. She concealed her lesbian identity because she worried that faculty and administrators at John Jay would foment homophobia in the campus community to undermine the founding of Black studies.[14] Lorde enjoyed more academic freedom and job security a few years later at Hunter College, as Distinguished Thomas Hunter Chair from 1981 to 1986. Her essays collected in *Sister Outsider* (1984) have become touchstones in the study of Black women's writing, queer theory, and Black feminism across disciplines. Lorde's work, particularly as it addresses the intersection of gender, race, and sexuality, currently occupies a prominent place in college classes in English; Black studies; ethnic studies; and women's, gender, and sexuality studies departments.

Alice Walker has located her work only partially in academic settings and has not taken on long-term employment at any one university. She has held appointments at HBCUs including Jackson State University and Tougaloo College; large public universities such as the University of Massachusetts at Boston; and small liberal arts schools such as Wellesley College. Walker maintained close, lasting friendships with academics including Robert Allen, Mary Helen Washington, and Howard Zinn. She has also consistently thought of academic institutions, especially Ivy League universities, as places that stifle creativity and authenticity. While teaching one course at Brandeis and regularly hanging out with both Washington and Zinn in the fall of 1982, Walker wrote in her journal, "A closer look at the Cambridge/Harvard scene made me joyful not to be there. Too much competition, acting & fear. People don't seem quite real." She later turned down an invitation to teach at Harvard for a semester, writing, "I couldn't imagine it. There is a stuffiness & a feeling of being trapped, even in the faculty club." In 1987, Walker wrote about Toni Morrison landing "a substantial position at Princeton," "I feel glad for her success. It isn't my kind of success . . . I know I couldn't stand Princeton for a day."[15] Walker kept her time on campuses brief, but her talks and writer-in-residence appointments allowed many students to have some direct contact with this prominent Black woman writer. Walker's essays, poetry, and novels—especially *The Color Purple*—are widely studied in academic settings. Zora Neale Hurston's *Their Eyes Were Watching God* (1937) is a regular part of American literature courses due in part to Walker's decades of work in print, films, and public lectures to emphasize Hurston's importance to the tradition. *The Color Purple* and *Their Eyes* are beloved, even sacred, texts for many readers, especially Black women.

Walker has maintained a large readership; her collection of essays *In Search of Our Mothers' Gardens* (1983) has stayed in print since it was published, and her recent book *Gathering Blossoms Under Fire: The Journals of Alice Walker* (2022), edited by scholar Valerie Boyd, was met with media coverage and acclaim, including a lengthy profile of Walker with excerpts and images from her journals in the *New York Times*. She continues to advocate for the power of reading and writing as "study" that does not depend on academic institutions. In 2021, even as she wondered amid a pandemic and worsening climate crisis, "Is there a future? . . . I'm not so sure we have a future," she continued to insist that "study" is the first and most urgent task, that we must "honor study" and read "to find wisdom and use it."[16] In other words, Walker has long been connected to the academy but not of it. Her notion of Black womanist "study," as in consciousness-raising groups and in The Sisterhood, does not depend on an academic setting.

June Jordan's Black feminist academic activism took many forms and was more rooted in academia than Walker's. She taught Black women's fiction and poetry to countless students, including at City College, Yale, and Stony Brook University, where she was promoted to full professor in the mid-1980s.[17] At Stony Brook, Jordan developed her courses "The Art of Black English" and "In Search of the Invisible Black Woman," which had a "large class" of students reading works by Black women writers, including *The Color Purple*.[18] Jordan wrote in detail about her work with students to "translate [the opening paragraphs of Walker's novel] into Standard English" to show the aesthetic value and specificity of Black English.[19] Her writing about pedagogy makes visible her classroom application of both the Black Arts tenet that Black writing must be evaluated according to its own criteria and The Sisterhood's commitment to Black women's writing as a distinct and important body of literature. From 1986 until her death in 2002, Jordan taught at the University of California, Berkeley, in the departments of English, African American studies, and women's studies.

Jordan navigated the academy to serve Black people's literature and liberation. She used her institutional affiliation and resources at Berkeley to establish the Poetry for the People Collective in 1991. Poetry for the People operated in and beyond the university as a writing workshop open to any student, a training ground for poetry teachers, a community organization that put on public readings and held fundraisers, and an outreach program that conducted poetry workshops in Berkeley's public schools, churches, and prisons.[20] Jordan established Poetry for the People as a project housed in, funded by, and staffed by the African American and African Diaspora Studies Department at UC Berkeley, where it continues today with "an academic focus on the reading, writing, and teaching of poetry" and programs to bridge "the gap between the university and the larger community, working with teens and young adults, schools, and community organizations, and activist projects in the greater Bay Area."[21] Jordan thus directed university resources into Black feminist literary organizing and to the study and creation of poetry by women, queer writers, Black writers, and other writers of color.

Poetry for the People lived up to its name; it advocated for all people to have access to poetry, as students, teachers, and writers. *June Jordan's Poetry for the People: A Revolutionary Blueprint* (1995), edited by Lauren Muller, documents the organization's work. Former Sisterhood members VèVè Clark and Ntozake Shange gave readings and workshops and contributed to Muller's volume. In creating Poetry for the People, Jordan continued The Sisterhood's efforts to balance practical matters and personal support, to advocate for writers, and to operate from a foundation of love for literature and each other. She relied on UC Berkeley's institutional resources, from spaces to meet and an annual operating budget to, as a professor, access to editors at Routledge, which published *June Jordan's Poetry for the People* alongside other titles by and for scholars and teachers.

The book both describes the collective's work and prescribes how others can continue that work. As it proclaims on the cover, it is "A Revolutionary Blueprint," a manual full of guidelines for poetry workshops, detailed instructions for fundraising and publishing, lists of tasks with timelines for organizing poetry readings, and suggested methods for outreach to elementary and high school students. The volume includes essays and poems by Jordan, Shange, Adrienne Rich, and other established poets as well as many essays and poems by a diverse group of writers who have participated in Poetry for the People as students, writers, teachers, and organizers. The book records the ways that Jordan spread Sisterhood principles and methods in the Bay Area—from The Sisterhood's practice of intellectual and culinary potluck to its careful negotiation of distributing the countless mundane labors needed to pull off a poetry reading, an anthology, or a class—giving others a "blueprint" to continue expanding the reach of this work.[22]

~

June Jordan and other Sisterhood members used their academic positions and institutional resources to support Black feminist books, thinking, and collaborations long after the group stopped meeting. As they were doing this work in the 1980s and '90s, Toni Morrison was using her platform to advocate for African American literature and Black studies, in her teaching, essays, and countless lectures on college campuses. She was a major intellectual who participated in debates over the literary canon and the direction of African American literary studies, and her novel *Beloved* firmly entered the canon of American literature and became a touchstone for Black studies.

In "Unspeakable Things Unspoken" (1988), a lecture she gave at the University of Michigan, Morrison called on scholars to "expand the traditional canon to include classic Afro-American works where generically and chronologically appropriate, and to devise strategies for reading and thinking about these texts."[23] This sounds like an argument for racially diversifying curricula in the 1980s, but Morrison is doing something more nuanced here. Her call was not primarily for incorporation into existing discourses. Like Alain Locke, Langston Hughes, Larry Neal, and many other Black thinkers before her, Morrison emphasized the ongoing need for specialists, arguing for "the development of a theory of literature that truly accommodates Afro-American literature: one that is based on its culture, its history, and the artistic strategies the works employ to negotiate the world it inhabits."[24] Morrison had an "intense interest in the development of African American literary criticism and pedagogy" that led her to use her roles as artist and academic to "help expand and deepen the arguments about the validity, necessity, and direction of African American scholarship," literary and otherwise.[25] Like other Black feminist scholars in the 1980s, she advocated for both the specific field of African American literary studies and the broader discipline of Black studies, asserting a principle that remains central to today: Black studies is its own thing and is also necessary to every other field of study. In practice, this means that Black studies requires autonomous academic departments able to hire faculty and award degrees, and it should reach into other areas and make science, social science, and humanities departments more racially just.

Morrison explains this dual place in the academy: "African American studies could, but need not, confine itself to itself because the project was like the so-called race problem itself. It was not a neighborhood thriving or struggling at the edge of campuses or at the outer rim of intellectual thought, nor was it an exotic, anthropologically interesting minority pulsing at the extremities of the body politic. It was and is at the heart of the heart of the nation."[26] At a moment when she was reaching more readers and listeners than ever, Morrison wrote and spoke about African American literature as a body of writing that requires both inclusion in existing canons and specialists trained to study, teach, and write about that specific tradition. By the early twenty-first century, she expanded the horizon of her assertions to make a similar claim about African American studies more broadly: it is a specific and distinct academic discipline that stands on its own and is important for every other academic discipline. In her vision for African American studies in the academy, Morrison applied both/and thinking, a central tenet of Black feminist thought.

Beloved is a paradigmatic example of how African American literature is both specific "to itself" and needed everywhere. In 1992, Morrison described the ways her novel was being taught in "twenty-three different subject-matter classes" at a "very large state university."[27] She acknowledges that the novel had been taken up by legal scholars, historians, literary scholars, political scientists, and others as "an all-purpose, highly serviceable source for some discourse in various disciplines and various genres and various fields," a "kind of shortcut to history."[28] The novel sated an intellectual hunger among students for the history of slavery, which is often absent from their education. Morrison transformed her extensive historical research into a compelling novel, so it was through fiction that many people learned that history.

It makes sense that *Beloved* and Morrison helped Black studies both get established as an autonomous academic discipline and reach into many other fields because the field of African American literature has an important place in the discipline of Black studies. Black women literary scholars were the driving force in establishing and maintaining Black studies departments throughout the 1970s, the 1980s, and beyond. A survey course in African American literature remains a requirement for most Black studies degrees, and many English departments have at least one expert in African American literature. Black studies and English departments were the most likely places for former Sisterhood members to find academic employment.

Even though some English departments had been or would prove welcoming to the study of African American literature, it was an uphill battle. Barbara Christian said that writing her indispensable first book, *Black Women Novelists* (1980), was possible only because she "was situated in an Afro-American studies rather than an English department, where not even the intercession of the Virgin would have allowed me to do research on black women writers."[29] At the University of California, Berkeley, Christian helped create and later chaired the African American studies department, and in 1978, she became the first Black woman at Berkeley to get tenure. Christian's commitment to the department and training in literary studies (she held a PhD in English from Columbia) were common among the Black women who brought their political and literary organizing into the academy in the 1980s.

Other scholars in this cohort worked in women's studies or ethnic studies departments. Beverly Guy-Sheftall describes Black feminists having to choose between Black studies and women's studies:

> During the late seventies, as the women's movement grew in momentum and as the Civil Rights Movement receded, it seemed, into the background, some Black women scholars left Black Studies or tried to infuse gender there—often a difficult enterprise. A few of us associated ourselves with Women's Studies and advocated loudly for paradigm shifts that would more adequately address race/class/ethnicity issues and eradicate frameworks that were constructed from the notion that "woman" is a monolithic category.[30]

Guy-Sheftall was among those who aligned themselves with women's studies. Black feminists who took this route were "few" because some women's studies departments institutionalized the racism of the 1970s women's liberation movement. As they got established at universities in the 1970s and '80s, many of these departments focused on the experiences of white, cisgender, straight women. A separation also came out of the fact that Black studies often gained institutional footholds through independent action rather than in coalition with women's and gender studies. Even at a school with both departments (almost every Ivy League university and many small liberal arts colleges) it is onerous to do academic service labor for more than one department or center. Decisions about a faculty member's tenure are often up to colleagues in traditional departments such as history, sociology, or English. This means that Black feminist academics officially appointed to those departments were (and are) taking on extra, uncompensated work to mentor students and junior faculty, organize talks and symposia, help apply for grants, or do other work to support Black studies and women's studies units, which (then and now) tend to be underfunded and understaffed compared to humanities departments such as English or history, and vastly under-resourced compared to social science and hard science departments, such as sociology and biology, respectively. Guy-Sheftall's words reflect the ways the complex relationships among academic disciplines operate differently at HBCUs. Being at Spelman, a Black women's college, has provided her with a strong base to do transformative Black studies work in women's studies and to create publication venues, archives, conferences, and classes that enable others to do the same kind of field-changing work.[31]

Women's studies may have been the best channel for institutionalizing Black feminist teaching and research at Spelman; at other schools, other departments or new methods of study were the route into academia for Black feminist teaching and research. Patricia Spears Jones observed the importance of cultural studies as part of this period of change: "I think between American studies, Black studies, Africana studies, and queer [studies], all kinds of people who had a master's and went on to get a PhD, then they could kind of start this move into cultural studies. I think cultural studies is a big deal here. I think that that kind of allowed a lot of Black thinkers into an academic space that might not have felt comfortable elsewhere."[32] This group of interdisciplinary fields and methods became visible in the academy in the 1980s and '90s and central to literary studies. Each turns away from or broadens the New Critical method of reading each work of literature in isolation with an exclusive focus on textual details. American studies, Black studies, queer studies, and cultural studies applied to literature have turned instead toward understanding every text and its particular details as produced in a set of historical, political, and social contexts. Each played a role in ushering "a lot of Black thinkers into an academic space," largely because each field and its methods focused on the ways that power works. For example, scholars Stuart Hall and Raymond Williams founded contemporary cultural studies at the University of Birmingham in the UK in 1964 in order to study, teach, and write about the roles of race, ethnicity, class, and gender in culture. Their definition of "culture" was broad, but it definitely included literature. In the 1980s and '90s, cultural studies gained ground in the United States in political science, history, sociology, and especially English departments. Black feminist intellectuals were also interested in power, identity, and culture, so the advent of this approach made a way for some of them to bring their ideas into the academy.

Alongside the development of new fields of study in the last two decades of the twentieth century, literary studies remained crucial to securing a lasting place for Black feminism in the academy. *The Norton Anthology of African American Literature* (*NAAAL*) is one important way that Black scholars, including many from The Sisterhood's cohort, changed the experience of countless students and teachers. *NAAAL* has, since its first edition in 1997, made undergraduate survey courses in African American literature possible and then standard in college English departments. In this sense, *NAAAL* shares the mission of anthologies from Alain Locke's *The New Negro* in 1925 to Toni Cade Bambara's *The Black Woman* in 1970 and Mary Helen

Washington's *Black Eyed Susans* in 1975: an anthology declares, by definition, that there is a distinct and coherent body of literature that must be studied as such. Collecting texts as a group in one place makes that kind of specific study possible. The *NAAAL* works much like Norton's anthologies of American literature, English literature, and world literature in the sense that the book both authorizes and enables survey courses. A Norton volume confers solidity and prestige; as Howard Rambsy puts it, "*The NAAAL* exudes indispensable symbolic capital and influence," such that being in the volume can shape an author's career, as when "inclusion in the anthology crucially assists poets in becoming part of canonical history."[33] Professors today do not need to replicate the photocopying of out-of-print works that Sisterhood members did so they could teach Black women's writing; the *NAAAL* has stayed in print through three editions, ready at hand with texts in chronological order and historical context for each period of African American literature from its beginnings to the present.

Neither the existence of the *NAAAL* nor the standardization of survey courses in African American literature was a foregone conclusion. Like every other success of Black studies, Black feminism, and African American literature charted in this book, creating the *NAAAL* was a battle that relied on the seemingly endless, daily, and often underrecognized work of Black women. Henry Louis Gates, Jr., served as general editor and shepherded the proposal for the volume through the process at with the publisher, W. W. Norton. Mary Helen Washington declined to join Gates in this work early on because "there were no other Black women" on board. A bit later, Nellie McKay joined Gates as general editor and helped bring in four other women—Barbara Christian, Frances Smith Foster, Deborah McDowell, and Hortense Spillers—each as editor of one of the chronological sections.[34] These women were already fierce, rigorous advocates for Black women's writing long before working on the *NAAAL*. From 1985 to 1993, McDowell's Black Women Writers' series at Beacon Press reissued fourteen out-of-print novels by African American women writers, including works by Alice Childress, Frances Harper, Ann Petry, Octavia Butler, and Gayl Jones.[35] This is just one example of scholarly and editorial labor akin to the efforts of The Sisterhood, but a particularly important one because of its lasting impact on which books by Black women scholars teach and study.

McKay understood the stakes, for both her career and her field, of having a leadership role with the *NAAAL* and getting McDowell, Christian, Foster, and Spillers to work on the anthology. As Shanna Benjamin narrates in

Half in Shadow, McKay took on the collaborative labor and the "day-to-day details to move the *NAAAL* forward" in ways that delayed her own writing and research but ensured that Black women's literature and Black women's expertise would define the book that remains the way countless students encounter African American literature every year.[36]

When the *NAAAL* came out in 1997, the first print run of 30,000 copies sold out rapidly, the volume went into a second printing, and Norton sold 72,717 copies by the end of that year. Henry Louis Gates, Jr., was getting calls from friends looking for a copy and Barbara Christian spotted copies at Costco.[37] This was just the first year of the anthology, which has unique reach and sales because a new crop of students purchases it each year for their African American literature courses.

Benjamin writes, "Now, more than twenty years after the publication of the first edition of the *NAAAL*, it seems almost inconceivable that there was ever a time when African American literature was not widely available to teachers, to scholars, and to the general public."[38] The third edition of *The Norton Anthology of African American Literature* (2014) is a popular textbook for college surveys of African American literature. My own experience is anecdotal, but instructive: I studied the first edition of the *NAAAL* as a college student majoring in English and African American studies in the late 1990s and have assigned the second and third editions to the forty students in my introductory survey of African American literature each of the roughly sixteen times I have taught that course as an English professor. My relationship with the *NAAAL* is fairly typical for a specialist in African American literature, particularly at a large public university.

The *Norton Anthology of African American Literature* is yet another example of the continuing influence of The Sisterhood: the second volume of the third edition includes the 1977 photo of the group and works by Sisterhood members June Jordan, Audre Lorde, Paule Marshall, Toni Morrison, Ntozake Shange, and Alice Walker. These writers were prolific, but in the difficult process of selecting which of their writings are most important for undergraduates to study, the editors of the *NAAAL* chose more works from the late 1970s and '80s period shaped by The Sisterhood's influence than from other periods of the authors' careers. The editors of the most current edition of the *NAAAL*, including Frances Smith Foster, Deborah McDowell, Valerie Smith, Hortense Spillers, and Cheryl Wall, continued Sisterhood work: they advocated for and made possible the study of Black women's writing on its own terms as part of a tradition of African American literature.

Literary scholars made the study of African American literature as a coherent tradition possible by creating and updating the *NAAAL*. In concert with these efforts, Black feminist scholars fought to make courses in Black women's writing standard offerings in English departments. They made Black women's intellectual traditions part of women's studies courses. They built Black studies departments. They hired Black faculty, recruited Black undergraduate and graduate students, and succeeded in making "Black feminism" and "intersectionality" common terms in academic settings.

∾

There were gains in the late twentieth century, but the story of Black feminism in the academy is also a story of compromise, co-optation, limits, and losses. Black feminist women changed the academy; academic institutions changed the meanings and uses of Black feminism. The afterlives of The Sisterhood in colleges and universities do not fit into easy binaries: their labor in educational institutions was not wholly radical or assimilationist and it was not entirely subversive or hegemonic; it was simultaneously all of these. Black feminist intellectuals made a place for Black women's writing and leveled critiques from within universities while also sustaining those institutions with their labor. They both resisted and were complicit with the capitalist, racist, misogynist, and homophobic institutions they worked in. This was and remains the bind for many Black feminist academics.[39]

These writers and scholars were sharply aware of the dangers of the institutionalization of African American literature and Black feminism as it was happening. In 1989, during the culture wars that were changing the American literary canon, but before the first edition of the *Norton Anthology African American Literature*, Barbara Christian wrote, "Canon formation has become one of the thorny dilemmas for the black feminist critic. Even as white women, blacks, people of color attempt to reconstruct that body of American literature considered to be *the* literature, we find ourselves confronted with the realization that we may be imitating the very structure that shut out our literatures in the first place."[40] Like Morrison working to get attention for many Black writers and simultaneously worrying about elevating one at a time, and like Michele Wallace working to bring Black feminism to a large audience and simultaneously worrying about the ways it might be co-opted into systems of oppression, Christian brought Black writers into "*the*" canon of American literature while also questioning the value of canon formation.

In the early 1990s, Barbara Christian and Nellie McKay wrote and spoke openly about what it meant for Black women to work in white universities. McKay wrote that, in the years following student uprisings of the late 1960s, "Few white institutions were interested in [Black scholars] other than for the calm they could bring to troubled campuses by way of Black Studies classes" and then, by the early 1990s, "a highly visible small group of brilliant, ambitious, achieving scholars now in well-placed positions in a few institutions signal no major changes in the general status of black women or men in higher education."[41] In 1994, Christian gave a talk titled "Diminishing Returns: Can Black Feminism(s) Survive the Academy?" Reflecting on about twenty-five years of work, she says, "black feminist thought and practice did not originate or does not now reside primarily in the academy . . . its roots were in popular movements, in the civil rights, black power, and women's movements of the 1960s and early 1970s as exemplified by the many voices of black women collected in Toni Cade's edition of *The Black Woman* (1970)." Christian insisted on the transformative power of social movements and saw clearly that she and her contemporaries faced "diminishing returns" in their efforts to bring Black and feminist liberation into academic contexts. She notes that "most studies conducted by American white women" do not consider "in any real way the ways in which African-American women call themselves 'womanist,' the word coined by Alice Walker."[42] Christian defines Black feminism through literature, in the works of Bambara and Walker; locates it in and outside of the academy; contextualizes it as intertwined with social movements; and insists on its racial specificity as signaled by the need for its own word, "womanist." When she asserted the continued significance of womanism in 1994, she was calling attention to the fact that white woman's racism in the women's movement of the 1960s and '70s continued well beyond that movement and was shaping colleges and universities in the 1980s and '90s.

Alice Walker created the term "womanism" to name a Black feminism distinct from white feminism, which often failed to address Black women's needs. "Womanism" named a difference that Sisterhood members had long been writing about. Toni Morrison's "What the Black Woman Thinks About White Women's Lib" (1971), an essay in the *New York Times*, described the justified distrust Black women felt toward that movement even as they supported women's liberation. Sisterhood member Vertamae Grosvenor's book

Thursdays and Every Other Sunday Off: A Domestic Rap (1972) illuminated the ways that white women's liberation depended on unacknowledged Black women's domestic work in white homes.

Building on Morrison's and Grosvenor's work and on Sisterhood discussions, Walker defined a womanist in 1983 as, in part, "A woman who loves other women, sexually and/or nonsexually. Appreciates and prefers women's culture . . . Committed to survival and wholeness of entire people, male *and* female." The last of her multiple definitions is perhaps the best known: "Womanist is to feminist as purple is to lavender."[43] Reflecting on the term in 1989, Walker explained its dense meaning:

> When I had to decide about the use of the word *feminist* for myself, it just didn't fit, especially when you had to say *Black feminist* . . . I wanted a word that was visible in itself, because it came out of my *own* culture . . . I thought about how Black women always say to their daughters, "You're acting womanish," which is the foundation of our self-love as Black women. The other thing is I really wanted a word in which you could be a lesbian or not a lesbian.[44]

When Black women intellectuals used "womanist" in the 1990s and beyond, they called on the power of 1970s Black feminist collectives. Using the word "womanism" in their teaching and writing was (and remains) one way that scholars indicate their obligation to love and liberate Black women in the world beyond the walls of the university. To speak and write that one is a "womanist" in a classroom, in an academic journal article, or on a conference panel is a declaration of one's Black feminist politics. The word "womanism" is "visible in itself" as coming out of Black American culture; it is a vernacular expression among women of both love and warning not to grow up too fast: "you're acting womanish." Blackness is the default and the center, so the word "Black" becomes unnecessary as a qualifier of one's feminism, gender, sexuality, or nation. "Womanist" signals "self-love as Black women" as a foundation for love among Black women, as between mothers and daughters, in writerly and political collaborations, and between lovers. "You could be a lesbian or not a lesbian," or experience and express desire for women without identifying as "lesbian," and be a womanist. Cheryl Wall writes that "womanism," "in distinguishing itself from feminism insists first of all on the right of black women to define their lives in their own terms." In her 2018 book *On Freedom and the Will to Adorn*, Wall explains that for

Walker, "black feminism" risks eliding "the history of resistance among African American women" and "assume[s] a minority position in someone else's discourse."[45] This is the ongoing utility of "womanism"; it assumes Blackness, values the vernacular, and speaks from one's own community, rather than in terms of "someone else's discourse."

In the mid-1990s, Barbara Christian was determined to hang on to the sense of possibility and love held out by Walker's womanism, but the facts on the ground were discouraging. As Jodi Melamed writes, "Although enrollment in public universities grew, there was a whitening at the top of an increasingly status-stratified system, while racial enrollment gaps increased and overall black enrollment declined from 1980 onwards."[46] In "Diminishing Returns," Christian described both the "small but influential place in the academy" that she and others created for "black women's studies" in the 1980s and their "substantive" "black feminist inquiry in all of the major disciplines of the university as well as in interdisciplinary areas," sometimes to the point of "restructuring of traditional disciplines" such as English and history.[47] Yet she titled her talk "Diminishing Returns" because, "though there have been some advances, they have been achieved at much cost and have not really changed the landscape or the population of the academy."[48] She was concerned about the dismally small number of Black PhD students and Black faculty. Christian saw both the change in objects of study and methodology created by "black feminist inquiry" and the painful limits to how much justice scholars had created.

The collaborative nature of The Sisterhood and other Black feminist collectives of the 1970s has persisted in informal and often invisible ways in teaching and administrative labor in the academy, especially for Black women and Black studies in white institutions. In a presentation she gave with Nellie McKay in 2000, Frances Smith Foster emphasized that collaboration is not only a matter of coauthored publications but also embedded in the daily tasks of women's jobs as professors.

> Think of all the years we've exchanged syllabi, consulted on which text would be most appropriate for a course, commiserated, ranted, raved, vented, and then planned how to solve the problem presented to us by yet another one or seven of our students, or justified why we ought to give up yet another hour of trying to sleep and write another letter of recommendation, tenure evaluation, or manuscript review for yet another colleague or someone who really needed a candid collegial comment.[49]

Part of what Foster describes is a sense of obligation to junior colleagues and graduate students. Teaching and service to the field of African American literary studies is the work of racial justice, which raises the stakes of every "letter of recommendation, tenure evaluation, or manuscript review" and is perhaps worth losing more sleep. McKay recognizes that she, Foster, and their cohort of Black women scholars of African American literature were themselves "beneficiaries of the barnstorming tactics of young black college students who, in the wake of the civil rights movement, demanded representation of the black experience in their education."[50] She explains that seeing or taking part in political activism on campuses in the late 1960s and early 1970s not only influenced Black feminist literary scholars who completed graduate degrees in the late 1970s and early 1980s but also created a sense of obligation as they went about their everyday, unseen, countless tasks as professors working to support Black studies and Black students.

Scholars including Frances Smith Foster, Nellie McKay, and Mary Helen Washington, like many members of The Sisterhood, continued their Black feminist literary labor well into the twenty-first century, even as they faced resistance and the retrenchment of systemic racism and sexism. Although "Black feminism" and "intersectionality" appeared regularly in course descriptions and faculty research, in 2018, only about 5.5 percent of college and university faculty in the United States identified as Black. This includes faculty across ranks (including tenured, untenured, adjunct, lecturers, visiting faculty), a disproportionate number of whom work at HBCUs. The percentage of Black faculty in tenure-track positions is even lower and the percentage of tenured faculty who identify as Black is just 2 percent. The numbers would be even lower if universities disaggregated African Americans from Black immigrants from across the Diaspora. This percentage, about 5.5, was the same in 2020 as it was in 2015 and has barely increased since Barbara Christian lamented "Diminishing Returns" in 1994. Many universities recruit Black faculty through widely publicized cluster hires without changing the hostile environment at predominantly white institutions and thus struggle to retain the few they do hire.[51]

The Sisterhood worked hard to make space for Black studies at universities. They also wanted those institutions to be safe for Black faculty and students and to be places where everyone could learn to liberate themselves and others. Toni Morrison spoke for many Black feminists when she said, "the function of freedom is to free somebody else."[52] Safety and liberation are goals that exceed the limited bureaucratic ideas of inclusion, diversity, and equity that define the contemporary university. I mean safety here in the sense that Erica Edwards uses it: "not as a private entitlement—as something that one can *have* or *enjoy*—but as a redistributive goal of abolitionist transformative justice, as a collective craft."[53] Safety as redistribution of resources and as "collective craft" is something scholars of African American literature are trying to make together every day, but it remains, as it did for Sisterhood members, something that happens largely outside of our official and visible jobs.

Doing radical Black feminist work within institutions that are able to absorb and instrumentalize that work can strip away its politics. Edwards explains an important example: "the phrase 'African American literature' rests neatly, unchallenged, in course catalogues, as a featured subcategory for online book shopping, or in polite conversation considering the latest bestseller about slavery," and this facilitates the use of Black books "to do the weighty ideological work of building a domestic multicultural consensus to post-Cold War US foreign policy."[54] The U.S. exercise of empire and repression at home and around the world is among the forms of racism and violence that studying African American literature does not automatically change, particularly when that literature is taught as part of a multicultural survey or an add-on, rather than in the context of its specific tradition. A student could, for example, read poems by June Jordan without encountering her "Poem About Police Violence" and thus not understand that Jordan is part of a long tradition of African American literature about racist police brutality. In a women's studies course, a student is likely to read essays by Audre Lorde without encountering her essay "Grenada Revisited" and thus miss entirely the Third World feminism and critique of U.S. foreign policy that was central to the way Lorde and her cohort understood Black feminism.

The co-optation of Black feminist writing and ideas is not a short-term reaction to the Black women writers' renaissance of the 1970s and '80s, nor exactly a backlash to the entry of Black feminists and their ideas into the academy in the 1980s and '90s. Rather, we are in another chapter of the long history of whiteness adapting to maintain power, in and far beyond the academy. Like the term "multiculturalism" in the 1990s, the term "diversity" since at least 2010 is largely anodyne and performative in the rhetoric of nearly every U.S. university, corporation, and governmental agency. Universities diffused the politics and goals of The Sisterhood and other Black feminist collectives by diverting radical knowledge into the project called diversity. After decades of defunding, higher education operates on an austerity model in which units compete for resources. Some Black Studies and other departments can only survive by taking on the mission of diversifying an institution, rather than pursuing teaching and research. This is one way that inclusion in an existing institution can depoliticize a formerly radical project. Most universities now have a high-level administrator charged with making their schools more racially diverse. Hiring diversity officers and establishing well-funded divisions of diversity, equity, and inclusion deforms the language of freedom into the work of administration. Research shows that this strategy is expensive and ineffective at increasing the number of Black faculty on a campus.[55] In effect, this means that universities are full of Black ideas but not Black people.[56]

Thus far in the twenty-first century, universities have absorbed Black feminist ideas without making substantial changes to material conditions for Black people. Even so, Black women intellectuals remain insurgent forces in the academy. Teaching, researching, writing, advising, and holding administrative roles while always being both hopeful and realistic, both acting for justice and acknowledging ongoing injustice, remains the situation of Black feminist workers in the academy in the twenty-first century.

Changes Black feminists wrought in the academy and the ways the academy has incorporated Black feminism for a variety of purposes raise the increasingly urgent question of whether colleges and universities can still, after decades of decreased federal and state funding and increasingly corporate practices, serve as a base for Black women's liberation. Understanding this defining ambivalence of Black feminist work in universities and knowing The Sisterhood and their generation of Black women made the choice to put their formidable intellectual powers to work in the academy is especially important now when scholars are rightly and increasingly pessimistic about the possibility of fomenting racial justice by working in academic institutions.

≈

Contemporary scholars in a number of fields turn to Black feminist writing by The Sisterhood and their cohort to imagine transformation of the social and political order. Grace Hong wrote in 2008 that Christian's "Diminishing Returns" "haunts me almost twenty years after its publication." Hong turns to "Black feminist thought" "to address how we might re-imagine and reconstitute this university formation so that it is no longer so violent toward black feminists" and to "find a method for reconstituting knowledge production within the university." She uses work by Audre Lorde, the Combahee River Collective, and Barbara Christian to apply the both/and thinking of Black feminism: "instead of positing epistemological and embodied politics as incommensurate opposites, I follow Christian in arguing that the materialist knowledge production pioneered by Black feminist thought allows us to see them as connected." This means simultaneously understanding the "university's violence toward Black feminists" and seeing how Black feminists are "central to this struggle" of "redistributing resources, producing counterknowledges, and critiquing white supremacy and imperialism." Hong remains hopeful that Black feminist thought can still make "the university a less hostile place for Black feminists."[57]

In *The Reorder of Things* (2012), Roderick Ferguson studies the ways that "institutional models" and "interpretive communities" that grew out of late 1960s student activism were "both disruptive *and* recuperative of existing institutions." These efforts, including the open admissions movement at City College, were "a rebellion against institutional forces" and also expressed "a desire for institutionality."[58] Higher education has proven adept at responding to student and faculty demands for change, quelling rebellion, by introducing discourses such as "multiculturalism" and "excellence" that speak to marginalized people's "desire for institutionality," but ultimately perpetuate racist, unequal distribution of power. Robin Kelley describes the "first wave" of student activism in the late 1960s that achieved a range of goals including establishing Black studies and ethnic studies units "at over 500 universities" and ensuring that "at least one Ethnic Studies course was taught at at least 13,000 universities." This student activism was "explicitly anti-capitalist and anti-imperialist." "Backlash" caused budget cuts and a "low point" for such programs by 1974, but a resurgence followed, resulting in what Kelley designates as a "high point" for Black and ethnic studies in 1994.[59]

That "high point"—in the same year Barbara Christian talked about "diminishing returns"—shows that it became possible, even common, to have an ethnic studies department without actually addressing student and faculty "anti-capitalist and anti-imperialist" stances or demands for racial justice. Kelley describes the 1990s as "the period of the culture wars" that "was also marked by the hegemony of liberal multiculturalism and the proliferation of Ethnic Studies classes and these two things coincided with one another, but they are not always in opposition." Some Black studies and ethnic studies departments established in this "second wave" were what Kelley calls "insurgent units" that practiced coalitional liberatory politics. But across the 1990s and to the present, "the neoliberal university . . . has no difficulty absorbing or incorporating commodified domestic difference . . . often in the name of diversity." This means, as Kelley observes, that contemporary "insurgent units" have to "fight" for resources, budgets, and hiring year after year.[60]

Even in the context of liberal multiculturalism and a constant struggle for resources, Black studies and ethnic studies departments provided an educational foundation that supported political movements outside the academy. In the 1990s, "young activists" who "came out of colleges and programs" where they learned about power, race, and capital in Black and ethnic studies classes founded political organizations including Critical Resistance, Domestic Workers United, the Black Radical Congress, and the Los Angeles Community Action Network.[61] Kelley traces a lineage of the "radical insurgency that formed the left wing of second wave Ethnic Studies" forward in time to the Occupy Movement, the Movement for Black Lives, the Dreamers, and the Black Youth Project in the twenty-first century.[62]

As these political movements have developed, Black feminist scholars of the twenty-first century follow in the footsteps of their teachers and mentors by continuing to invest their skills and intellect in the academy. As Jennifer Nash asserts, "it is crucial to note that black feminism—and black feminists—have long been attached, optimistically or self-destructively (or maybe both)—to the university . . . while black feminists have long traced the violence of the university, few have advocated for abandoning the institutional project of black feminism." In her study of the idea of intersectionality in women's studies over the past several decades, Nash grapples with the fact that Black feminist scholars have "largely retained a faith in the institution's capacity to be remade, reimagined, or reinvented in ways that will do less violence to black feminist theory and black feminists' bodies."[63] This "faith" is somewhat surprising given that Black scholars, Black studies, and Black feminism are still precarious at many universities. At a 2021 symposium celebrating her mentor Barbara Christian, Arlene Keizer remarked that "Black Studies is still an outsider within the traditional academy," even in departments such as women's studies and English that often declare a commitment to intersectionality.[64] Keizer expressed continued concern about the same dangers of exceptionalism that concerned her predecessors: "I am worried about a future in which the fruits of individual success for Black Studies faculty will replace a collective notion of the success of the field . . . we find ourselves in roughly the same position that Barbara [Christian] and her pathbreaking generation did."[65] Nash, Keizer, and others, though, stay the course alongside members of that generation.

Cheryl Wall was writing Black feminist scholarship, mentoring postdoctoral fellows and graduate students, running programs to prepare Black students for graduate school, and teaching many undergraduates right up until her passing in the spring of 2020, just as she was officially retiring from Rutgers University. Wall was a truly great teacher, scholar, and institution builder, but she did not do this work alone. Farah Griffin, Maryemma Graham, Trudier Harris, Joycelyn Moody, and Mary Helen Washington, among many other Black feminist literary scholars, have done or are now doing Sisterhood work in the academy. From Graham's History of Black Writing project, going strong at the University of Kansas since 1983, to Moody editing the seventeen volumes of Cambridge's *African American Literature in Transition* series and Griffin serving as the inaugural chair of the African American and African Diaspora Studies Department at Columbia University, Black feminists have stayed committed to colleges and universities as places to do just and meaningful work.

Black feminists, in the mode of The Sisterhood, also continue to support one another in ways that are adjacent to but not embedded in academic institutions. The Wintergreen Women Writers' Collective is one long-lasting example. In 1987, scholar Joanne Gabbin brought a group of Black women poets, scholars, playwrights, and novelists together in the Blue Ridge Mountains for what became Wintergreen. The collective welcomed about fifty women intellectuals into this annual "gathering of writers who gain strength and direction from communion with one another."[66] In 2009, Gabbin edited the volume of essays *Shaping Memories: Reflections of African American Women Writers*. The book is a record of Black women writers' experiences in and out of academic settings and of the way that "being writers drew them to this group, but their friendship kept them in communion with one another for more than twenty [now thirty] years."[67] Unlike The Sisterhood, Wintergreen members commented on one another's writings, met annually at a remote location away from the obligations of jobs and families, and published a book that collects their writings as members of the group. Poet and founding Wintergreen member Nikki Giovanni writes that the first meeting was "A weekend of girl-friend-getting-to-know-each-other. Some of us were famous; some not. Some were students; some faculty. Some poets and writers; some critics. . . . We played cards, swam, walked in the woods . . . read poetry to the group, cooked and ate, and it was great. It was supposed to be a one-time thing, but we all said: *Let's do it again* . . . It is a safe place. To relax. To be surrounded by love. To be. A haven."[68] Twenty years after their first meeting, Giovanni describes Wintergreen as rooted in love and a necessary refuge for members, among them accomplished scholars of African American literature Gabbin, Daryl Cumber Dance, Maryemma Graham, Trudier Harris, Karla Holloway, and Lovalerie King and poets Giovanni, Nikki Finney, Toi Derricote, Opal Moore, and Sonia Sanchez. Paule Marshall is the one Sisterhood member who also attended Wintergreen.

Wintergreen does not necessarily take collaborative aim at cultural institutions the way that The Sisterhood did, but its members have shaped the cultural landscape. Three key examples are Cave Canem, Furious Flower, and Penn State Africana Studies. In 1996, Derricote and Cornealius Eady founded Cave Canem, a national nonprofit literary organization for African American poets and poetry that is an important and effective example of Black literary organizing. Howard Rambsy explains prizes as one key facet of Cave Canem's literary activism: "Each year since 1999, the Cave Canem Foundation has sponsored an annual poetry prize" that "was responsible for launching the publishing careers of Kyle Dargan, Rickey Laurentiis, Tracy K. Smith, and Natasha Trethewey"; "for the nearly two dozen African American poets who earned Cave Canem Book Prizes since 2000, winning the competition was vital to book publication and served as gateways to other major professional opportunities" such as academic jobs. Every Black poet who has won a Pulitzer for poetry since the organization was founded, from Tretheway in 2007 through Jericho Brown in 2020, has been "affiliated in some way with Cave Canem."[69]

Wintergreen's founder, Joanne Gabbin, established another crucial site of literary organizing: the Furious Flower Poetry Center. Furious Flower was the first academic center in the United States for Black poetry and has been home since 1994 to the Furious Flower Poetry Conferences. The center gives poets opportunities to gather, produces teaching materials, and awards fellowships, among other forms of literary activism. At Penn State, Lovalerie King directed the Africana Research Center, organized African American literature conferences, and edited several volumes of scholarly essays about African American literature. These were not Wintergreen projects but all included Wintergreen members, and work on each of them was celebrated and sustained by the support Black women intellectuals found in the Wintergreen Women Writers' Collective. In this sense, Wintergreen achieved what Alice Walker hoped The Sisterhood would: incubating and sustaining a variety of Black feminist academic and literary projects.

The women of The Sisterhood, Wintergreen, and the first couple of generations of Black feminist scholars built a strong foundation. A generation of Black feminists now at mid-career is building on that foundation. In the 1970s and '80s, Black women writers and scholars used groups like The Sisterhood to talk privately about the racism and misogyny they faced every day at their jobs. Today, Black women academics have platforms in academia and beyond, including social media, podcasts, and television. Some of them choose to talk publicly about this racism and misogyny. Patricia Matthew and Koritha Mitchell have both taken on the risk and the labor of making academic institutions more racially just. Both hold PhDs in English; Matthew is an expert in British abolitionist literature and culture and Mitchell is an expert in African American literature. For both scholars, academic institutional racism has become a secondary area of expertise out of necessity.

Matthew's volume *Written/Unwritten: Diversity and the Hidden Truths of Tenure* (2016) makes plain how the racism of academia keeps Black, Indigenous, and other people of color out of the tenured ranks of the professoriate. The scholars who contributed to *Written/Unwritten* "hold the academy to account, but they do so from the vantage point of those committed to its success."[70] Matthew and the contributors take an unflinching look at the ways academic institutions simultaneously declare a commitment to diversity yet make "unwritten" demands that faculty of color do the invisible, onerous work of increasing racial diversity while also serving as hypervisible physical evidence of it. Most contributors understand the impossible burdens of this position but remain committed to racial justice in academia. *Written/Unwritten* reflects conversations that have become more and more visible in academic settings and formalizes those conversations as a text available for use in settings such as education studies classrooms and reading groups of faculty and administrators.

Like Matthew, Koritha Mitchell is in demand to offer talks, workshops, and consulting at universities working to address their own institutional racism. Her writing and speaking about how and why not to use the n-word in the classroom has become an important resource for teachers across the country.[71] In addition to writing important scholarly books and articles about African American literature and culture, Mitchell regularly gives talks, informed by her literary research, that address urgent current issues such as racist violence in the United States and the connections between America's history of lynching Black people and current anti-LGBTQIA violence. She has also spoken about these topics on *CNN*, *Good Morning America*, and NPR's *Morning Edition*.

Mitchell is part of a cohort of Black feminist scholars, including Salamishah Tillet and Brittney Cooper, who regularly write for and speak to broad print, radio, and television audiences. Tillet writes scholarly books and articles, serves as faculty at Rutgers University-Newark, curates art exhibits, and cofounded A Long Walk Home (a nonprofit organization that uses art to end violence against girls and women). She won a 2022 Pulitzer Prize for her cultural criticism in the *New York Times*. Cooper, a professor of women's, gender, and sexuality studies at Rutgers-New Brunswick, has written scholarly and popular books, cofounded the Crunk Feminist Collective, writes regularly for *New York Magazine*'s *The Cut*, and is prominent on social media and television news offering commentary on race, gender, and politics. In these ways, today's Black feminist scholars use the academic base that The Sisterhood's generation built for Black feminist activism in and outside of the academy.

≈

There is so much to celebrate in the work and legacies of The Sisterhood and of Black feminist scholars of the late twentieth century. They brought Black feminist thought and writing into political, literary, and academic spheres. They sustained Black studies, African American literature, and Black feminism at colleges and universities and gave scholars such as Erica Edwards, Grace Hong, and Roderick Ferguson the tools to critique the ways the academy has coopted and depoliticized those fields and ideas. They paved the way for Black feminist activism in the academy by scholars such as Patricia Matthew and in mass media by scholars such as Salamishah Tillet. This generation of Black thinkers and writers also made it possible for many people, including me, to study, teach, and write about Black women's literature.

These scholars and writers were often the first Black woman faculty member in their respective academic departments. Transforming the academy was a lonely endeavor, it was hard work, and the costs were high. Nellie McKay describes some of what her cohort faced as a "generation" of Black women who "had gone to white graduate schools between the late 1960s and early 1970s and were the first as a group (by race and sex) to find employment at predominantly white colleges and universities . . . as a rule, black women did not feel welcome or appreciated in their new positions, but having broken the barriers of this stronghold of sex prejudice, they planned no retreat from gains hard won." Black women may have had at least some Black peers in graduate school, but if they managed to land an academic job, then as now, there would be "few if any black colleagues, especially women."[72] Within a couple of decades, the toll of these working conditions was painfully clear: Black women scholars who made African American literature an established field of study were uncredited, being erased, and often suffering physically and emotionally as a result of outrageously demanding jobs. Shanna Benjamin describes this emergency:

> As Black women's ideas became indispensable within the mainstream academy, the women who produced them became disposable . . . Black women's recovery work and intellectual interventions were changing higher education, but Black women themselves were consistently marginalized, their ideas invoked without reference to the Black women responsible, to the battles Black women fought, or to the price Black women paid to document Black women's literature.[73]

Black women scholars chose, again and again, to do the work of liberation at colleges and universities, despite and amid the severe hostility to Black women that continues in predominantly white institutions of higher education. The choice to stay in the academy and the losses that wrought shape contemporary Black feminist work.

For some Sisterhood members and many Black women intellectuals, their stunning careers were woefully short. An inescapable fact of the recent history of Black feminism is that many of its brightest lights died at a relatively young age. When Barbara Christian said in 1994 that "though there have been some advances, they have been achieved at much cost," she understood that the greatest costs were the lives of Black women.[74] Grace Hong writes that "Christian's archive reveals some of her own institutional difficulties," including "a level of university and professional service . . . that would defy belief if it were not still so common among women academics of color" and "appeals for leave and funding" that "note that she was the only Black humanities professor at Berkeley at the time" and mention "health problems even prior to her cancer diagnosis."[75] Layered obligations can make the professoriate an impossibly hard career for Black women; Shanna Benjamin describes her mentor Nellie McKay's list of the main "challenges facing Black women in higher education: isolation within the department, disrespect from students, and the burden of being the primary figure charged with attending to the personal, professional, and even emotional needs of Black women students."[76] The exceptionalism I describe in chapter 6 amplifies these burdens. As Myisha Priest observed in 2008, "The hypervisibility of writers like Toni Morrison and Alice Walker gives a false impression of both institutional power and economic prosperity in the lives of black women cultural workers," but the far more common experience is "hopping from one short-term teaching appointment to the next . . . overburdened with departmental duties, admission and funding committees, advising and mentoring, and outreach and community service . . . hobbled by the lack of institutional and financial support for their work."[77] This was, and remains, the more common career path for members of The Sisterhood, their contemporaries, and still and now, the Black women scholars whom they trained.

The persistence of dire circumstances means that Black feminist scholarship has to keep on narrating and historicizing these dangers and losses. McKay examined the obstacles in 1983, and they remained severe when Benjamin wrote about them in her 2021 book about McKay. Scholars including McKay, Benjamin, Ann duCille, P. Gabrielle Foreman, Farah Jasmine Griffin, and Grace Hong have all had to write about and contextualize these losses because, as Priest wrote in 2008, "Death is becoming an occupational hazard of black female intellectual life. Black women intellectuals are sickening and dying at alarming rates."[78] Priest understands Barbara Christian's worsening illness and eventual cancer diagnosis in the 1990s as intertwined with the erosion of gains for both Black students and Black studies: "when her life's work began to crumble around her, she got tired. Hers was a progressive debilitation, a slow chipping away of power and energy that was a precise mirror of the slow destruction of progress she saw around her."[79]

Black feminist writers, scholars, and activists of the late twentieth century were well aware that their work to transform the academy, the literary marketplace, and the world took a toll, every single day, on their physical health. Audre Lorde passed in 1992 at age fifty-eight and was surely on Christian's mind when she spoke in 1994 of few "advances" at "much cost."[80]

Lorde's papers repeatedly document the conflict between individual survival and institutional change. Alexis Gumbs writes that Lorde "was denied medical leave" and "had to turn down prestigious fellowships . . . that required residency in places too cold for her to live during her fight against cancer." Lorde tried to strategize ways to do her work and stay healthy, but, as Gumbs explains, "The English Department at Hunter, which recently honored Lorde with a conference 20 years after her death, rejected her proposals at the end of her life to teach on a limited residency basis that would allow her to teach poetry intensive classes for students during warm weather in New York and to live in warmer climates during the winter based on her health needs."[81]

Less than a year after Christian's consideration of "Diminishing Returns," Toni Cade Bambara passed away at age fifty-six, the same age as Christian when she passed in 2000. June Jordan and VèVè Clark lived only to their early sixties. Although Jordan successfully used the academy to foment justice, attempts to preserve her health were met with resistance: "June Jordan's records show that even as she was battling breast cancer, UC Berkeley would not grant her medical leave or the breaks from teaching that she repeatedly wrote her administration to request in 2001, months before she died, less than two years after her Black feminist Berkeley colleague, Barbara Christian died" and less than a year before Black feminist scholar Claudia Tate died of lung cancer at age fifty-five in 2002.[82] The pain of these losses is acute for many reasons, including that, as Hong writes, "to observe that those of Christian's generation of Black women in the academy have been decimated by premature death is to say that this happened to the *first* to be able to even be called a 'generation.'"[83] To write about this "generation" is to grapple with loss. Vertamae Grosvenor, Lovalerie King, Paule Marshall, Toni Morrison, Ntozake Shange, and Cheryl Wall passed on as I was writing this book.

To tell the story of The Sisterhood is to reckon with the costs Black women intellectuals paid, are paying, to make the world more just. Their collective story is one of struggle between laboring in the institutions they worked to gain access to and survival. Their story is not just one of costs and loss; it is also a story of the wild joy of Black feminist thinkers at work. In her last piece of published writing, Cheryl Wall reveled in the fact that "In the twenty-first century, Black women, either by virtue of their academic careers or their vocations outside of institutional settings, pursue intellectual work for its own sake as well as in pursuit of collective goals. That is to say, they can acknowledge intellectual work as a source of personal fulfilment, indeed a source of joy in ways that earlier Black women could not," even though "it remains difficult for Black women to own the joy that their engagement with ideas produces."[84] She and her generation of Black feminist literary scholars, in collaboration with The Sisterhood and other writers, created this landscape of profound pleasure in intellectual work for Black women. Sisterhood work is collaborative advocacy for Black women's writing rooted in love. Black women's joyful engagement with ideas, the historicizing impulse in contemporary Black feminist scholarship, the circulation and celebration of the 1977 photo, and hopefully this book, are Sisterhood work for the twenty-first century.

CONCLUSION

In a 2018 essay, Jamey Hatley, a contemporary Black woman writer and filmmaker, contemplated the 1977 photo of The Sisterhood and asked, "How could such black literary luminaries all be in one space?" These women became "literary luminaries" partly as a result of the collaborative labor of those in the photo and of the many members and interlocutors of The Sisterhood not pictured. Hatley understands the photo as inspiration for building literary community: "How could they not all be in one space? Wouldn't you try to be in a room full of excellent peers if you had the chance?"[1] The meaning of the photo for Hatley and other writers is among the stakes of The Sisterhood's place in literary history. She also finds inspiration in Toni Morrison and Toni Cade Bambara's friendship:

> That the writers of *Sula* and *The Salt Eaters* had made a way just like my friends and I were trying to, let me dream. This kind of everyday care may not have charted as an epic hero's journey, but it has made space for my work and for my friends' work. This is how our art gets made. We steal time from our employers. We cook for each other and make drinks. We charge up credit cards when we have them. We stand up for each other at funerals. We use our library privileges at institutions to get each other the books we need. Make photocopies on our day jobs. Write dazzling letters of support. We read drafts. Take children to camp. We cuss and cry over whatever insult the world brings. It is the guiding light of these friendships, the razor sharpness of this love that

cuts through the muck of a world that tells us our stories are not important, are not worthy, are not enough.[2]

This "everyday" work may seem utterly ordinary and personal while it is happening. However, the story of The Sisterhood reveals that ordinary collaborative work among Black women writers can have extraordinary results. This story tells Hatley, and many other Black women writers, teachers, and scholars, not only that their work is "worthy" and "enough" but also that their personal and intimate "friendships" are a network of support that can change what people read, think, and do in the world.

The name "The Sisterhood" may seem outdated today, but in 1977, it was thick with political connotations and racial and gender specificity. "The Sisterhood" signals Black women united in kinship and activism doing culture work rooted in love for self, for one another, and for Black women's writing. The Sisterhood aimed to transform public culture, but they did this work through personal and affective bonds. Their decision at the first meeting to call themselves "The Sisterhood" created a condition of possibility; it could have turned out to mean almost any of the infinite number of things that a group of Black women writers could create together. Over the course of the two years the group met, "Sisterhood" came to describe collaborative activism to get Black women's writings published and publicized in the literary marketplace and seriously studied in the academy.

The influence of The Sisterhood is, from the vantage point of the twenty-first century, undeniable. Judith Wilson reflects that "the 1970s were ground-zero for the emergence of black literary feminism and The Sisterhood was a brilliant embodiment of the forces that emergence involved."[3] This book has told the story of The Sisterhood to make that "ground-zero," that women's work, visible in its multiple cultural, political, historical, and institutional contexts. The 1977 photo is one snapshot, one moment, in a long history of Black feminist collaborative labor.

Telling the story of that moment becomes more urgent with each passing year. Members of The Sisterhood and many other Black women writers and intellectuals have passed on since the late 1970s. Recording the history of the group, the broader network around it, and the lasting results of their collaboration is a way to honor those women and to document some of the less visible aspects of their labor. The move to online communication in the 1990s and early 2000s means that The Sisterhood and their contemporaries are among the last writers to have ample but dispersed paper archives that reflect a network of literary, political, and academic work. Erica Edwards writes, "As Black women passed through the institutions that wanted to eat them alive, their writing left a trail of instructions for how to work in, and how to carve one's way out of, the belly of the beast."[4] That "trail of instructions" requires recovery, attention, and study.

Those whom Spelman College archivist Holly Smith calls "memory workers" are following that trail by preserving, archiving, and caring for Sisterhood members' papers.[5] Alexis Gumbs organized Cheryll Y. Greene's papers to be housed and available to researchers at Emory University's Stuart A. Rose Manuscripts, Archives, and Rare Book Library. Emory is also home to Alice Walker's archive, which preserves Walker's careful organization of a lifetime of papers, recordings, and materials in other formats. Morrison ensured the future of her papers as a research repository by placing them at Princeton, where the Firestone Library quickly processed the archive and opened it to researchers in 2016. The exhibit "Toni Morrison: Sites of Memory" opened at Princeton in 2023 with more than ninety items from Morrison's papers on display. Scholar Autumn Womack curated the exhibit with a team of scholars and researchers. Womack and scholar Kinohi Nishikawa co-organized three days of programming in March 2023 titled "Sites of Memory: A Symposium on Toni Morrison and the Archive" and are coediting a volume of essays about the archive in Morrison's life, imagination, and writings.[6]

Kim Hall, the Department of Africana Studies, the Barnard College Library, and other collaborators brought Ntozake Shange's archive to Barnard and made a beautiful, welcoming place for it on campus. Toni Cade Bambara's and Audre Lorde's archives are in the Women's Resource and Research Center at Spelman College, which (by design) binds them to active feminist research and where, over time, college President Johnetta Cole, scholar Beverly Guy-Sheftall, and memory workers Smith, Taronda Spencer, and Kassandra Ware acquired, valued, and organized the materials and have tended them with archival practices of "care, celebration, and repair."[7] This memory work is literary and academic organizing in the tradition of The Sisterhood. Some of it is radical simply by making specific Black women viscerally present in an archive at an academic institution through actions such as archiving Lorde's dreadlocks at Spelman and building an altar to Shange in the Barnard archives reading room, complete with a two-liter bottle of her favorite beverage, Diet Pepsi.[8]

Other Sisterhood members' papers are not so readily available: Vertamae Grosvenor's and Paule Marshall's letters are among those that are scattered across several other peoples' archives, not currently gathered and held at one repository, or not yet available to researchers. Grosvenor lost much of what might have comprised her archive due to hurricanes and moves. It will be, as ever, Black feminist culture workers and scholars who find, assemble, and write these women's stories. Filmmaker Julie Dash is making a documentary about Grosvenor, and Mary Helen Washington is writing a biography of Paule Marshall.

Print archives of some Black women intellectuals at libraries and universities around the country contain folders of letters, syllabi, and photographs. Many of these folders end abruptly with funeral programs and obituaries. Correspondence among Sisterhood members about their lives and writings, flyers for events that Black women writers organized, and even some Black periodicals exist only as hard copies, many unlikely to be digitized. In this book, I have gathered some of these materials to tell a story of Black women's work in political, literary, and academic spheres. I hope this book also serves as invitation: there are so many other stories to tell and so much work yet to be done to gather, care for, and put to use Black women's archives.

It remains to be seen how younger generations of Black writers will continue to make use of The Sisterhood's legacies. There are several exciting currents happening in literature. One area of collaborative literary organizing is in the broad array of Black print culture happening outside of trade publishing, literary fiction, and academic study. Maryemma Graham describes a tradition of self-publishing and independent Black presses that runs from "wildly popular" poet and novelist Frances Harper in the nineteenth century through presses established during the Black Arts Movement, such as Haki Madhubuti's Broadside Press, and continuing in today's "improved print-on-demand technology, e-books, e-marketing, and guerilla marketing . . . and black distributors like AALBC and Black Books Direct."[9] There is a lot of popular Black writing today, including "romance novels, mysteries, speculative fiction, historical fiction" along with "graphic novels, self-help books, and Christian fiction." These genres vary in form and content, but they share some conditions of reception: they have fervent fan bases and their authors tend to engage fans directly. Specialized podcasts, online groups, and book clubs embrace these authors and their books. These sectors of Black print culture sometimes produce best-selling writers, including Terry McMillian, E. Lynn Harris, and Zane, all of whom "self-published their first books." More recently Nikki Turner went from self-publishing her popular street lit novels to publishing best-selling multivolume books series with

One World (an imprint of Random House) and Urban Books (an imprint of Kensington Press, distributed by Random House), and best-selling romance novelist Jasmine Guillory is remarkably accessible to fans through her newsletter, website, and podcast interviews, in which she regularly explains using Twitter to find an agent and pitch her first book. Contemporary Black genre fiction, especially romance novels and street lit, are big categories of African American writing circulating among readers alongside the literary fiction and poetry that scholars tend to focus on. Graham calls on teacher-scholars to "acknowledge the chasm between our teaching canon and the vast domain of print culture" that our students are reading outside of the classroom.[10] It might be hard for some professors (me included!) to imagine teaching any one of the steamy six novels in Guillory's The Wedding Date series in a class about Black women's fiction, but it was once hard to imagine that Ntozake Shange's experimental and challenging *for colored girls* would be a staple of countless classes and college theater productions. The Sisterhood's success bringing contemporary Black women's writing into the canon of African American literature offers a useful model for scholars who would follow Graham's lead in teaching and writing about a more diverse body of Black print culture.

In another important strain of contemporary African American literature, men novelists have had a period of critical and commercial success thus far in the twenty-first century. Paul Beatty, Mat Johnson, Victor LaValle, Maurice Carlos Ruffin, Colson Whitehead, and others write novels that are dense in their cultural references, often darkly funny, sometimes satirical, and widely celebrated, particularly when they are directly or implicitly about slavery. Most of this cohort of Black men hold MFAs, and several of them teach in creative writing departments. They write self-consciously in the wake of late twentieth-century Black feminist literature. Morrison's presence looms especially large for them, as with Johnson's *Pym* (2011), which is in direct dialogue with Morrison's *Playing in the Dark* (1992), and Whitehead's *The Underground Railroad* (2016), which alludes to *Beloved* in many ways, including giving an enslaver the last name Garner.

Black women fiction writers of the African Diaspora have enjoyed substantial interest among readers in the United States thus far in the twenty-first century. This group includes Chimamanda Adichie, Edwidge Danticat, Helen Oyeyemi, and Zadie Smith.[11] These writers both benefit from doors The Sisterhood opened and fulfill The Sisterhood's hopes for an increasing awareness of Black literature of the Diaspora among American readers. However, the justified attention for their books sometimes comes at the expense of

African American women writers. This is in part because the problem that Toni Morrison described in 1981 persists: "the market can only receive one or two [Black women writers]. Dealing with five Toni Morrisons would be problematic . . . the marketplace receives only one or two Blacks in days when it's not fashionable."[12]

Mainstream publications are paying more attention to personal essays and memoirs by Black authors including Ta-Nehisi Coates, Brittney Cooper, Tressie McMillian Cottom, Roxane Gay, and Kiese Laymon. Black writers are not necessarily producing more first-person writing than they did in the past, but that genre is widely read, and these authors write for magazines and newspapers and appear on popular podcasts and television news programs. The bestseller status of Coates's *Between the World and Me* (2016) depended partly on Morrison anointing him this generation's James Baldwin in her blurb for the book and made clear that readers were eager for non-fiction that narrates personal experience and diagnoses the ongoing effects of racism in United States. Since 2015, many white readers, universities, and corporations have responded to their newfound awareness of police murder of Black people and to the Movement for Black Lives by forming book clubs about, assigning to students, or selecting for undergraduate common reading works of "antiracist nonfiction."[13] This could be a legacy of The Sisterhood in the sense that collective reading and study are central to political consciousness raising. However, through no fault of their authors, these works have become part of the antiracist reading lists that do not necessarily lead to substantive change.

Kenton Rambsy and Howard Rambsy, in their 2020 article "Black Books and Dead Black Bodies: Twitter, Hashtags, and Antiracist Reading Lists," document the rise in sales of "books about racism and white privilege" after Minneapolis police officer Derek Chauvin murdered George Floyd in May 2020. As Rambsy and Rambsy explain, each week in May 2020, *Publisher's Weekly*'s top ten list included one specific book by a Black writer—Michelle Obama's memoir *Becoming*—and no books specifically about race. In the first week of June 2020, the list was dominated by "antiracist nonfiction" by Black writers Ijeoma Oluo and Ibram X. Kendi and white writer Robin D'Angelo.[14] These books are for white readers and focus on transforming individual white sentiment, rather than ending systemic racism. Because the marketplace remains narrow, sales, reviews, and media for "antiracist nonfiction" are drawing attention away from works of literature by, for, and about Black people. As Rambsy and Rambsy write, "Ultimately, antiracist reading lists privilege explaining race and racism, especially to white people, while diminishing the possibility of black readers exploring varied considerations, especially in artistic and creative genres." Unlike on the reading lists of the National Black Feminist Organization and other 1970s political groups, "relatively few novels, collections of short stories, and volumes of poetry have appeared on antiracist reading lists."[15]

Amid the constraints of market competition, ongoing racism in publishing and academia, and the difficulty earning a living through writing, contemporary African American women write self-consciously into the spaces that The Sisterhood created. Danzy Senna's remarkable novel *New People* (2017) takes a stance of justified racial and gendered paranoia that is both formally innovative and informed by earlier novels by Toni Cade Bambara and Gloria Naylor.[16] Tayari Jones regularly names her debt to two Black women writers: her mentor Pearl Cleage, who was a friend of Bambara's and a member of the Southern Collective of African American Writers, and Toni Morrison, whose recursive storytelling, respect for Black children's intellect, and idea of the past persisting in the present all appear in each of Jones's four novels. In *Leaving Atlanta* (2002), Jones writes about the Atlanta child murders of 1979–1981 and includes a note that explains the influence on her of Bambara's posthumous novel about those murders, *Those Bones Are Not My Child* (2000).[17]

Some of the best African American women's writing so far this century has been poetry, including Evie Shockley's *the new black* (2011), *semiautomatic* (2017), and *suddenly we* (2023) and short fiction, including Danielle Evans's *Before You Suffocate Your Own Fool Self* (2010) and *The Office of Historical Corrections* (2020) as well as Nafissa Thompson-Spires's *Heads of the Colored People* (2018). Shockley, Evans, and Thompson-Spires hold appointments at universities, and each writes self-consciously in relationship to a long tradition of African American women's writing reaching back to the late eighteenth century. The influence of The Sisterhood's generation of Black feminist writers is visible in so many places, from Shockley's poem "double bop for ntozake shange" in *a half-red sea* (2006) to Evans titling *Before You Suffocate Your Own Fool Self* after a line from Kate Rushin's "The Bridge Poem," which appeared in the 1981 feminist anthology *This Bridge Called My Back* (1981).[18] All of these Black women authors, and others, write directly or indirectly about how to live in a United States defined by state-sanctioned or state-enacted murder of Black people, especially at the hands of police. These women write poems, stories, and novels that, like the works of The Sisterhood, are tools for a survival that includes grief, but also play, pleasure, and complex interior lives.

Queer identities, sexuality, desire, and embodiment are central to recent books by Black women who locate themselves in The Sisterhood's lineage. Bettina Judd's *Patient* (2014) is a volume of poetry that weaves together the speaker's contemporary experiences with the history of medical racism and gynecological experimentation on Black women. Audre Lorde's *The Cancer Journals* (1980) is a clear predecessor to Judd's formally experimental writing that connects one Black woman's experience to larger systems of medical racism, sexism, and homophobia. In Mecca Jamilah Sullivan's *Big Girl* (2022), protagonist Malaya Clondon works to inhabit her big, Black body, her hungers and desires, and her place in both her family and her gentrifying 1990s New York neighborhood. In its close attention the protagonist's physicality, the complexity of a Black mother-daughter relationship, and the navigation of sexual and physical desire with both pleasure and confusion, *Big Girl* is a descendant of Lorde's book *Zami: A New Spelling of My Name* (1982). The short story writer Deesha Philyaw and genre-defying writer Alexis Pauline Gumbs are among this cohort of current Black feminist writers whose works show that desire and sex among women, queer politics, and deep investment in a Black feminist lineage are parts of The Sisterhood's legacy that have become even more visible in the work of their descendants.

The Sisterhood remains a useful example for readers, writers, students, and teachers right now. Their collaborative everyday work was largely invisible and often mundane; it also sustained them and transformed two major cultural institutions—publishing and the academy. There were limits to this transformation: they worked in a period of disappointment that the civil rights and Black Power movements had not achieved many of their goals, and in recent decades white supremacy has adapted and reasserted itself in both spheres. The women of The Sisterhood continued from the 1970s on, knowing and naming these limits and dangers. The everyday labor, dissent, collaboration, and consequences of their collective efforts offer both models and cautionary tales, particularly for the many young people who have in recent years marched, sat in, and otherwise engaged in direct political actions against racist police violence and for racial justice.

Some Sisterhood members were still working in universities in 2015 when, following the police murder of Michael Brown, student activism across the country again created a wave of support for Black studies units and hiring of Black faculty. It simply cannot continue to be the burden of college students, particularly of Black students at predominantly white universities, to make our educational institutions more just. Sisterhood members—editors, journalists, writers, intellectuals, teachers—are models for how those of us committed to Black literature and liberation can work for justice using the skills we have. A refuge for Black women intellectuals is as necessary right now as it was when The Sisterhood began meeting over four decades ago. The academy remains hostile to and dangerous for Black people and Black studies, from the everyday racism that Black people at predominantly white institutions face, to the increase of hate crimes in countless college towns over the past several years, to faculty job insecurity created by the current wave of legislation against an inaccurate and misunderstood idea of "critical race theory." What Barbara Christian named as "Diminishing Returns" in 1994 persists, and scholars are rightly skeptical about the increasingly corporate university as a site of liberation. Even so, as the women of The Sisterhood knew, it is important to send young people into the world armed with an understanding of Black studies and especially of African American literature.

Something shifted between student protests in 2015 and the uprising against racist police violence in 2020. In a way that struck me as new, students in my undergraduate classes assumed the interdependence of literary study and direct political action. They understood it as entirely of a piece to read June Jordan's poetry and then march in the streets, masked during a pandemic, to protest police brutality including the murders of Ahmaud Arbery, George Floyd, and Breonna Taylor. In this time of intersecting crises, this time of change and loss and maybe possibility, young people on and beyond college campuses are practicing consciousness raising and mutual aid. They are rightly interested in the radical imagination of Black feminists in the 1970s who demanded free child care, free college tuition, and open admissions; advocated for Black women's writing; and wrote fiction, poetry, and plays. The lessons and literature of The Sisterhood are resources for students, writers, and activists who are, right now, imagining and making a better world.

ACKNOWLEDGMENTS

A Public Scholars Award from the National Endowment for the Humanities in 2018–19 made it possible for me to complete this book. At the University of Oregon, summer stipends in 2016 and 2021 from the Office of the Vice President for Research and Innovation, summer 2018 support from the College of Arts and Sciences, and a 2016–17 sabbatical provided necessary time for research and writing. A subvention from the The Oregon Humanities Center and the College of Arts and Sciences funded the index.

Every stage of work on this book has depended on archivists and librarians. I owe a particular debt to years of correspondence and collegiality offered by Kathy Shoemaker at Emory University's Stuart A. Rose Manuscript, Archives, and Rare Book Library; Holly Smith, Taronda Spencer, and Kassandra Ware at the Spelman College Archives in the Women's Research and Resource Center; and Martha Tenney at the Barnard Archives and Special Collections. I am grateful to every single photographer, writer, son or daughter, brother or sister, literary estate, repository, and other rights holders who granted permission to include images, poetry, and unpublished archival materials. This is one of what I hope will be many books made possible by the foresight of Black women writers and intellectuals—Toni Cade Bambara, Lucille Clifton, Audre Lorde, Toni Morrison, Ntozake Shange, Michele Wallace, Alice Walker, and others—who valued and preserved their archives and made them available to researchers. Margo Jefferson, Patricia Spears Jones, Renita Weems, and Judith Wilson-Pates, thank you for your generosity with your time, memories, and intellect. Thank you for your Sisterhood work, then, now, and still to come.

Kathleen Anderson helps me dream big for the life of my writing. Philip Leventhal is a smart and generous interlocutor who made this book better. I am grateful to Philip, Monique Laban, Caitlin Hurst, and their colleagues at Columbia University Press for rigorous and careful work rooted in a love of books. Four insightful and careful anonymous readers for the Press seriously engaged with my work (during the academic labor demands of a pandemic, no less!) in ways that sharpened my thinking and writing. Leslie Kriesel is a precise copyeditor who paid profoundly close and generous attention to my writing. Ben Kolstad managed the production process with clear and kind communication. Catherine Huff approached obtaining permissions for material in this book with intellectual curiosity, grace, and expertise.

For their enthusiasm for this work and for kindness that sustained me in an academic workplace while I wrote this book, I am grateful to University of Oregon scholars and friends past and present: Leslie Alexander, Curtis Austin, Faith Barter, Joel Black, Liz Bohls, David Bradley, Lara Bovilsky, Kirby Brown, Karen Ford, Miriam Gershow, Mat Johnson, Carmel Ohman, Paul Peppis, Taylor McHolm, Tres Pyle, Shoniqua Roach, Angie Rovak, Ben Saunders, Casey Shoop, Avinnash Tiwari, David Vazquez, Mary Wood, and Mark Whalan.

There have been many moments when brilliant people offered a research tip, words of encouragement and inspiration, useful questions, gentle correction, or crucial practical advice. Among those who helped me and this book along our way are Michael Awkward, Sarah Jane Cervenak, Margo Crawford, Gabrielle Foreman, Alexis Gumbs, Beverly Guy-Sheftall, Kim Hall, Aida Levy-Hussen, Tricia Matthew, Koritha Mitchell, Harryette Mullen, Ed Pavlić, Kevin Quashie, Anthony Reed, Evie Shockley, Mecca Jamilah Sullivan, Michele Wallace, and Mary Helen Washington.

For conversations that shaped this work, for the models of beauty and rigor their writing offers, for believing that this book was necessary and urgent, and especially for thinking I was the person to write it, I am grateful to Erica Edwards, Farah Griffin, Emily Lordi, Howard Rambsy, Matt Sandler, Carol Stabile, and Cheryl Wall. Erica, Matt, and Carol read drafts of this book and offered feedback that made it better. Emily helped me find the courage to write the book I wanted to. Howard sets the bar for how to be in this profession. Writing in conversation with Erica has been among the greatest joys of this project. Farah, beloved mentor and friend, lights the way.

I wish Cheryl were here to see this book in print. I hope some of what Matt has taught me about how friendship can define life and work is clear in these pages.

I'm lucky enough to have more supportive friends and family than I can name here, but a few require special mention. Shout out to the quaranteam: Carol Stabile, Mark Unger, and Tony Unger, who toasted every stage of this book. Millie Smith is righteous and kind. Anna Ford, Jason Hershman, and Ava Hershman make me laugh and play, and they have been excited about this book from the start. Duncan Haberly, Matt Sandler, and Jenn Sharp are spectacular, smart people and true, forever, ride-or-die friends who make me have fun, feel most myself, and remember that there's life outside of work. Thora Colot is generous with her whole heart. I hope to someday be half as good as she is at making family and community. Christine Rothman, the best mom there is, listens and loves unconditionally. I've finally figured out that if I am becoming more like my mother with every passing day, then I am doing something right. Peter Colot Thorsson gets more interesting, impressive, fun, and enthusiastic about my writing and teaching with each passing year. The life we've made together is more than I ever dared to expect. What a thing to love and be loved by my favorite person!

PERMISSIONS

MEMBERS OF THE SISTERHOOD

Zita Allen attended March 20, 1977, and May 15, 1977, meetings. A dance writer since the 1970s, Allen was the first African American critic at *Dance Magazine* and a founding contributor to *The Feet*, a 1970s Black dance publication. Her articles have appeared in the *Amsterdam News, New York Times, Village Voice, SoHo Weekly News,* and *Essence.* She is the author of *Black Women Leaders of the Civil Rights Movement* (1996), a book aimed at middle school and high school readers, and the souvenir book *Alvin Ailey American Dance Theater, 25 Years* (1983). Allen is a contributor to *Ain't Nothing Like the Real Thing: How the Apollo Theater Shaped American Entertainment* (2010) and the *Encyclopedia of African-American Culture and History.* She holds an MA in dance history from New York University and is completing her PhD at Temple University.

Audreen Ballard (1938–), also known as Audreen Buffalo, appears in the famous 1977 photo; attended the February 10, 1977, lunch meeting with Morrison and Abike; and was at other meetings of the group. Ballard served as co-chair of Black Perspective, a group that organized and lobbied on behalf of Black journalists. She worked as a journalist and editor at *Essence, Redbook,* and *Lear's* and is the author of a biography of Oprah Winfrey. She acted in a dramatization of Toni Cade Bambara's "The Johnson Girls."[1]

Rosemary Bray, now Rosemary Bray McNatt, does not appear in any extant meeting minutes, but Renita Weems recalls that she was a member of the group and invited Weems to attend. Bray was an editor at *Essence* when The Sisterhood started meeting.[2] She earned her BA from Yale; has worked at *The New York Daily News*, *The Wall Street Journal*, *Ms.*, and *The New York Review of Books*; and is the author of a memoir, *Not Afraid of the Dark* (1998).[3] Bray earned her master's of divinity at Drew Theological Seminary, served as senior minister of the Fourth Universalist Society in New York, and served as president of Starr King School for the Ministry in Berkeley, California.

Nancy Clare is listed as an attendee in Wilson's minutes for the April 10, 1977, meeting.

Vèvè Clark (1944–2007) attended the April 10, 1977; March 20, 1977; and May 15, 1977, meetings per Wilson's minutes. Clark was a professor of African American studies at the University of California, Berkeley for sixteen years and a literary scholar known for coining the term "diaspora literacy." She also taught at Tufts and served as a fellow-in-residence at Brown. She coedited *The Legend of Maya Deren* (1984), *Kaiso! Writings by and about Katherine Dunham* (1978, 2006), *Revising the Word and the World: Essays in Feminist Literary Criticism* (1993), and *Anti-feminism in the Academy* (1996).

Andaye De La Cruz attended the March 20, 1977, meeting per Wilson's minutes. De La Cruz worked for the New York City Department of Education.

Audrey Edwards (1947–) is a journalist and the author of children's books about Stevie Wonder and Muhammad Ali. She earned her BA from the University of Washington in 1969 and her MA from Columbia University in 1974. Edwards became associate editor at *Black Enterprise* magazine in 1977 and senior editor at *Family Circle* in 1978. She was the executive editor of *Essence* from 1981 to 1986. In 1990, she returned to *Black Enterprise* magazine as executive editor and vice president of editorial operations, and in 1998, she became a senior editor at *More* magazine. Edwards coauthored, with Craig Polite, *Children of the Dream: The Psychology of Black Success* (1992); coauthored, with Patricia Hinds, *Essence: 25 Years of Celebrating Black Women* (1995); and wrote *Emil Holzhauer: Portrait of an Artist* (2001). She is coauthor of Edward Lewis's biography *The Man from Essence: Creating a Magazine for Black Women* (2014). Edwards also ran a real estate company for over twenty years and has taught journalism courses at Columbia and NYU.

Phyl Garland (1935–2006) attended the February 20, 1977, and May 15, 1977, meetings and hosted the April 10, 1977, meeting. A journalist and teacher, she worked as a writer and editor at *The Pittsburg Courier* from 1958 to

1965 and as associate editor at *Ebony* from 1967 to 1969. She taught at the State University of New York at New Paltz, where she was acting chair of the Black studies department. In 1981, Garland became the first African American to earn tenure in Columbia's School of Journalism. She is the author of a history of Black music, *The Sound of Soul* (1969), a writer on the documentary film *Adam Clayton Powell* (1989), and the author of many articles in *Ebony* and other periodicals.

Vertamae Grosvenor (1938–2016) appears in the 1977 photo and attended several Sisterhood meetings. Grosvenor was a culinary anthropologist and author of books including *Vibration Cooking or, the Travel Notes of a Geechee Girl* (1970) and *Thursdays and Every Other Sunday Off: A Domestic Rap* (1974). She danced with Sun Ra's Arkestra, appeared in Julie Dash's *Daughters of the Dust* (1992), commented regularly for NPR, and created the PBS show "The Americas' Family Kitchen" and wrote two companion cookbooks for that show: *Vertamae Cooks in the Americas' Family Kitchen* (1996) and *Vertamae Cooks Again: More Recipes from the Americas' Family Kitchen* (1999).

Rosa Guy (1922–2012) attended the May 15, 1977, meeting and other meetings. She was a Trinidadian-born playwright, short story author, novelist, and helped start the Harlem Writers' Guild. Guy is the author of many books for both adults and young adults. Her best-known novel, *Ruby* (1976), is part of a trilogy with *The Friends* (1973) and *Edith Jackson* (1978).

Jessica Harris (1948–) attended the February 20, 1977, meeting. Harris is a scholar of food and foodways of the African Diaspora and the author of cookbooks and culinary studies including *Iron Pots and Wooden Spoons: Africa's Gifts to New World Cooking* (1989) and *High on the Hog* (2011) and a memoir, *My Soul Looks Back* (2017). As a journalist, Harris has written reviews and articles on various subjects for many periodicals including *Essence*. She is a founding member of the Southern Foodways Alliance and hosted the radio show and podcast *My Welcome Table*. Harris has long been a professor of English at Queens College in the City University of New York system.

Joan Harris is copied on Patricia Spears Jones's letter to Renita Weems of March 3, 1978, about The Sisterhood. Harris cohosted the 1970s television show *Positively Black*.

Margo Jefferson (1947–) attended the February 20, 1977, and April 10, 1977, meetings, hosted one later meeting, and attended other meetings of the group. She earned her BA from Brandeis and her MS from the Columbia

University Graduate School of Journalism. She worked at *Newsweek* from 1973 to 1978 and was an assistant professor at the Department of Journalism and Mass Communication at NYU from 1979 to 1983 and again from 1989 to 1991. Jefferson began working at the *New York Times* in 1993 as a book critic. She is currently a professor of professional practice in writing at Columbia University School of the Arts. Jefferson is the author of *On Michael Jackson* (2006); *Negroland* (2015), which won a National Book Critics Circle Award; and *Constructing a Nervous System* (2022). She won a Pulitzer Prize for her cultural criticism, which has appeared in *Newsweek*, the *New York Times*, *New York Magazine*, and *Harper's*, among many other publications.

Patricia Spears Jones (1951–) attended the May 15, 1977, meeting and later meetings. Jones is a poet and playwright. She worked as the grant program director for the Coordinating Council of Literary Magazines in New York from 1977 to 1981. Jones holds an MFA from the Vermont College of Fine Arts. Her poetry collections include *Painkiller* (2010), *Femme du Monde* (2006), *The Weather That Kills* (1995), and *A Lucent Fire: New and Selected Poems* (2015). Her work has been featured in anthologies including *Angles of Ascent: A Norton Anthology of Contemporary African American Poetry* (2013), *Starting Today: 100 Poems for Obama's First 100 Days* (2010), *Black Nature: Four Centuries of African American Nature Poetry* (2009), and *Best American Poetry* (2000). Jones has taught at LaGuardia Community College, Parsons, The New School, Hunter College, and the College of New Rochelle. She won the Jackson Poetry Prize in 2017. Her book *The Beloved Community* is forthcoming from Copper Canyon Press.

June Jordan (1936–2002) cofounded The Sisterhood and attended most or all meetings. Jordan was a poet, essayist, activist, teacher, and author of many books. Her works include a biography of Fannie Lou Hamer for young readers and twenty-seven volumes of poetry, among them *Some Changes* (1971), *Living Room* (1985), and *Kissing God Goodbye: Poems 1991–1997* (1997). Her books of essays include *Civil Wars: Selected Essays 1963–1980* (1981) and *On Call: Political Essays* (1985).

Audre Lorde (1934–1992) attended the March 20, 1977, meeting and likely attended later meetings. Lorde was a poet, essayist, teacher, and activist. Her books include the "biomythography" *Zami: A New Spelling of My Name* (1982); the essay collection *Sister Outsider* (1984); *The Cancer Journals* (1980); and the volumes of poetry *Cables to Rage* (1970), *From a Land Where Other People Live* (1973), *New York Head Shop and Museum* (1974), *Coal* (1976), and *The Black Unicorn* (1978).

Paule Marshall (1929–2019) attended the February 20, 1977; March 20, 1977; April 10, 1977; and May 15, 1977, meetings. She is the author of novels including *Brown Girl, Brownstones* (1959), *The Chosen Place, the Timeless People* (1969), *Praisesong for the Widow* (1983), and *The Fisher King* (2001); the story collections *Soul Clap Hands and Sing* (1961) and *Reena and Other Stories* (1983); the memoir *Triangular Road* (2009); and the essay "From the Poets in the Kitchen" (1983). Marshall taught English and creative writing at Virginia Commonwealth University, New York University, Yale, the Iowa Writers' Workshop, and the University of California, Berkeley.

Nana Maynard, now Dr. Sananda Ananda-Maynard, appears in the photo from the February 6, 1977 meeting; is listed as an attendee in Wilson's minutes for the April 10, 1977, and May 15, 1977, meetings; and hosted the March 20, 1977, meeting at the home in Brooklyn she shared with Abike. She is an advanced teacher of Transcendental Meditation.[4]

Susan McHenry does not appear in minutes for meetings in the first months of The Sisterhood, but joined later. Margo Jefferson recalls that McHenry was part of The Sisterhood and "the only Black editor" at *Ms.* when the group was meeting. Patricia Spears Jones recalls that McHenry was "definitely at meetings" of The Sisterhood.[5] McHenry holds a BA in American history and literature from Harvard-Radcliffe and an MA in literature from Boston University. She was a senior editor at *Ms.* from 1978 to 1987, founded *Emerge* in 1990, helped launch *Black Issues Book Review*, worked for *Essence*, and has taught at New York University, Medgar Evers College, and Borough of Manhattan Community College.

Madeline Moore attended the May 15, 1977, meeting per Wilson's minutes.

Toni Morrison (1931–2019) attended the first meeting of The Sisterhood; a smaller February 10, 1977, meeting about publishing; and the April 10, 1977, meeting. She earned her MA at Cornell University and taught literature and writing courses at Texas Southern University, Howard, Yale, SUNY Purchase, Bard College, SUNY Albany, and Princeton. She retired from Princeton in 2006.[6] Morrison wrote eleven novels and won the Nobel Prize for Literature, among many other awards.

Patricia Murray is listed as an attendee in Wilson's minutes for the February 20, 1977; March 20, 1977; and April 10, 1977, meetings. During the time The Sisterhood met, Murray was known as Abike. As Abike, she wrote a letter to the group in March 1977 with detailed minutes from meetings on February 6, 1977, and February 20, 1977, as well as notes from the lunch meeting she attended on February 10, 1977, with Audreen Ballard and Toni Morrison. She lived with Nana Maynard in Brooklyn, and they hosted the March 20, 1977, meeting. June Jordan identifies Murray as her lawyer in correspondence with Random House in 1979.

Pamela Roach is listed as an attendee in Wilson's minutes for the April 10, 1977, meeting.

Sheila Rush (1940–) attended the April 10, 1977; March 20, 1977; and May 15, 1977, meetings and hosted meetings on July 12, 1977, and later. She sometimes used her married name, Sheila Okpaku, while she was married to publisher Joseph Okpaku. Rush coauthored *How to Get Along with Black People. A Handbook for White Folks. And Some Black Folks Too* (1971) with Chris Clark, published scholarly articles on legal subjects, graduated from Harvard Law School in 1964, worked as a lawyer including for the NAACP Legal Defense Fund, taught at Hofstra University, and was a full professor at Harvard Law School. Rush resigned from Harvard and moved to California in 1980 to join the Ananda spiritual community, where she also used the name Nayaswami Naidhruva. At Ananda, Rush did various forms of work including as a lawyer for the group through at least 1998, editor for their publications at least through the early 2000s, and as a minister and speaker.[7]

Ntozake Shange (1948–2018) appears in the 1977 photo and attended later meetings. Shange was a poet, playwright, novelist, essayist, and author of several books for children. Her writings include the "choreopoem" *for colored girls who have considered suicide/when the rainbow is enuf* (1975); the novels *Sassafrass, Cypress and Indigo* (1982) and *Lillane* (1995); and the hybrid memoir-cookbook *If I Can Cook You Know God Can* (1999). Shange earned a BA in American studies from Barnard College and an MA in American studies from the University of Southern California.

Lori Sharpe appears in the photo and also attended meetings on February 20, 1977; March 20, 1977; April 10, 1977; and May 15, 1977. Sharpe was a founding member of the National Black Feminist Organization and wrote the section "Supplemental Guidelines for Black Women" for the 1975 edition of the Women's Action Alliance booklet *Consciousness-Raising Guidelines*. She worked at *Ms.* in the 1970s.

Donna Simms attended the April 10, 1977, and May 15, 1977, meetings. Under the name Donna Allegra, she was the host and producer of WBAI radio shows including *The Lesbian Show* and *The Velvet Sledgehammer*, both of which featured poets including June Jordan and Pat Parker.[8]

Alice Walker (1944–) cofounded The Sisterhood, hosted the first meeting, and attended most meetings of the group. Walker is a prolific novelist, poet, essayist, and activist. Her novels include *The Third Life of Grange Copeland* (1970), *Meridian* (1976), and *The Color Purple* (1982), which won the National Book Award and the Pulitzer Prize for Fiction. Her many other works include *Revolutionary Petunias and Other Poems* (1973) and the essay collection *In Search of Our Mothers' Gardens: Womanist Prose* (1983).

Diane Weathers (1950–) attended the May 15, 1977, meeting and hosted the November 20, 1977, meeting. She holds a BA in journalism from Syracuse University. She was a writer and editor for *Newsweek* for eight years, a senior editor at *Redbook*, and editor in chief of *Essence* from 2001 to 2005. Weathers has written for many publications including *Black Enterprise*, the *Atlanta Black Star*, and *Black World*. She served as the assistant vice president of communications and marketing at Bronx Community College.

Renita Weems (1954–) attended the May 15, 1977, meeting; organized the December 18, 1977, meeting; attended other meetings of the group; and served as correspondence secretary for The Sisterhood. Weems is an ordained minister in the African Methodist Episcopal Church and holds a PhD from Princeton Theological Seminary. She is the author of books about faith, scripture, and women's spirituality including *Showing Mary: How Women Can Share Prayers, Wisdom, and the Blessings of God* (2002) and *Just a Sister Away: A Womanist Vision of Women's Relationships in the Bible* (1988). Weems has held faculty positions in the Divinity School at Vanderbilt University, as the Cosby Professor of the Humanities at Spelman College, and at American Baptist College. She has written for *Beliefnet.com* and *Essence* and is copastor of the Ray of Hope Community Church in Nashville, Tennessee.

Judith Wilson (1952–), now Judith Wilson-Pates, served as secretary for The Sisterhood and attended the February 20, 1977; March 20, 1977; April 10, 1977; May 15, 1977; and other meetings. She holds a BA from Bennington College and a PhD in art history from Yale. She has held faculty positions at Yale, the University of Virginia, Syracuse University, Barnard College, and the University of California, Irvine. She has published articles in venues including the *Village Voice, Art in America,* and *Women's Art Journal* and written numerous catalogue essays for art exhibitions including *Lorraine O'Grady: Critical Interventions* (1991), *The Decade Show* (1990), and *Next Generation: Southern Black Aesthetic* (1990). Wilson retired from UC Irvine in 2006 and lives in San Francisco.

MEETINGS OF THE SISTERHOOD

February 6, 1977: At June Jordan's home, 75 Eighth Avenue, Brooklyn, NY (Park Slope), attended by Jordan, Alice Walker, Lori Sharpe, Toni Morrison, Ntozake Shange, Vertamae Grosvenor, Nana Maynard, and Audreen Ballard

February 10, 1977: Abike, Audreen Ballard, and Toni Morrison lunch meeting

February 20, 1977: At June Jordan's home, 75 Eighth Avenue, Brooklyn, NY (Park Slope), attended by Jordan, Alice Walker, Judith Wilson, Patricia Murray, Margo Jefferson, Paule Marshall, Phyl Garland, Lori Sharpe, and Jessica Harris

March 20, 1977: 2 p.m. at Abike and Nana Maynard's home, 73 Eighth Avenue, Brooklyn, NY (Park Slope), attended by Zita Allen, Vèvè Clark, Andaye DeLaCruz, June Jordan, Audre Lorde, Paule Marshall, Nana Maynard, Patricia Murray (Abike), Sheila Okpaku (Sheila Rush), Lori Sharpe, Alice Walker, and Judith Wilson

April 10, 1977: 2 p.m. at Phyl Garland's home, 60 East Eighth Street, #23, New York, NY (between Mercer and Broadway in the East Village), attended by Nancy Clare, Vèvè Clark, Phyl Garland, Margo Jefferson, Paule Marshall, Nana Maynard, Patricia Murray, Pamela Roach, Sheila Rush, Lori Sharpe, Donna Simms, Alice Walker, and Judith Wilson

May 15, 1977: At Alice Walker's home, 216 Garfield Place, Brooklyn, NY (Park Slope), attended by Zita Allen, VèVè Clark, Phyl Garland, Rosa Guy, Patricia Spears Jones, June Jordan, Paule Marshall, Nana Maynard, Madeline Moore, Patricia Murray, Sheila Rush, Lori Sharpe, Donna Simms, Alice Walker, Diane Weathers, Renita Weems, and Judith Wilson

June 12, 1977: 2 p.m. at Sheila Rush's home, 685 West End Avenue, New York, NY (at Ninety-Third Street on the Upper West Side), attended by Rush, Patricia Spears Jones, Toni Morrison, and others

July–September 1977: One meeting at Margo Jefferson's home, one meeting at Paule Marshall's home, and at least one meeting at Sheila Rush's home

October 1977: At June Jordan's home

November 20, 1977: At Diane Weathers's home, 470 Lenox Avenue, #171, New York, NY

December 18, 1977: At Wellesley Club in the Biltmore Hotel, 335 Madison Avenue, New York, NY

February 1978: Meeting canceled

March 1978–December 1978: Meetings continued

January or February 1979: Last meeting

NOTES

INTRODUCTION

1. Evelyn C. White, *Alice Walker: A Life* (New York: Norton, 2004), n.p.
2. "The Sisterhood, 1977," photograph, 1977, box 184, folder 12, Alice Walker Papers, Stuart A. Rose Manuscripts, Archives, and Rare Book Library, Emory University.
3. See Rudolph P. Byrd, "Introduction," in *The World Has Changed: Conversations with Alice Walker*, ed. Rudolph P. Byrd (New York: The New Press, 2010), 22–23; Jamey Hatley, "Read My World," *Oxford American*, March 13, 2018; and Michael D. Hill, *The Ethics of Swagger: Prizewinning African American Novels, 1977–1993* (Columbus: Ohio State University Press, 2013), 57.
4. I am grateful to poet and scholar Harryette Mullen for our July 2022 email exchange of research confirming that Ballard is the woman in the archival photo of The Sisterhood. A 1974 photo of Ballard in Alabama Department of Archives and History is the same woman in the Sisterhood photo (https://digital.archives.alabama.gov /digital/collection/photo/id/40857/rec/1); Our Mothers' Kitchens, a community organization inspired by members of The Sisterhood, confirmed in consultation with Vertamae Grosvenor's daughter Kali Grosvenor that the woman pictured is Ballard (https://www.eventbrite.com/e/in-search-of-the-body-is-not-an-apology-tickets -355064145417?aff=erelexpmlt); and writer Jacqui Shine confirmed in 2018 that it is Ballard and not Edwards pictured by asking Edwards directly (https://medium .com/@jacquishine/free-space-feminism-consciousness-raising-and-the-black-radical -imagination-eed40e85b770).
5. Alice Walker, "'Outlaw, Renegade, Rebel, Pagan': Interview with Amy Goodman from *Democracy Now!*," 2006, in Byrd, *The World Has Changed*, 278.
6. Walker, "Outlaw," 278. Jordan and Walker both had that photo of Bessie Smith by Carl Van Vechten framed and hung in their apartments. Patricia Spears Jones, "Creation Is Everything You Do: Shange, The Sisterhood & Black Collectivity," panel and discussion with Mecca Jamilah Sullivan and Courtney Thorsson, Barnard College, New York, March 16, 2021, https://www.youtube.com/watch?v=tv322Y_qZgc.

7. Alice Walker, "On Raising Chickens: A Conversation with Rudolph P. Byrd," in Byrd, *The World Has Changed*, 318.

8. One prominent example of resisting competition is Audre Lorde, Adrienne Rich, and Alice Walker's response to being nominees for the 1974 National Book Award for poetry. They wrote a collective feminist statement "refusing the terms of patriarchal competition," and Rich, when she and Allen Ginsberg won the award, read that statement aloud at the ceremony. Alexis De Veaux, *Warrior Poet: A Biography of Audre Lorde* (New York: Norton, 2004), 133–134.

9. VèVè Clark, "In-House Proposal: re. Publishing in Popular Magazines," box 102, folder 2, Alice Walker Papers, Stuart A. Rose Manuscripts, Archives, and Rare Book Library, Emory University, 3.

10. Journalist Emma Brockes writes that Morrison "was supported at home by a network of women friends, who helped her with the kids, and some of whose fiction she published." "Toni Morrison: 'I want to feel what I feel. Even if it's not happiness,'" *Guardian*, April 13, 2012. This mention of a "network" that centers Morrison and suggests casual friendships rather than organized, collective work is typical of references to The Sisterhood in journalism and scholarship. Evelyn White describes The Sisterhood in similar terms as "composed of black women who gathered, informally, to socialize, share their creative work, and debate the political issues of the day" (288–289). The 2014 edition of the *Norton Anthology of African American Literature* includes the photo and describes the group as "informal" (919).

11. Renita Weems, interview by Courtney Thorsson, January 8, 2019.

12. See appendix 1 for information about each member of The Sisterhood.

13. Kimberly Springer writes, "Use of terms such as *social movement community, protest fields*, and *sisterhood* create a space for inserting black feminist organizations into women's movement history." *Living for the Revolution: Black Feminist Organizations, 1968–1980* (Durham, NC: Duke University Press, 2005), 171.

14. Patricia Spears Jones to Renita Weems, 3 March 1978, box 101, folder 3, June Jordan Papers, Schlesinger Library, Radcliffe Institute, Harvard University, 2.

15. Margo Jefferson, interview by Courtney Thorsson, May 31, 2018.

16. Jefferson, interview by Thorsson.

17. Farah Griffin's *If You Can't Be Free, Be a Mystery: In Search of Billie Holiday* (2001) opens with the sentence "This is not a biography of Billie Holiday." Griffin's approach shaped Gayle Wald's *Shout, Sister, Shout!: The Untold Story of Rock-and-Roll Trailblazer Sister Rosetta Tharpe* (2007) and at the September 2022 conference at Yale celebrating Griffin's work, Wald offered this insight: "Black feminist biographies of Black women are by definition 'experimental.'"

18. Audre Lorde, "Learning from the 60s," 1982, in *Sister Outsider* (Berkeley, CA: Ten Speed Press, 1984), 140.

19. Farah Jasmine Griffin, "That the Mothers May Soar and the Daughters May Know Their Names: A Retrospective of Black Feminist Literary Criticism," 2007, in *Still Brave: The Evolution of Black Women's Studies*, ed. Stanlie M. James, Frances Smith-Foster, and Beverly Guy-Sheftall (New York: Feminist Press, 2009), 336–337.

1. "REVOLUTION IS NOT A ONE-TIME EVENT"

1. Audre Lorde, "Learning from the 60s," 1982, in *Sister Outsider* (Berkeley, CA: Ten Speed Press, 1984), 140, 134, 137.

2. Toni Cade Bambara, interview by Claudia Tate, in *Black Women Writers at Work*, ed. Claudia Tate (New York: Continuum, 1984), 13.

3. As Kim Phillips-Fein explains, "The view of higher education as a right that could be claimed by any New York resident" "articulated a conception of citizenship that was much more expansive than any to be found at the national level" and it was thus a prime target of President Gerald Ford and others as "a symbol of the city's excessive generosity." *Fear City: New York's Fiscal Crisis and the Rise of Austerity Politics*. 2017 (New York: Picador, 2018), 243.

4. Phillips-Fein, *Fear City*, 2.

5. Phillips-Fein, *Fear City*, 3.

6. Kimberly Springer describes this arc: "Like many social movement organizations of the period, the black feminist organizational cycle began with the opening of political opportunities in the late 1960s and ended with the backlash against civil rights and women's rights gains during the Reagan presidency . . . black feminists . . . often found their activism institutionalized in social services, governmental bodies, higher education institutions, and other organizations they could attempt to influence with antiracist and antisexist ideology" (*Living for the Revolution: Black Feminist Organizations, 1968–1980* [Durham, NC: Duke University Press, 2005], 9–10).

7. Sherie M. Randolph writes that Flo "Kennedy's story forces us to recognize the Black Power movement's central role in shaping radical feminism. Strategies and theories understood to have originated in Black Power struggles were absorbed, if at times unevenly, by both black and white feminists." *Florynce "Flo" Kennedy: The Life of a Black Feminist Radical* (Chapel Hill: University of North Carolina Press, 2015), 5.

8. Alexis De Veaux, *Warrior Poet: A Biography of Audre Lorde* (New York: Norton, 2004), 131; Christoph Keller and Jan Heller Levi, eds., *We're On: A June Jordan Reader* (Farmington, ME: Alice James Books, 2017), 94. BAM venues were more likely than white journals and presses to publish works by Black women writers (De Veaux, *Warrior Poet*, 91–92, 116).

9. See Courtney Thorsson, *Women's Work: Nationalism and Contemporary African American Women's Novels* (Charlottesville: University of Virginia Press, 2013), 14–24.

10. *The Black Book* (1974), which Morrison edited, makes a related implicit claim that text is a form of collectivity. See Toni Morrison, "Behind the Making of the Black Book," *Black World* 23, no. 4 (February 1974): 86–90, and Cheryl A. Wall, "Toni Morrison, editor and teacher," in *The Cambridge Companion to Toni Morrison*, ed. Justine Tally (Cambridge: Cambridge University Press, 2007), 143.

11. Springer, *Living for the Revolution*, 1–2. Robin Kelley notes that the Third World Women's Alliance was the "offspring" of the Black Women's Liberation Committee of the Student Non-Violent Coordinating Committee (SNCC). Robin Kelley, *Freedom Dreams: The Black Radical Imagination* (Boston: Beacon, 2002), 143.

12. Springer, *Living for the Revolution*, 1.

13. Beverly Davis, "To Seize the Moment: A Retrospective on the National Black Feminist Organization," *SAGE* 5, no. 2 (Fall 1988): 43. See Randolph, *Florynce "Flo" Kennedy*, 205–210.

14. Davis, "To Seize the Moment," 44.

15. Vertamae Smart Grosvenor, *Thursdays and Every Other Sunday Off: A Domestic Rap by Verta Mae* (New York: Doubleday, 1972), 31.

16. Grosvenor, *Thursdays*, 9, 66.

17. Grosvenor, *Thursdays*, 153.

18. Davis, "To Seize the Moment," 44, 46.

19. National Black Feminist Organization (NBFO), Statement of Purpose, 1973, box 14, folder "Black Women's Organizations 1973–1976," Michele Wallace Papers, Manuscripts, Archives, and Rare Books Division, Schomburg Center for Research in Black Culture, The New York Public Library.

20. Davis, "To Seize the Moment," 45.

21. James Smethurst, "Retraining the Heartworks: Women in Atlanta's Black Arts Movement" in *Want to Start A Revolution?: Radical Women in The Black Freedom Struggle*, ed. Dayo F. Gore, Jeanne Theoharis, and Komozi Woodard (New York: New York University Press, 2009), 218.

22. National Black Feminist Organization (NBFO), Newsletter, September 1975, box 14, folder "Black Women's Organizations 1973–1976," Michele Wallace Papers, Manuscripts, Archives, and Rare Books Division, Schomburg Center for Research in Black Culture, The New York Public Library.

23. Springer, *Living for the Revolution*, 1; Davis, "To Seize the Moment," 46.

24. "Trying to Make the Personal Political," reprint of 1975 "Consciousness-Raising Guidelines" with new foreword by Mariame Kaba and afterword by Jacqui Shine (Chicago: Half Letter Press, 2017), 42; National Black Feminist Organization (NBFO), Writers' Workshop Program, box 14, folder "Black Women's Organizations 1973–1976," Michele Wallace Papers, Manuscripts, Archives, and Rare Books Division, Schomburg Center for Research in Black Culture, The New York Public Library, 1; Springer, *Living for the Revolution*, 102; Margo Jefferson, interview by Courtney Thorsson, May 31, 2018; Judith Wilson, interview by Courtney Thorsson, February 12, 2019; National Black Feminist Organization (NBFO), "First Eastern Regional Conference on Black Feminism," November 30, 1973–December 2, 1973, box 14, folder "Black Women's Organizations 1973–1976," Michele Wallace Papers, Manuscripts, Archives, and Rare Books Division, Schomburg Center for Research in Black Culture, The New York Public Library.

25. Springer, *Living for the Revolution*, 56; Keeanga-Yamahtta Taylor, ed., *How We Get Free: Black Feminism and The Combahee River Collective* (Chicago: Haymarket Books, 2017), 77. Around this time, future Sisterhood cofounder June Jordan was writing speeches for James Farmer, national director of CORE. See Alexis De Veaux, "Creating Soul Food: June Jordan," *Essence* 11, no. 82 (April 1981): 145.

26. Springer, *Living for the Revolution*, 56–59.

27. Taylor, *How We Get Free*, 41.

28. Combahee River Collective, "The Combahee River Collective Statement," 1977, *Home Girls: A Black Feminist Anthology*, ed. Barbara Smith (New York: Kitchen Table Women of Color Press, 1983), 272; Springer, *Living for the Revolution*, 60–61.

29. Combahee River Collective, "Statement," 279.

30. Wilson, interview by Thorsson.

31. Kelley, *Freedom Dreams*, 148.

32. De Veaux, *Warrior Poet*, 188.

33. Combahee River Collective, "Statement," 280.

34. Springer, *Living for the Revolution*, 75.

35. Farah Jasmine Griffin, "That the Mothers May Soar and the Daughters May Know Their Names: A Retrospective of Black Feminist Literary Criticism," 2007, in *Still Brave: The Evolution of Black Women's Studies*, ed. Stanlie M. James, Frances Smith-Foster, and Beverly Guy-Sheftall (New York: Feminist Press, 2009), 342.

36. Combahee River Collective, "Statement," 273.

37. Combahee River Collective, "Statement," 281.
38. De Veaux, *Warrior Poet*, 102–103; Linda Janet Holmes, *A Joyous Revolt: Toni Cade Bambara, Writer and Activist* (Santa Barbara, CA: Praeger, 2014), 42; Toni Morrison, "In Depth with Toni Morrison," CSPAN, 2001, http://blog.loa.org/2011/02/on-toni-morrison-80th-birthday.html; Jessica Harris, *My Soul Looks Back: A Memoir* (New York: Scribner, 2017), 4, 41. Poet Adrienne Rich also taught in SEEK in the 1960s and '70s (Shanna Greene Benjamin, *Half in Shadow: The Life and Legacy of Nellie Y. McKay* [Chapel Hill: University of North Carolina Press, 2021], 37).
39. See https://lehman.edu/seek/history.php.
40. Benjamin, *Half in Shadow*, 31.
41. Benjamin, *Half in Shadow*, 37.
42. Benjamin, *Half in Shadow*, 31.
43. Barbara Christian, "Does Theory Play Well in the Classroom?," 1996, in *New Black Feminist Criticism, 1985–2000*, ed. Gloria Bowles, M. Giulia Fabi, and Arlene R. Keizer (Chicago: University of Illinois Press, 2007), 53.
44. Wilson, interview by Thorsson.
45. See https://blackactivism.library.northeastern.edu/african-american-institute/. Several boxes in Shange's papers at Barnard College contain materials from her work in Black Studies at Northeastern. Later, when she began teaching at John Jay College in 1970, Audre Lorde worked to establish a Black studies department, which required "a radical restructuring of the institution in terms of hiring more black faculty and staff, and institutionalizing a black intellectual presence" (De Veaux, *Warrior Poet*, 105–106, 120). Scholar Barbara Christian also "participated in these early movement-based struggles for ethnic studies and access to education in the student strikes in 1968–69 at the City College of New York, where she was teaching while finishing her PhD at Columbia University" (Grace Kyungwon Hong, *Death Beyond Disavowal: The Impossible Politics of Difference* [Minneapolis: University of Minnesota Press, 2015], 133–134).
46. June Jordan, "Black Studies: Bringing Back the Person," 1969, in *Civil Wars: Observations from the Front Lines of America*, 1981 (New York: Simon & Schuster, 1995), 46.
47. Roderick A. Ferguson, *The Reorder of Things: The University and Its Pedagogies of Minority Difference* (Minneapolis: University of Minnesota Press, 2012), 77.
48. Jodi Melamed, *Represent and Destroy: Rationalizing Violence in The New Racial Capitalism* (Minneapolis: University of Minnesota Press, 2011), 102–103.
49. "Trying to Make the Personal Political," 32.
50. Sonia Sanchez, interview by Susan Kelly, *African American Review* 34, no. 4 (Winter 2000): 683; De Veaux, *Warrior Poet*, 117.
51. Dana Murphy, "Praisesong for Margaret Walker's *Jubilee* and the Phillis Wheatley Poetry Festival," *African American Review* 53, no. 4 (Winter 2020): 305.
52. Carole A. Parks, "Report on a Poetry Festival: Phillis Wheatley Comes Home," *Black World* 23, no. 4 (February 1974): 92–97.
53. Phillis Wheatley Poetry Festival Program, November 1973, Institute for The Study of History, Life, and Culture of Black People, Jackson State College, Jackson, Mississippi, box 55, folder 12, Lucille Clifton Papers. Stuart A. Rose Manuscripts, Archives, and Rare Book Library, Emory University.
54. Murphy, "Praisesong," 307.
55. Mary Helen Washington, "'Disturbing the Peace: What Happens to American Studies If You Put African American Studies at the Center?': Presidential Address to the

American Studies Association, October 29, 1997," *American Quarterly*, 50, no. 1 (March 1998): 1.

56. Nellie Y. McKay, "Black Women's Literary Scholarship: Reclaiming an Intellectual Tradition," *SAGE* 6, no. 1 (Summer 1989): 89.

57. Washington, "Disturbing the Peace," 2.

58. Mary Helen Washington, "Teaching *Black-Eyed Susans*: An Approach to the Study of Black Women Writers," 1977, *African American Review*, 50, no. 4 (Winter 2017): 557. On Washington's editorial work, see SaraEllen Strongman, "The Archaeological Impulse, Black Feminism, and *But Some of Us Are Brave*," *Feminist Studies* 48, no. 1 (2022): 44.

59. McKay, "Black Women's Literary Scholarship," 90.

60. Kelley, *Freedom Dreams*, 154.

61. Barbara Christian, "But What Do We Think We're Doing Anyway: The State of Black Feminist Criticism(s) or My Version of a Little Bit of History," 1989, *New Black Feminist Criticism, 1985–2000*, ed. Gloria Bowles, M. Giulia Fabi, and Arlene R. Keizer (Chicago: University of Illinois Press, 2007), 9.

62. Alice Walker, "The Unglamorous but Worthwhile Duties of the Black Revolutionary Artist, or of the Black Writer Who Simply Works and Writes," 1971, *In Search of Our Mothers' Gardens: Womanist Prose* (New York: Harcourt, 1983), 132–133.

63. Griffin, "That the Mothers May Soar," 340.

64. Cheryl A. Wall, *On Freedom and the Will to Adorn: The Art of the African American Essay* (Chapel Hill: University of North Carolina Press, 2018), 178.

65. Thulani Davis, "Family Plots: Black Women Writers Reclaim Their Past," *Village Voice*, March 1987.

66. Benjamin, *Half in Shadow*, 54. In 1972, Alice Walker was also in Cambridge on a fellowship at Radcliffe and teaching one course at Wellesley College (*Gathering Blossoms Under Fire: The Journals of Alice Walker*, ed. Valerie Boyd [New York: Simon & Schuster, 2022], 44).

67. Shanna Greene Benjamin, "Breaking the Whole Thing Open: An Interview with Nellie Y. McKay," by *PMLA* 121, no. 5 (October 2006): 1679; McKay, "Black Women's Literary Scholarship," 89.

68. Christian, "But What Do We Think We're Doing Anyway," 13; Benjamin, *Half in Shadow*, 67.

69. Christian, "But What Do We Think We're Doing Anyway," 11.

70. Arlene Keizer, "Barbara Christian and the Futures of Black Studies," panel at University of California, Berkeley, January 25, 2021.

71. Anne Tyler, "Writers in Place and Writers in Motion," *New York Times*, May 29, 1983.

72. Christian, "But What Do We Think We're Doing Anyway," 7.

73. Ann duCille, "Of Race, Gender, and the Novel; or, Where in the World is Toni Morrison?," *Novel* 50, no. 3 (November 2017): 381.

74. Renita Weems, interview by Courtney Thorsson, January 8, 2019.

75. Wilson, interview by Thorsson. Paula Giddings and Cheryl Wall, both important scholars, worked at Random House while Morrison was a senior editor there. Giddings was among those in the in the secretarial pool who helped Morrison out by typing up the manuscript for *The Bluest Eye*. See Timothy Greenfield-Sanders, dir., *Toni Morrison: The Pieces I Am*, Magnolia Films, 2019.

76. Wilson, interview by Thorsson.

77. Margo Jefferson, "From 'I' to 'We': The Role of the Citizen-Critic," Kritikos Lecture in the Humanities, Oregon Humanities Center "We the People" Series, University of Oregon, Eugene, Oregon, May 30, 2018.

78. Weems, interview by Thorsson; Renita Weems, email to author, January 8, 2019.

79. Kristen Hogan, "Women's Studies in Feminist Bookstores: 'All the Women's Studies women would come in,'" *Signs* 33, no. 2 (Spring 2008): 603.

80. Weems, interview by Thorsson.

81. Hogan, "Women's Studies in Feminist Bookstores," 601.

82. Hogan, "Women's Studies in Feminist Bookstores," 599.

83. Taylor, *How We Get Free*, 57; De Veaux, *Warrior Poet*, 186.

84. Barbara Smith, letter to Audre Lorde, January 10, 1978, series 1.1, folder 123. Audre Lorde Papers, Spelman College Archives.

85. Springer, *Living for the Revolution*, 106–107, VèVè Clark, "In-House Proposal: re. Publishing in Popular Magazines," box 102, folder 2, Alice Walker Papers, Stuart A. Rose Manuscripts, Archives, and Rare Book Library, Emory University, 1. For details of Combahee's Black feminist retreats in 1977 and 1979, see series 1.2, folder 14, Audre Lorde Papers, Spelman College Archives.

86. Springer, *Living for the Revolution*, 111. Springer names debates over the relationship of academic writing to activism; economic class differences among members; and diverging paths as some earned postgraduate degrees, academic positions, and tenure as among the conflicts that grew toward the end of Combahee's existence (*Living for the Revolution* 128–129). Also see Taylor, *How We Get Free*, 46–47.

87. Barbara Smith, "Introduction," *Home Girls: A Black Feminist Anthology*, ed. Barbara Smith (New York: Kitchen Table Women of Color Press, 1983), xxxi.

88. Smith, "Introduction," xlix.

89. Strongman, "The Archaeological Impulse," 33.

90. Smith, "Introduction," xlix.

91. Cheryl Clarke, "The Failure to Transform: Homophobia in the Black Community," in *Home Girls: A Black Feminist Anthology*, ed. Barbara Smith (New York: Kitchen Table Women of Color Press, 1983), 204.

92. Clarke, "The Failure to Transform," 204.

93. Barbara Christian, "No More Buried Lives: The Theme of Lesbianism in Audre Lorde's *Zami*, Gloria Naylor's *The Women of Brewster Place*, Ntozake Shange's *Sassafras, Cypress and Indigo*, and Alice Walker's *The Color Purple*," 1984, *Black Feminist Criticism: Perspectives on Black Women Writers* (New York: Teachers College Press, 1997), 187.

94. Jefferson, interview by Thorsson.

95. De Veaux, *Warrior Poet*, 139.

96. Patricia Spears Jones, interview by Courtney Thorsson, December 11, 2019. De Veaux describes Toni Cade Bambara, June Jordan, Paule Marshall, and Toni Morrison as "mentors" and describes the ways Jordan "really put her stamp on me" "as a writer and as a woman" (De Veaux, interview by Sharon Bridgeforth, *Who Yo People Is* podcast, episode 16, December 30, 2019; https://www.whoyopeopleis.com /podcast/2019/12/19/episode-16-alexis-de-veaux).

97. Jordan, "Civil Wars," in *Civil Wars: Observations from the Front Lines of America*, 1981 (New York: Simon & Schuster, 1995), 181.

98. This move is fairly common among Black writers from at least the Harlem Renaissance on and is exemplified by James Baldwin. See Courtney Thorsson, "James Baldwin and Black Women's Fiction," *African American Review* 46, no. 4 (Winter 2013): 615–631.

99. Walker sent a copy of her letter about *Sula* to Morrison; Morrison replied expressing gratitude (Evelyn C. White, *Alice Walker: A Life* [New York: Norton, 2004], 258–259).

100. Harris, *My Soul Looks Back*, 49, 74.

101. Wilson, interview by Thorsson.

102. Mary Helen Washington, *The Other Blacklist: The African American Literary and Cultural Left of the 1950s* (New York: Columbia University Press, 2014), 16–17.

103. Rosa Guy, interview by Louise Meriwether, September 22, 2002, Series 6, video recording, Camille Billops and James V. Hatch Archives, Stuart A. Rose Manuscript, Archives, and Rare Book Library, Emory University. Also see Shanna Greene Benjamin, *Half in Shadow: The Life and Legacy of Nellie Y. McKay* (Chapel Hill: University of North Carolina Press, 2021), 129.

104. Harris, *My Soul Looks Back*, 16, 81–2, 84–5. Judith Wilson lists Harris as an attendee in the minutes of one meeting. Harris's memoir *My Soul Looks Back* (2017) does not describe The Sisterhood even as Harris writes about her relationships in the 1970s with various members of the group. This suggests that The Sisterhood was not an especially formative influence on Harris and her writing, but rather adjacent to the circle of literary luminaries, including James Baldwin and Maya Angelou, that shaped Harris in 1970s New York.

105. Toni Morrison, Letter to Paule Marshall, May 12, 1972, box 1511, folder "Bambara, Toni Cade. Miscellaneous," Random House Records, Rare Books and Manuscript Library, Columbia University.

106. See box 1511, folder "Bambara, Toni Cade. Miscellaneous." Random House Records, Rare Books and Manuscript Library, Columbia University.

107. The dedication of *Things That I Do in the Dark* reads, "With gratitude for the beautiful work of the writer Toni Morrison, who, as my editor, has kept on believing this book into print. And with loving to Patricia, who helps me keep the faith," almost certainly referring to Sisterhood member Patricia Murray.

108. Patricia Spears Jones, "Four Women, Two Objects," *Killens Review of Arts & Letters* 9, nos.1 and 2 (Fall/Winter 2018): 5.

109. June Jordan, Note to Toni Morrison and "Statement on the Editorial Policy of *American Poetry Review*," December 12, 1976, box 1522, folder "Jordan, June. Author Correspondence," Random House Records, Rare Books and Manuscript Library, Columbia University, 2–3.

110. Jones, "Four Women," 5.

111. Patricia Spears Jones, "We're On: Writers in Conversation about how the *June Jordan Reader* can carry us into new forms of revolution," panel and discussion, May 18, 2018, The City University of New York. https://vimeo.com/271271706.

112. Keller and Levi, eds., *We're On*, 182; Jordan, Note to Toni Morrison and "Statement on the Editorial Policy of *American Poetry Review*," 3.

113. Jordan, Note to Toni Morrison and "Statement on the Editorial Policy of *American Poetry Review*," 5.

114. See White, *Alice Walker*, 199, 201, and Wall, *On Freedom*, 176–178. Walker and Jordan met when Walker gave a lecture at Sarah Lawrence, where Jordan was on the faculty, in 1972. See Jordan's letters to Walker from her time in 1970–71 at the American Academy in Rome, box 3, folder 5, Alice Walker Papers, Stuart A. Rose Manuscript, Archives, and Rare Book Library, Emory University.

115. Alice Walker, "Reaping What We Sow: A Conversation with Pulitzer Prize Winner Alice Walker," panel with Darieck Scott and Ra Malika Imhotep, February 15, 2021, University of California, Berkeley.

116. June Jordan, interview by Karla Hammond, 1978, in Keller and Levi, eds., *We're On*, 234.

117. See Morrison's business correspondence in the Random House Records at Columbia University. See chapter 6 of this book on the 1988 open letter in the *New York Times* protesting the lack of prizes for Morrison's novels.

118. For one example, see Toni Morrison, "Faulkner and Women," 1986, *The Source of Self-Regard: Selected Essays, Speeches, and Meditations* (New York: Knopf, 2019), 302.

119. Richard Jean So writes that period turned out to be tragically "passing and ephemeral." *Redlining Culture: A Data History of Racial Inequality and Postwar Fiction* (New York: Columbia University Press, 2021), 14.

120. Toni Morrison, Monthly Expense Reports, April 1976 to November 1976, box 1269, folder "Expense Reports," Random House Records, Rare Books and Manuscript Library, Columbia University. These members of The Sisterhood are just a few of the many authors Morrison met with in the 1970s and early 1980s. Expense reports and correspondence in the Random House Records reflect that Morrison was in touch in the 1970s with others including Toni Cade Bambara, Camille Billops, Octavia Butler, Bebe Moore Campbell, Barbara Christian, Lucille Clifton, Angela Davis, Toi Derricotte, Rita Dove, Mari Evans, Paula Giddings, Gayl Jones, Carlene Polite, Eleanor Traylor, Hortense Spillers, and Mary Helen Washington.

121. Toni Morrison, Letter to Richard Curtis, May 21, 1975, box 1526, folder C, Random House Records, Rare Books and Manuscript Library, Columbia University. Also see Box 1528, Folder A Pre-1981 and Box 1529, Folder C 1981–1983 in the Random House Records at Columbia University.

122. Toni Morrison, Monthly Expense Report, 1972, box 1269, folder "Expense Reports," Random House Records, Rare Books and Manuscript Library, Columbia University.

123. For example, dance scholar, journalist, and Sisterhood member Zita Allen turned to Morrison for suggestions of "new, interesting Black writers" who might write for *Travel & Leisure* magazine, where Allen was an associate editor. Zita Allen, Letter to Toni Morrison, March 19, 1975, box 1526, folder A, Random House Records, Rare Books and Manuscript Library, Columbia University. Morrison and Allen corresponded at least through 1979 while Allen worked on a book about dancer and choreographer Judith Jamison. See Box 1529, Folder C 1981–1983 in the Random House Records at Columbia University.

2. "AN ASSOCIATION OF BLACK WOMEN WHO ARE WRITERS/POETS/ARTISTS"

1. Margo Jefferson, interview by Courtney Thorsson, May 31, 2018. The title of this chapter comes from Abike, Letter to The Sisterhood, March 15, 1977, box 22, folder 13, June Jordan Papers, Schlesinger Library, Radcliffe Institute, Harvard University, 4.

2. Patricia Spears Jones, "Creation Is Everything You Do: Shange, The Sisterhood & Black Collectivity," panel and discussion with Mecca Jamilah Sullivan and Courtney Thorsson, Barnard College, New York, March 16, 2021, https://www.youtube.com /watch?v=tv322Y_qZgc.

3. Ntozake Shange, *for colored girls who have considered suicide/when the rainbow is enuf*, 1975 (New York: Macmillan, 1989), 7, 8, 17, 26, 45.

4. Barack Obama, *Dreams from My Father: A Story of Race and Inheritance*, 1995 (New York: Crown, 2004), 204–206.

5. Shange, *for colored girls*, 63.

6. Kim Hall, "Finding God in Ourselves: *For Colored Girls* at 40," *Ebony*, September 15, 2016. Scholar Moya Bailey created the term "misogynoir" to name anti-Black sexism.

7. Hilton Als, "Color Vision: Ntozake Shange's Outspoken Art," *New Yorker*, November 1, 2010.

8. See Deborah McDowell, *The Changing Same: Black Women's Literature, Criticism, and Theory* (Bloomington: Indiana University Press, 1995), chapter 7; Courtney Thorsson, *Women's Work: Nationalism and Contemporary African American Women's Novels* (Charlottesville: University of Virginia Press, 2013), 9–10; and Salamishah Tillet, *In Search of The Color Purple: The Story of an American Masterpiece* (New York: Abrams, 2021). Walker felt "betrayed" by novelist David Bradley's "dishonest" profile of her and review of *The Color Purple* in the *New York Times Magazine* (Walker, *Gathering Blossoms Under Fire: The Journals of Alice Walker*, ed. Valerie Boyd [New York: Simon & Schuster, 2022], 216–220). In February 1984, the magazine published Walker's response to Bradley's piece.

9. When *The Color Purple* came out in 1972, Walker and her partner Robert Allen had a "falling out" because "he felt his work had been overshadowed" by hers. Allen, an editor at *The Black Scholar*, wanted to have a table featuring the journal at the book launch party for Walker's novel; she declined (Walker, *Gathering Blossoms*, 195).

10. To get a sense of Ishmael Reed's position, see his March 2021 essay, "The Alice Walker Cult," in *Tablet*, https://www.tabletmag.com/sections/arts-letters/articles/alice-walker-ishmael-reed.

11. Ishmael Reed, "Ishmael Reed: A Conversation with John Domini," 1977, in *Conversations with Ishmael Reed*, ed. Bruce Dick and Amritjit Singh (Jackson: University of Mississippi Press, 1995), 128.

12. Reed, "A Conversation with John Domini," 129, 130, 132.

13. Reed, "A Conversation with John Domini," 133.

14. Reed, "A Conversation with John Domini," 142–143. Ellipses in original.

15. Toni Morrison, Letter to Jim Silberman, May 16, 1974, box 1054, folder "Morrison, Toni 1973," Random House Records, Rare Books and Manuscript Library, Columbia University.

16. Reed, "A Conversation with John Domini," 135.

17. Ntozake Shange, Journal, 1981–2009, box 9, folder 5, Ntozake Shange Papers, 1966–2016, Barnard Archives and Special Collections, Barnard Library, Barnard College.

18. Patricia Spears Jones, interview by Courtney Thorsson, December 11, 2019.

19. Margo Jefferson, *Negroland* (New York: Random House, 2015), 175–176; Jones, interview by Thorsson; Linda Janet Holmes, *A Joyous Revolt: Toni Cade Bambara, Writer and Activist* (Santa Barbara, CA: Praeger, 2014), 91. See Zita Allen's 2016 article in *The Amsterdam News* about Shange's work, http://amsterdamnews.com/news/2016/dec/01/ntozake-shange-colored-girl-whom-rainbow-not-enuf-/.

20. Judith Wilson, interview by Courtney Thorsson, February 12, 2019.

21. Michele Wallace, "For Colored Girls, the Rainbow is Not Enough," 1976, in *Invisibility Blues: From Pop to Theory*, 1990 (New York: Verso, 2016), 131.

22. Jones, interview by Thorsson.

23. Abike, Letter to The Sisterhood, 4.

24. Wilson, interview by Thorsson.

25. Abike, Letter to The Sisterhood, 4–5.

26. Jones, "Creation Is Everything You Do."

27. Abike, Letter to The Sisterhood, 5.

28. Wilson, interview by Thorsson; Judith Wilson, email to author, February 16, 2019.

29. Vertamae Smart Grosvenor, Note to June Jordan, Undated (early 1977), box 101, folder 3, June Jordan Papers, Schlesinger Library, Radcliffe Institute, Harvard University, Cambridge.

30. Judith Wilson, "Meeting of the Sisterhood Sunday, February 20, 1977," box 101, folder 3, June Jordan Papers, Schlesinger Library, Radcliffe Institute, Harvard University, Cambridge.

31. Toni Cade Bambara, interview by Claudia Tate, in *Black Women Writers at Work*, ed. Claudia Tate (New York: Continuum, 1984), 34.

32. Adrienne Rich was an important white friend, poet, and collaborator for Lorde and Jordan especially, but, as a white woman, would never have been invited to a Sisterhood meeting. Rich, Lorde, Michelle Cliff, and others were in another writers' group that met once a month at therapist Bernice Goodman's apartment (Alexis De Veaux, *Warrior Poet: A Biography of Audre Lorde* [New York: Norton, 2004], 181–182).

33. James Smethurst, "Retraining the Heartworks: Women in Atlanta's Black Arts Movement" in *Want to Start A Revolution?: Radical Women in The Black Freedom Struggle*, ed. Dayo F. Gore, Jeanne Theoharis, and Komozi Woodard (New York: New York University Press, 2009), 207.

34. Rudolph P. Byrd, "Introduction," in *The World Has Changed: Conversations with Alice Walker*, ed. Rudolph P. Byrd (New York: The New Press, 2010), 6.

35. Alexis Pauline Gumbs, "Dread Archive: Audre Lorde and What We Are Afraid to Want," *The Black Scholar* 52, no. 2 (May 2022): 28.

36. June Jordan, note to Audre Lorde, January 29, 1977, series 1.2, folder 123, Audre Lorde Papers, Spelman College Archives.

37. Abike, Letter to The Sisterhood, 1. Abike appears by one name only in all Sisterhood materials. Harryette Mullen confirmed through correspondence with Sisterhood member Dr. Sananda Ananda-Maynard that lawyer Patricia Murray was also known as Abike.

38. Alice Walker, "'Outlaw, Renegade, Rebel, Pagan': Interview with Amy Goodman from *Democracy Now!*," 2006, in Byrd, *The World Has Changed*, 278.

39. Renita Weems, interview by Courtney Thorsson, January 8, 2019.

40. Patricia Spears Jones, "Four Women, Two Objects," *Killens Review of Arts & Letters* 9, nos.1 and 2 (Fall/Winter 2018): 5.

41. Wilson, interview by Thorsson.

42. Jones, "Creation Is Everything You Do."

43. Patricia Spears Jones, email to author, January 4, 2019.

44. Wilson, interview by Thorsson. Harryette Mullen corresponded with Dr. Sananda Ananda-Maynard and confirmed that Dr. Sananda is the Nana Maynard in "The Sisterhood, 1977" archival photo.

45. Wilson, interview by Thorsson.

46. Jones, interview by Thorsson. Marie Brown was, like Morrison, the sole Black woman in an editorial role at a trade publishing house. Brown was at Doubleday and went on to found her own literary agency. She worked on books by Mary Helen Washington, Vertamae Grosvenor, Jean and Carole Darden, and Mari Evans, among other Black women writers. See https://www.shondaland.com/inspire/books/a14428057 /marie-dutton-brown-profile/. Washington recalls, "I sent Marie a proposal for

Black-Eyed Susans, and within three weeks I had a contract," Mary Helen Washington and Shaun Myers, "'Cobbling It All Together': Mary Helen Washington and Shaun Myers, in Conversation," *Los Angeles Review of Books*, July 14, 2021, https://www.lareviewofbooks.org/article/cobbling-it-all-together-mary-helen-washington-and-shaun-myers-in-conversation/.

47. Charles Rowell, "Above the Wind: An Interview with Audre Lorde," *Callaloo* 14, no. 1 (Winter 1991): 95.

48. Jones, "Four Women," 5.

49. Jones, interview by Thorsson; Jones, "Four Women," 5.

50. Jones, "Four Women," 5.

51. Jones, "Four Women," 5.

52. Jones, interview by Thorsson.

53. Judith Wilson, email to author, December 3, 2018.

54. "Trying to Make the Political Personal," reprint of 1975 "Consciousness-Raising Guidelines" with new foreword by Mariame Kaba and afterword by Jacqui Shine (Chicago: Half Letter Press, 2017), 12. Lori Sharpe wrote "Supplemental Guidelines for Black Women" for the 1975 version of this pamphlet.

55. Renita Weems, email to author, January 8, 2019.

56. Kim Phillips-Fein, *Fear City: New York's Fiscal Crisis and the Rise of Austerity Politics*. 2017 (New York: Picador, 2018), 205–206.

57. Evelyn C. White, *Alice Walker: A Life* (New York: Norton, 2004), 296.

58. Alice Walker, *Good Night Willie Lee, I'll See You in The Morning* (New York: Harcourt Brace Jovanovich, 1979), 20.

59. Alice Walker, "One Child of One's Own: A Meaningful Digression within the Work(s)," December 9, 1979, *In Search of Our Mothers' Gardens: Womanist Prose* (New York: Harcourt, 1983), 391.

60. Walker, "One Child," 392.

61. Walker, "One Child," 393.

62. Jessica Harris, "I Will Always Be a Writer," profile of Toni Morrison, *Essence*, December 1976, in *Toni Morrison: Conversations*, ed. Carolyn C. Denard (Jackson: University of Mississippi Press, 2008), 4. Walker's published journals include the related reflection following her 1972 tubal ligation surgery that "Motherhood, when one really wants to write, is too heavy a burden" (*Gathering Blossoms* 46). She writes often in her journals about how much she loves Rebecca and about mothering as one among many competing demands on her time (*Gathering Blossoms* 51).

63. Judith Wilson, review of *Good Night Willie Lee, I'll See You in The Morning* by Alice Walker, *Essence*, December 1979, 16.

64. Toni Morrison, interview by Terry Gross, *Fresh Air*, National Public Radio, April 15, 2015.

65. Angela Davis, eulogy for Toni Morrison, November 21, 2019, Cathedral of St. John the Divine, New York, https://vimeo.com/374796939.

66. Harris, "I Will Always Be a Writer," 4.

67. Toni Morrison quoted in Mel Watkins, "Talk with Toni Morrison," *New York Times*, September 11, 1977.

68. See Dorothy Roberts, *Killing the Black Body: Race, Reproduction, and the Meaning of Liberty*, 1997 (New York: Vintage, 2017), 90 and Robin Kelley, *Freedom Dreams: The Black Radical Imagination* (Boston: Beacon, 2002), 145.

69. The Moynihan Report, https://www.dol.gov/general/aboutdol/history/webid-moynihan.

70. Sherie M. Randolph, *Florynce "Flo" Kennedy: The Life of a Black Feminist Radical* (Chapel Hill: University of North Carolina Press, 2015), 182–183.
71. Jefferson, interview by Thorsson.
72. Abike, Letter to The Sisterhood, 1.
73. Abike, Letter to The Sisterhood, 1–2.
74. Abike, Letter to The Sisterhood, 2–3.
75. Abike, Letter to The Sisterhood, 3.
76. Abike, Letter to The Sisterhood, 3–4.
77. Ballard spoke on behalf of Black Perspective in a 1972 court case in which the group, with the support of *Essence* and Second Front (another organization of Black journalists), defended their right to keep sources confidential. Paul L. Montgomery, "Statute for Newsman Immunity Pushed by Congress Democrats," *New York Times*, July 1, 1972. "Black Journalists Criticize U.S. Supreme Court Ruling," *Jet*, July 20, 1972. I am grateful to Harryette Mullen, who alerted me to this aspect of Ballard's career.
78. Timothy Greenfield-Sanders, dir., *Toni Morrison: The Pieces I Am*, Magnolia Films, 2019. Morrison lists 1965 as the start date of her employment on various forms in the Random House Records at Columbia University.
79. White, *Alice Walker*, 466.
80. Alice Walker, Note to Toni Morrison, February 19, 1977, box 1522, folder "Jordan, June. Poetry," Random House Records, Rare Books and Manuscript Library, Columbia University.
81. Walker, Note to Morrison, February 19, 1977. In February 1977, Morrison wrote both Walker and Shange to solicit comments on Jordan's volume for use in promoting the book.
82. Judith Wilson, "March 20, 1977 Meeting of The Sisterhood," box 22, folder 17, June Jordan Papers, Schlesinger Library, Radcliffe Institute, Harvard University, Cambridge, 2.
83. Wilson, "Meeting of the Sisterhood Sunday, February 20, 1977," 2.
84. Wilson, "Meeting of the Sisterhood Sunday, February 20, 1977," 3.
85. Wilson, "Meeting of the Sisterhood Sunday, February 20, 1977," 2.
86. VèVè Clark, "In-House Proposal: re. Publishing in Popular Magazines," box 102, folder 2, Alice Walker Papers, Stuart A. Rose Manuscripts, Archives, and Rare Book Library, Emory University, 1.
87. De Veaux, *Warrior Poet*, 180.
88. See series 1.1, folder 63, Audre Lorde Papers, Spelman College Archives.
89. June Jordan, note to Audre Lorde, October 24, 1977, series 1.1, folder 63, Audre Lorde Papers, Spelman College Archives.
90. Patricia Spears Jones, card to Audre Lorde, November 30, 1977, series 1.1, folder 62, Audre Lorde Papers, Spelman College Archives.
91. Clark, "In-House Proposal," 1.
92. Wilson, "March 20, 1977," 1.
93. National Black Feminist Organization (NBFO), Statement of Purpose, 1973, box 14, folder "Black Women's Organizations 1973–1976," Michele Wallace Papers, Manuscripts, Archives, and Rare Books Division, Schomburg Center for Research in Black Culture, The New York Public Library.
94. Kimberly Springer, *Living for the Revolution: Black Feminist Organizations, 1968–1980* (Durham, NC: Duke University Press, 2005), 29.
95. Wilson, "March 20, 1977," 1–2.

96. Clark, "In-House Proposal," 1.

97. Harris, "I Will Always Be a Writer," 6.

98. Clark, "In-House Proposal," 1–2.

99. Clark, "In-House Proposal," 2.

100. Wilson, "March 20, 1977," 1–2.

101. Judith Wilson, "April 10, 1977 Meeting of The Sisterhood," box 102, folder 2, Alice Walker Papers, Stuart A. Rose Manuscripts, Archives, and Rare Book Library, Emory University, 2.

102. Many issues of *Black World* are available online at https://books.google.com/books /serial/MbIDAAAAMBAJ?rview=1. Also see Howard Rambsy's blog entries on *Black World* indexed at http://www.culturalfront.org/2015/09/blogging-about-black -world-magazine.html.

103. Roderick A. Ferguson, *The Reorder of Things: The University and Its Pedagogies of Minority Difference* (Minneapolis: University of Minnesota Press, 2012), 113.

104. For examples see the April 1973, March 1972, and May 1970 issues of *Black World* at https://books.google.com/books/serial/5LIDAAAAMBAJ?rview=1&rview=1.

105. James Smethurst, *Behold the Land: The Black Arts Movement in the South* (Chapel Hill: University of North Carolina Press, 2021), 160.

106. Washington and Myers, "'Cobbling It All Together.'"

107. Smethurst, *Behold the Land*, 160.

108. *First World* 1, no. 1 (January/February 1977): 37–39, 50.

109. *First World* 1, no. 2 (March/April 1977): 10; 1, no. 3 (May/June 1977): 6, 37; 2, no. 1 (Spring 1978): 39, 41; 2, no. 2 (1979): 55; 2, no. 4 (1980): 23.

110. Judith Wilson, "May 15, 1977 Meeting of the Sisterhood," box 101, folder 3, June Jordan Papers, Schlesinger Library, Radcliffe Institute, Harvard University, Cambridge, 2.

111. Wilson, "April 10, 1977," 2. In 2018, Jefferson said, "I don't remember *Chrysalis* . . . because I was a journalist, someone from *Chrysalis* must have gotten in touch with me" (Jefferson, interview by Thorsson). Lorde began working with the quarterly magazine leading up to its 1977 launch and shepherding its publication of poems by Patricia Spears Jones and June Jordan, among others (De Veaux, *Warrior Poet*, 177–178, 181). Lorde and Jordan resigned from *Chrysalis* in 1979 because of the magazine's failure to include work by and about Black women (Jordan, Letter to the Editors of *Chrysalis*, September 10, 1979, series 1.1, folder 63, Audre Lorde Papers, Spelman College Archives). Soon after this, Jones worked at *Heresies* for a few years (Jones, interview by Thorsson).

112. Abigail Pogrebin, "How do You Spell Ms.," *New York*, October 19, 2011.

113. Walker, *Gathering Blossoms*, 65.

114. Wilson, interview by Thorsson.

115. Wilson, interview by Thorsson.

116. Lindsy Van Gelder, a contributor to *Ms.* from 1977–1992, quoted in Pogrebin, "How do You Spell Ms."

117. For Jefferson's letter, Wallace's other 1975 correspondence with *Ms.*, and the WSABAL manifesto, see box 14, folder "Women Students and Artists for Black Art Liberation (WSABAL) 1975," Michele Wallace Papers at the Manuscripts, Archives, and Rare Books Division at the Schomburg Center for Research in Black Culture, New York Public Library.

118. "*Ms.* magazine 10 years later," *Christian Science Monitor*, December 29, 1981.

119. Springer, *Living for the Revolution*, 33; White, *Alice Walker*, 268; Tillet, *In Search of The Color Purple*, 69, 72. Walker remained a contributing editor until 1986 (Pogrebin, "How do You Spell Ms.").

120. Pogrebin, "How do You Spell Ms."

121. Marcia Ann Gillespie, "The History Makers: Marcia Ann Gillepsie," July 14, 2013, https://www.thehistorymakers.org/biography/marcia-ann-gillespie.

122. Michele Wallace, "Introduction," in *Dark Designs and Visual Culture* (Durham, NC: Duke University Press, 2004), 17. Also see Michele Wallace, "Variations on Negation and the Heresy of Black Feminist Creativity," 1989, in *Invisibility Blues: From Pop to Theory*, 1990 (New York: Verso, 2016), 223, and a panel in 2000 at Howard University including Susan McHenry, https://www.c-span.org/video/?160091-1/future-black-books.

123. Walker, *Gathering Blossoms*, 263.

124. Walker, *Gathering Blossoms*, 263–264.

125. Quoted in Pogrebin, "How do You Spell Ms."

126. Pogrebin, "How do You Spell Ms."

127. Gillespie, "The History Makers."

128. *Essence*, July 1975; Jessica Harris, *My Soul Looks Back: A Memoir* (New York: Scribner, 2017), 48, 85.

129. Jacqueline Trescott, "The Battle for *Essence*," *Washington Post*, April 26, 1977; Deirdre Carmody, "Women's Magazines Are More Than Fashionable," *New York Times*, February 15, 1978.

130. Wilson, "April 10, 1977," 1.

131. Gillespie, "The History Makers."

132. Toni Morrison, Letter to Audreen Ballard, January 31, 1977, box 1511, folder "Bambara, Toni Cade. *The Sea Birds Are Still Alive*," Random House Records, Rare Books and Manuscript Library, Columbia University.

133. Toni Morrison, Monthly Expense Reports, July 1977 and August 1977, box 1269, folder "Expense Reports," Random House Records, Rare Books and Manuscript Library, Columbia University.

134. Cheryl A. Wall, *On Freedom and the Will to Adorn: The Art of the African American Essay* (Chapel Hill: University of North Carolina Press, 2018), 188.

135. See Erica R. Edwards, *The Other Side of Terror: Black Women and the Culture of US Empire* (New York: New York University Press, 2021), chapters 1 and 5.

136. Tillet, *In Search of The Color Purple*, 65.

137. Wilson, "April 10, 1977," 1, 3.

138. Wilson, "April 10, 1977," 3.

139. Wilson, "May 15, 1977," 2.

140. Jones, "Four Women," 5.

3. "TO MOVE THE NEEDLE IN BLACK WOMEN'S LIVES"

1. Judith Wilson, "May 15, 1977 Meeting of the Sisterhood," box 101, folder 3, June Jordan Papers, Schlesinger Library, Radcliffe Institute, Harvard University, Cambridge, 2. The title of this chapter comes from Renita Weems, interview by Courtney Thorsson, January 8, 2019.

2. Wilson, "May 15, 1977," 1.

3. Wilson, "May 15, 1977," 1. This is one of several examples where Nana Maynard's first name appears with alternate capitalization as NaNa.

4. Wilson, "May 15, 1977," 1–2.

5. Judith Wilson, interview by Courtney Thorsson, February 12, 2019.

6. Wilson, "May 15, 1977," 1.

7. Patricia Spears Jones, letter to June Jordan, June 3, 1977, box 35, folder 13, June Jordan Papers, Schlesinger Library, Radcliffe Institute, Harvard University, Cambridge.

8. Margo Jefferson, interview by Courtney Thorsson, May 31, 2018.

9. Ntozake Shange, interview by Henry Blackwell, *Black American Literature Forum* 13, no. 4 (Winter 1979): 134.

10. Alexis De Veaux, *Warrior Poet: A Biography of Audre Lorde* (New York: Norton, 2004), 166.

11. Wilson, "May 15, 1977," 2.

12. See a review of a 2015 exhibit of the L.A. rebellion filmmakers' works at the Tate Modern at https://www.theguardian.com/film/2015/apr/09/the-la-rebellion-when-black-film-makers-took-on-the-world-and-won and the UCLA archive of their works at https://www.cinema.ucla.edu/la-rebellion.

13. Wilson, "May 15, 1977," 2.

14. Judith Wilson, "Rosa Guy: Writing with Bold Vision," *Essence*, October 1979, 14.

15. Patricia Spears Jones, "Four Women, Two Objects," *Killens Review of Arts & Letters* 9, nos.1 and 2 (Fall/Winter 2018): 6.

16. Patricia Spears Jones, interview by Courtney Thorsson, December 11, 2019.

17. De Veaux, *Warrior Poet*, 335; Audre Lorde, "Grenada Revisited: An Interim Report," *Sister Outsider* (Berkeley: Ten Speed Press, 1984), 176.

18. Lorde, "Grenada Revisited," 177, 178.

19. Lorde, "Grenada Revisited," 177.

20. Lorde, "Grenada Revisited," 179–180.

21. Lorde, "Grenada Revisited," 183.

22. Lorde, "Grenada Revisited," 189.

23. For more on how one Sisterhood member theorized this relationship in one text, see Courtney Thorsson, "Kitchen, Nation, Diaspora: Ntozake Shange's African American Foodways," in *Foodscapes: Food, Space, and Place in a Global Society*, ed. Carlnita Greene (New York: Peter Lang, 2018), 199–222.

24. Toni Morrison, *Tar Baby*, 1981 (New York: Random House, 2004), 215.

25. Morrison, *Tar Baby*, 221–222.

26. Morrison, *Tar Baby*, 219.

27. Patricia Spears Jones, Letter to June Jordan, June 20, 1977, box 35, folder 13, June Jordan Papers, Schlesinger Library, Radcliffe Institute, Harvard University, Cambridge.

28. Jones, interview by Thorsson.

29. Jones, interview by Thorsson.

30. Jefferson, interview by Thorsson; Weems, interview by Thorsson; Judith Wilson, email to the author, December 3, 2018.

31. Jefferson, interview by Thorsson.

32. Renita Weems, "Dear Sisters," December 5, 1977, series 1.2, folder 123, Audre Lorde Papers, Spelman College Archives.

33. Weems, "Dear Sisters."

34. Weems, interview by Thorsson. Weems recalls, "at the end of each meeting I was told what to send for the next meeting.".

35. Weems, "Dear Sisters."

36. Wilson, interview by Thorsson; Judith Wilson, email to Courtney Thorsson, December 3, 2018; Weems, interview by Thorsson.

37. Weems, interview by Thorsson.

38. Patricia Spears Jones, letter to Renita Weems, March 3, 1978, box 101, folder 3, June Jordan Papers, Schlesinger Library, Radcliffe Institute, Harvard University, Cambridge, 1–2.

39. Jones to Weems, March 3, 1978, 1.

40. Weems, interview by Thorsson.

41. Jones, Letter to Jordan, June 20, 1977.

42. Alice Walker, "'Outlaw, Renegade, Rebel, Pagan': Interview with Amy Goodman from *Democracy Now!*," 2006, in *The World Has Changed: Conversations with Alice Walker*, ed. Rudolph P. Byrd (New York: The New Press, 2010), 278; Alice Walker, "On Raising Chickens," in Byrd, *The World Has Changed*, 318; Weems, interview by Thorsson.

43. Weems, interview by Thorsson; Wilson, interview by Thorsson.

44. Jones to Weems, March 3, 1978, 1.

45. Jones to Weems, March 3, 1978, 1–2.

46. Weems, interview by Thorsson.

47. Weems, interview by Thorsson.

48. Jones, interview by Thorsson.

49. Weems, interview by Thorsson.

50. Evelyn C. White, *Alice Walker: A Life* (New York: Norton, 2004), 308.

51. Weems, interview by Thorsson; Wilson, interview by Thorsson.

52. Weems, interview by Thorsson.

53. June Jordan, "Letter to My Friend Ntozake Shange," 1980, in *Directed by Desire: The Collected Poems of June Jordan*, ed. Jan Heller Levi and Sara Miles (Port Townsend, WA: Copper Canyon Press, 2007), 291–292. I am grateful to Erica Edwards for drawing my attention to this poem.

54. Shange, interview by Blackwell, 137.

55. Jordan, "Letter to My Friend Ntozake Shange," 292.

56. Alexis De Veaux, "In Celebration of Our Triumph," 1979, in *Conversations with Paule Marshall*, ed. James C. Hall and Heather Hathaway (Jackson: University Press of Mississippi, 2010), 43.

57. Paule Marshall, "Reena," 1962, *Reena and Other Stories* (New York: The Feminist Press, 1983), 83.

58. De Veaux, "In Celebration," 45.

59. Wilson, interview by Thorsson.

60. June Jordan, Note to Toni Morrison, January 29, 1977, box 1522, folder "Jordan, June. Author Correspondence," Random House Records, Rare Books and Manuscript Library, Columbia University.

61. Weems, email to author, January 8, 2019.

62. On her uses of scripture in her novels, see Toni Morrison, "God's Language," May 10, 1996, *The Source of Self-Regard: Selected Essays, Speeches, and Meditations* (New York: Knopf, 2019), 246–270. On Afro-Protestantism in twentieth-century African American literature, see Josef Sorett, *Spirit in the Dark: A Religious History of Racial Aesthetics* (Oxford: Oxford University Press, 2016).

63. Jones, interview by Thorsson.

64. Cheryl A. Wall, *On Freedom and the Will to Adorn: The Art of the African American Essay* (Chapel Hill: University of North Carolina Press, 2018), 188.

65. June Jordan, "Where is the Love?," 1978, in *Civil Wars: Observations from the Front Lines of America*, 1981 (New York: Simon & Schuster, 1995), 140.

66. Jordan, "Where Is the Love?," 140–141.

67. Tom Dent, "1978 Howard Writers Conference and SBCA," *Callaloo* 4 (October 1978): 161–162.

68. Hollie West, "Sexual Politics and the Afro-American Writer," *Washington Post*, May 8, 1978.

69. Toni Cade Bambara, "The Black Woman and Her Image," *Washington Post*, February 18, 1979.

70. Michele Wallace, *Black Macho and the Myth of the Superwoman*, 1978 (New York: Verso, 1999), 6.

71. *Ms*, "Black History Month: The Myth of the Black Superwoman, Revisited," *Ms.*, February 16, 2011.

72. Wilson, interview by Thorsson.

73. Michele Wallace, "For Whom the Bell Tolls: Why Americans Can't Deal with Black Feminist Intellectuals," 1995, *Dark Designs and Visual Culture* (Durham, NC: Duke University Press, 2004), 153.

74. Jefferson, interview by Thorsson.

75. Judith Wilson, review of *Black Macho and the Myth of the Superwoman* by Michele Wallace, *Essence*, February 1979, 27.

76. As Wallace considered whether to be on the cover of *Ms.* and after Wilson's review of *Black Macho* came out, Wallace and Wilson "had some very long conversations" and thus "got to be friends" (Wilson, interview by Thorsson).

77. June Jordan, "Black History as Myth," review of *Black Macho and the Myth of the Superwoman* by Michele Wallace, 1979, in *Civil Wars: Observations from the Front Lines of America*, 1981 (New York: Simon & Schuster, 1995), 163.

78. Alice Walker, "To *The Black Scholar*," 1979, in *In Search of Our Mothers' Gardens: Womanist Prose* (New York: Harcourt, 1983), 323.

79. Walker, "To *The Black Scholar*," 324.

80. Alice Walker, *Gathering Blossoms Under Fire: The Journals of Alice Walker*, ed. Valerie Boyd (New York: Simon & Schuster, 2022), 140.

81. Bambara, "The Black Woman and Her Image."

82. Walker, "To *The Black Scholar*," 320.

83. Wilson, interview by Thorsson.

84. Claudia Tate, "Introduction," in *Black Women Writers at Work*, ed. Claudia Tate (New York: Continuum, 1985), xix.

85. Audrey Edwards, "The History Makers: Audrey Edwards," December 12, 2013, https://www.thehistorymakers.org/biography/audrey-edwards.

86. Edwards, "The History Makers: Audrey Edwards." From 1970 to about 2000, Susan L. Taylor worked her way up at *Essence* from freelancer to beauty editor to editor-in-chief.

87. Susan L. Taylor, interview for "In Black America," October 1, 1989, KUT Radio, Austin, Texas, American Archive of Public Broadcasting, https://americanarchive .org/catalog/cpb-aacip_529-086348hj46.

88. Taylor, "In Black America."

89. See Mary Helen Washington, *Invented Lives: Narratives of Black Women, 1860–1960* (New York: Doubleday, 1987), especially the introduction.

90. In a 2021 *New Yorker* profile of Ishmael Reed, Julian Lucas writes that Reed "continues to argue that the media disproportionately emphasizes Black male misogyny, which he believes 'honorary Black feminists' of other races use to distract from sexism in their own ethnic groups." Lucas cites bell hooks and Michele Wallace as, in more recent years, finding value in some of Reed's ideas while critiquing others, and he notes that Reed continues to criticize Alice Walker, in particular for "her praise of an anti-Semitic book by conspiracy theorist David Ickes." Lucas's profile begins to reveal some of the kinds of complicated intraracial intellectual exchanges between Black men and women writers that are obscured or rendered impossible by white media's sensational and exaggerated interest in conflict among Black people. Julian Lucas, "Ishmael Reed Gets the Last Laugh," *New Yorker*, July 19, 2021.

91. Jacqueline Bobo, "Sifting Through the Controversy: Reading *The Color Purple*," *Callaloo* 39 (Spring 1989): 332.

92. Bobo. "Sifting Through the Controversy," 333–334.

93. Bobo, "Sifting Through the Controversy," 335, 337.

94. Bobo, "Sifting Through the Controversy," 337.

95. Thulani Davis, "Family Plots: Black Women Writers Reclaim Their Past," *Village Voice*, March 1987.

96. *The Phil Donahue Show*, episode "Black Women Writers," aired July 14, 1989, CBS, Videocasette (VHS). Films for the Humanities.

97. Donahue, "Black Women Writers."

98. Alexis De Veaux, "Alice Walker," *Essence*, September 1989, 56.

99. Donahue, "Black Women Writers."

100. Wilson, interview by Thorsson.

101. Jones, interview by Thorsson.

102. Jones, interview by Thorsson. Quoting Jane Galvin-Lewis of the NBFO, Kimberly Springer describes Black feminist organizers at the end of the 1970s as "war weary warriors" (*Living for the Revolution: Black Feminist Organizations, 1968–1980* [Durham, NC: Duke University Press, 2005], 139).

103. Edwards, "The History Makers: Audrey Edwards."

4. "A COMMUNITY OF WRITERS EVEN IF THEY ONLY SLAP FIVE ONCE A MONTH"

1. Michele Wallace, "Anger in Isolation: A Black Feminist's Search for Sisterhood," 1975, *Invisibility Blues: From Pop to Theory*, 1990 (New York: Verso, 2016), 20. The title of this chapter comes from Toni Cade Bambara, *"Realizing the Dream of a Black University" & Other Writings, Part I*, Lost & Found: The CUNY Poetics Document Initiative, series 7, no. 2, part I (Fall 2017), ed. Makeba Lavan and Conor Tomás Reed (New York: Small Press Distribution and lostandfoundbooks.org, 2017), 30.

2. Wallace, "Anger in Isolation," 21.

3. Wallace, "Anger in Isolation," 24; Michele Wallace, "For Whom the Bell Tolls: Why Americans Can't Deal with Black Feminist Intellectuals," 1995, *Dark Designs and Visual Culture* (Durham, NC: Duke University Press, 2004), 152.

4. Michele Wallace, "To Hell and Back: On the Road with Black Feminism in the '60s and '70s," 1998, *Dark Designs and Visual Culture* (Durham, NC: Duke University Press, 2004), 104.

5. Michele Wallace, "Variations on Negation and the Heresy of Black Feminist Creativity," 1989, in *Invisibility Blues: From Pop to Theory*, 1990 (New York: Verso, 2016), 225.

6. Wallace, "Anger in Isolation," 19.

7. Wallace, "To Hell and Back," 103.

8. Wallace, "To Hell and Back," 104.

9. Wallace, "Variations on Negation," 225; Wallace, "To Hell and Back," 107; Margo Jefferson, interview by Courtney Thorsson, May 31, 2018.

10. Wallace, "To Hell and Back," 105.

11. Wallace, "To Hell and Back," 106, 103, 107.

12. Wallace, "To Hell and Back," 106; Barbara Omolade, "Sisterhood in Black and White," *The Feminist Memoir Project: Voices from Women's Liberation*, ed. Rachel DuPleiss and Ann Snitow (New York: Three Rivers Press, 1998), 387.

13. Wallace, "For Whom the Bell Tolls," 152.

14. Michele Wallace, Letter to Alice Walker, March 25, 1977, box 4, folder "Walker, Alice," Michele Wallace Papers, Manuscripts, Archives, and Rare Books Division, Schomburg Center for Research in Black Culture, The New York Public Library, 1.

15. Beverly Guy-Sheftall, "Commitment: Toni Cade Bambara Speaks," in *Sturdy Black Bridges: Visions of Black Women in Literature*, ed. Roseann P. Bell, Bettye J. Parker, and Beverly Guy-Sheftall (New York: Anchor, 1979), 232.

16. Alice Walker, Letter to Michele Wallace, April 7, 1977, box 4, folder "Walker, Alice," Michele Wallace Papers. Manuscripts, Archives, and Rare Books Division, Schomburg Center for Research in Black Culture, The New York Public Library, 1.

17. Michele Wallace, Letter to Gloria Steinem, May 27, 1975, box 14, folder "Women Students and Artists for Black Art Liberation (WSABAL) 1975," Michele Wallace Papers, Manuscripts, Archives, and Rare Books Division, Schomburg Center for Research in Black Culture, The New York Public Library, 1–2.

18. VèVè Clark, "In-House Proposal: re. Publishing in Popular Magazines," box 102, folder 2, Alice Walker Papers, Stuart A. Rose Manuscripts, Archives, and Rare Book Library, Emory University, 2.

19. Omolade, "Sisterhood in Black and White," 387–388.

20. Wallace, Letter to Steinem, May 27, 1975, 2.

21. Michele Wallace, "If You Can't Join 'Em, Beat 'Em: Stanley Crouch and Shaharazad Ali," 1995, *Dark Designs and Visual Culture* (Durham, NC: Duke University Press, 2004), 305.

22. Wallace, "To Hell and Back," 109, 108.

23. Wallace, "For Whom the Bell Tolls," 155.

24. Wallace, "If You Can't Join 'Em," 305; "For Whom the Bell Tolls," 155.

25. Wallace, "Variations on Negation," 213.

26. Wallace, "Variations on Negation," 214.

27. Wallace, "Variations on Negation," 220.

28. Linda Janet Holmes, *A Joyous Revolt: Toni Cade Bambara, Writer and Activist* (Santa Barbara, CA: Praeger, 2014), xix.

29. Miriam Atkin and Imanjá Brown, "Introduction," in *"I Teach Myself in Outline": Notes, Journals, Syllabi & an Excerpt from* Deotha *by Audre Lorde*, Lost & Found: The CUNY Poetics Document Initiative, series 7, no. 1 (Fall 2017) (New York: Small

Press Distribution and lostandfoundbooks.org, 2017); Makeba Lavan and Conor Tomás Reed, "Introduction," in *"Realizing the Dream of a Black University" & Other Writings, Part I*, Lost & Found: The CUNY Poetics Document Initiative, series 7, no. 2, part I (Fall 2017) (New York: Small Press Distribution and lostandfoundbooks. org, 2017). Holmes dates the start of the program as 1966 (*A Joyous Revolt*, 42) while Bambara's resumés in her papers at Spelman, the Random House records at Columbia, and the Cheryll Y. Greene Papers at Emory list the start date for Bambara's work at SEEK as 1965. Lorde's appointment as a part-time lecturer teaching creative writing in the SEEK program began in 1968 (Mina Shaughnessy, Letter to Audre Lorde, July 29, 1968, series 1.2, folder 17A, Audre Lorde Papers, Spelman College Archives). June Jordan started teaching at City College in 1967 when her friend Herb Kohl called her the night before the first meeting of a class to ask her to fill in for him so he could "write, full-time" (Jordan, "Black Studies: Bringing Back the Person," 1969, in *Civil Wars: Observations from the Front Lines of America*, 1981 [New York: Simon & Schuster, 1995], 45).

30. Toni Cade Bambara, Letter to June Jordan, 1977, June Jordan Papers, 1936–2002, Schlesinger Library, Radcliffe Institute, Harvard University, Cambridge, 2.
31. Judith Wilson, "May 15, 1977 Meeting of the Sisterhood," box 101, folder 3, June Jordan Papers, Schlesinger Library, Radcliffe Institute, Harvard University, Cambridge, 2.
32. Bambara, Letter to Jordan, 1977, 2.
33. Holmes, *A Joyous Revolt*, 46, 43, 50. The NBFO also supported Bambara's work although she was a not a member. Her anthology *The Black Woman* (1970) and collection of short stories *Gorilla, My Love* (1972) are the only works containing poetry and fiction that appear on a reading list the NBFO distributed. National Black Feminist Organization (NBFO), Suggested Reading List, box 14, folder "Black Women's Organizations 1973–1976," Michele Wallace Papers, Manuscripts, Archives, and Rare Books Division, Schomburg Center for Research in Black Culture, The New York Public Library.
34. Bambara, Letter to Jordan, 1977, 2.
35. Other recipients include James Baldwin, Frances Beale at Third World Women's Alliance, Barbara Christian at UMBRA, Hoyt Fuller at First World Publishing, Flo Kennedy, and Mary Helen Washington at the University of Detroit. Mailing Labels for *The Sea Birds Are Still Alive*, Undated (1977), box 1276, folder "Bambara, Toni Cade. *Sea Birds*," Random House Records, Rare Books and Manuscript Library, Columbia University.
36. Patricia Spears Jones, interview by Courtney Thorsson, December 11, 2019.
37. Bambara, "Realizing the Dream," 30.
38. See Thorsson, "'They Could Be Killing Kids Forever': The Atlanta Child Murders in African American Literature," *African American Review*. 53.4 (Winter 2020): 315–332.
39. Bambara, "Realizing the Dream," 38.
40. James Smethurst, "Retraining the Heartworks: Women in Atlanta's Black Arts Movement" in *Want to Start A Revolution?: Radical Women in The Black Freedom Struggle*, ed. Dayo F. Gore, Jeanne Theoharis, and Komozi Woodard (New York: New York University Press, 2009), 207.
41. Smethurst, "Retraining the Heartworks," 215, and James Smethurst, *Behold the Land: The Black Arts Movement in the South* (Chapel Hill: University of North Carolina Press, 2021), 163–167.

42. The Southern Collective of African American Writers (SCAAW), *The Newsletter of the Southern Collective of African-American Writers* 1, no. 5 (1979), box 17, Toni Cade Bambara Papers, Spelman College Archives.

43. The Southern Collective of African American Writers (SCAAW), *The Newsletter of the Southern Collective of African-American Writers* 1, no. 8 (1979), box 17, Toni Cade Bambara Papers, Spelman College Archives.

44. Smethurst, *Behold the Land*, 158; The Southern Collective of African American Writers (SCAAW), *The Newsletter of the Southern Collective of African-American Writers* 1, no. 1 (November 1978), box 17, Toni Cade Bambara Papers, Spelman College Archives.

45. SCAAW, *Newsletter* 1, no. 1, November 1978.

46. Nikky Finney, "Ambrosia," in *Shaping Memories: Reflections of African American Women Writers*, ed. Joanne Gabbin (Jackson: University of Mississippi Press, 2009), 144.

47. The Southern Collective of African American Writers (SCAAW), Second Annual Conference Program, October 19–21, 1979, box 7, folder "SCAAW," Cheryll Y. Greene Papers, Stuart A. Rose Manuscripts, Archives, and Rare Book Library, Emory University.

48. SCAAW, Second Annual Conference Program, October 19–21, 1979.

49. The Southern Collective of African American Writers (SCAAW), *The Newsletter of the Southern Collective of African-American Writers* 2 (1980), box 17, Toni Cade Bambara Papers, Spelman College Archives.

50. Finney, "Ambrosia," 145.

51. SCAAW, *Newsletter* 1, no. 8 (1979) and *Newsletter* 2, 1980; on the Institute of the Black World (IBW), see Smethurst, *Behold the Land*, 102–105.

52. SCAAW, Second Annual Conference Program, October 19–21, 1979.

53. Toni Cade Bambara, Letter to Cheryll Y. Greene, October 9, 1979, box 7, folder "SCAAW," Cheryll Y. Greene Papers, Stuart A. Rose Manuscripts, Archives, and Rare Book Library, Emory University.

54. Toni Cade Bambara, Letter to Cheryll Y. Greene, September 11, 1979, box 7, folder "SCAAW," Cheryll Y. Greene Papers, Stuart A. Rose Manuscripts, Archives, and Rare Book Library, Emory University, 2.

55. SCAAW, Second Annual Conference Program, October 19–21, 1979.

56. Smethurst, "Retraining the Heartworks," 216.

57. Photographer Susan J. Ross dates the photo of Bambara at a SCAAW conference included in this book as being taken in 1988.

58. Holmes, *A Joyous Revolt*, 49, 181.

59. Bambara, Interview by Kay Bonetti, American Audio Prose Library, KOPN Radio, Columbia, Missouri, February 1982. Cheryl A. Wall wrote, "Morrison was a hands-on editor who was closely involved with every step of the publishing process from acquisition to marketing" (Wall, "Toni Morrison, editor and teacher," in *The Cambridge Companion to Toni Morrison*, ed. Justine Tally [Cambridge: Cambridge University Press, 2007], 142). Correspondence in the Random House records at Columbia University's Rare Books and Manuscript Library demonstrates Morrison's detailed labor in "every step of the publishing process."

60. Vertamae Smart Grosvenor, postcard to Toni Cade Bambara, 1980, Toni Cade Bambara Papers, Spelman College Archives.

61. Books in African American literary studies that devote a full chapter to *The Salt Eaters* include David Ikard's *Breaking the Silence: Toward a Black Male Feminist Criticism* (2007), my *Women's Work* (2013), and Carter Mathes's *Imagine the Sound* (2015). An August 2021 search in the JSTOR and MUSE databases shows scholarly essays that use the opening line of *The Salt Eaters* as a theoretical touchstone in work that spans the disciplines of literary studies, education, health, folklore, religious studies, women's studies, and bioethics.

62. Linda Janet Holmes and Cheryl A. Wall, "*Savoring the Salt*: An Introduction," in *Savoring the Salt: The Legacy of Toni Cade Bambara*, ed. Linda Janet Holmes and Cheryl A. Wall (Philadelphia: Temple University Press, 2008), 4.

63. Holmes, *A Joyous Revolt*, 175. Morrison's words are from a research interview that Holmes conducted in 2012.

64. See Hilton Als, "Ghost in the House," *New Yorker*, October 19, 2003.

65. Toni Morrison and Junot Díaz, Public Conversation, December 12, 2013, Stephen A. Schwartzman Building, New York Public Library.

66. Toni Morrison, Letter to Toni Cade Bambara, March 1, 1977, box 101, folder 4, Toni Morrison Papers, Department of Rare Books and Special Collections, Princeton University Library. Morrison also thought of Gayl Jones as among the few "*living black women writing good fiction*." For a 1981 example of Bambara and Jones as the two important Black women writers Morrison mentions in interviews, see Judith Wilson, "A Conversation with Toni Morrison," *Essence*, July 1981, 128.

67. Morrison and Díaz, Public Conversation, December 12, 2013.

68. Bambara, "Gorilla, My Love," in *Gorilla, My Love*, 1972 (New York: Random House, 1992), 16.

69. Bambara, "Gorilla, My Love," 20.

70. Alexis P. Gumbs, "Spelling Soul: For Cheryll Y. Greene," *Souls* 18, no. 1 (January–March 2016): 142, note 1. Greene wrote reviews and articles for *Essence* in the early 1970s before her full-time employment at the magazine. She also regularly consulted on special projects and occasionally contributed after 1985. In 1990, she officially became an editor-at-large for *Essence* (Cheryll Y. Greene, Letter to Susan Taylor, May 22, 1990 [Revised 20 September 1990], box 8, folder "Transition—*Essence* 1990," Cheryll Y. Greene Papers, Stuart A. Rose Manuscripts, Archives, and Rare Book Library, Emory University).

71. Gumbs, "Spelling Soul," 136.

72. Cheryll Y. Greene, Resume, Undated (circa 1979), box 7, folder "Lecture Agency," Cheryll Y. Greene Papers, Stuart A. Rose Manuscripts, Archives, and Rare Book Library, Emory University, 1; Toni Morrison, Letter to Cheryll Y. Greene, February 13, 1975, box 1520, folder "Gayl Jones. *Corregidora*," Random House Records, Rare Books and Manuscript Library, Columbia University; Toni Morrison, Letter to Cheryll Y. Greene, February 24, 1975, box 1, folder "Essence—Book Reviews," Cheryll Y. Greene Papers, Stuart A. Rose Manuscripts, Archives, and Rare Book Library, Emory University.

73. Studio Museum of Harlem, First Annual Lewis H. Michaux Book Fair Program, 1976, box 1, Cheryll Y. Greene Papers, Stuart A. Rose Manuscripts, Archives, and Rare Book Library, Emory University; Cheryll Y. Greene, Comments on "Black Producers" by Jessica Harris, Handwritten Notes, box 1, folder "Essence—1977 Free-Lance," Cheryll Y. Greene Papers, Stuart A. Rose Manuscripts, Archives, and Rare Book Library, Emory University; Cheryll Y. Greene, Comments on "Guess Who's

Coming to Dinner?" by Vertamae Smart Grosvenor, Handwritten Notes, box 1, folder "Essence—1977 Free-Lance," Cheryll Y. Greene Papers, Stuart A. Rose Manuscripts, Archives, and Rare Book Library, Emory University; Cheryll Y. Greene, Background on Cheryll Y. Greene for distribution to potential clients of New World Lecture Bureau, Undated (circa October 1979), box 7, folder "Lecture Agency," Cheryll Y. Greene Papers, Stuart A. Rose Manuscripts, Archives, and Rare Book Library, Emory University. "Black Women's Anger" was retitled as "Eye to Eye: Black Women, Hatred, and Anger" in Lorde's 1984 volume of essays *Sister Outsider*. Alexis De Veaux, *Warrior Poet: A Biography of Audre Lorde* (New York: Norton, 2004), 320.

74. De Veaux, *Warrior Poet*, 330–331; James Baldwin and Audre Lorde, "Revolutionary Hope," *Essence*, 1984. Republished online by The Museum of Contemporary African Diaspora Arts at https://mocada-museum.tumblr.com/post/73421979421/revolutionary-hope-a-conversation-between-james.

75. Baldwin and Lorde, "Revolutionary Hope."

76. De Veaux, *Warrior Poet*, 331.

77. Baldwin and Lorde, "Revolutionary Hope."

78. Rich Blint, Alexis De Veaux, and Imani Perry, "Ancestral Witnesses: James Baldwin and Audre Lorde: A Revolutionary Hope," panel discussion moderated by Josef Sorett, December 4, 2014, Columbia University.

79. Some of the writers Greene worked with in the late 1970s were Sisterhood members Audrey Edwards, Vertamae Grosvenor, Rosa Guy, June Jordan, Audre Lorde, Paule Marshall, and Toni Morrison as well as other important Black writers including Toni Cade Bambara, Lucille Clifton, Jayne Cortez, Thulani Davis, Alexis De Veaux, Larry Neal, Beverley Guy-Sheftall, Eleanor Traylor, and Mary Helen Washington. See box 7, Cheryll Y. Greene Papers, Stuart A. Rose Manuscripts, Archives, and Rare Book Library, Emory University.

80. See box 12, folders "MSS & Comments FOB Essays Speak—May 85," "MSS & Comments—Our Lives Together May 85," "MSS & Comments—Claiming Our Power May 85," "MSS & Comments—Woman to Woman May 85," and "MSS & Comments—Our Style May 85" in Cheryll Y. Greene Papers, Stuart A. Rose Manuscripts, Archives, and Rare Book Library, Emory University. At the time of this issue, Bambara was on the magazine's editorial advisory board (*Essence*, May 1985). The May 1985 special issue of the magazine includes contributions by former Sisterhood members Garland, Grosvenor, Jordan, Marshall, Morrison, Shange, and Walker. Greene edited a piece by Bambara about the Atlanta child murders that did not ultimately not appear in this issue; the piece includes phrases and sentences that later appeared in Bambara's posthumously published novel *Those Bones Are Not My Child* (1999). Diane Weathers, Sisterhood member and contributor, wrote Edwards congratulating her on the beauty and courage of the contents (Diane Weathers, Letter to Ed, Susan, and Audrey, April 30, 1985, box 8, folder "PR & Promo Info & Responses—May 85," Cheryll Y. Greene Papers, Stuart A. Rose Manuscripts, Archives, and Rare Book Library, Emory University). Weathers, who would go on to serve as the magazine's editor-in-chief in the 2000s, says of *Essence*, "I don't think it was a frivolous magazine . . . I am very proud of the work I did. I'm very proud of the articles I wrote when I was a writer. I am very proud of the leadership that I provided when I was editor-in-chief . . . It's an important vehicle for Black female writers . . . we supported a lot of writers, Gloria Naylor, Terry McMillan's first pieces were in *Essence*. I finally got Jamaica Kincaid in there" (Diane Weathers, Interview by Stanley Crouch, video

recording, October 15, 2006, series 6, Camille Billops and James V. Hatch Archives, Stuart A. Rose Manuscript, Archives, and Rare Book Library, Emory University.)

81. "Essence Writers' Retreat, Nassau, Bahamas, 1988," photograph and list of participants, box 7, folder "Pictures," Toni Cade Bambara Collection, Spelman College Archives.

82. See memos and drafts of retreat schedule in box 8, folder "Writers' Retreat," Cheryll Y. Greene Papers, Stuart A. Rose Manuscripts, Archives, and Rare Book Library, Emory University.

83. Alexis De Veaux, "A Message of Support and Greetings," box 8, folder "Writers' Retreat," Cheryll Y. Greene Papers, Stuart A. Rose Manuscripts, Archives, and Rare Book Library, Emory University.

84. Toni Morrison, "Toni Morrison's Statement," November 9, 1988, box 8, folder "Writers' Retreat," Cheryll Y. Greene Papers, Stuart A. Rose Manuscripts, Archives, and Rare Book Library, Emory University.

85. Jordan, "Message from June Jordan—11/5/88," Box 8, Folder "Writers' Retreat," Cheryll Y. Greene Papers, Stuart A. Rose Manuscripts, Archives, and Rare Book Library, Emory University.

86. Cheryll Y. Greene, Letter to Lucille Clifton, October 21, 1988, box 52, folder 6 "Essence Writers' Conference November 1988," Lucille Clifton Papers, Stuart A. Rose Manuscripts, Archives, and Rare Book Library, Emory University.

87. Cheryll Y. Greene, "Editorial Services," Undated (circa 1999), box 13, Cheryll Y. Greene Papers, Stuart A. Rose Manuscripts, Archives, and Rare Book Library, Emory University, 3.

88. Toni Cade Bambara, Letter to Cheryll Y. Greene, March 12, 1980, box 7, folder "Lecture Agency," Cheryll Y. Greene Papers, Stuart A. Rose Manuscripts, Archives, and Rare Book Library, Emory University.

89. This is evident in Bambara's letters to Greene throughout 1979 and 1980, in which Bambara provides names and contact information of potential clients for Greene, explanations of her process and fees for giving readings and talks in various venues, and suggestions of various organizations that Greene might work with to build her new business. See folder "Lecture Agency" in box 7, Cheryll Y. Greene Papers. Stuart A. Rose Manuscripts, Archives, and Rare Book Library, Emory University.

90. Toni Cade Bambara, Letter to Cheryll Y. Greene, December 5, 1979, box 7, folder "SCAAW," Cheryll Y. Greene Papers, Stuart A. Rose Manuscripts, Archives, and Rare Book Library, Emory University.

91. Cheryll Y. Greene, Letter to Toni Cade Bambara, November 5, 1979, box 7, folder "SCAAW," Cheryll Y. Greene Papers, Stuart A. Rose Manuscripts, Archives, and Rare Book Library, Emory University.

92. See box 22, padded envelope, "Estate of Toni Cade Bambara," Cheryll Y. Greene Papers, Stuart A. Rose Manuscripts, Archives, and Rare Book Library, Emory University.

5. "A REGULAR PROFUSION
OF CERTAIN/UNIDENTIFIED ROSES"

1. June Jordan, interview by Karla Hammond, 1978, in Christoph Keller and Jan Heller Levi, eds., *We're On: A June Jordan Reader* (Farmington, ME: Alice James Books, 2017), 242. Correspondence in Cheryll Y. Greene's papers at Emory suggests that

Hammond unsuccessfully pitched this interview for publication in *Essence*. The title of this chapter comes from June Jordan, "Letter to the Local Police," 1980, in Keller and Levi, eds., *We're On*, 329.

2. Alexis De Veaux, "Creating Soul Food: June Jordan," *Essence* 11, no. 82 (April 1981): 150.
3. June Jordan, "Poem About My Rights," 1978, in Keller and Levi, eds., *We're On*, 344.
4. Judith Wilson, interview by Courtney Thorsson, February 12, 2019.
5. For information about MoMA's 2022–23 exhibit of the work and artists of JAM, see https://www.moma.org/calendar/exhibitions/5078.
6. Thomas (T.) Jean Lax and Lilia Rocio Taboada, eds., *Just Above Midtown: Changing Spaces* (New York: The Museum of Modern Art and The Studio Museum in Harlem, 2022), exhibition catalogue.
7. The catalogue "was ultimately not realized." Lax and Taboada, eds., *Just Above Midtown*, 97–98.
8. Judith Wilson, *Lorraine O'Grady: Critical Interventions* (New York: INTAR Gallery, 1991), exhibition catalogue.
9. Wilson, interview by Thorsson.
10. Alexis P. Gumbs, "Black (Buying) Power: The Story of *Essence* Magazine," in *The Business of Black Power: Community Development, Capitalism, and Corporate Responsibility in Postwar America*, ed. Laura Warren Hill and Julia Rabig (Rochester, NY: Boydell & Brewer, 2012), 95.
11. Gumbs, "Black (Buying) Power," 96.
12. Gumbs, "Black (Buying) Power," 97.
13. See Gumbs's readings of ways the magazine framed poems by and profiles of Giovanni and Lorde in "Black (Buying) Power," 108–110.
14. Alice Walker to Judith Wilson, February 23, 1979, box 1, folder 47, Judith Wilson Papers, 1966–2010, Smithsonian Archives of American Art. The two women exchanged letters about their romantic relationships; works by Toni Cade Bambara, W. E. B. Du Bois, and Zora Neale Hurston; Walker's visits to New York; Walker's efforts to get published or reviewed in *Essence*; and an interview Wilson conducted with Walker that was never published. Wilson conducted and recorded this interview during a two-week trip to California during which she did interviews for pieces for *Ms.*, *Essence*, and *Black Enterprise*. At Walker's request, Wilson returned the audiotapes of their unpublished interview to her. Wilson's interviews with artists in the Bay Area and Los Angeles became part of her essay in the 1980 special issue of *Black Enterprise* on the business of art collecting (Wilson, email to author, February 15, 2019). See the Judith Wilson Papers in the Smithsonian Archives of American Art. Box 1, folder 47 contains correspondence with Alice Walker from 1978 to 1981.
15. *Essence*, July 1980, 15–16.
16. *Essence*, October 1979, 14, 20; *Essence*, October 1980, 18, 21; *Essence*, June 1981, 14.
17. *Essence*, September 1980, 14; *Essence*, September 1981, 17.
18. Alexis De Veaux, *Warrior Poet: A Biography of Audre Lorde* (New York: Norton, 2004), 246–248.
19. De Veaux, *Warrior Poet*, 258; Erica R. Edwards, *The Other Side of Terror: Black Women and the Culture of US Empire* (New York: New York University Press, 2021), 240–241.
20. De Veaux, *Warrior Poet*, 276–277.
21. Alexis De Veaux, "Alice Walker," *Essence*, September 1989, 120.

22. De Veaux, *Warrior Poet*, 264.

23. Charles Rowell, "Above the Wind: An Interview with Audre Lorde," *Callaloo* 14, no. 1 (Winter 1991): 93.

24. Wilson, interview by Thorsson.

25. De Veaux, *Warrior Poet*, 264, 407 note 2. Though neither was a member, De Veaux and Thulani Davis were important friends and collaborators for The Sisterhood and both took part in NATWW. Davis was a close friend of Shange. Shange dedicated the first chapbook of *for colored girls* to her sisters Ifa and Bisa, June Jordan, and Davis and gave her daughter Savannah two middle names: Eloise, after Shange's mother, and Thulani, after Thulani Davis (Ntozake Shange, Journal, 1981–2009, box 9, folder 5, Ntozake Shange Papers, 1966–2016, Barnard Archives and Special Collections, Barnard Library, Barnard College).

26. A database of NEA grant awardees is available at https://www.arts.gov/grants/recent -grants. A detailed history of the NEA from its founding through 2008 is available at https://www.arts.gov/sites/default/files/nea-history-1965-2008.pdf.

27. See a 2014 National Endowment for the Arts interview with Morrison at https://www.arts.gov/stories/magazine/2014/4/art-failure-importance-risk-and -experimentation/toni-morrison and a complete list of Carter's 1980 NEA appointees at https://www.presidency.ucsb.edu/documents/national-endowment-for-the-arts -appointment-seven-members-the-national-council-the-arts.

28. Rowell, "Above the Wind," 83–84; Audre Lorde, "Sisters in Arms," *Feminist Studies* 14, no. 3 (Autumn 1988): 443.

29. Evelyn C. White, *Alice Walker: A Life* (New York: Norton, 2004), 365.

30. Alice Walker, *Gathering Blossoms Under Fire: The Journals of Alice Walker*, ed. Valerie Boyd (New York: Simon & Schuster, 2022), 352–353, 406.

31. Linda Janet Holmes, *A Joyous Revolt: Toni Cade Bambara, Writer and Activist* (Santa Barbara, CA: Praeger, 2014), 157; De Veaux, *Warrior Poet*, 347. Bambara returned to Cuba in early 1989 as part of a Writers' Guild of America trip.

32. See Edwards, *The Other Side of Terror*, chapters 1 and 5.

33. See Mary Helen Washington's introduction in *Invented Lives: Narratives of Black Women, 1860–1960* (New York: Doubleday, 1987).

34. De Veaux, "Alice Walker," 56.

35. See Simone Browne, *Dark Matters: On the Surveillance of Blackness* (Durham, NC: Duke University Press, 2015).

36. See Kevin Quashie, *The Sovereignty of Quiet: Beyond Resistance in Black Culture* (New Brunswick, NJ: Rutgers University Press, 2012).

37. Jordan, "Letter to the Local Police," 329, 330.

38. In the volume *Revolutionary Petunias* (1973), Walker begins section IV of the poem "Mysteries . . . The Living Beyond" with an epigraph drawn from a letter Jordan wrote to Walker in 1970.

39. June Jordan, "Poem About Police Violence," in Keller and Levi, eds., *We're On*, 330–331.

40. Renita Weems, interview by Courtney Thorsson, January 8, 2019.

41. Renita Weems, *Just a Sister Away: A Womanist Vision of Women's Relationships in the Bible* (San Diego: LuraMedia, 1988), ix.

42. Weems, *Just a Sister Away*, x.

43. Weems, *Just a Sister Away*, 20, 50, 126, 69.

44. Patricia Spears Jones, interview by Courtney Thorsson, December 11, 2019.

45. See Howard Rambsy, "A Notebook on prizes, awards, and fellowships," http://www
    .culturalfront.org/2015/01/a-notebook-on-prizes-and-awards.html.
46. Patricia Spears Jones, "Glad All Over," in *The Weather That Kills* (Minneapolis:
    Coffee House Press, 1995), 43.
47. Sterling Brown, "Strong Men," 1931, in *The Collected Poems of Sterling A. Brown*, ed.
    Michael S. Harper (Evanston, IL: Northwestern University Press, 1980), 58.
48. Margo Jefferson, interview by Courtney Thorsson, May 31, 2018.
49. Margo Jefferson, *Negroland: A Memoir* (New York: Pantheon, 2015), 7–8.
50. Jefferson, *Negroland*, 160.
51. Jefferson, *Negroland*, 166.
52. Jefferson, *Negroland*, 170.
53. Jefferson, *Negroland*, 171–172.
54. Jefferson, *Negroland*, 174.
55. Jefferson, *Negroland*, 173.
56. Jefferson, *Negroland*, 176.

6. "THE FUNCTION OF FREEDOM IS TO FREE
SOMEBODY ELSE"

1. See https://archive.nytimes.com/www.nytimes.com/ref/books/fiction-25-years.html
   ?emc=th&th. Howard Rambsy and Kenton Rambsy document that "In every decade
   since the 1970s, the *Times* has cited Morrison in more total articles than [Alice]
   Walker and every other Black writer except [James] Baldwin." See Howard Rambsy
   and Kenton Rambsy, "How the *New York Times* Covers Black Writers," *Public Books*,
   October 12, 2022. The title of this chapter comes from Toni Morrison, "Cinderella's
   Stepsisters," May 13, 1979, in *The Source of Self-Regard: Selected Essays, Speeches, and
   Meditations* (New York: Knopf, 2019), 110–112.
2. See http://www.culturalfront.org/2019/08/coverage-of-toni-morrisons-passing.html
   and https://www.hashtagfeminism.com/hashtag-feminism-blog/2019/8/13/black-women
   -tribute-toni-morrison.
3. Morrison's simultaneous dependence on and advocacy for Black studies is in keeping
   with a tradition: "in many early Black Studies departments and programs . . . it was
   the artists who put those departments on the map, not the young (for the most part)
   academics who accompanied them." In the 1960s and '70s, this included Black Arts
   poets Amiri Baraka and Sonia Sanchez at San Francisco State and Sterling Brown,
   Toni Cade Bambara, John O. Killens, Margaret Walker, and Audre Lorde at HBCUs
   across the U.S. South (James Smethurst, *Behold the Land: The Black Arts Movement
   in the South* [Chapel Hill: University of North Carolina Press, 2021], 112–113).
4. Hilton Als, "Ghost in the House," *New Yorker*, October 19, 2003.
5. In the foreword to the 2002 edition of *Sula*, Morrison notes that, living in Queens
   while writing the novel in the late 1960s, she was trying to balance raising her
   children and "commuting to Manhattan to an office job" (Toni Morrison, *Sula*, 1973
   [New York: Random House, 2002], xiv). She had help with child care from her parents and struggled to make ends meet financially.
6. Toni Morrison and Junot Díaz, Public Conversation, December 12, 2013, Stephen A.
   Schwartzman Building, New York Public Library.
7. Margo Jefferson, interview by Courtney Thorsson, May 31, 2018.

8. Boris Kachka, "Who Is the Author of Toni Morrison?," *New York*, April 29, 2012.
9. See Joe Karaganis and David McClure, "Did Harold Bloom or Toni Morrison Win the Literary Canon Wars?," *New York Times*, October 19, 2019.
10. Margalit Fox, Obituary for Toni Morrison, *New York Times*, August 6, 2019.
11. Emily Langer, Obituary for Toni Morrison, *Washington Post*, August 6, 2019.
12. Als, "Ghost in the House."
13. Shanna Benjamin told this story at a book launch talk for her scholarly biography of McKay, *Half in Shadow: The Life and Legacy of Nellie Y. McKay* (Chapel Hill: University of North Carolina Press, 2021).
14. Morrison, interview by Nellie McKay, *Contemporary Literature* 24, no. 4 (Winter 1983): 426.
15. https://www.youtube.com/watch?v=u7vXnbEd8z4.
16. Als, "Ghost in the House."
17. Kachka, "Who Is the Author of Toni Morrison?"
18. Alice Walker, *Gathering Blossoms Under Fire: The Journals of Alice Walker*, ed. Valerie Boyd (New York: Simon & Schuster, 2022), 147. It was only a few years later that Harcourt bought Walker's novel *The Temple of My Familiar* for $2.5 million (279).
19. Walker, *Gathering Blossoms*, 250, 367.
20. Richard O. Moore, dir., *The Writer in America: Toni Morrison*, Perspective Films, Chicago, May 4, 1978, https://archive.org/details/thewriterinamericatonimorrison.
21. Judith Wilson, "A Conversation with Toni Morrison," *Essence*, July 1981, 84.
22. Morrison, "Cinderella's Stepsisters," 111.
23. Morrison, "Cinderella's Stepsisters," 112.
24. Morrison and Díaz, Public Conversation, December 12, 2013.
25. See Richard Jean So, chapter 1, "Production: On White Publishing," in *Redlining Culture: A Data History of Racial Inequality and Postwar Fiction* (New York: Columbia University Press, 2021).
26. Cheryl A. Wall, "Toni Morrison, editor and teacher," in *The Cambridge Companion to Toni Morrison*, ed. Justine Tally (Cambridge: Cambridge University Press, 2007), 139.
27. Morrison and Díaz, Public Conversation, December 12, 2013.
28. Wilson, "A Conversation with Toni Morrison," 84.
29. Jacqueline Trescott, "Toni Morrison's Success by the Book," *Washington Post*, April 8, 1981.
30. For examples, see box 1528, folder B 1981, Random House Records, Rare Books and Manuscript Library, Columbia University.
31. Wall, "Toni Morrison, editor and teacher," 139.
32. Patricia Spears Jones, interview by Courtney Thorsson, December 11, 2019.
33. Henry Louis Gates, Jr., "Afterword: Zora Neale Hurston: 'A Negro Way of Saying,'" 1990, *Their Eyes Were Watching God*, 1937 (New York: Harper Perennial, 2006), 198.
34. June Jordan, "Notes Toward a Black Balancing of Love and Hatred," 1974, *Civil Wars: Observations from the Front Lines of America*, 1981 (New York: Simon & Schuster, 1995), 85, 86, 87.
35. Gates, "Afterword," 195–196.
36. I am grateful to the anonymous reader for Columbia University Press who reminded me of these layers of advocacy for Hurston's novel.
37. Walker, *Gathering Blossoms Under Fire*, 63.

38. Christoph Keller and Jan Heller Levi, eds., *We're On: A June Jordan Reader* (Farmington, ME: Alice James Books, 2017), 189.

39. Jordan, "Notes Toward a Black Balancing," 89.

40. Wilson, "A Conversation with Toni Morrison," 128, 130; bracketed text in original.

41. See Richard Jean So, *Redlining Culture*, and Howard Rambsy, "A Notebook on prizes, awards, and fellowships," http://www.culturalfront.org/2015/01/a-notebook-on-prizes-and-awards.html.

42. See Howard Rambsy and Kenton Rambsy, "How the *New York Times* Covers Black Writers."

43. Michele Wallace, "Negative Images: Towards a Black Feminist Cultural Criticism," 1991, *Invisibility Blues: From Pop to Theory*, 1990 (New York: Verso, 2016), 253.

44. Michael D. Hill, *The Ethics of Swagger: Prizewinning African American Novels, 1977–1993* (Columbus: Ohio State University Press, 2013), 45.

45. Edwin McDowell, "48 Black Writers Protest By Praising Morrison," *New York Times*, January 19, 1988.

46. The sense of Baldwin's death as a monumental personal and cultural loss is apparent in the way many African American authors of the period documented the funeral in their now-archived papers. Bambara, Morrison, Grosvenor, and many others kept copies of the program. Bambara made handwritten notes documenting attendees and each part of the funeral. Poets Thomas Sayers Ellis and Sharan Strange traveled from Boston to attend Baldwin's funeral in New York. As they left the service, they decided to found the Dark Room Collective, a group that lasted about a decade and shaped the writing and careers of members including Pulitzer Prize winner Natasha Trethewey and Pulitzer Prize winner and 2017–2019 U.S. Poet Laureate Tracy K. Smith. See Jeff Gordiner, "The Dark Room Collective: Where Black Poetry Took Wing," *New York Times*, May 27, 2014.

47. McDowell, "48 Black Writers."

48. June Jordan, Houston Baker, et al., "Black Writers in Praise of Toni Morrison," *New York Times*, January 24, 1988. On the meanings, impact, and legacy of the *Times* letter, see Howard Rambsy's post at http://www.culturalfront.org/2015/07/from-baldwin-to-morrison-coates-brief.html.

49. Jordan, Baker, et al., 36.

50. Jordan, Baker, et al., 36.

51. Jordan, Baker, et al., 36.

52. Walker, *Gathering Blossoms Under Fire*, 63.

53. Walker, *Gathering Blossoms Under Fire*, 143.

54. Edwin McDowell, "An Upset at The National Book Awards," *New York Times*, November 10, 1987.

55. McDowell, "48 Black Writers."

56. Toni Morrison, Letter to Toni Cade Bambara, December 29, 1987, box 1, folder "Personal Correspondence, Toni Morrison, 1972–1994, n.d.," Toni Cade Bambara Papers, Spelman College Archives; ellipses in original.

57. Henry Louis Gates, Jr., Letter to Toni Morrison, June 7, 1983, box 78, folder 3, Toni Morrison Papers, Department of Rare Books and Special Collections, Princeton University Library, 4.

58. Henry Louis Gates, Jr., Letter to Toni Morrison, December 22, 1987, box 78, folder 3, Toni Morrison Papers, Department of Rare Books and Special Collections, Princeton University Library. Gates was among those disappointed that Gloria Naylor, in her

role as a fiction judge for the 1987 NBA, apparently did not argue for giving the award to Morrison. See Gates's letters to Morrison and June Jordan's letter to Naylor in the Toni Morrison Papers at Princeton University, box 78, folder 3 and box 81, folder 4.

59. Excerpts of this broadcast appear in Timothy Greenfield-Sanders, dir., *Toni Morrison: The Pieces I Am*, Magnolia Films, 2019.

60. In a 1989 letter, Gates suggests to Morrison that her winning the Nobel is inevitable, if a few years away (Henry Louis Gates, Jr., Letter to Toni Morrison, January 31, 1989, box 78, folder 3, Toni Morrison Papers, Department of Rare Books and Special Collections, Princeton University Library). For more on the meanings of and reactions to Morrison winning the Nobel, see Ann duCille, "Of Race, Gender, and the Novel; or, Where in the World is Toni Morrison?," *Novel* 50, no. 3 (November 2017):

61. Jordan, Baker, et al., 36. Former members of The Sisterhood continue to shore up Morrison's place in African American literature. Patricia Spears Jones dedicated her 2011 poem "Dream Book" to Morrison; that poem alludes to Morrison's *Sula* (1973) and its setting, "the Bottom" (Jones, *A Lucent Fire: New and Selected Poems* [Buffalo, NY: White Pine Press, 2015], 140). In a 2018 lecture, Margo Jefferson drew on Morrison's *The Origin of Others* as a theoretical tool to understand "image" and "language" and read a section of her memoir *Negroland* that uses Morrison's term "rememory" from *Beloved* (Jefferson, "From 'I' to 'We': The Role of the Citizen-Critic," Kritikos Lecture in the Humanities, Oregon Humanities Center "We the People" Series, University of Oregon, Eugene, Oregon, May 30, 2018).

62. Stephen Best, *None Like Us: Blackness, Belonging, Aesthetic Life* (Durham, NC: Duke University Press, 2018), 68.

63. "Contemporary narratives of slavery" is Arlene Keizer's term, which I find more capacious and useful than the more narrow "neo-slave narrative." See Arlene Keizer, *Black Subjects: Identity Formation in the Contemporary Narrative of Slavery* (Ithaca, NY: Cornell University Press, 2004).

64. See Ashraf H. A. Rushdy, *Neo-slave Narratives: Studies in the Social Logic of a Literary Form* (New York: Oxford University Press, 1999); Angelyn Mitchell, *The Freedom to Remember: Narrative, Slavery, and Gender in Contemporary Black Women's Fiction* (New Brunswick, NJ: Rutgers University Press, 2002); and Madhu Dubey, "Neo-Slave Narratives," in *A Companion to African American Literature*, ed. Gene Andrew Jarrett (Hoboken, NJ: Wiley-Blackwell, 2013).

65. About 130 million viewers watched *Roots* on ABC in early 1977. By the time of Alex Hayley's death in 1992, over six million copies of *Roots* had been sold. Bart Barnes, "Alex Hayley, Who Found His 'Roots,' Dies," *Washington Post*, February 11, 1992.

66. Best, *None Like Us*, 68.

67. *How to Read African American Literature: Post-Civil Rights Fiction and the Task of Interpretation* (New York: New York University Press, 2016), 133.

68. Emma Brockes, "Toni Morrison: 'I want to feel what I feel. Even if it's not happiness,'" *Guardian*, April 13, 2012. Some of Morrison's letters to Bambara from the 1980s in Bambara's papers in the Spelman College Archives are signed "Clo" or "Chloe."

69. Kachka, "Who Is the Author of Toni Morrison?"

70. Farah Jasmine Griffin, "Toni Morrison Talks Racism, Readers and Her New Novel," *Essence*, April 17, 2015.

71. Greenfield-Sanders, *Toni Morrison*.

72. Edwidge Danticat, eulogy for Toni Morrison, November 21, 2019, Cathedral of St. John the Divine, New York. https://vimeo.com/374796939.

73. In the acknowledgments in her 1974 autobiography, Angela Davis writes, "The writing of this book allowed me to work with and get to know a person who is a magnificent writer and inspiring Black woman. As my editor, Toni Morrison not only gave me invaluable assistance, but she was patient and understanding when the work on the book had to be continually interrupted by my responsibility to the movement to free political prisoners. I am deeply grateful to the Cuban Communist Party and its First Secretary Fidel Castro for having invited me to spend several months in Cuba to work full time on the manuscript" (*Angela Davis: An Autobiography*, 1974 [New York: International Publishers, 1988], xiii).

74. Danticat, eulogy for Morrison.

75. Jessica Harris, "I Will Always Be a Writer," profile of Toni Morrison, *Essence*, December 1976, in *Toni Morrison: Conversations*, ed. Carolyn C. Denard (Jackson: University of Mississippi Press, 2008), 8.

76. Harris, "I Will Always Be a Writer," 9.

77. Toni Morrison, "Unspeakable Things Unspoken: The Afro-American Presence in American Literature," October 7, 1988, in *The Source of Self-Regard: Selected Essays, Speeches, and Meditations* (New York: Knopf, 2019), 183.

78. Toni Morrison, "Goodbye to All That: Race, Surrogacy, and Farewell," April 3, 2001, in *The Source of Self-Regard: Selected Essays, Speeches, and Meditations* (New York: Knopf, 2019), 335.

7. "MAKING USE OF BEING USED"

1. Danica Savonick's *Insurgent Knowledge: The Poetics and Pedagogy of Toni Cade Bambara, June Jordan, Audre Lorde, and Adrienne Rich in the Era of Open Admissions* (forthcoming from Duke University Press), will be an important contribution to knowledge about the radical teaching of Sisterhood members and other feminists of their era. The title of this chapter comes from Paule Marshall's recollection of going on a U.S. State Department tour in her memoir *Triangular Road* (2009). My use of Marshall's phrase is indebted to Erica Edwards's reading of it in *The Other Side of Terror: Black Women and the Culture of US Empire* (New York: New York University Press, 2021).

2. Mary Helen Washington and Shaun Myers, "'Cobbling It All Together': Mary Helen Washington and Shaun Myers, In Conversation," *Los Angeles Review of Books*, July 14, 2021, https://www.lareviewofbooks.org/article/cobbling-it-all-together-mary -helen-washington-and-shaun-myers-in-conversation/.

3. June Jordan, "Black Studies: Bringing Back the Person," 1969, in *Civil Wars: Observations from the Front Lines of America*, 1981 (New York: Simon & Schuster, 1995), 47, 52.

4. Toni Cade Bambara, interview by Kay Bonetti, American Audio Prose Library, KOPN Radio, Columbia, Missouri, February 1982.

5. Mecca Jamilah Sullivan, "Pedagogies of the 'Irresistible': Imaginative Elsewheres of Black Feminist Learning," *Journal of Feminist Scholarship* 20 (Spring 2022): 2.

6. Barbara Smith, Letter to Audre Lorde, January 5, 1979, series 1.1, folder 123, Audre Lorde Papers, Spelman College Archives.

7. Patricia Spears Jones, interview by Courtney Thorsson, December 11, 2019.

8. Edwards, *The Other Side of Terror*, 193.

9. https://bcrw.barnard.edu/publications/digital-shange/.

10. https://sfonline.barnard.edu/worlds-of-ntozake-shange/.

11. https://barnard.edu/what-we-do/shange-magic.

12. Toni Cade Bambara's papers serve similar purposes at Spelman College, where her archive is held and where Beverly Guy-Sheftall, with faculty and students, organizes a biannual "Toni Cade Bambara Scholar-Activist-Writer Conference" on Bambara's birthday. Holly Smith, "'Wholeness Is No Trifling Matter': Black Feminist Archival Practice and the Spelman College Archives," *The Black Scholar* 52, no. 2 (May 2022): 24.

13. For a fictional portrait of Lorde's intellectual, administrative, and emotional labor of building the Black studies department at John Jay, see her unfinished novel *Deotha* (Audre Lorde, *"I Teach Myself in Outline," Notes, Journals, Syllabi & an Excerpt from Deotha by Audre Lorde*, Lost & Found: The CUNY Poetics Document Initiative, series 7, no. 1 [Fall 2017] [New York: Small Press Distribution and lostandfoundbooks .org, 2017], 43–65).

14. Alexis De Veaux, *Warrior Poet: A Biography of Audre Lorde* (New York: Norton, 2004), 139.

15. Alice Walker, *Gathering Blossoms Under Fire: The Journals of Alice Walker*, ed. Valerie Boyd (New York: Simon & Schuster, 2022), 198, 410, 276.

16. Alice Walker, "Reaping What We Sow: A Conversation with Pulitzer Prize Winner Alice Walker," Panel with Darieck Scott and Ra Malika Imhotep, February 15, 2021, University of California, Berkeley.

17. June Jordan, "Notes Toward a Black Balancing of Love and Hatred," 1974, *Civil Wars: Observations from the Front Lines of America*, 1981 (New York: Simon & Schuster, 1995), 94; Christoph Keller and Jan Heller Levi, eds., *We're On: A June Jordan Reader* (Farmington, ME: Alice James Books, 2017), 134.

18. June Jordan, "Nobody Mean More to Me Than You and the Future Life of Willie Jordan," 1985, *We're On: A June Jordan* Reader, eds. Christoph Keller and Jan Heller Levi (Farmington, ME: Alice James Books, 2017), 134–136.

19. Jordan, "Nobody Mean," 137.

20. Valerie Kinloch, *June Jordan: Her Life and Letters* (Westport, CT: Praeger, 2006), 122–123. See https://www.berkeley.edu/news/media/releases/2002/06/17_jordan.html and https://senate.universityofcalifornia.edu/_files/inmemoriam/html/JuneJordan .htm. Barbara Christian's work in Berkeley public schools and for University Without Walls were also acts of educational access and justice that were possible partly because of Christian's position at Berkeley but far exceeded the prescriptions and confines of the university. See Grace Kyungwon Hong, *Death Beyond Disavowal: The Impossible Politics of Difference* (Minneapolis: University of Minnesota Press, 2015), 138.

21. https://africam.berkeley.edu/poetry-for-the-people/.

22. *Poetry for the People* thus resembles the earlier contents and aims of *But Some of Us Are Brave* (1982), which SaraEllen Strongman describes as "consciously constructed as a classroom tool. A large portion of the anthology is devoted to actual teaching resources in the form of bibliographic essays, bibliographies, and syllabi" (Strongman, "The Archeological Impulse, Black Feminism, and *But Some of Us Are Brave*," *Feminist Studies* 48, no. 1 [2022]: 34).

23. Toni Morrison, "Unspeakable Things Unspoken: The Afro-American Presence in American Literature," October 7, 1988, in *The Source of Self-Regard: Selected Essays, Speeches, and Meditations* (New York: Knopf, 2019), 170.

24. Morrison, "Unspeakable Things Unspoken," 172.

25. Toni Morrison, "Academic Whispers," March 10, 2004, in *The Source of Self-Regard: Selected Essays, Speeches, and Meditations* (New York: Knopf, 2019), 202–203.

26. Morrison, "Academic Whispers," 203.

27. Toni Morrison, "The Source of Self-Regard," March 19, 1992, in *The Source of Self-Regard: Selected Essays, Speeches, and Meditations* (New York: Knopf, 2019), 304.

28. Morrison, "The Source of Self-Regard," 304–305. The same year that Morrison made this observation, Nellie McKay wrote, "I wanted Black Studies to grow and develop into a force on college and university campuses across the country, but I was also concerned that our scholarship and teaching permeate the disciplines in Arts and Sciences curriculum and thus completely transform them" ("A Troubled Peace: Black Women in the Halls of the White Academy," *The Bucknell Review* 36, no. 2 (January 1992): 23).

29. Barbara Christian, "But What Do We Think We're Doing Anyway: The State of Black Feminist Criticism(s) or My Version of a Little Bit of History," 1989, *New Black Feminist Criticism, 1985-2000*, ed. Gloria Bowles, M. Giulia Fabi, and Arlene R. Keizer (Chicago: University of Illinois Press, 2007), 10.

30. Beverly Guy-Sheftall, "Sisters in Struggle: A Belated Response," *The Feminist Memoir Project: Voices from Women's Liberation*, ed. Rachel DuPleiss and Ann Snitow (New York: Three Rivers Press, 1998), 486.

31. Among other labors, Guy-Sheftall participated in the Southern Collective of African American Writers (SCAAW), edited *Sturdy Black Bridges* (1979), cofounded *Sage: A Scholarly Journal on Black Women* in 1983, edited *Words of Fire: An Anthology of African American Feminist Thought* (1995), and founded the Women's Research and Resource Center at Spelman College, which is the repository of Toni Cade Bambara's and Audre Lorde's papers.

32. Jones, interview by Thorsson.

33. Howard Rambsy, "The Consequences of Competition: Book Awards and Twenty-first Century Black Poetry," *Book History* 25, no. 1 (Spring 2022): 286.

34. Shanna Greene Benjamin, *Half in Shadow: The Life and Legacy of Nellie Y. McKay* (Chapel Hill: University of North Carolina Press, 2021), 135–137.

35. Strongman, "The Archeological Impulse," 51.

36. Benjamin, *Half in Shadow*, 140–141.

37. Henry Louis Gates, Jr., interview in *Harvard Magazine*, circa 1998, https://harvardmagazine.com/sites/default/files/html/1998/07/norton.3.html. Barbara Christian, "An African-American Canon," interview in *Berkeleyan* campus newspaper, March 19, 1997, https://www.berkeley.edu/news/berkeleyan/1997/0319/canon.html.

38. Benjamin, *Half in Shadow*, 147–148.

39. Strongman writes, "Black feminists, including the editors of *But Some of Us Are Brave*, realized that although the academy was partially responsible for the silencing of Black women's writing, it also paradoxically provided the resources that Black women academics needed to redress that absence" (Strongman, "The Archeological Impulse," 47).

40. Christian, "But What Do We Think We're Doing Anyway," 15.

41. McKay, "A Troubled Peace," 22, 32. Benjamin notes an important exception: "Exclusionary practices and isolation may characterize the experiences of Black women at predominantly white institutions, especially elite ones, but those same terms

don't necessarily describe the experiences of Black women with PhDs who taught at HBCUs" (*Half in Shadow*, 83).

42. Christian, "Diminishing Returns: Can Black Feminism(s) Survive the Academy?" 1994, in *New Black Feminist Criticism, 1985–2000*, ed. Gloria Bowles, M. Giulia Fabi, and Arlene R. Keizer (Chicago: University of Illinois Press, 2007), 205.

43. Alice Walker, *In Search of Our Mothers' Gardens: Womanist Prose* (New York: Harcourt, 1983), xi–xii.

44. Alexis De Veaux, "Alice Walker," *Essence*, September 1989, 122.

45. Cheryl A. Wall, *On Freedom and the Will to Adorn: The Art of the African American Essay* (Chapel Hill: University of North Carolina Press, 2018), 180.

46. Jodi Melamed, *Represent and Destroy: Rationalizing Violence in the New Racial Capitalism* (Minneapolis: University of Minnesota Press, 2011), 31. Melamed relies partly on Christopher Lucas's *American Higher Education: A History* (1994) for this information. The *Chronicle of Higher Education* reports a 13 percent decline in Black student college enrollment from 2010 to 2019; https://www.chronicle.com/article/why-has-black-student-enrollment-fallen/?cid=gen_sign_in.

47. Christian, "Diminishing Returns," 206–207.

48. Christian, "Diminishing Returns," 209. Nellie McKay writes in 1992, "I am not as optimistic over material changes in our situation as I was a decade ago" ("A Troubled Peace," 30).

49. Nellie Y. McKay and Frances Smith Foster, "A Collective Experience: Academics Working and Learning Together," *Profession* (2001): 17.

50. McKay and Foster, "A Collective Experience," 18–19.

51. Colleen Flaherty, "The Souls of Black Professors," *Inside Higher Ed*, October 21, 2020.

52. Toni Morrison, "Cinderella's Stepsisters," May 13, 1979, in *The Source of Self-Regard: Selected Essays, Speeches, and Meditations* (New York: Knopf, 2019), 111.

53. Edwards, *The Other Side of Terror*, 31.

54. Edwards, *The Other Side of Terror*, 18.

55. See Steven W. Bradley, James R. Garven, Wilson W. Law, and James E. West, "The Impact of Chief Diversity Officers on Diverse Faculty Hiring," National Bureau of Economic Research, August 2018, https://www.nber.org/papers/w24969?utm_campaign=ntw&utm_medium=email&utm_source=ntw.

56. A performance of investment in racial justice without substantive change is not unique to the academy. One insidious way that systemic racism adapts is that the federal government incorporates Black people whom it deems exceptional and uses those few as an alibi for ongoing racist oppression. This dynamic persists and reached its apex with the election of Barack Obama. Erica Edwards describes the U.S. war on terror as a period that spans from the repression and murder of Black Americans in 1968 through instruments such as the FBI's COINTELPRO and continued in the U.S. exercise of empire and domination in countries including Grenada and Nicaragua and wars in Iraq and Afghanistan. Edwards demonstrates that "domestic public culture" in this post–Cold War period of 1968–2012 "also *affirmed* Blackness as the sign of enlightenment, with officials like Condoleeza Rice and Colin Powell announcing the nation's fitness as a world leader in multiracial democracy" (*The Other Side of Terror*, 10). Patricia Harris in Jimmy Carter's cabinet, Harriet Tubman on a stamp or U.S. currency, Obama, Rice, and Powell are examples.

57. Hong, *Death Beyond Disavowal*, 125, 130, 131, 132, 146.
58. Roderick A. Ferguson, *The Reorder of Things: The University and Its Pedagogies of Minority Difference* (Minneapolis: University of Minnesota Press, 2012), 16, 102. See Melamed on "official antiracisms and literary studies as liberal modes of institutionalizing power" (*Represent and Destroy*, xv). Melamed theorizes and historicizes three periods of official antiracisms since World War II in which literary studies, though not works of literature themselves, did much of the work to disseminate liberal discourses that obscure injustice and racist material conditions.
59. Robin Kelley, "Over the Rainbow: Second Wave Ethnic Studies Against the Neoliberal Turn," lecture at the University of San Diego, May 18, 2016.
60. Kelley, "Over the Rainbow."
61. Kelley, "Over the Rainbow."
62. Kelley "Over the Rainbow." This specific hopeful note about the potential futures of past radical thought is in keeping with Kelley's analysis in *Freedom Dreams: The Black Radical Imagination* (Boston: Beacon, 2002).
63. Jennifer C. Nash, *Black Feminism Reimagined: After Intersectionality* (Durham, NC: Duke University Press, 2019), 4.
64. Arlene Keizer, "Barbara Christian and the Futures of Black Studies," panel at University of California, Berkeley, January 25, 2021.
65. Keizer, "Barbara Christian and the Futures of Black Studies." For a view of how such diminishing returns, valorization of one or two exceptions, and retrenchment of white dominance function in trade publishing, book reviewing, and literary prizes, see Richard Jean So, *Redlining Culture: A Data History of Racial Inequality and Postwar Fiction* (New York: Columbia University Press, 2021).
66. Joanne Gabbin, "Acknowledgements," in *Shaping Memories: Reflections of African American Women Writers*, ed. Joanne Gabbin (Jackson: University of Mississippi Press, 2009), xi.
67. Joanne Gabbin, "Introduction," in *Shaping Memories: Reflections of African American Women Writers*, ed. Joanne Gabbin (Jackson: University of Mississippi Press, 2009), xv.
68. Nikki Giovanni, "A Distant Star Called Possibility: Wintergreen," in *Shaping Memories: Reflections of African American Women Writers*, ed. Joanne Gabbin (Jackson: University of Mississippi Press, 2009), 6.
69. Rambsy, "The Consequences of Competition," 270, 276.
70. Patricia Matthew, "Written/Unwritten: The Gap Between Theory and Practice," in *Written/Unwritten: Diversity and the Hidden Truths of Tenure*, ed. Patricia Matthew (Chapel Hill: University of North Carolina Press, 2016), 2.
71. See https://www.korithamitchell.com/teaching-and-the-n-word/.
72. McKay, "A Troubled Peace," 21–22.
73. Benjamin, *Half in Shadow*, 126.
74. Christian, "Diminishing Returns," 209.
75. Hong, *Death Beyond Disavowal*, 142.
76. Benjamin, *Half in Shadow*, 98.
77. Myisha Priest, "Salvation is the Issue," *Merdians* 8, no. 2 (2008): 119.
78. Priest, "Salvation is the Issue," 116–117. Also see P. Gabrielle Foreman, "A Riff, a Call, and a Response," *Legacy* 30, no. 2 (2013): 306–322.
79. Priest, "Salvation is the Issue," 117.
80. Christian, "Diminishing Returns," 209.

81. Alexis Gumbs, "The Shape of My Impact," *The Feminist Wire*, October 29, 2012.

82. Gumbs, "The Shape of My Impact."

83. Hong, *Death Beyond Disavowal*, 134.

84. Cheryl A. Wall, "Black Women and The Pleasures of Intellectual Work," *The Southern Journal of Philosophy* 59, no. 1 (2021): 17.

CONCLUSION

1. Jamey Hatley, "Read My World," *Oxford American*, March 13, 2018.

2. Hatley, "Read My World."

3. Judith Wilson, email to author, December 3, 2018.

4. Erica R. Edwards, *The Other Side of Terror: Black Women and the Culture of US Empire* (New York: New York University Press, 2021), 187.

5. Holly Smith, "'Wholeness Is No Trifling Matter': Black Feminist Archival Practice and the Spelman College Archives," *The Black Scholar* 52, no. 2 (May 2022): 16.

6. See https://library.princeton.edu/news/general/2021-10-28/groundbreaking-pul -exhibition-toni-morrison-open-spring-2023 and https://sitesofmemorysymposium .org/.

7. Alexis Pauline Gumbs, "Dread Archive: Audre Lorde and What We Are Afraid to Want," *The Black Scholar* 52, no. 2 (May 2022): 28; Smith, "'Wholeness Is No Trifling Matter,'" 16.

8. On the many and complex meanings of Lorde's hair in her archive and as a theory of Black archives, see Gumbs, "Dread Archive."

9. Maryemma Graham, "Black is Gold: African American Literature, Critical Literacy, and Twenty-First-Century Pedagogies," in *Contemporary African American Literature: The Living Canon*, ed. Lovalerie King and Shirley Moody-Turner (Bloomington: Indiana University Press, 2013), 75.

10. Graham, "Black is Gold," 82. I use the term "street lit" in the way I have heard Graham use it to refer both to novels set on Black urban streets and to the fact that these works are sold on tables on the street, such as the card tables that line the sidewalks of 125th Street in Harlem.

11. Howard Rambsy and Kenton Rambsy show that in the *New York Times* in the 1990s and 2000s, Black diasporic writers including "Zadie Smith, who is British; Chimamanda Ngozi Adichie, who is Nigerian; and Edwidge Danticat, who is Haitian . . . appear in articles much more frequently than their Black women peers from the US" ("How the *New York Times* Covers Black Writers," *Public Books*, October 12, 2022).

12. Judith Wilson, "A Conversation with Toni Morrison," *Essence*, July 1981, 128, 130, bracketed text in original.

13. For a useful analysis of the 2020 focus on "antiracist nonfiction" and the stakes for African American literature, see Kenton Rambsy and Howard Rambsy II, "Black Books and Dead Black Bodies: Twitter, Hashtags, and Antiracist Reading Lists," *CLA Journal* 63, no. 2 (September 2020): 179–183.

14. Rambsy and Rambsy, "Black Books," 179–180.

15. Rambsy and Rambsy, "Black Books," 181, 183.

16. On paranoia as "a form of occult knowledge" in Black women's writing, see Edwards, *The Other Side of Terror*, 300–307.

17. See Courtney Thorsson, "'They could be killing kids *forever!*': The Atlanta Child Murders in African American Literature," *African American Review* 53, no. 4 (Winter 2020): 315–332.

18. See Lizzy LeRud, "Radical Revision: Rewriting Feminism with *This Bridge Called My Back* and Kate Rushin's 'The Bridge Poem,'" *Tulsa Studies in Women's Literature* 39, no. 2 (Fall 2020): 303–327.

APPENDIX 1. MEMBERS OF THE SISTERHOOD

1. Linda Janet Holmes, *A Joyous Revolt: Toni Cade Bambara, Writer and Activist* (Santa Barbara, CA: Praeger, 2014), 50.

2. Renita Weems, interview by Courtney Thorsson, January 8, 2019.

3. See Henry Kisor, "A Welfare Success Story," *New York Times*, March 8, 1998, https://www.nytimes.com/1998/03/08/books/a-welfare-success-story.html and https://www.sksm.edu/people/rosemary-bray-mcnatt/..

4. See https://drsananda.com/.

5. Margo Jefferson, interview by Courtney Thorsson, May 31, 2018; Patricia Spears Jones, email to author, November 5, 2018.

6. Cheryl A. Wall, "Toni Morrison, editor and teacher," in *The Cambridge Companion to Toni Morrison*, ed. Justine Tally (Cambridge: Cambridge University Press, 2007), 147.

7. George Beinhorn, "Sheila Rush: A Lawyer Turns to Yoga," *Yoga Journal*, May/June, 1982, 43–44, 57. Rush wrote a letter to the editors of *Yoga Journal* on behalf of The Ananda Church of Self-Realization in 2003. Sheila Rush, "By Any Other Name," *Yoga Journal*, September/October 2003, 19.

8. An audio archive of Donna Allegra's radio shows is online at https://www.pacificaradioarchives.org/contributors/donna-allegra.

INDEX

Note: The photo insert images are indexed as *p1, p2, p3*, etc.

Abike. *See* Murray, Patricia

academia, 13, 196, 233n3, 263n13; activism in, 23–26, 198–199, 235n45; Black faculty in, 191–192, 199–200, 211; Black feminism in, 9–10, 172–174, 191, 194–195; Black studies in, 24–26, 175, 194; Black women and, 187–193, 200–202, 206, 265n41; careers in, 88–89, 175–176; Christian on, 187–188; collaboration and, 23, 190–191; HBCUs and, 93, 118, 178, 183, 191, 265n41; interdisciplinarity and, 183–184; Jordan and, 23–24, 173, 179–180; lesbianism in, 177–178; liberation and, 14, 133–134, 191–192; McKay on, 191, 264n28, 265n48; members and, 88, 173–175; misogyny in, 24, 107; Morrison and, 171, 180–182; racism in, 198–199, 211; resources in, 176, 179–180, 213, 263n20, 264n39; SEEK Program and, 22–23, 113, 251n29; student activism and, 212–213

academics, Black women, 21, 25, 59, 183, 187, 264n39

activism, 11–13, 138, 197; in academia, 23–26, 198–199, 235n45; literary, 39–42,

66–67, 105, 108–109; love and, 10, 37, 93, 160, 180, 189–190; student, 212–213

administrative work, 61, 183, 190–191, 263n13; burden of, 83, 176

advocacy: for Black woman writers, 129–130; collaboration and, 203; editorial, 53, 63, 146–147, 252n59, 262n73

African American literature, 151, 209; *Beloved* and, 182; canon and, 180–181; Christianity and, 91–92; *NAAAL* and, 186–187

African Diaspora, 38, 209–210, 246n23, 267n11; collaboration with, 77–80

agents, literary, 124–125, 254n79

Alice Walker: A Life (White), 1–2

Allegra, Donna. *See* Simms, Donna

Allen, Robert, 162, 178, 240n9

Allen, Zita, 4, 6, 48, 63, 221, 239n123

allies, of The Sisterhood, 105, 107–108, 128

Als, Hilton, 45, 147–148

American Poetry Review (*APR*), 46–47; protest of, 39–40

Ananda-Maynard, Sananda. *See* Maynard, Nana

Angelou, Maya, 101, 103, *p8–p9*

anthologies, 15–16, 175; Black studies and, 26–27; collective action and, 233n10; *Home Girls*, 34–35; *NAAAL* and, 184–187

APR. See American Poetry Review

archives, 2, 51–52, 77, 176–177, 206–208, 267n8

art: collaboration in, 43; experimental, 76–77; performance, 131–132; visual, 177

Atlanta, GA, 114–115; Bambara and, 116–118

attendance, of meetings, 82–86

awards, 5–6, 40, 142, 239n117; committees for, 159, 162–164, 261n58; *for colored girls* and, 43–44; NBA, 61, 232n8; Pulitzer Prize, 143, 159–160, 163; Alice Walker and, 162, 232n8

backgrounds, of members, 4–5, 92

backlash, 36, 49, 93, 104; Black feminists and, 96–97

Baker, Houston, 159–160, 164–165

Baldwin, James, 159–160, 238n98, 251n35, 260n46; "Revolutionary Hope," 123–125

Ballard, Audreen, 60, 221, 243n77, *p4*; "The Sisterhood, 1977" and, 2, 231n4

BAM. *See* Black Arts Movement

Bambara, Toni Cade, 11–12, 51, 74, 136, 174, 202; on *Black Macho*, 95, 98; *The Black Woman*, 15–16; extended community and, 113–122; *Gorilla, My Love*, 38–39, 121–122, 251n33; Greene and, 127–128, 255n89; Jordan and, 113, 251n29; Morrison and, 38–39, 113, 118–122, 151–152, 205–206, 253n66, 261n68; *The Salt Eaters*, 96, 119, 253n61; SCAAW and, 113, 115–117, 252n57, *p7*; *The Seabirds Are Still Alive*, 114, 119, 251n35; Spelman and, 113–115, 117, 207, 263n12

Baraka, Amina, 162, *p9*

Baraka, Amiri, 15, 121, 161–162

Barnard College, 152–153; Shange and, 176–177, 207

Batchelder, Eleanor Olds, 32–33

Bay Area, CA, 75–77. *See also* West Coast, U.S.

Beloved (Morrison), 146, 167–168; African American literature and, 182; contemporary slave narratives and, 165–166; NBA and, 159–165, 260n48; review of, 110–111

Benjamin, Shanna, 185–186, 200–201, 265n41

Best, Stephen, 165–168

Black Arts Movement (BAM), 12, 15–16, 115, 153–154, 208, 233n8; homophobia and misogyny in, 34; literature and, 21–22

Black Book, The (Morrison), 37, 233n10

Black feminism, 5, 33–34, 75, 112, 181–182; in academia, 9–10, 172–174, 191, 194–195; activism and, 197–199; backlash and, 96–97; Black lesbians and, 94; Black nationalism and, 51; criticism of, 101, 249n90; intellectuals of, 10, 31–32, 193; literary criticism and, 150–151, 156–157; literary studies and, 9–10, 12, 25–26, 31–32, 149–150; in magazines, 66–71, 132–134; reproductive justice and, 17–18; scholarship of, 12, 26–27, 31–32, 196, 201; white Women's Liberation and, 58, 188–189

"Black Feminist Statement, A" (Combahee River Collective), 21–22, 34

Black lesbianism, 11, 35–36; Black feminism and, 94

Black Macho and the Myth of the Superwoman (Wallace), 8, 94–96, 98, 100–103; *Ms.* and, 68, 96–97; Alice Walker on, 98–99; Toni Cade Bambara, on, 95

Black men: Black women and, 45–46, 93, 95–96, 99–103; NBA open letter and, 161–162

Black nationalism, 51, 115–116, 144

Black Power movement, 12–13, 15, 31, 106, 144, 233n7; criticism of, 7, 20, 85, 95

"Black Sexism Debate, The," 99

Black studies, 24–25, 28–29, 194, 235n45; anthologies and, 26–27, 175; City College and, 177, 263n13; contemporary slave narratives and, 165–168, 192; HBCUs and, 258n3; interdisciplinarity and, 167–168; intersectionality and, 187; specialists in, 181–182; women's studies and, 183–184

Black Woman, The (Bambara), 15–16

Black women, 7, 50–51, 73, 90; academia and, 187–193, 200–202, 206, 265n41; as academics, 21, 25, 59, 183, 187, 264n39; Black men and, 45–46, 93, 95–96, 99–103; motherhood and, 58–59; publications of, 30, 108–111; white Women's Liberation and, 16–18; work of, 17, 138, 196

Black Women Novelists (Christian), 182

Black women writers, 15–16, 210–212; advocacy for, 129–130; misogyny and, 14, 44–45, 48–50, 101, 104, 137; Morrison on, 121, 253n66; Reed and, 46–47, 240n10; visibility for, 5–6, 36, 41, 63, 86, 92

"Black Women Writers" episode, of *The Phil Donahue Show*, 101–104, *p8*

Black World (magazine), 31, 64–65. *See also First World*

Black Writers Conference, Howard University, 92–94

Bloom, Harold, 149

Bluest Eye, The (Morrison), 32, 169–170, 236n75

Bobo, Jacqueline, 101

both/and thinking, 27, 167, 181–182, 194

Bray, Rosemary, 33, 221–222

Brockes, Emma, 232n10

Brown, Sterling, 143

Buffalo, Audreen. *See* Ballard, Audreen

burdens, of work, 83, 104, 176, 249n102

burnout, members and, 74, 86

Byrd, Rudolph, 3, 52

California (CA), Bay Area, 75–77

Callaloo (journal), 93–94

canon, literary, 42, 187; African American literature and, 180–181; Morrison and, 149–150

capitalism, goals and, 53–54

careers, 91–92; in academia, 88–89, 175–176; misogyny and racism and, 81, 89–90, 187, 198. *See also* jobs; work

Caribbean, 77–78; New York City compared to, 79–80

celebrity, literary, 5, 111–112; power and, 107

childcare, 55

China, 136

Christian, Barbara, 27–31, 235n45, 251n35, 263n20; on academia, 187–188; *Black Women Novelists*, 182; "Diminishing Returns," 190–191, 193–195, 213, 266n65

Christianity, African American literature and, 91–92

Chrysalis (magazine), 66, 134, 244n111

City College: Black studies and, 177, 263n13; protests at, 23–24

civil rights movement, 12, 21; criticism of, 7, 85, 95–96, 103

Clare, Nancy, 222

Clark, Vèvè, 63–64, 202, 222; visual art and, 75

Clarke, Cheryl, 35–36

Clifton, Lucille, *p1*

collaboration, 3, 5, 9, 73–74, 205–206, 241n32; academia and, 23, 190–191; advocacy and, 203; with African Diaspora, 77–80; in art, 43; Bambara and Morrison and, 113, 118–122; erasure of, 97; NBA open letter and, 160–162; power of, 80–81; SCAAW and, 116

collective action, 5–6, 12, 36, 232n10; anthologies and, 233n10; *APR* protest and, 39–40; NBA open letter and, 162–163; poetry and, 140; skills for, 19, 50–51

collectives, 14; Combahee River Collective, 16–17, 237n86; Dark Room Collective, 260n46; Poetry for the People Collective, 179–180; SCAAW, 118; Wintergreen Women Writers' Collective, 196–198

Color Purple, The (Alice Walker), 45, 101, 240n9; *Donahue* and, 102–103

Color Purple, The (film), 45, 101, 240n8

Combahee River Collective, 16–17, 237n86; "A Black Feminist Statement" of, 21–22, 34; NBFO and, 19–20

commitment, to The Sisterhood, 82–85

committees, for awards, 159, 162–164, 261n58
community, extended, 105
competition, ranking and: hierarchy and, 67, 84; NBA and, 232n8; refusal of, 3–4, 52–53, 116; for university resources, 193, 195
conflicts, 93–94, 100–101, 249n90; Combahee River Collective and, 237n86; goals and, 62, 80–81, 83, 86
Congress of Racial Equity (CORE), 19, 234n25
contemporary narratives of slavery, 161, 165–66, 209, 261n63
CORE. See Congress of Racial Equity
correspondence, 62; of Greene, 122, 127, 255n89; of Morrison, 163–164, 261n60; poetry as, 86–88, 138–139, 257n25; of The Sisterhood, 50, 52, 72, 82–86; of Alice Walker and Wilson, 256n14; of Wallace and Alice Walker, 108–109
Crenshaw, Kimberlé, 22
criticism, 46–47; of Black feminism, 101, 249n90; of Black Macho, 96–98; of Black Power movement, 7, 20, 85, 95; of civil rights movement, 7, 85, 95–96, 103; of The Color Purple film, 101; of for colored girls, 44–45; literary, 150–151, 156–157
Crouch, Stanley, 110–111
Cuba, 136
cultural capital, 86, 162–163
cultural institutions, 14, 33–34, 41–42; museums, 131–132

Danticat, Edwidge, 169
Dark Room Collective, 260n46
Davis, Angela, p9; Donahue and, 101–103, p8; Morrison and, 57, 262n73; Shange and, 257n25
Davis, Beverly, 16
Davis, Thulani, 28–29, 49, 101, 125, 161, 177, 257n25
deaths, of members, 200–202, 206–207
debates, 111, 180; "The Black Sexism Debate," 99; in organizations, 84, 86, 92
De La Cruz, Andaye, 222

demands, 86–88; of jobs, 84–85
Dent, Tom, 93–94
depression, 71–72, 145
De Veaux, Alexis, 26, 36, 123–125, 135, 161, 237n96, 257n25
differences, among members, 88–92
"Diminishing Returns" (Christian), 190–191, 193–195, 213, 266n65
dissolution, of The Sisterhood, 4–5, 8, 85, 89, 101, 141–142
diversity, 58, 151, 155, 165, 198; performative, 14, 137, 191–193, 195, 210, 265n56
documentation, record keeping and, 2, 77, 108, 206, 260n46
Dodson, Howard, p9
Donahue. See Phil Donahue Show, The
Dumas, Henry, 153–154

Ebony (magazine), 37, 44–45, 109–110; poetry in, 63–64
economic class, 54, 143–144
editorial work, 185–186; advocacy as, 53, 63, 146–147, 252n59, 258n3, 262n73
education, 13, 78; of members, 4–5, 32; Open Syllabus Project and, 150; Title IX and, 16–18. See also academia
Edwards, Audrey, 4, 71, 99–100, 104, 124–125, 222; "The Sisterhood, 1977" and, 2, 231n4
Edwards, Erica, 176, 192, 199, 207, 265n56
emotional support, 71–73, 138
enrollment, in universities, 190, 265n46
erasure, 9–10, 149; of collaboration, 97; of lesbianism, 35–36
Essence (magazine), 31, 48, 100, 132–133, 256n13; Greene and, 71, 122–126, 253n70, 254n80; interviews in, 256n1; reviews in, 70–71, 97; The Sisterhood and, 69–71, 124–125, 254n80; Wilson and, 133, 256n14; writers' retreat of, 125–126
Evans, Mari, 26, p9, 127, 136, 161, 239n120, 242n48
exceptionalism, 111, 195–196, 266n65; death and, 201; Jordan on, 155–156; Morrison and, 146–147, 149–150, 155, 165

experimental art, 76–77
extended community, 105; Bambara and, 113–122; Greene and, 122–128; Wallace and, 106–112

faculty, Black, 191–192, 199–200, 211
Faison, George, *p9*
feminism, 108–109, 170; backlash and, 93; Black, 5, 33–34, 75, 112, 181–182; interracial, 51, 241n32; legislation and, 17–18; Third World, 78–79, 135; white, 17, 133–134, 136, 138
"Feminism and the Black Woman Writer" panel (Jordan), 93–94
feminist bookstores, 32–33
Ferguson, Roderick, 24, 65, 194, 199
first meeting, of The Sisterhood, 3, 37, 59
First World (magazine), 47, 64–66, 113
forced sterilization, reproductive justice and, 58
for colored girls who have considered suicide (Shange), 43–45, 47–49, 70, 76; *Donahue* and, 101–103
Ford, Gerald, 13, 233n3
Foster, Frances Smith, 31, 185–186, 190–191
friendship, 87–88; of Greene and Bambara, 127–128, 255n89; of Morrison and Bambara, 120, 205–206
Fuller, Hoyt, 47, 63–65, 113, 115, 127, 251n35
fun, The Sisterhood and, 81–82
funding, NEA and, 134–135. *See also* resources
Furious Flower Poetry Center, 197

GA. *See* Georgia
Gabbin, Joanne, 196–198
Garland, Phyl, 4, 6, 37, 41, 64, 113, 124–125, 222–223; on Southern U.S., 74–75
Gates, Henry Louis, Jr., 103, 156, 260n58; Morrison and, 163–164, 261n60; *NAAAL* and, 185–186
Gathering Blossoms Under Fire (Walker), 178
genre fiction, 209, 267n10
Georgia (GA), Atlanta, 114–115
Giddings, Paula, 26, 124–125, 140, 161, 236
Gillespie, Marcia Ann, 48, 63, 68–71, 100
Ginsberg, Allen, 232n8

"Glad All Over" (Patricia Spears Jones), 142–143
goals, of The Sisterhood, 6–8, 50–51, 84; capitalism and, 53–54; conflicts and, 62, 80–81, 83, 86; feminism and, 108–109; publishing and, 60–61
Gorilla, My Love (Bambara), 38–39, 121–122, 251n33
Greene, Cheryll Y.: Bambara and, 127–128, 255n89; *Essence* and, 71, 122–126, 253n70, 254n80; as literary agent, 124–125, 254n79
"Grenada Revisited" (Lorde), 77–79
Griffin, Farah Jasmine, 1, 9–10, 21, 28, 196, 201, 232n17
Grosvenor, Vertamae, 37, 58, 223, *p4*; *Vibration Cooking*, 113–114; on white Women's Liberation, 16–17, 188–189
Gumbs, Alexis Pauline, 52, 122, 132–133, 256n13
Guy, Rosa, 38, 223
Guy-Sheftall, Beverly, 117, 183, 207, 263n12, 264n31

Haley, Alex, *Roots*, 60, 166, 261n65
Hammond, Karla, 256n1
Harlem Renaissance, 15, 26–27, 157
Harlem Writers' Guild (HWG), 38
Harris, Jessica, 37, 57, 223, 238n104; *High on the Hog*, 223; *My Soul Looks Back*, 223
Harris, Joan, 223
HBCUs. *See* historically Black colleges and universities
health, of members, 201–202; mental, 71–72, 145
Heresies (magazine), 66, 244n111
hierarchy, 67, 84
High on the Hog (Harris), 223
Hill, Anita, 142
historically Black colleges and universities (HBCUs), 93, 118, 178, 183, 191, 265n41; Black studies and, 258n3
Holmes, Linda Janet, 119–120
Home Girls (Lorde and Barbara Smith), 34–35
homophobia, 20, 35–36, 132, 177; BAM and, 34

Hong, Grace, 193–194, 199–202
hostility, 7–8, 104, 191, 200, 213
hosts, of meetings, 53, 82–83
Howard University, 106; Black Writers
    Conference, 92–94
Hurston, Zora Neale, 260n36; *Their Eyes
    Were Watching God*, 33, 98, 155–157,
    174, 178
HWG. *See* Harlem Writers' Guild

identity, 11–12, 27, 157; privacy and, 36;
    queer, 9, 123–124, 211–212
independence, from academia, 178–179
influence, of The Sisterhood, 141–142,
    196, 206–207; collaboration and, 74,
    190–191. *See also* legacies
In Search of our Mothers' Gardens
    (Walker), 28, 98, 178, 227
institutions, 88–89; cultural, 14, 33–34,
    41–42; power in, 175–176
intellectuals, Black feminist, 10, 31–32,
    193
interdisciplinarity, 183–184; Black studies
    and, 167–168
international work, of members, 135–136
interracial feminism, 51, 241n32
interracial solidarity, 51, 96
intersectionality, 22, 27, 191; Black studies
    and, 187; in women's studies, 195
interviews, 49, 67, 90, 129–130, 256n1; of
    members, 30; with Morrison, 151
invisible labor, 6, 61, 146, 212; Greene and,
    122–123; *The Salt Eaters* and, 96

JAM. *See* Just Above Midtown gallery
Jefferson, Margo, 7–8, 47, 59, 107, 223–224;
    Morrison and, 261n61; *Negroland*,
    143–145; reviews by, 37, 154; on West
    Coast, 76
jobs, 107, 152, 213; demands of, 84–85; of
    members, 4, 41, 53–54; whiteness in, 8,
    148, 175, 188, 199–200. *See also* work
Johnson, Joyce, 96
Jones, Gayl, 26, 28, 31, 46–47, 122–123, 152,
    154, 158, 185, 253n66
Jones, Patricia Spears, 76, 176, 184, 224,
    261n61; on commitment, 83–85; "Glad
    All Over," 142–143; *Heresies* and, 66,

244n111; literary activism and, 39–40;
    on meetings, 72, 80–81, 92; privacy
    and, 141–142; on visibility, 155; on Alice
    Walker, 52–53
Jordan, June, 1, 47, 202, 224, *p1*, *p4*;
    academia and, 23–24, 173, 179–180;
    APR protest and, 39–40; Bambara
    and, 113, 250n29; on *Black Macho*, 97;
    in California, 75–76; *Chrysalis* and,
    244n111; CORE and, 234n25; *Essence*
    and, 70–71, 255n1; on exceptionalism,
    155–156; "Feminism and the Black
    Woman Writer" panel of, 93–94;
    interviews with, 129–130; "Letter to
    My Friend the Poet Ntozake Shange,"
    86–87; "Letter to the Local Police,"
    137–140; Lorde and, 61–62; NBA open
    letter and, 159–160, 164–165; "Poem
    About Police Violence," 137–140;
    Shange and, 86–88; student activism
    and, 23–26, 172; *Things That I Do in
    the Dark*, 39, 60, 238n107, 243n81;
    Alice Walker and, 40, 238n114, 257n25;
    "Where Is the Love," 70–71
journals: *Callaloo*, 93–94; *Kalliope*,
    129–130; niche, 65–66. *See also*
    magazines
Just Above Midtown gallery (JAM), 131,
    256n7
Just a Sister Away (Renita Weems), 5, 137,
    140–141, 227
justice, 104, 112, 202; racial, 12–14, 198, 212;
    reproductive, 25, 66

Kachka, Boris, 149–151
Kalliope (journal), 129–130
Keizer, Arlene, 29–30, 195–196, 261n63
Kelley, Robin, 27, 194–195, 266n62
Kennedy, Florynce, 16, 233n7, 251n35
Kennedy, John F., 135
King, Lovalerie, 197
King, Rodney, 142
Kitchen Table Press, 134
Kizzy Enterprises, Inc., 59–60, 62

labor, invisible, 6, 61, 212
leadership, 14, 18, 54, 67, 84, 156
Lee, Spike, 101

legacies, 8–9, 199–203, 208–209, 211–213; Morrison and, 146–149
legislation, feminism and, 17–18
lesbianism, 11, 34–36, 177–178. *See also* queer identities
"Letter to My Friend the Poet Ntozake Shange" (Jordan), 86–87
"Letter to the Local Police" (Jordan), 137–140
Levy-Hussen, Aida, 167
LGBTQIA identities. *See* queer identities
liberation, 15; academia and, 14, 133–134, 191–192; literature and, 156–157, 213; white women and, 7, 16–18
literary activism, 39–42, 66–67, 105, 108–109; Combahee River Collective and, 20–22; SCAAW and, 115–116
literary agents, 124–125, 254n79
literary celebrity, 5, 111–112
literary criticism, Black feminist, 150–151, 156–157, 170–171; recovery imperative and, 27–29, 167–168
literary studies, Black feminist, 9–10, 12, 25–26, 31–32, 149–150
literature, 21–22; liberation and, 156–157, 213; racial justice and, 173–174
Lorde, Audre, 76, 201–202, 224, *p1, p6;* academia and, 23, 177–178, 235n45, 263n13; archives of, 52, 207, 267n8; Bambara and, 113, 250n29; *Chrysalis* and, 134, 244n111; "Grenada Revisited," 77–79; *Home Girls,* 34–35; Jordan and, 61–62; lesbianism and, 11, 36; "The Master's Tools Will Never Dismantle the Master's House," 133; NBA and, 61, 232n8; "Revolutionary Hope," 123–125; *Sister Outsider,* 133; Barbara Smith and, 33–35, 134, 175; Virgin Islands and, 135–136; *Zami,* 57
love, 6, 206; activism and, 10, 37, 93, 160, 180, 189–190; "The Sisterhood, 1977" and, 2, 203; in writings, 35–36, 44, 56–57, 62, 140, 197, 203
Love (Morrison), 122

magazines, 254n80; Black feminism in, 66–71, 132–134; *Black World,* 31, 64–65; *Chrysalis,* 66, 134, 244n111; *Ebony,* 37;
44–45, 109–110; *Essence,* 31, 48, 100, 132–133, 256n13; *First World,* 47, 64–66, 113; *Heresies,* 66, 244n111; *Ms.,* 31, 49, 66, 70; *Newsweek,* 32, 37, 47, 107, 154
market forces, 111, 158, 162
Marshall, Paule, 38–39, 89, 197, 225; mentorship and, 90–91; *Praisesong for the Widow,* 57–58; "Reena," 90
"Master's Tools Will Never Dismantle the Master's House, The" (Lorde), 133
Matthew, Patricia, 198
Maynard, Nana, 1, 225, 241n44, 246n3, *p4*
McHenry, Susan, 66, 68, 225
McKay, Nellie, 29, 150–151, 185, 201; on academia, 191, 264n28, 265n48
media, 154–155; whiteness and, 100, 249n90
meetings, of The Sisterhood, 1–2, 6, 54–55, 60, 91; attendance of, 82–86; first, 3, 37, 59; hosts of, 53, 82–83; Patricia Spears Jones on, 72, 80–81, 92; queer identities and, 35–36; record keeping and, 50–52
Melamed, Jodi, 24, 190, 265n46, 266n58
members, of The Sisterhood, 1, 15, 30, 254n80; academia and, 88, 173–175; African Diaspora and, 79, 246n23; archives of, 206–208; backgrounds of, 4–5, 92; burnout and, 74, 86; Caribbean and, 77; criticism of, 46–47; deaths of, 200–202, 206–207; differences among, 88–92; health and, 71–72, 145, 201–202; international work and, 135–136; jobs of, 4, 41, 53–54; mentorship between, 37–38; networks of, 37–42, 150–152; publications of, 5–6, 22, 136–137, 140–145; publishing industry and, 60–61, 64; relationships between, 9, 61–62, 86–88; religion and, 91–92; relocation of, 85–86; self-directed study of, 32–33; Southern U.S. and, 74–75
mental health, members and, 71–72, 145
mentorship, 65, 90–91, 237n96; between members, 37–38
misogyny, 8, 18, 142, 240n6, 249n90; in academia, 24, 107; BAM and, 34; Black Power and, 7, 20, 106; Black women writers and, 14, 44–45, 48–50, 101, 104, 137; careers and, 81, 89–90, 187, 198; Morrison and, 170

Mitchell, Koritha, 198–199
Moore, Madeline, 83, 225
Moraga, Cherríe, 134
Morrison, Toni, 166, 191–192, 225, *p2*, *p4*;
    academia and, 171, 180–182; archives
    of, 207; Bambara and, 38–39, 113, 118–122,
    151–152, 205–206, 253n66, 261n68;
    Beloved, 146, 167–168; *The Black
    Book*, 37, 233n10; *The Bluest Eye*, 32,
    169–170, 236n75; correspondence of,
    163–164, 261n60; Angela Davis and,
    57, 262n73; editorial advocacy of, 53,
    63, 146–147, 252n59, 258n3, 262n73;
    exceptionalism and, 146–147, 149–150,
    155, 165; Gates and, 163–164, 261n60;
    Love, 122; motherhood and, 57, 259n5;
    NBA and, 159–165, 260n48; networks
    and, 125, 232n10; Nobel Prize of, 164,
    260n58, *p9*; public persona of, 90, 148,
    168–171, 261n68; Pulitzer Prize of, 164;
    Random House and, 40–41, 60, 148,
    152, 154–155, 239n120, 239n123, 243n78;
    scholarship on, 29–30, 169; scripture
    and, 247n62; *Song of Solomon*, 40–41;
    success of, 85, 146, 152–155, 258n1; *Sula*,
    37, 122, 238n99, 259n5; support and,
    120–121, 125, 147–148, 259n5; *Tar Baby*,
    79–80; visibility and, 158, 169–170;
    Alice Walker and, 37, 149–151, 178,
    237n99
motherhood, 55–56, 58–59; Morrison and,
    57, 259n5; Alice Walker on, 242n62
Movement for Black Lives, 210
movements, 21, 195–196, 210; BAM, 12,
    15–16, 115, 153–154, 208, 233n8; Black
    Power, 12–13, 15, 31, 106, 144, 233n7
Moynihan, Daniel, *The Negro Family*,
    58–59, 94–95, 103
Ms. (magazine), 31, 49, 67, 69–70, 245n121;
    Black Macho and, 68, 96–97; Wallace
    and, 109–110, *p5*; white feminism and,
    63, 66, 109–110
multiculturalism, 137, 192, 194–195. *See
    also* diversity
multimedia projects, 75–76
Murphy, Dana, 25
Murray, Patricia, 61, 66, 225–226; as Abike,
    52, 241n37; Jordan and, 238n107

museums, in New York City, 131–132
My Soul Looks Back (Harris), 223

NAAAL. *See Norton Anthology of African
    American Literature*
NAC. *See* Neighborhood Art Center
Nash, Jennifer, 195–196
National Association of Third World
    Writers (NATTW), 134–135, 257n25
National Black Feminist Organization
    (NBFO), 14, 16–17, 62–63, 106, 118,
    251n33; Combahee River Collective and,
    19–20; "Statement of Purpose" of, 18–19
National Black Theatre (NBT), 106
National Book Award (NBA), 61, 232n8;
    open letter for, 159–160, 163–164,
    260n48
National Endowment for the Arts (NEA),
    134–135, 257n26
nationalism, Black, 51, 115–116, 144
National Organization of Women
    (NOW), 106
NATTW. *See* National Association of
    Third World Writers
Naylor, Gloria, 28, 104, 124, 162, 211,
    254n80, 260n58
NBA. *See* National Book Award
NBFO. *See* National Black Feminist
    Organization
NBT. *See* National Black Theatre
NEA. *See* National Endowment for the
    Arts
Negro Family, The (Moynihan), 58–59,
    94–95, 103
Negroland (Jefferson), 143–145
Neighborhood Art Center (NAC), 115
networks, 105, 117, 128, 206–207; Bambara
    and, 114, 127; of members, 37–42,
    150–152; Morrison and, 125, 232n10
Newsweek (magazine), 32, 37, 47, 107, 154
New York City, U.S., 1, 4, 53, 84, 114;
    Caribbean compared to, 79–80;
    publishing industry in, 14, 130; visual
    art in, 131–132, 256n7; West Coast
    compared to, 75–76
New York Times: *Magazine* of, 240n8;
    open letter to, 159–165, 260n48
Nobel Prize, of Morrison, 164, 260n58, *p9*

Norton Anthology of African American Literature (*NAAAL*), 184–187
NOW. *See* National Organization of Women
"Now That the Book Is Finished" (Alice Walker), 55–56

Obama, Barack, 44–45, 150, 265n56
Obama, Michele, 210
Okpaku, Sheila. *See* Rush, Sheila
open letter, for NBA, 159–160, 163–164, 260n48; signatories of, 161–162, 165, 168
Open Syllabus Project, 150
oppression, 18, 20, 94, 99, 133, 265n56; academia and, 25; systems of, 129–131, 187–188
organizations, 107–108, 116; collective action and, 6, 232n10; debates in, 84, 86, 92; NBFO, 14, 16–17, 62–63, 106, 118, 251n33; political, 9–10, 25, 41, 175
out-of-print books. *See* recovery imperative

paranoia, in writing, 211, 268n16
performance art, 131–132
performative diversity, 14, 137, 191–193, 195, 210, 265n56
personal lives, 36, 120, 128; Black feminism and, 123–124; motherhood and, 55–57; record keeping and, 72
Phil Donahue Show, The (*Donahue*), "Black Women Writers" episode, 101–104, *p8*
Phillips-Fein, Kim, 233n3
Phillis Wheatley Poetry Festival (1973), 25–26, *p1*
"Poem About My Rights" (Jordan), 129–130
"Poem About Police Violence" (Jordan), 137–140
poetry, 44, 211; collective action and, 140; as correspondence, 86–88, 138–139, 257n25; in *Ebony*, 63–64; by Jordan, 86–87, 125–126, 137–140; by Alice Walker, 139, 257n38
Poetry for the People Collective, 179–180
police violence, 123, 137–139, 212–213
political organizations, 9–10, 25, 41, 175; Black feminist, 12, 195; NBFO, 14, 16–20, 62–63; work in, 81
Pomoja Writers' Guild, 117

popular magazines, 69–71
power: celebrity and, 107; of collaboration, 80–81; institutional, 175–176
practical matters, 51, 81–82, 127, 180
Praisesong for the Widow (Marshall), 57–58
pressures, 5, 81, 94, 104, 134–135, 144–145
Priest, Myisha, 201
privacy: identity and, 36, 237n98; Patricia Spears Jones and, 141–142; Marshall and, 89–91
projects, 197–198; multimedia, 75–76; for The Sisterhood, 51, 54, 60–61, 71–72
promotion, of publications, 38, 60, 84–85, 115, 243n81
protagonists, 57–58, 91, 98, 121–122, 139, 212
protest, 213; of *APR*, 39–40; at City College, 23–24; of *The Color Purple* film, 45; NBA open letter of, 159–165, 260n48
publications, of Black women, 30, 108–111; *Essence* and, 123–124; genre fiction and, 209; Morrison on, 154; protagonists of, 57–58, 91, 98, 121–122, 139, 212; self-publishing and, 208–209. *See also* recovery imperative
publications, of members, 5–6, 22, 136–137, 140–145; promotion of, 38, 60, 84–85, 115, 243n81
public persona, of Morrison, 90, 148, 168–171, 261n68
publishing industry, 5, 81, 206; editorial work and, 185–186; literary activism and, 66–67; members and, 60–61, 64; in New York City, 14, 130; popular magazines in, 69–71; racism in, 158, 211; Random House and, 236n75; small presses and, 134
Pulitzer Prize, 143, 159–160, 163; of Morrison, 164

queer identities, 9, 123–124, 211–212; meetings and, 35–36

racial justice, 12–14, 198, 212; literature and, 173–174; performative, 265n56; teaching and, 190–191, 193 racism, 7–8, 13, 18, 107, 183; in academia, 198–199, 211; careers and, 89–90; exceptionalism and, 149; in publishing industry, 158, 211; systemic, 58–59, 140, 191, 210, 265n56

radical imagination, 7–8, 213

Ramsby, Howard, 185, 197, 244n102, 258n45, 260n41, 260n48

Ramsby, Howard and Kenton, 210, 258n1, 260n42, 267n11

Randolph, Sherie M., 233n7

Random House, 236n75; Morrison and, 40–41, 60, 148, 152, 154–155, 239n120, 239n123, 243n78; Wallace and, 106–107

ranking. *See* competition, ranking and

Reagan, Ronald, 8, 13; NEA and, 135; "welfare queen" of, 59

record keeping: documentation and, 2, 77, 108, 206, 260n46; meetings, 50–52; personal lives, 72

recovery imperative, 31; feminist bookstores and, 33; Hurston and, 156–157; literary criticism and, 27–29, 167–168

Reed, Ishmael, 98; Black women writers and, 46–47, 240n10; on misogyny, 249n90

"Reena" (Marshall), 90

refusal, of competition, 3–4, 52–53, 116

relationships, 96; between members, 9, 61–62, 86–88

religion, members and, 91–92

relocation, of members, 85–86

reproductive justice, 25, 66; Black feminism and, 17–18; forced sterilization and, 58

resources, 33, 116, 264n22; university, 176, 179–180, 213, 263n20, 264n39

reviews, 30; by Als, 45; of *Beloved*, 110–111; in *Essence*, 70–71, 97; Greene and, 122–124; by Jefferson, 37, 154; in *Ms.*, 68; by Wilson, 56–57, 71, 97

"Revolutionary Hope" (Baldwin and Lorde), 123–125

Revolutionary Petunias (Alice Walker), 139, 257n38

Rich, Adrienne, 129, 180, 232n8, 235n38, 241n32

Ringgold, Faith, 19, 106–107

Roach, Pamela, 226

Roe v. Wade, 17–18

roles: secretary, 50–51, 61; of Weems, 82–83, 247n34

Roots (Haley), 60, 166, 261n65

Rush, Sheila, 54, 80–83, 226, 268n7

Salt Eaters, The (Bambara), 27, 119, 122, 127, 130, 133, 205, 253n61; invisible labor and, 96

Savonick, Danica, 262n1

SCAAW. *See* Southern Collective of African American Writers

scholarship, 98, 108, 157, 161; Black feminist, 12, 26–27, 31–32, 196, 201; *Black World* and, 65; on Morrison, 29–30, 169. *See also* literary studies, Black feminist

scripture: Morrison and, 247n62; Weems and, 140–141

Seabirds Are Still Alive, The (Bambara), 114, 119, 251n35

secretary role, of Wilson, 50–51, 61

SEEK (Search for Education, Elevation, and Knowledge), 22–23, 113, 251n29

self-directed study, members and, 32–33

self-interview, of Shange, 49, 67

self-publishing, 208–209

sexism. *See* misogyny

Shakur, Assata, 136

Shange, Ntozake, 1, 107, 145, 226, *p3–p4*; academia and, 23, 235n45; Barnard and, 176–177, 207; Bay Area and, 76; celebrity and, 111; Thulani Davis and, 257n25; *Donahue* and, 101, 103, *p8*; *for colored girls*, 43–45, 47–49, 70, 76; institutions and, 88–89; Jordan and, 86–88; SCAAW and, 116; self-interview of, 49, 67

Sharpe, Lori, 25, 226, *p4*

signatories, of NBA open letter, 161–162, 165, 168

Simms, Donna, 66, 226, 268n8

"Sisterhood, 1977, The," 1, 3, 10, 231n4, *p4*; love and, 2, 203; *NAAAL* and, 186

Sister Outsider (Lorde), 133

skills, for collective action, 19, 50–51

slave narratives, contemporary. *See* contemporary narratives of slavery

Sloan, Margaret, *Ms.* and, 66–67

small presses, 134

Smethurst, James, 65, 115

Smith, Barbara, 19–22, 93–94; *Home Girls*, 34–35; Lorde and, 33–34, 134, 175

Smith, Bessie, 1, 3, 231n6

Smith, Beverly, 19–20

SNCC. *See* Student Nonviolent Coordinating Committee

Sojourner Truth Festival of the Arts, 107

solidarity, 46, 141; African Diaspora and, 78–79; interracial, 51, 96

Song of Solomon (Morrison), 40–41

Southern Collective of African American Writers (SCAAW), 118; Bambara and, 113, 115–117, 252n57, *p7*; Guy-Sheftall and, 264n31

Southern U.S., members and, 74–75

specialists, in Black studies, 181–182

Spelman College, 183–184, 264n31; Bambara and, 113–115, 117, 207, 263n12

spirituality, in writings, 91–92. *See also* scripture

Springer, Kimberly, 20–21, 232n13, 233n6, 237n86, 249n102

Staples, Robert, 99

"Statement of Purpose," of NBFO, 18–19

Steinem, Gloria, 67, 96, 109–110; Alice Walker and, 68

"street lit" genre, 209, 267n10

Strongman, SaraEllen, 34, 264n39

student activism, 212–213; Jordan and, 23–26, 172

Student Nonviolent Coordinating Committee (SNCC), 95

success, 84, 86, 88, 141–142, 158–159; of Morrison, 85, 146, 152–155, 258n1; visibility and, 112, 136–137, 155; of Alice Walker, 153, 259n18

Sula (Morrison), 37, 122, 237n99, 259n5

Sullivan, Mecca Jamilah, 9, 174, 212

Sullivan, Ruth, 68

support, 61–62, 81; in academia, 175–176; emotional, 71–73, 138; Morrison and, 120–121, 125, 147–148, 259n5

survival, 14, 59, 201–202, 211–212

sustaining, of groups, 82, 114, 117, 174

systemic racism, 140, 191, 210, 265n56; *The Negrᵢ ᴿamily* and, 58–59

systems, of oppression, 129–131, 187–188

Tar Baby (Morrison), 79–80

Tate, Claudia, 99

Taylor, Susan, 100, *p9*, 248n86

teaching, 172, 190–191, 193; recovery imperative and, 28

textual work, 26, 109, 141, 143, 184

Their Eyes Were Watching God (Hurston), 33, 98, 155–157, 174, 178

Things That I Do in the Dark (Jordan), 39, 238n107; promotion for, 60, 243n81

Third World Feminism, 78–79, 135, 192

Third World Women's Alliance, 16–17, 233n11, 251n35

Title IX, 16–18

Traylor, Eleanor, *p9*, 161, 239n120, 254n79

UCLA. *See* University of California Los Angeles

United States (U.S.): California, 75–77; Georgia, 114–115; New York City, 1, 4, 53, 84; Southern, 74–75; West Coast, 74, 77

universities: enrollment in, 190, 265n46; HBCUs, 93, 118, 178, 183, 191, 265n41. *See also* academia

University of California Los Angeles (UCLA), filmmaking program of, 76–77

university resources, 176, 179–180, 213, 263n20, 264n39; competition for, 193, 195

University Without Walls, 263n20

"Variations on Negation and the Heresy of Black Feminist Creativity" (Wallace), 111–112

Vibration Cooking (Grosvenor), 113–114

violence, police, 123, 137–139, 212–213

Virgin Islands, Lorde and, 135–136

visibility, 5–6, 36, 41, 63, 86, 92; Morrison and, 158, 169–170; of *NAAAL*, 186; success and, 112, 136–137, 155

visual art, 177; Clark and, 75; in New York City, 131–132, 256n7; Wallace and, 107; Wilson and, 130–132

Walker, Alice, 3, 62, 85, 227, *p1–p2, p4*; archives of, 2, 51–52, 207; awards and, 162, 232n8; Bambara and, 113; on *Black Macho*, 98–99; *The Color Purple*, 45, 101, 240n9; *Donahue* and, 101–103, *p8*;

Walker, Alice (*continued*)
Essence and, 71, 133, 256n14; HBCUs
and, 178–179; on Hurston, 157; *In
Search of our Mothers' Gardens*, 28, 98,
178, 227; *Gathering Blossoms Under
Fire*, 178; Patricia Spears Jones on,
52–53; Jordan and, 40, 238n114, 257n25;
Morrison and, 37, 149–151, 178, 237n99;
on motherhood, 242n62; *Ms.* and,
66, 68–69, 245n121; *New York Times
Magazine* profile of, 240n8; "Now That
the Book Is Finished," 55–56; poetry
by, 139, 257n38; publishing industry
and, 60; *Revolutionary Petunias*, 139,
257n38; success of, 153, 259n18; Wallace
and, 108–109; Wild Tree Press of, 134;
womanism and, 188–190
Walker, Margaret, 25–26, 166
Wall, Cheryl, 40, 196, 202–203, 252n59; on
Bambara, 119; on womanism, 189–190
Wallace, Michele, 105–107; *Black Macho*,
8, 94–95, 100–103; celebrity and,
111–112; *Donahue* and, 101, 103, *p8*; *for
colored girls* and, 49; *Ms.* and, 109–110,
p5; "Variations on Negation and the
Heresy of Black Feminist Creativity,"
111–112; Alice Walker and, 108–109;
Wilson and, 248n76
Washington, Mary Helen, 27–28, 30, 65,
173, 251n35
Weathers, Diane, 131–132, 227, 254n80
Weems, Renita, 32–33, 74, 227; *Just a Sister
Away*, 5, 137, 140; on commitment,
82–83, 85; role of, 82–83, 247n34;
scripture and, 140–141
"welfare queen," of Reagan, 59
Wesling, Frances Cress, 94
West, Hollie, 94
West Coast, U.S., 74, 77; multimedia projects
and, 75–76; New York City compared to,
75–76; small presses and, 134
"Where Is the Love" (Jordan), 70–71
White, Evelyn, 1–2, 232n10
white feminism, 17, 133–134, 136, 138; *Ms.*
and, 63, 66, 109–110; womanism and,
188–189

whiteness, 10, 210; feminist bookstores
and, 33; in jobs, 8, 148, 175, 188, 199–200;
media and, 100, 249n90; at *Ms.*, 67–69
white supremacy, 212
white Women's Liberation, 7, 16–18; Black
feminism and, 58, 188–189
Wideman, Edgar, 159, 162
Wild Tree Press, 134
Wilson, Judith, 20, 37–38, 53–54, 99, 206,
227; academia and, 23, 177; archives
and, 77; *Essence* and, 133, 256n14;
Morrison and, 32; *Ms.* and, 66–68;
reviews by, 56–57, 71, 97; secretary role
of, 50–51, 61; visual art and, 130–132;
Wallace and, 248n76
Winfrey, Oprah, 54, *p9*
Wintergreen Women Writers' Collective,
196–198
Wofford, Chloe, 168–171, 261n68. *See also*
Morrison, Toni
womanism, 140, 190; white feminism and,
188–189
women's studies: Black studies and, 183–184;
intersectionality in, 195
Women Students and Artists for Black Art
Liberation (WSABAL), 107, 109
work, 3–4, 64, 206; administrative, 61, 183,
190–191, 263n13; archival, 77; of Black
women, 17, 138, 196; burdens of, 83,
104, 176, 249n102; editorial, 185–186;
gendered, 85; international, 135–136;
invisible labor and, 6, 61, 212; political,
81; textual, 26, 109, 141, 143, 184
Wright, Richard, 155–157
writers, 108, 152; Black women as, 15–16,
210–212; motherhood and, 55–58
writers' retreat, of *Essence*, 125–126
writings, 86–88; love in, 35–36, 44, 56–57,
62, 140, 197, 203; paranoia in, 211,
268n16; spirituality in, 91–92. *See also*
poetry; publications, of members;
specific titles
WSABAL. *See* Women Students and
Artists for Black Art Liberation

Zami (Lorde), 5, 57, 137, 212